# Robert Burns

## *The Tinder Heart*

Also by Hugh Douglas

*The Underground Story* (Robert Hale)
*Crossing the Forth* (Robert Hale)
*Portrait of the Burns Country* (Robert Hale)
*Edinburgh, a Children's History* (Longman)
*Burke and Hare, the True Story* (Robert Hale)
*Charles Edward Stuart, the Man, the King, the Legend* (Robert Hale)
*Robert Burns – a Life* (Robert Hale)
*Burns Supper Companion* (Alloway Publishing)
*Hogmanay Companion* (Neil Wilson Publishing)
*Flora MacDonald, the Most Loyal Rebel* (Alan Sutton Publishing)
*Bonnie Prince Charlie in Love* (Alan Sutton Publishing)

# ROBERT BURNS
## *The Tinder Heart*

*Hugh Douglas*

*My heart was compleatly tinder, and was eternally lighted up by some Goddess or other; and like every warfare in this world, I was sometimes crowned with success, and sometimes mortified with defeat.*

Letter from Robert Burns
to Dr John Moore, 2 August 1787

ALAN SUTTON PUBLISHING LIMITED

First published in the United Kingdom in 1996
Alan Sutton Publishing Ltd · Phoenix Mill · Far Thrupp · Stroud
Gloucestershire

British Library Cataloguing in Publication Data

A catalogue record for this book is available from the British Library.

ISBN 0-7509-1213-8

Typeset in 10/13pt New Baskerville.
Typesetting and origination by
Alan Sutton Publishing Limited.
Printed in Great Britain by
Butler & Tanner, Frome, Somerset.

*For Cathie Crosbie
and in memory
of Tom
with love and thanks
for a lifetime's friendship*

———

*Also for Lin, Dick and Molly Thomas*

# Contents

# List of Illustrations

## PICTURE ACKNOWLEDGEMENTS

Illustrations by courtesy of:

Trustees of Burns Cottage and Monument Nos 13, 19, 36, 46; National Galleries of Scotland 1, 4, 6, 11, 22, 23, 25, 27, 28, 29, 33, 34, 35, 42, 52; National Library of Scotland 10, 30, 31; Church of Scotland, Presbytery of Ayr. Strathclyde Archives 16, 17, 18, 32; Irvine Burns Club 24, 41; Mitchell Library, Glasgow 26, 47; Peter Westwood 2, 5, 8, 9, 12, 15, 37, 38, 39, 40, 48, 49; Ewart Library, Dumfries 44, 51; R. McChlery, Dunoon 20; Burniston Studios, Greenock 21; from the *Life of Burns* by P. Hateley Waddell 3, 14, 43, 50; from Allan Cunningham's *Life and Complete Works of Burns* 7; from *Burns and Mrs Dunlop* by W. Wallace 53; National Trust 45.

# Acknowledgements

It is impossible to thank everybody who has helped with this book because the material for it has been gathered over more than thirty years. However, I must express my gratitude to the London Library, Peterborough Central Library, Carnegie Library, Ayr, Edinburgh City Libraries, Mitchell Library, Glasgow, National Library of Scotland, British Library, Ewart Library, Dumfries, Dick Institute, Kilmarnock, Strathclyde Archives and the Scottish Record Office, all of which have assisted recently.

I have had help from John Inglis, Hon. Secretary of the Burns Federation and his staff, Allister Anderson, former Secretary of the Burns Federation, Peter Westwood, Hon. President of the Burns Federation, John Manson, Curator, Burns Cottage, Irvine and Greenock Burns Clubs, staff of various Burns centres and museums, especially Burns Cottage and the Writers' Museum, Edinburgh. Sheena Andrew, at the Carnegie Library, Ayr, has given generous help as always, and the following individuals deserve special thanks – Dr Richard Oram, University of Aberdeen, Miss A. Gardiner, Strathclyde Archives, Hamish Whyte, Mitchell Library, Graham Roberts, Ewart Library, Dumfries. Donald F. MacDonald, Edinburgh, Dr George Cardno, Fife, Dr John Gordon, Peterborough, Dr James Bruce, Edinburgh, Professor J.A. Raeburn, Nottingham, John Horsburgh QC, Edinburgh, Wilson Ogilvie, Dumfries, Wendy Glavis, Peterborough, and David Kiltie, Maybole. Keeta and John Campbell have read the manuscript and given me much advice and encouragement. To all of these must be added my wife, Sheelagh, and family and friends, who have listened, discussed, read and advised on aspects of the Poet's life – they may have believed they were just humouring me by talking about my latest writing project, but I assure them they were providing essential support and help. Thanks to all of them.

James Mackay, author of *A Biography of Robert Burns*, has researched a number of details of the Poet's story, including the backgrounds to his children, Nelly Kilpatrick, Alison Begbie, Clarinda and Ann Park, which has been invaluable to my own work. I am grateful to him and to a number of other writers on Burns, and have acknowledged their help in the notes to the text. Alloway Publishing and James Mackay have kindly allowed me to quote from their editions of Burns' *Complete Works* and *Complete Letters*: these, too, are acknowledged in the notes.

# *Preface*

My father was a farmer upon the Carrick border, O,
And carefully he bred me in decency and order, O.
He bade me act a manly part, though I had ne'er a farthing, O,
For without an honest manly heart, no man was worth regarding, O.

I was born on an Ayrshire farm beside the River Doon, into a background very similar to that of Robert Burns. My father was a farmer and life was easier for us than it had been in the 1700s, there is no doubting that, but it had not changed out of recognition from Robert Burns' time – the horse still pulled the plough and farm-cart, and the men spent back-breaking hours in the field or later sitting on the corn-kist in the stable gossiping and day-dreaming; the women did most of the byre and dairy work as well as the housework. It was endless toil for small reward, yet there was always time for enjoyment – dancing, concerts, summer ice (a kind of indoor curling), drinking, darts and gossiping at Miss Martin's pub, or, for the bolder ones, a while with the lassies.

Attitudes to sex have changed since Burns' time, passing through the prim, censorious nineteenth century, to move slowly towards the more open attitudes of the present day. In writing about Burns, his women and the influence of love on his poetry, biographers have followed the mores of their own day, rather than his, so that for two centuries his sex life has been denied, glossed over, or bowdlerized out of recognition – even though it was the catalyst for so much of his poetry and songs. In all this the real Robert Burns has been lost.

So let us explore the life of the *real* Robert Burns. If you look closely you see him as clearly today as in 1785, when he was a twenty-six-year-old and just about to make his mark as a poet. He is good-looking, and might be really handsome were it not for a slight coarseness of facial features: he stands five feet nine inches tall, but seems rather smaller because of a stoop that has resulted from bending over a heavy plough. None the less he is a person to be noticed, for his dark, glowing eyes have the appearance of a man who looks deeply into life.

Can this be the man others see as a pauper passing himself off as a laird as he struts around Mauchline, hair tied back to catch the eye? Is this the man who has given the dour kirkmen of the district a roasting with his poetry, yet has just fathered a love child by Lizzie Paton, the servant girl at Lochlie? Can it be he who drinks overmuch and overlong with a crowd of rebellious young men at Johnnie Dow's pub?

Robert Burns was as hard to identify in 1785 as he is today, although remarkably few of those who profess to care for him and his work ever read or listen to a line of his poetry except on 25 January when the Scots get excited about their National Bard (always with a capital N and a capital B). They call it Burns Nicht (a capital again), and they greet the haggis with whisky drams and drink toasts to the lassies in the fond belief that they are emulating this man who was quite a lad for the bottle and girls.

In *The Tinder Heart* I have examined Robert Burns' relationships with women, not just to show that he was a bit of a lecher, seducer, a Don Juan, Casanova, rake, roué, fornicator, and womanizer – which he was – but to demonstrate the love and humanity that beat in his ardent heart, and discover the poetry and song which resulted therefrom. In love Robert Burns ran the gamut from cad to adoring husband: he could treat his women roughly then show them the deepest respect. And those unfathomable, enigmatic relationships were the catalyst for many of his actions and the poetry and songs he produced. Life and love were a battlefield on which Burns waged many campaigns, sometimes to win a great victory, but often to be routed ignominiously. He fought his love battles with all the passion his heart could command, and in the end he can stand up and be judged by the verse which his tinder heart inspired – poetry as movingly beautiful in defeat as it was in victory.

> Fare-thee-weel, thou first and fairest!
> Fare-thee-weel, thou best and dearest!
> Thine be ilka joy and treasure,
> Peace, Enjoyment, Love and Pleasure!
> Ae fond kiss, and then we sever!
> Ae fareweel, alas, for ever!
> Deep in heart-wrung tears I'll pledge thee,
> Warring sighs and groans I'll wage thee.

# Chronology – the Life of Robert Burns 1759–96

This book is not a biography of Robert Burns, but a view of an aspect of his life. The reader may find this chronology helpful.

## ALLOWAY 25 January 1759–66

| | |
|---|---|
| 1759 | Robert Burns, first child of William Burnes and his wife, Agnes Brown, born 25 January at Alloway, Ayrshire |
| 1760 | Brother Gilbert born |
| 1762 | Sister Agnes born |
| 1764 | Sister Annabella born |
| 1765 | Began lessons with John Murdoch |

## MOUNT OLIPHANT 1766–77

| | |
|---|---|
| 1766 | Moved to Mount Oliphant Farm, which his father rented |
| 1767 | Brother William born |
| 1769 | Brother John born |
| 1771 | Sister Isabella born |
| 1772 | Robert and Gilbert attended Dalrymple School |
| 1773 | Studied with Murdoch again. Wrote first song, *Handsome Nell,* for Nellie Kilpatrick |
| 1775 | Sent to Kirkoswald to study surveying |

## LOCHLIE 1777–84

| | |
|---|---|
| 1777 | Moved to Lochlie Farm at Tarbolton |
| 1780 | Bachelors' Club formed |
| 1781 | Courted Alison Begbie. Became a Freemason. Went to Irvine to learn flax-dressing |

Father quarrelled with landlord

1782 Flax shop burned down and Robert returned to Lochlie

1783 Began *Common Place Book*

Dispute with landlord went to law

Robert and Gilbert secretly rented Mossgiel

## MOSSGIEL 1784–6

1784 William Burnes died (13 February)

Moved to Mossgiel

1785 His *annus mirabilis*. Composed much poetry, including *Cotter's Saturday Night*, *The Twa Dogs*, *To a Mouse*, *The Holy Fair* and satires on Kirk

Elizabeth ('Dear bought Bess'), Burns' first love-child born (22 May). Mother was Elizabeth Paton, servant girl at Lochlie

Brother John died

Met Jean Armour

1786 Planned to emigrate to West Indies

Proposal for publication of book of poems

(Spring) Jean Armour pregnant. Burns rejected as husband

'Highland Mary' Campbell affair. Parted mid-May. Mary died (autumn)

Rebuked for fornication in Mauchline Kirk (9 July)

Armour issued writ against him

Transferred share of Mossgiel to brother (22 July)

Kilmarnock Edition published (31 July)

Twins born to Jean Armour (3 September). Boy and girl, named Robert and Jean

First letter from Mrs Frances Dunlop

Abandoned emigration plan and left for Edinburgh (27 November)

## EDINBURGH, TOURING SCOTLAND AND MAUCHLINE 1786–8

1787 Edinburgh Edition of poems published 21 April. Sold copyright to Creech for 100 guineas

Met James Johnson, editor of *Scots Musical Museum*, and began song-collecting

Border Tour with Robert Ainslie (5 May–1 June)

Returned Mauchline 8 June

West Highland Tour (late June)

Meg Cameron, Edinburgh barmaid, pregnant
Highland Tour (25 August–16 September)
Jean Armour pregnant again
In Edinburgh during winter. Affair with Agnes McLehose (Clarinda) began

1788   First meeting with Clarinda (4 January). Passionate meetings and correspondence followed
Returned Mauchline 23 February, Jean in last stages of pregnancy. 'Scalade' incident
Second set of twins born to Jean (about 10 March). Both died
Took lease of Ellisland Farm, Dumfriesshire
Accepted Jean as his wife (about April)
Began instruction for joining Excise Service
Took over Ellisland (11 June)
Another Edinburgh girl, Jenny Clow, had a son by him
Tour to Stirling and Clackmannan (4–20 October)

1789   Son Francis Wallace born (18 August)
Began work as Excise officer as well as farmer (1 September)

1790   Promoted to Dumfries Third Excise Division
Wrote *Tam o' Shanter* for Francis Grose's *Antiquities of Scotland*

1791   Daughter born to Dumfries barmaid, Ann Park (31 March)
Son William Nicol born to Jean (9 April)
Gave up Ellisland lease (10 September) and moved to Wee Vennel, Dumfries (11 November)
Visited Edinburgh to arrange for Jenny Clow's baby and say farewell to Clarinda, who was going to join husband in Jamaica

1792   Promoted to Dumfries Port Division of Excise
Met Maria Riddell
Bought guns from *Rosamond*, captured smuggling ship, and attempted to send them to France
Began association with George Thomson, writing songs for his *Select Collection of Scottish Airs*
Daughter Elizabeth Riddell born (21 November)
End December–January 1793, Inquiry by Excise into Burns' loyalty

1793   Second Edinburgh Edition of poems published
Moved to house in Mill Hole Brae
Thomson's Select Collection published

1794   'Rape of the Sabines' incident. Quarrel with Riddells
Son James Glancairn born (12 August)
Estrangement from Mrs Dunlop over his views on French Revolution

1795    Acting Superintendent of Excise during illness of superior
Resumed correspondence with Maria Riddell
Joined Dumfries Volunteers to defend south-west Scotland in
event of French invasion
Daughter Elizabeth died (September)
Burns seriously ill

1796    Health deteriorated
At Brow-on-Solway for sea-bathing on doctor's orders (June/July)
Saw Maria Riddell for last time (7/8 July)
Sent last letter to Mrs Dunlop
Worried about family and finances
Died Dumfries (21 July)
Funeral and birth of son, Maxwell (25 July)

# CHAPTER ONE

# *Auld Sang – New Song*

And why shouldna poor folk mowe*, mowe, mowe,      *copulate
  And why shouldna poor folk mowe:
The great folk hae siller*, and houses and lands,      *money
  Poor bodies hae naething but mowe.

Song by Robert Burns, 1792[1]

'I now began to be known in the neighbourhood as a maker of rhymes.' Thus Robert Burns recalled the year 1785,[2] but he was being over-modest for this was not only the twelve months during which he reached maturity as a poet, it was the time when he came of age as a lover too. This year has been called the Poet's *annus mirabilis*,[3] and that is not putting it too high – it really was the miraculous year when the young farmer at Mossgiel scaled the highest peak of his creativity, when he produced poetry as stunning in its quantity as in its quality. During the ten brief years still left to him Burns wrote scores more poems and songs, some touching those same heights of genius, but 1785 saw him at his most prolific, his most creative and composing the majority of his important poems.

  The *annus mirabilis* brought the first fruits of a rich sexual life also, for in May of that year he became a father for the first time when Lizzie Paton gave birth to a daughter, the first of eight children born out of wedlock. Robert accepted Lizzie's daughter as his without demur, and provided for her; she was partly brought up by his patient mother at Mossgiel, just as another was reared by his wife, Jean, as her own. Rab Mossgiel was proud rather than ashamed of having seduced Lizzie Paton and when friends in Mauchline teased him about his predicament, he dashed off light-hearted verses in which he compared himself to a poacher bagging some game.

'Twas ae night lately, in my fun,
I gaed a rovin wi the gun,
An brought a paitrick* to the grun'*      *partridge  *ground

1

> A bonie hen;
> And, as the twilight was begun,
> Thought nane wad ken*.[4]          *none would know

Lizzie's child was just the start of a sexual phase as fertile as his *annus mirabilis* had been for poetry, which produced at least five other children, admittedly including two sets of twins. But that all lay ahead in the unseen future as his twenty-seventh birthday passed on 25 January, 1786. This was the start of a year that brought the publication of *Poems Chiefly in the Scottish Dialect*, his first book, which catapulted him to fame overnight: it was also the start of the new amorous adventures which were responsible for shaping his life and future poetry. However, no one could have divined any of that from the ill-omened way in which the *annus mirabilis* closed and the new year opened. For one thing there was the business of Geordie Gibson's jurr*. Mauchline, let alone any other parish in the south-west of Scotland, had rarely seen a commotion like it.

What happened was this: one night a group of lads in the town seized hold of Geordie's jurr and stanged her through the village – that is to say they carried her astride a rough-hewn tree trunk to punish her for being a whore and to take revenge for the disease she spread among them as she plied her trade. Needless to say the experience was excessively painful and caused such lacerations to the girl's nether regions that she would not be able to whore again for some time to come.

Agnes Wilson, who was stanged so brutally, was a maidservant of George Gibson, landlord of Poosie Nansie's, an inn-cum-doss-house in Mauchline with a particularly unsavoury reputation. Years before, in January 1773, Gibson, who had been nick-named 'Black-bearded Geordie' by Burns, had been summoned before the Kirk Session of Mauchline along with his wife, Agnes Ronald, and daughter, Jess, on charges of resetting† but failed to appear.[5] Throughout the spring the kirk authorities, who took responsibility upon themselves to uphold law and order in the town, investigated the matter, and on 22 April reached the decision that Gibson kept 'a very irregular house' and his wife and daughter were found guilty of selling stolen goods. All three were ordered to present themselves before the minister to be rebuked, but failed to appear. By 29 April the Kirk Session had a further complaint

---

* servant, derived from English journeywoman or daily help. *The Concise Scottish Dictionary*
† receiving stolen goods for re-sale

against Gibson's wife, this time of being 'habitually drunk (and) troublesome to her neighbours': again she ignored the summons, but the kirk elders eventually caught up with her only to be rebuffed and forced to record in their minutes 'that she is resolved to continue in her disorderly way, declares her resolution to continue in the sin of Drunkenness.' She was excluded from all the privileges of the Church 'until she shall profess her repentance.'[6] With a woman of Agnes Ronald's spirit there was little chance of that.

Men and women in the south-west of Scotland had minds of their own and were often resistant to church discipline in the time of Burns. Ian D. Whyte, who examined this aspect of life in his recent economic history of Scotland prior to the Industrial Revolution, commented that it was technically easy to get married in Scotland in those days, yet the average age of marriage was relatively high and a significant proportion of the population never married at all. The mean age for Lowland women to marry during the century from 1660–1760 was between twenty-six and twenty-seven, with men marrying a year or two later. Although the Kirk managed by and large to keep sexual activity firmly within marriage by the early eighteenth century, these relatively late marrying ages left plenty of scope for illicit sex, and the south-west, particularly Ayrshire and Wigtownshire, displayed a higher level of illegitimacy than other regions of the country. These figures climbed rapidly during the second half of the eighteenth century. It has been suggested that a significant factor behind this trend lay in the strong tradition in the region, dating back to the Reformation, if not earlier, of resistance to the moral disciplinarianism of the Kirk, and clearly there was a higher level of illicit sexual activity evident in the local culture, which led to pregnancies. As Ian Whyte commented:

The inhabitants of the south-west showed more resistance to church discipline than other Lowland regions. This is seen in the proportion of women who refused to give the names of the fathers of their illegitimate children, the number who ran away rather than face kirk discipline, and the percentage of men who would not admit responsibility.[7]

The Gibsons fitted well into the pattern of recalcitrant and unrepentant parishioners who gave the Reverend William Auld, minister of Mauchline, and his elders so much trouble. Their daughter, who was summoned with her mother on the charge of resetting, was every bit as bad as her parents, and was dubbed 'Racer Jess' by Burns, who summed up the young woman's position in Mauchline society in a couple of pithy lines in his poem, *The Holy Fair.*

> There Racer Jess, an twa-three whores,
>   Are blinkin at the entry*[8]          *flirting in doorways

Agnes Wilson, who came to live at Poosie Nansie's during the latter half of 1785, was no better than her employers, and like 'Racer Jess' spent much of her time 'blinkin at entries', plying her trade as a whore. She may have been the woman Burns referred to in *The Jolly Beggars* as a 'tozie drab'* but even as victim (quite literally the injured party) of the stanging affair, the kirk elders could not find a good word to say about the girl: they simply described her as 'a vagrant woman of bad fame in the parish and places whence she came', and recorded that they wanted her banished from the district. Clearly the Kirk Session held Agnes as being as much to blame for the ordeal as young Armour and the other perpetrators of the crime. On 6 March the elders minuted: 'The bad reputation of this woman as being lewd and immoral in her practices has been the occasion of a late disturbance in this place which the Session greatly disapprove of and resolve to inquire into.'[9]

The 'stanging of the jurr' caused quite a stir around Mauchline, a quiet well doing wee Ayrshire town, where such ongoings had rarely occurred throughout the half century in which the Revd William Auld had been minister of the parish. The minister, known to his parishioners as 'Daddy' Auld, could honestly describe his twelve hundred or so parishioners as sober, industrious, charitably disposed and of decent appearance, although he did regret that the town no longer had the right to appoint magistrates who 'might contribute to the public good, by checking riots and disorders, which are at present too frequent.' Townswomen, in their silk caps and cloaks, now looked 'as fine as ladies of quality were formerly,' he wrote. They were also punctual attenders at church on Sundays, something that could not be said of many other places, where it was the custom for worshippers to gossip at the kirk door until the minister climbed into the pulpit, then make an unseemly dash to their pews, chattering to friends even as he uttered the word of God. Mauchline was a more sober place nowadays also: in half of the parish tea had replaced the 'good two-penny, strong-ale' that used to be drunk there in large quantities.[10]

*dishevelled hussy

Perhaps it was the 'stanging of the jurr' and the presence of the young poet Robert Burns within the parish that made the old minister preface his flattering picture of his parishioners with the ominous words, 'In such a number there must be some exceptions.'

Robert Burns was certainly numbered among the exceptions. He was born at Alloway, near Ayr, on 25 January 1759, the son of a gardener and market gardener who later became a farmer, and he had already made a name for himself locally as a writer of verse. As the eldest son of the family who had moved into Mossgiel Farm just a year before, he stood out from the common throng as he walked around the district; his appearance as a strong, mature farmer belying the toll hard farm work had already taken on his health. In his dark, glowing eyes he had the look of a poet.

The Burns family in Mossgiel was known to be in penury, yet tenant farmer, Rab, strutted through Tarbolton and Mauchline with his hair tied jauntily back to flaunt the fact that he was a poet, whose verse was good enough to catch the eye of people who knew about such things. Some folk even said his poems should be printed. Rab was well aware of his importance, not just as a writer of rather clever verse, but as head of the family since the death of his father in 1784. Yet he did not behave with the *gravitas* expected of a man in such a position: he was leader of a pack of wild blades in the town – a gang in which the closest to him were John Richmond, James Smith and David Brice, none of them a good influence on the young lads who had stanged Geordie Gibson's jurr.

At the head of the group who set upon the whoring servant was Adam Armour, a lad, barely fifteen, and small for his age – 'scarce as lang's a guid kail-whittle'* in the words of Rab Burns from Mossgiel, who admired the boy's spirit. Adam was wiry, fast on his feet and full of mettle. His father, James Armour, was a well-doing, dour and 'kirky' man, a successful stonemason in the town, so Adam was the last person one would expect to find involved in such a scandal. Naturally, the jurr and Geordie both raised such a hue and cry that the authorities instituted a search to bring young Armour to book, but he vanished and was not seen again until the noise calmed down: nobody knew that he was in hiding out at Mossgiel. Burns enjoyed the joke and, as if sheltering the culprit were not enough, he sat down and wrote a poem about it to entertain his friends. It certainly did that, but it also shocked the townsfolk and kirk session, for Burns' poem, although entitled *Adam Armour's Prayer*,[11] was far from a

*knife for cutting kale

penitent's confession and plea for forgiveness – it was a boastful telling of the unedifying tale:

> An now Thou kens our woefu case:
> For Geordie's jurr we're in disgrace,
> Because we stang'd her through the place,
>> An hurt her spleuchan;*       *tobacco pouch=genitalia
> For whilk* we daurna* show our face      *which *dare not
>> Within the clachan.

In the final verse Burns admitted that the jurr had suffered enough, but warned her that she might be subjected to greater retribution if she continued to whore:

> As for the jurr – puir worthless body!–
> She's got mischief enough already:
> Wi stanget hips and buttocks bluidy
>> She suffer'd sair;
> But may she wintle in a woody*,      *swing from a noose
>> if she whore mair.

By the time Adam Armour emerged from hiding at Mossgiel and his stanging of Geordie's servant came before the Kirk Session on 6 March 1786,[12] Burns had sinning of his own to confess to – and this also involved the Armours. Adam's sister, Jean, had confessed to her parents that she was pregnant and she named Rab Burns from Mossgiel as the father. In the autumn of 1786 when Jean Armour's term came, the whole world of Robert Burns, the Armours and 'Daddy' Auld and his parishioners had changed: Robert's *Poems Chiefly in the Scottish Dialect*, the Kilmarnock Edition, had appeared, and the name Robert Burns was known in every cottage and mansion as far away as Edinburgh – and that was a very different world from Mauchline.

The capital of Scotland, as elsewhere, had indeed seen great changes during the first half of the eighteenth century, culminating in a period that is rightly called the Scottish Enlightenment. The birth of this golden age had not been easy, and on the first day of May in 1707, when the bells of St Paul's Cathedral in London and the High Kirk of St Giles in Edinburgh rang out to mark the fusion of the nations of Scotland and England into a single sovereign state, they pealed very different tunes. While Queen Anne gave thanks in her English capital, the Earl of Seafield in Edinburgh expressed the true feelings of many of his countrymen. 'There's ane end to ane auld sang,'* he said as his ancient, proud, war-scarred country ceased to exist as an independent state. How wrong he was: Scotland and England were far too different in character for a Treaty of Union to alter them. In the short term the Union was painful; in the longer run it proved not to be the end of an old song at all, but the beginning of a new one – a song of the Scottish people's love for their nation, one still being sung.

At the start, the Union was far from the economic and social success its supporters predicted. For one thing, the Parliament in London which was still predominantly English with only a token Scottish representation, soon began to flout the spirit and even the letter of the treaty. While the linen and tobacco trades increased, so did taxes, and the country's woollen industry was devastated. No effective body was set up to govern Scotland, so the country drifted, and as it did so, the English Parliament high-handedly gave back to landowners the right to choose ministers of the Church of Scotland, a right which had been abolished a number of years before the Union – a right which the Scottish people did not wish to see restored. Even the use of the old Scottish tongue was frowned upon in this new Scotland.

There were advantages in the Union too: it reduced political strife in the country and allowed a more liberal element to flourish within the Kirk. This was something that was to affect Burns and his poetry-making.

In this new Scotland born in 1707, Edinburgh, no longer the capital of a nation, became the capital of the Scottish Enlightenment, a golden city, which reached out to the whole world and touched every intellectual activity – economics, philosophy, law, architecture, science, medicine and literature. The list of great men of the Enlightenment is almost endless, but among the giants were philosopher David Hume, economist Adam Smith, architect Robert Adam, anatomist Alexander Monro, artists Alexander Nasmyth and Henry Raeburn, and a host of brilliant lawyers and ministers. Burns was already well read when he first arrived in Edinburgh in 1786, having grown up with the Bible, Ossian, Pope, Sterne, Addison and Steel, and of course those brilliant Scottish poets, Allan Ramsay and Robert Fergusson, who influenced him so much. In the capital he found himself in an intoxicating literary circle headed by Henry Mackenzie, author of *The Man of Feeling*, whom he admired and who had actually reviewed his *Poems Chiefly in the Scottish Dialect* favourably in *The Lounger*.

---

*'There's an end to an old song.'

One great advantage all these men enjoyed was that Edinburgh was still a small city, so they were thrown together socially and shared their thoughts, their erudition, and their lives. It all made for an exciting, stimulating city, where the great lived cheek by jowl with lesser, but useful men and women, who made Edinburgh live – right down to the girls in the taverns and Burns' namesake, Margaret Burns, who plied her trade as a whore in Rose Street.

Edinburgh of the Enlightenment and the rest of Scotland were two countries, utterly foreign to one another. Robert Burns lived in both from 1786 onwards. Dr Ian Whyte summed up his relationship with these two nations in the closing paragraph of his book:

> Burns' life typifies the ambivalence and restlessness of Scottish society in the mid-eighteenth century. His romantic Jacobite leanings led him to look back at the Union of 1707 and condemn the 'parcel of rogues' who had caused Scotland to be 'bought and sold for English gold'. At the same time, like the Edinburgh literati who encouraged him, he wrote in English rather than Scots when he was trying to impress most. His unsuccessful career as a farmer was influenced by the changes in agriculture and rural society which were affecting Ayrshire by the 1770s. His later post as an exciseman was gained by shrewd use of the system of patronage.[13]

In the first of these two Scotlands of Burns' day, the nobility and growing intellectual classes spent their lives in elegant comfort that increased in splendour year upon year, but the other nation was peopled with decaying derelicts – those who were tenants or employees, undercapitalised tenant farmers like the Burns family, ill-paid labourers and servant girls, and a host of out-of-work, homeless people who had been driven off the land, or cast out of the Army or Navy when they became unfit to fight or King George III had no more need of them. The authorities were sympathetic enough towards those they considered the 'deserving poor', but other beggars were dealt with severely. Thieves, sorners,* gypsies and tinkers wandered the countryside, existing as best they could and often their only comfort and solace was the company they found in ale houses such as Poosie Nansie's. Geordie Gibson's jurr was one of those comforts.

In the Poet's day Ayrshire looked uninviting: the Burns family lived

---

*people who begged or demanded lodging as they wandered around the country

on three farms during the Poet's childhood and early manhood. The first, Mount Oliphant (1766–77), only a few miles from Alloway was poor, with unimproved soil which could not provide a living; the second, Lochlie at Tarbolton (1777–84) was larger and better, but still not good enough for the growing family; the third, Mossgiel, to which they moved in 1784 following William Burnes'* death, came too late for by then they had too many debts and troubles to succeed in it. At the time they farmed Lochlie, the Reverend John Mitchell described the face of the county as 'rough and dark, consisting greatly of heath, moss, patches of straggling wood and rudely cultivated grounds.' Roads were pitted with holes and flanked by ditches and hedges, which were never pruned or clipped, but 'allowed to shoot forth into all their wild luxuriance'.[14] Fortunately this desolate picture was changing, as forward-sighted landlords like the Earls of Eglinton and Loudon worked to improve the land, enclosing it into tenanted farms, which in time would provide those who farmed them with a reasonable living. When compiling his report for the Board of Agriculture in 1793, William Fullarton noticed such enormous improvement that he believed Ayrshire would soon rank among the most productive districts in Great Britain.[15]

Robert Burns was born a generation too soon to enjoy that, and he saw the well-shod 'improving lairds' and burgeoning coal-mining and manufacturing entrepreneurs against the background of the suffering of those who were sacrificed to make way for the promised better Ayrshire. So the Poet did not fit comfortably into either of the two nations which formed his Scotland. Had he done so, life might have been easier, but his poetry poorer.

It took a foreigner to see clearly the motivations, which made Burns such an acute observer of human nature and a writer of verse that commented on it. Hans Hecht, the German author of a remarkably perceptive biography of Burns, observed that close proximity obscures the vision and too great love blinds the judgement as much as too violent antipathy. In the case of Burns, he said, there was a further difficulty because 'the controversial points [in his life] move along the dangerous lines of sexuality, alcoholism, religion, politics, and class prejudices or preferences.'[16]

Let us first consider the drink and the smirking innuendoes so often made by those who know least about Robert Burns. Of course, Burns

*Burns' father spelt his name Burnes; Robert dropped the 'e'

drank and to excess, but who did not in the Scotland of those days when funerals were said to be far merrier than weddings in England? The Poet, like others in his social class, grew up on the twopenny ale so commonly drunk at the time, and moved on to whisky and fine wines at gentlemen's tables as he became accepted by society. There were times when drink left him intoxicated at bedtime and full of remorse next morning. He drank for many reasons: for company, with drinking friends, and even one night while snowbound at Ecclefechan because the choice was to suffer the noise of 'a Scraper . . . torturing catgut, in sounds that would have insulted the dying agonies of a Sow under the hands of a Butcher' or to get drunk. 'I, of the two evils have chosen the least, & am very drunk – at your service!' he wrote next morning.[17]

It was a deliberate choice to get drunk at Ecclefechan that night; at other times it was not, as when the Reverend William McMorine of Caerlaverock arrived too early to baptize Burns' daughter and found the Poet's guests still recovering from the night before through drinking toasts from a historic drinking cup Mrs Frances Anna Dunlop of Dunlop had sent him; or when the Riddells of Glenriddell entertained him too well and the result was a piece of horseplay which cost him his friendship with the family. The libel of alcoholism pursued Burns beyond the grave with Dr James Currie, his first biographer, going so far as to link his death to a night at a tavern when he returned home about three o'clock in a very cold morning, benumbed and intoxicated.[18] It was only a short step from that to the stories, nudges and winks that have pursued his memory ever since – fuelled by the countless Burns Suppers which mark the anniversary of his birth each year.

In politics the republican spirit which moved Burns also affected Wordsworth, Coleridge and Keats. He had romantic Jacobite leanings with no respect or admiration for the Hanoverian royal family of his day, and he also had deep sympathy for the French revolutionaries for whom he unwisely bought some guns seized from the ship *Rosamond* and attempted to send them to France – a dangerous ploy for a man who worked for His Majesty's Excise Service at this time. Later, however, he enlisted in the Dumfries Volunteers when French invasion threatened. Sympathy for the French up to the moment the Revolution became a bloodbath cost him one of his most valued women friends: old Mrs Dunlop, a mother figure to him for years, had French sons-in-law, and she cut him off because of tactless sympathetic references he made to the French revolutionaries. This loss of her support came at a time when he needed it most: politics cost Burns dear.

He got away with the 'squibs' he produced during elections at home, which were closely linked to his own position as a member of the tenant farming class. Even after the door was opened to allow him to pass through and join intellectual and aristocratic Scotland he remained true to the heritage into which he had been born. He cultivated the image of the ploughman poet, and always considered himself a farmer or a working exciseman rather than anything higher up the social scale. This made him extremely sensitive to any rebuff (imagined or otherwise) from his social superiors, whom he could attack with a viciously poisoned pen whenever he felt slighted. Caution was never Burns' watchword: one of his election 'squibs' savaged the Duke of Queensberry, a powerful landowner, who lived at Drumlanrig Castle, not far from where he settled in Dumfriesshire, and consequently a man who could have done him great harm:

> Drumlanrig's towers hae tint* the powers      *lost
>    That kept the lands in awe, man:
> The eagle's dead, and in his stead
>    We've gotten a hoodie-craw*, man . . .     *hooded crow

> The lads about the banks o' Nith,
>    They trust his Grace for a' man:
> But he'll sair* them as he sair't his King,     *serve
>    Turn tail and rin awa, man.[19]

Even in death it was possible to give offence to the touchy Burns: one wild, snowy winter's night in 1788 on his way to Ayrshire he had just settled down in front of a bowl of punch at Whigham's Inn at Sanquhar 'the only tolerable inn in the place' when the cortege arrived carrying the body of old Mrs Mary Oswald of Auchincruive. Poor Robert had to get out to make way for the mourners. As he rode 12 miles through the icy blizzard to the next inn at New Cumnock in Ayrshire he remembered that among her servants and tenants, whom he had known when he was younger, 'she was detested with the most heartfelt cordiality', and, having reached the New Cumnock inn at last, he sat down and wrote an ode 'sacred' to the memory of this woman 'laden with unhonoured years'.[20]

> View the wither'd beldam's face:
> Can thy keen inspection trace
> Aught of humanity's sweet, melting grace?
> Note that eye, 'tis rheum o'erflows –
> Pity's flood there never rose.

See these hands, ne'er stretch'd to save,
Hands that took, but never gave.
Keeper of Mammon's iron chest,
Lo, there she goes, unpitied and unblest,
She goes, but not to realms of everlasting rest![21]

While one can understand his feeling at being thrown out into a stormy winter night, the poem was surely too bitter. He admitted he never knew the woman, and it was not she who turned him out of the inn. It is surprising that he thought enough of the poem to send it to an admirer, Dr John Moore, fifteen months later.

Burns was always too insecure, much too sensitive, and responded too sharply, and for a man who was so easily hurt, he could inflict lasting injury on others.

Religion was a thorny topic in Scottish life generally in Burns' day, and the Kirk gave the Poet much trouble. Robert Burns had deep religious convictions but by the latter half of the eighteenth century religion had come a long way from the church of a hundred years earlier when blasphemy was a capital offence. By the time Burns was a young man, known for his satirical poetry, there was a great cleavage of view between the old-style traditional Calvinists and the more liberal Moderates, and it is hardly surprising that Burns supported the latter group in direct opposition to the old Mauchline minister. Burns' poetic satires on Church and churchmen were not attacks on the Kirk itself, but on the hypocrites within it. Every one of his verse attacks was right on target and viciously exposed the wrongs Burns saw around him, yet the strange thing is that none of them – *The Ordination, The Twa Herds, Holy Willie's Prayer* or *The Holy Fair* – brought out the 'holy beagles': it was sex that achieved that, and it has remained so right down to the present day. Mention Burns' criticism of the Church and few will say a bad word about him; say he was a drunkard and they will not like it but will admit there was truth in the charge. But sex is another matter. Cyril Pearl's comment was as sharply to the point as anything Burns wrote about the Kirk:

The recoil from sex, the reluctance to admit that a man can lead an enthusiastic and unashamed sex-life, and still write tender lyrics about a tim'rous mouse, or stirring lyrics about Scots who bled wi' Wallace, has given Burns' biographers a lot of trouble; few of them present him as a man of flesh and blood, of very eager flesh and very ardent blood.[22]

Many generations of Burns lovers have chosen to disregard this aspect of his life. Robert Louis Stevenson has never really been forgiven for suggesting that womanizing was Burns' greater sin than his drinking. This, and other comments Stevenson made about the Poet, has been given as one reason why a statue of Stevenson has never been erected in Edinburgh.

In sex, as in every other aspect of his life, Robert Burns lived joyfully. He would never have subscribed to the aphorism attributed to that great Scottish character of the early part of the twentieth century, R. B. Cunninghame-Grahame, who said, 'The Scots fornicate gravely but without conviction.'[23] It is true, there is a certain Puritanism in the character of the Scot, especially the Lowland one, which does make him appear earnest even in his enjoyment. But surely it can never be said that he is grave in the act of love-making, and certainly he does not lack conviction. Robert Burns approached sex with gusto, which came from the very soul of the man, and he was always in love with the girl who was his current partner. In Tarbolton and Mauchline he loved them all, and to be rebuffed or rejected by any of them was a mortifying experience.

Burns lived and wrote for the moment, his biographer, Christina Keith, believed. 'It is for the moment he is read. You do not take him up in a library, as you would Shakespeare or Milton, to dig for hidden treasure . . . All the reactions are obvious and on the surface,'[24] she said.

It is true, Burns' verse was based on life around him, often crafted while he worked on the farm and set down on paper in the evening. All it took to fire his imagination was a chance remark or meeting – an incident like that brief visit to Poosie Nansie's which resulted in his glorious long cantata, *The Jolly Beggars*.[25]

The Bard had spent an evening at Johnnie Dow's tavern in Mauchline with his cronies, Richmond and Smith, and on their way home they passed Poosie Nansie's, where the walls were bursting with music, singing, laughter, shouting and argument, a look inside was irresistible, although this was not a place where Burns usually drank. There they discovered that 'other Scotland' of vagrants and beggars, singing, quarrelling, telling their tales, fiddling, loving and whoring. Just a few days later Burns showed Richmond a draft of his great lyrical drama, *The Jolly Beggars* or *Love and Liberty* as it was also named.[26] For the young farmer-poet to produce this series of solos and choruses at all was remarkable – to have done so within the space of a few days was superhuman.

It was from 'this ragged crew' as Thomas Crawford calls them in his study of Burns' poems,[27] he assembled his *dramatis personae* (some real, others possibly invented in his own fertile mind), who each sing their songs in turn: the old soldier describes his campaigns while his doxy holds up her 'greedy gab'* for his 'skelpan kisses't, then goes on to describe her own conquests; Merry-Andrew 'a fool by profession' shows he may be an idiot, but he has as sound a view of society as anyone around him; his tinker companion grieves for her man, a common thief deserving of the hanging which was his fate, but still *her* 'braw John Highlandman'; the 'pygmy scraper wi' his Fiddle', a 'wee Apollo', comforts her with his song until another tinker draws 'a roosty§ rapier' and takes her from him; and the poet himself had to be in the cast of course – 'a bard of no regard', to toast the lasses and bring the cantata to its climax with a final glorious chorus to the tune, *Jolly Mortals, Fill your Glasses*:

A fig for those by law protected!
  Liberty's a glorious feast!
Courts for cowards were erected,
  Churches built to please the priest!

| | |
|---|---|
| Here's to budgets*, bags and wallets! | *leather bags |
|   Here's to all the wandering train! | |
| Here's our ragged brats and callets* | *trollops |
|   One and all, cry out, Amen! | |

It is that glorious final line, *One and all, cry out, Amen!* that is so typical of Burns' response to being with or writing about people; he joyed in their company, he sorrowed in their suffering, he exalted in their sexuality and in his own. For him neither carousing nor seducing was done gravely or without conviction.

Wherever Rab Mossgiel went it was rarely the scenery or surroundings that moved him, for his was always a landscape with people. On visiting Perthshire during the summer of 1787, he wrote a poem about the birk (or birch) woods, the tentative summer sun on the hills, and the deep, roaring river alongside. But he could not leave a lassie out of his picture: he turned his poem into a song based on a traditional Aberdeenshire ballad, *The Birks of Abergeldie*, so that its chorus ran:

Bonie lassie, will ye go,
Will ye go, will ye go?
Bonie lassie, will ye go
  To the birks of Aberfeldie?[28]

*mouth, tsmacking kisses, §rusty

Even back home in Ayrshire when he wrote about the rivers Ayr, Doon, or Lugar, the result was a song of deeply felt love.

By the 1785–6 watershed in his career, the Bard had already produced a staggering amount of poetry, which displayed maturity beyond his years. To such poems as *A Prayer*, *Under the Pressure of Violent Anguish* and *Man was made to Mourn* he brought a profound understanding of the frailty and suffering of mankind. He observed acutely the way of life of country folk like his own family in *The Cotter's Saturday Night* and *Hallowe'en*, and *The Jolly Beggars*. As if that were not enough he had also produced *To Ruin*, *The Twa Dogs*, *To a Louse*, *To a Mouse* – a sheaf of poems about friends and comments on the kirk and hypocritical kirkmen. His *Address to the Unco Guid*, *The Holy Tulzie*, *Holy Willie's Prayer* and *Epitaph on Holy Willie*, *The Holy Fair*, and the *Address to the Deil* all caused a stir within the church and outside it too.

We must not forget his prose writings, however, but should not take it for granted that these always reveal the true Burns. It is hard, when reading the frank letters he wrote to his friends, always in superbly constructed prose, that he did not sense the world looking over his shoulder. Was Burns writing for posterity? Was he deliberately putting on an act for his friends? Should we not be cautious therefore about accepting every word of every letter as gospel?

In his letters, as in his poems, he bragged about the women in his life, and was nothing if not frank about them. Humility and repentance for his sins were usually absent too. It was as if he did not respect the institution of marriage or the women with whom he became so passionately involved: he told a young friend, John Tennant junior of Glenconner, 'Who would not be in raptures with a woman that will make him £300 richer? And then to have a woman to lye with when one pleases without running any risk of the cursed expence of bastards and all the other concomitants of that species of Smuggling. These are solid views of matrimony.'[29]

On the very morning on which he had to go to Mauchline church to do penance for fornication with Jean Armour he was more interested in sales of his book of poems, which was about to be published, than in his sin, and bragged to his bosom pal, John Richmond, that he was to be allowed to sit in his own seat in church to do penance instead of being obliged to stand before the congregation on the sinner's cutty stool. There was little sympathy for poor Jean Armour, and neither sackcloth nor ashes in his own attitude.[30]

Yet just three weeks later he could write about the same woman, 'If you see Jean tell her, I will meet her, So help me Heaven in my hour of need!'[31]

Whatever he wrote, verse or prose, women had a part in it: these were seldom great ladies, but the women of his own layer of society, farm girls, barmaids, wives of hard-working friends and acquaintances. Among his peers his sexual appetite and candour caused comment, for even in his day, a time of sexual frankness such as has not been known again until the present time, the Mossgiel farmer-poet's conduct was different from that of those around him; whereas others who made local girls pregnant went meekly to church to stand alongside the girl they had wronged and be chastized by the minister, Burns showed defiance. Rab Mossgiel's swagger in life and when he put pen to paper caused offence and alarm. When Lizzie Paton fell pregnant by him he produced the boastful, aggressive, *Rantin Dog the Daddie o't* and *The Fornicator*, yet when her daughter, his love-child, was born, he welcomed her with the tender and beautiful *Poet's Welcome to his Love-begotten Daughter*:

> Welcome my bonie, sweet, wee dochter!
> Tho ye come here a wee unsought for,
> And tho your comin I hae fought for,
>     Baith kirk and queir*;                                    *choir
> Yet, by my faith, ye're no unwrought for
>     That I shall swear![32]

No wonder Scotland did not know what to make of Robert Burns in his time. And still does not!

Love in all its forms was never far from Robert Burns' heart or pen: of all the subjects about which he wrote, it was the one which propelled him most surely towards poetry. In his *Common Place Book* in August 1783, he wrote, 'I never had the least thought or inclination of turning Poet till I got once heartily in Love, and then Rhyme and Song were, in a manner, the spontaneous language of my heart.'[33] And all through life this was the catalyst for his most intense creativity. Love was as essential to Burns' life as breath itself. He confided, again in his *Common Place Book* in April the same year, when he was just twenty-four:

Notwithstanding all that has been said against Love, respecting the folly and weakness it leads a young unexperienced mind into; still I think it, in a great measure, deserves the highest enconiums that have been passed upon it. If any thing on earth deserves the name of rapture or transport, it is the feelings of green eighteen in the company of the mistress of his heart when she repays him with an equal return of affection.[34]

The moment Burns set eyes on a woman his heart was tinder: he admitted that the first response came from deep within him, immediate, sexual, fiery, and rarely as controlled as might have been wise. Women responded, from the barmaid, Ann Park, in Dumfries to loyal, loving Jean Armour. In the course of making a radio programme some years ago, I discussed the Poet's sexuality with a young woman from the Scottish-English Border, and received an instant and frank answer: 'He was very sensuous and very sensual, and had gentle understanding. I just need to look at his picture and I would respond. If there were someone around like Burns today, I would be making a pass at him.'[35]

If even today, two centuries on, Burns can still provoke such a response, what chance had those who encountered him in the flesh in Ayrshire, Edinburgh, or Dumfriesshire? Perhaps it is fear that Burns still has the power to 'seduce' their wives today that makes so many men treat the Bard as a kind of Don Juan, whose affairs, however procreative, were short-lived and shallow, an affront to womankind. Nothing could be further from the truth, for Burns had enormous respect for women.

In an essay on the role of women in Burns' poems and songs, Dr William Murray summed this up:

For Burns women were not just objects of desire, devoid of will or responses; on the contrary they were the female equivalent of his independent, honest man. At all times Burns avoided the two poles of general attitudes to women: treating them with contempt, or that more subtle form of denigration, placing them on a pedestal. Indeed in an oppressive age in which women, especially poor women, suffered most, Burns' poetry can be seen as a plea for them to be treated as individuals in their own right.[36]

Such a view frees Burns from the 'male chauvinist' label that the ignorant have attached to him, and makes him a forerunner of the liberation of women, which has taken two centuries to flower.

Burns' relationships with women were set at four levels – casual, carnal encounters; purely intellectual friendships; acquaintanceships which stirred both heart and intellect; and those wholly of the heart, which resulted in marriage to Jean Armour and, dare one say it, the much argued meeting with 'Highland Mary' Campbell.

At the first and lowest of these levels were the chance acquaintances he made wherever he went, ranging from Lizzie Paton, the maid on the farm at Lochlie, to Edinburgh servant lassies, Meg Cameron and Jenny Clow. One quality these women all had in common was that they, and he, were so fertile that each bore him a child. It is not known how many others there were who rejoiced to have him between their loins, but Burns himself would have admitted to quite a few.

Fame brought a new type of woman into Burns' life, the wives, sisters and daughters of the nobility and literati of Scotland who befriended him. With them there was no question of a sexual dimension to the relationship – no more than the flattery allowed in polite social circles – except for once, with the Riddells of Glenriddell, a family of high social standing who befriended him at Dumfries during the latter part of his life. This friendship was brought to an abrupt end when Robert overstepped the bounds of gentlemanly conduct during some horseplay following a rather alcoholic dinner.

These women welcomed him into their homes, sent him gifts, and pestered him with their own attempts at verse, which usually he read dutifully. In return he amused and entertained them, and charmed them with his own work. In one case this friendship grew into something deep enough to hurt both him and the woman when it came to an end. Mrs Frances Anna Dunlop of Dunlop was nearly thirty years older than Burns, but for years they carried on a correspondence which meant much to both of them.

Mrs Dunlop belonged to the old Scottish aristocracy, yet she always treated Burns, not merely as a social equal, but as an intellectual superior. 'I feel I imbibe your graces,' she told him once.[37] She constantly poured out kindly, motherly advice in interminably long letters (which he probably seldom read to the end, and whose content he often ignored when he did), but he was always careful to describe her chastising as 'the cruel act of a friendly surgeon.'[38] She handled his genius with great sensitivity. When she knew he was seriously troubled about something she wrote to him: 'I don't like to ask what is busying or troubling you since you don't like to say', adding, 'I truly sympathize with you.'[39]

The friendship only came to an end in 1794, when Burns sent her that tactless letter in praise of the French revolutionaries, and he regretted the loss of her friendship to the end of his life. She refused to write to him again, and only relented as he lay on his death-bed.

Heart and mind fused into passion three times for Robert Burns, and the combination always proved explosive – ending 'deep in heart-wrung tears', which were a catalyst for great poetic creativity. The first and last of these three intellectual loves, Margaret (Peggy) Chalmers and Maria Riddell, both had fine minds, which sparked Burns' genius, but Peggy rejected his offer of marriage and Maria never reached the starting gate as a marriage prospect or even a mistress – for one thing, both she and the Poet were already married by the time they met, and for another,

Maria was far above his social class and was guarded by the waspish wife of her brother-in-law.

The third intellectual lover, Agnes (Nancy) McLehose, may have been the least scholarly and mentally able, but she inspired the most beautiful love songs. Nancy schemed to meet Burns in Edinburgh just at the time he lost Peggy Chalmers, so his heart was even more combustible than usual. A husband and unhappy marriage proved small deterrent to Nancy who, while protesting that she was a married woman, was soon exchanging poems with Burns and teetered over the brink into rapture. Throughout that winter of 1787–8 they often met and, whenever apart, corresponded under high-flown classical *noms de plume*, Clarinda and Sylvander, but this all came to a mean, unworthy end when Sylvander suddenly upped and married Jean Armour without even telling his Clarinda. The affair was dead, but its legacy belongs to us:

> Ae* fond kiss, and then we sever!        *one
> Ae farewell, and then forever!
> Deep in heart-wrung tears I'll pledge thee,
> Warring sighs and groans I'll wage thee.[40]

Jean Armour deserves a love category all to herself since the relationship between her and Robert was based solely on love, without deep intellectual thoughts interposing, or poems and precious letters being exchanged. Love between them was strong from the first, although Burns would probably not have admitted that. It was basic, it was sexual, it was far more profound than anyone realized – apart probably from Jean herself, who was as shrewd as Burns' mother and would have settled for marriage the moment she sensed the first changes within her body that told her she was pregnant. It is remarkable that, just as Burns' mother took his love child into her home and raised it as her own, Jean also took his child by Ann Park and added it to her own brood. Both mother and wife were remarkable women.

Jean had a good voice and a good ear, so was able to help him with the song-writing which was his inspiration during their years together. She made no deliberate attempt to further his literary creativity other than to supply him with some old tunes and sing them over for him. However, she did make one vital contribution to his Poet's needs: she provided him with the security of home and family that he needed to write, a rock to which he could anchor his life. When he settled down with her he was on Parnassus hill, he loved her with all his heart, and he was happy to boast his adoration to the world:

I see her in the dewy flowers –
  I see her sweet and fair.
I hear her in the tunefu birds –
  I hear her charm the air.
There's not a bonie flower that springs
  By fountain, shaw*, or green,               *small wood
There's not a bonie bird that sings,
  But minds me o my Jean.[41]

During the early part of 1786, when Jean Armour first found herself pregnant and her father refused to consider Young Mossgiel as a son-in-law, Burns was driven to distraction. Not even the imminent publication of his first volume of poems could disperse the stormclouds that hung overhead, and it was against this background that he met and fell deeply in love with the only other person who ever competed with Jean Armour for Burns' pure love, Mary Campbell. Their relationship was as brief and as passionate as were all the Poet's affairs, it may well have resulted in a promise of marriage and an invitation to Mary to emigrate to the West Indies with him, and it may also have led to pregnancy.

Whatever the truth about Mary Campbell, her relationship with Burns and her death affected him profoundly, and troubled his conscience in time to come. She may not have inspired Burns to his best verse, but even allowing for poetic licence and the colouring of his memories by time, the songs about the Highland lassie suggest that for a time at least Jean had a real rival in Mary:

Wi monie a vow and lock'd embrace
  Our parting was fu tender:
And, pledging aft to meet again,
  We tore oursels asunder.
But O! fell Death's untimely frost,
  That nipt my flower sae early!
Now green's the sod, and cauld's the clay,
  That wraps my Highland Mary![43]

So it was that from 1786 Burns turned his immense talent from poetry to song-writing. The music and singing he heard in Edinburgh and on his travels through Scotland stirred memories of those songs he had heard as a child, and awakened a love of folk-song which quickly became a passion that filled his life. He teamed up with two editors who were compiling volumes of Scottish songs, first James Johnson and then George Thomson, and virtually took over their works. In all Burns provided

Johnson with 160 songs and Thomson with 114, which in terms of sheer volume was a superhuman achievement, but in range and quality nothing short of genius.

As for the contribution Burns' songs made to Scottish life and culture, that is incalculable. Thomas Carlyle said that in his songs Burns 'found a tone and words for every mood of man's heart,'[44] and there can be no denying that they do touch on almost every emotion experienced by man or woman, not just in Scotland but round the world – manhood, nationhood, patriotism, politics, conviviality, bawdiness, joy, satire, Jacobitism, companionship, friendship, and love, especially love.

It took a perceptive Frenchman to discover no fewer than twenty-five different types of love song among Burns' work.[45] In *Robert Burns: la Vie, les Oeuvres*[46] Auguste Angellier classified Burns' songs as ranging from a simple mingling of landscape with sentiment to pure, unadulterated physical passion. There are songs of courtship, copulation, parting, separation and death. They span life from the young girl not yet ready for marriage to serene companionship of old age. Whatever aspect of love Robert Burns touched upon, he imparted to it a timeless, classless majesty. Burns' lyrics are the songs of an earthy countryman who understood what love was all about and was not too inhibited to express it. He had the ability to capture feelings which he could not have experienced himself: in *I'm O'er Young to Marry Yet*, for example, he took an old traditional chorus and added the thoughts of a young girl to turn it into a magical song of a girl's fear of her first wooing:

| | |
|---|---|
| I am my mammie's ae* bairn, | *one/only |
| Wi unco folk* I weary, Sir: | *strangers |
| And lying in a strange bed, | |
| I'm fley'd* it make me eerie*, Sir. | *frightened *afraid |

I'm o'er young, I'm o'er young,
   I'm o'er young to marry yet!
I'm o'er young, 'twad be a sin
   To tak me frae my mammie yet.[47]

He was equally at home writing of love at the opposite end of life's span to produce the hauntingly serene *John Anderson, my Jo*. It seems impossible that a recently married man just turned thirty could produce such a timeless gem. He started from an old bawdy ballad, which has been printed in his *Merry Muses of Caledonia*, and fashioned this into a song of the undying love as old age approaches, when sexual powers have waned, but are not forgotten. The wife remembers proudly the way her husband had loved her when both were young and she goes on to tell him she is still as deeply in love with him now that they are on the verge of old age. One can only rejoice that love can endure so strongly that even at the end of a long life together they remain as devoted as young sweethearts.

| | |
|---|---|
| John Anderson my jo*, John | *sweetheart |
| When we were first acquent*, | *acquainted |
| Your locks were like the raven, | |
| Your bonie brow was brent*; | *smooth |
| But now your brow is beld*, John, | *bald |
| Your locks are like the snaw*, | *snow |
| But blessings on your frosty pow*, | *head |
| John Anderson, my jo![48] | |

Life had not always been easy, as the singer confesses in the second and final verse of this gentle, touching song. The wife recalls the joys they have shared through the uphill struggle their time together has been – but there is no regret at the end, just total serenity as she looks forward to their resting together in eternal peace when it is over.

| | |
|---|---|
| John Anderson my jo, John, | |
| We clamb the hill thegither, | |
| And monie* a cantie* day, John, | *many  *happy |
| We've had wi ane anither*: | *one another |
| Now we maun* totter down, John, | *must |
| And hand in hand we'll go, | |
| And sleep thegither at the foot, | |
| John Anderson my jo! | |

No poet ever summed up a lifetime's love more beautifully than Burns in that song.

Between these extremes Burns explored all the themes of love that he had experienced in life: constancy in *A Red, Red Rose*, warmly remembered friendship in *Auld Lang Syne*, the glory of marriage in *I Hae a Wife o my Ain*:

| | |
|---|---|
| I hae a wife o my ain*, | *own |
| I'll partake wi naebody: | |
| I'll tak cuckold frae nane*, | *from none |
| I'll gie cuckold to naebody.[49] | |

The sheer, unashamed physical passion of a cheekily stolen sexual triumph in the harvest field is experienced too. *The Rigs o Barley*, like so many of his other songs, had a long pedigree before Burns touched it, for it had already been published in various versions through the preceding century. In Burns' hands the music became the rhythm of sexual intercourse and the words its climax. It all starts innocently enough, as no doubt did many of Burns' own encounters which ended in copulation: the lad slips away into the cornfield with his girl, but soon she is locked in his fond embrace, and is his:

> The sky was blue, the wind was still,
>   The moon was shining clearly;
> I set her down, wi right good will,
>   Amang the rigs o barley:
> I ken't* her heart was a' my ain*;          *knew  *own
>   I lov'd her most sincerely;
> I kiss'd her owre* and owre again,             *over
>   Amang the rigs o barley.

> Corn rigs, an barley rigs,
>   An Corn rigs are bonie:
> I'll ne'er forget that happy night,
>   Amang the rigs wi Annie.

*The Rigs o Barley* is more than a celebration of a stolen sexual encounter by a country couple on a harvest evening: it encapsulates the joy that copulation gives to the couple who share it, the intense emotion it releases, and the lasting effect it leaves in the heart.

> I lock'd her in my fond embrace;
>   Her heart was beating rarely:
> My blessings on that happy place,
>   Amang the rigs o barley!
> But by the moon and stars so bright,
>   That shone that hour so clearly!
> She ay shall bless that happy night
>   Amang the rigs o barley.

> I hae been blythe wi comrades dear;
>   I hae been merry drinking;
> I hae been joyfu gath'rin gear*;          *possessions
>   I hae been happy thinking:

But a' the pleasures e'er I saw,
  Tho three times doubl'd fairly –
That happy night was worth them a',
  Amang the rigs o barley.


Robert Burns elevated the joy of love to the greatest pleasure life could offer the common man: for him the act of coming together, whether merely spiritually or physically, was the finest blessing on earth. He was a genius at loving as well as a genius at composing verse, and to find the secret of his ability to love and to generate love, one must go back to his roots.

Men, and women too, learn about love and how to love at their mother's knee and from the shared parental affection they see around the childhood home. Robert Burns was fortunate to have the best of tutors in his mother, Agnes Brown and his father, William Burnes.[50] His mother's easy, outgoing affection was complemented by his father's quiet, stolid, earnest devotion, which may have lacked rapture, but was warm and enduring. Young Robert's sharp eyes and quick mind noted both, and from them he learned the art of loving.

CHAPTER TWO

# *Apprentice to Love*

There is certainly some connection between Love, Music, and Poetry . . .
I never had the least thought or inclination of turning Poet till I got
once heartily in love, and then Rhyme and Song were, in a manner, the
spontaneous language of my heart.

Robert Burns' *Common Place Book*,
August 1783[1]

In the old parish church at the foot of the Kirkwynd in Maybole one
Sunday in November 1757, the minister, the Reverend James McKnight,
called the banns for a proposed marriage between Agnes Brown,[2] a local
girl, and William Burnes from the neighbouring parish of Alloway.
Minnibolers (as people of this Ayrshire town are known) sat up and
listened: the future bride was now a mature 25-year-old and there had
been much gossip the previous year when she called off her seven-year-
long engagement to a local ploughman, William Nelson who had been
unfaithful.

Not much of a catch for either of them, some thought, as they studied
Agnes's bridegroom, for he had passed his thirty-sixth birthday, which put
him then on the edge of middle age. Outward appearances suggested a
thoroughly ill-matched couple, but Burnes and his wife proved to be as
devoted a pair as were to be found in the whole of Ayrshire, and they
remained so throughout their twenty-six years together.

William Burnes was the kind of man one noticed: he was tall and
reserved to the point of shyness, while Agnes was tiny and still looked no
more than a simple country lass in spite of her twenty-five years. Her red
hair and blazing brown eyes betrayed the temper she could show at times,
but that quality was countered by a jaunty smile, which suggested she had
not a care in the world. Agnes retained her attractive looks right up to her
death in 1820. Her daughter, Isabella, left a detailed description of her:

She was rather under the average height: inclined to plumpness, but
neat, shapely, and full of energy; having a beautiful pink-and-white

complexion, a fine square forehead, pale red hair, but dark eyebrows and dark eyes often ablaze with a temper difficult to control. Her disposition was naturally cheerful; her manner, easy and collected; her address, simple and unpresuming; and her judgment uncommonly sound and good. She possessed a fine musical ear, and sang well.[3]

Agnes contrasted oddly with her man's sober demeanour, but in all probability her pleasant look was the quality which first attracted her to him. William Burnes certainly did not choose Agnes for her intellect because he was not only more mature, he also had a far better brain. William always gave the impression that he carried more than his fair share of the world's cares on his shoulders, partly because he scarcely knew a day during the whole of his married life when financial troubles were not pressing down on him.

Yet the very different characters of Robert Burns' parents complemented each another; his reserve and her outgoing openness which could flare into anger so easily did not separate the couple, but brought them closer together. Not a breath of a quarrel between them was ever recorded by their children or others who met them, although there must have been differences of opinion between the upright William and fiery Agnes. After her husband's death in 1784, Agnes, still a presentable woman, might have found herself a second husband who could have made life easier, but she chose not to. Throughout thirty-six years of widowhood she remained loyal to the memory of the man who had entered her life so many years before.

William Burnes and his wife were both descended from farming stock: he from the dour north-east of Scotland and she from the more mellow south-west. William was born on 11 November 1721, and grew up at Clochnahill, near Dunottar, in Kincardineshire. It is not certain exactly when or where Agnes was born. Tradition gives the date as 17 March 1732, and the place as Whitestone Cottage at Culzean, near Maybole.

William Burnes grew up with all the dour, upright, open honesty expected of a man bred from solid north-east farming stock. It has been suggested, however, that the family's earlier roots lay in Argyll in the West of Scotland when an ancestor had to leave there because he offended his clan chief by siding with the Jacobites at the time of the Glorious Revolution in 1688. The family then settled in the parish of Glenbervie in Kincardineshire.[4] This tale was perpetuated by family tradition and the fact that they came to live in a part of Scotland where staunch Jacobites, the Keiths, were one of the principal families. Earl Marischal, head of the Keiths, remained stubbornly loyal to the Stuart Pretenders and abandoned them only after Bonnie Prince Charlie treated him badly and the Prince's wild behaviour destroyed the Cause.

Robert Burns himself helped to keep this story alive. He genuinely believed his family had suffered by supporting the exiled James Stuart, and told John Ramsay of Ochtertyre that his grandfather had worked as gardener to the Earl Marischal at Inverugie Castle in Aberdeenshire, but had been 'plundered and driven out in the year 1715.'[5] He confirmed this in his autobiographical letter to Dr John Moore in 1787. 'My Fathers rented land of the noble Keiths of Marshal, and had the honor to share their fate,' he told Moore.[6]

Subsequent writers have taken tradition and the Poet's words as the truth, but there is no known evidence that Burns' grandfather ever supported the Old Pretender during the 1715 Rising. Biographer James Mackay suggests, however, that the earlier story of being forced to leave Argyll may be true, but if so, it must relate to Covenanting times around the middle of the seventeenth century rather than to the Glorious Revolution towards the end of it.[7]

Whatever misfortune struck the Burneses, they fell on hard times, and in 1748, the Poet's father and his brothers, had to strike out for themselves. One moved to Montrose and another to Ayrshire, but William walked to Edinburgh where he found work on private estates and later helped to lay out the parkland of what is now the Meadows on the south side of the old city. Two years later he headed west to Ayrshire, where his brother, Robert, had already settled, and for a time he worked for Alexander Fairlie of Fairlie in the north of the county before moving south in 1754 to become gardener to John Crawford at Doonside, near Alloway.

William lodged just across the River Doon at Doonside Mill, and settled down to work hard and save hard, even tendering successfully at one point to build a short stretch of road at Alloway for the local authorities, and helping Provost William Fergusson to lay out the gardens of his estate at Doonholm. There was precious little Burnes could not turn his hand to.

His ambition was to be independent and possess his own market garden and, by June 1756, he had gathered together enough money to feu (or lease) some land at Alloway from Dr Alexander Campbell, a doctor in Ayr, and here he planned to create a market garden. He named his holding New Gardens and on the eastern edge of the $7\frac{1}{2}$ acre holding, started to build a dwelling house, Burns Cottage, which is still standing today.

All he needed now was a wife, but the canny William had that in hand too. He was courting a girl at Alloway Mill nearby and according to tradition – it is amazing how tradition always comes to our rescue by filling the gaps in Burns' story – he had his marriage proposal written out and all ready in his pocket to hand to her when the time was ripe. This was when he went to one of the fairs in Maybole and discovered, as his son was also to find later, that the best laid plans of men 'gang aft agley.'*. This time, however, it was a piece of good fortune, for instead he met Agnes Brown of the red hair and bewitching smile and fell in love.

Agnes was the eldest of six children of Gilbert Broun and his wife Agnes Rennie, and had grown up at Craigenton Farm, near Turnberry, when her parents joined her paternal grandfather who was tenant farmer there. When Agnes was only ten, her mother died, leaving the girl to look after her siblings and help her father to run the house.

It is reputed that while Gilbert Brown's wife lay dying, her sister asked her, 'Are you not sorry to leave your husband and your children?' The dying woman replied: 'No – I leave my children to the care of God, and Gilbert will soon get another wife.'[8] Gilbert did find himself another wife within two years and Agnes, no longer needed to care for her brothers and sisters, was packed off to her Granny Rennie in Maybole. There she helped her grandmother and a blind uncle who lived with them. Agnes worked hard both indoors and out, spinning, helping to cultivate the Rennies' small patch of land just outside the town and to harvest the crops and thresh the grain. Agnes Brown had virtually no schooling at Craigenton or in Maybole, and all she ever learnt was the Bible and how to be an uncomplaining domestic drudge; she could not even sign her own name. The only relaxation she enjoyed was singing the old ballads which her grandmother taught her. Agnes picked up more songs from William Nelson, the hired man beside whom she worked in the fields; a bond grew between them which eventually led to a promise of marriage. Poor Nelson could not afford to marry, however, and Agnes was too high principled to allow him pre-marital sex, so the engagement dragged on for seven years without hope or sexual gratification until Nelson fell from grace by getting another girl into trouble, and Agnes refused to have anything more to do with him.

It was at that moment that she encountered William Burnes during one of the fairs in Maybole's steep High Street; the spot is marked by a bust of their poet son, but nobody notices it unless it is pointed out as it is set

*often go wrong

high on the gabled roof of Willie Ross's butcher's shop, far above eye level.

On 15 December the following year, 1757, William and Agnes were married and settled down to life together in the cottage William had built with his own hands at Alloway. There, fifteen months later, on 25 January 1759, their first child was born. They named him Robert after William's father.

Robert was the first of seven children born to William and Agnes Burnes. Gilbert followed in 1760, then Agnes (1762), Annabella (1764), William (1767), John (1769) and Isabella (1771). The Burnses reared their children well and, at this time when infant mortality was high, every one of their children survived early childhood with all its hazards. Only John died young, at the age of sixteen, and William fell victim to an epidemic of some kind in London in 1790.

Life at Alloway was not easy: William never had enough capital and the climate was always against him and his market garden failed to prosper as he had hoped. He continued with his gardening job at Doonholm, and eventually sold off part of his New Gardens land. While her husband worked at Provost Fergusson's gardens, Agnes was left at home to do much of the work in the market garden, milk the cows, make cheese, run the house and look after her growing brood. She found no problem in this with those years of experience at Craigenton and Maybole behind her. Betty Davidson, the poor widow of one of her cousins, came to live with them and helped her.

As his boys began to grow up, William worried that they would end up virtual slaves working for some farmer, so he decided to take a farm of his own, where the whole family could remain together and earn a comfortable living. His employer at Doonholm owned a farm called Mount Oliphant, only a couple of miles away from Alloway, and he offered Burnes a twelve-year tenancy on a lease which contained a break clause half way through. There were problems, however, for Mount Oliphant was poor with unimproved soil and Burnes was unable to dispose of the lease of New Gardens to raise the capital he needed to start in the farm. Once more Provost Fergusson came to the rescue, and offered a loan of £100, so at Whitsun 1766, when Robert was just seven and his brother, Gilbert five, the Burnes family moved to Mount Oliphant full of hope.

Before the move it had become plain to William and Agnes that their eldest child was remarkably clever. From his youngest days he had listened spellbound to his mother's singing and Betty Davidson's stories. 'I owed much to an old Maid of my Mother's, remarkable for her ignorance, credulity and superstition,' he told Dr Moore:

She had, I suppose, the largest collection in the county of tales and songs concerning devils, ghosts, fairies, brownies, witches, warlocks, spunkies, kelpies, elf candles, dead-lights, wraiths, apparitions, cantraips, giants, inchanted towers, dragons and other trumpery. This cultivated the latent seeds of Poesy; but had so strong an effect on my imagination, that to this hour, in my nocturnal rambles, I sometimes keep a sharp look-out in suspicious places: and though nobody can be more sceptical in these matters than I, yet it often takes an effort of Philosophy to shake off these idle terrors.[9]

Betty did not need to make up all the tales of ghosts that frightened young Robert around Alloway. When he was about nine years of age a stray Highland bullock made its way into the roofless old kirk in the village, and became trapped there without food or water. A day or two later a local woman passing by saw a horned head staring at her through an unglazed window. It let out a loud bellow when it saw her, and she fled in terror, convinced that the Devil had been in the Auld Kirk and now was after her.[10] Burns' imagination raced at the thought of the ghostly ruin, and he recounted a number of adventures around it – how someone had dared to steal a cauldron from its infernal inhabitants, and how a shepherd boy once flew away to Bordeaux with the witches of Alloway. There was also the story of a farmer who encountered the warlocks and witches there as he rode home, a wee bit the worse for wear with drink one night.[11] Years later that last tale was turned into *Tam O' Shanter*, when he agreed to write a poem to accompany a drawing by Captain Francis Grose of the old haunted kirk:

> Before him Doon pours all his floods;
> The doubling storm roars thro the woods;
> The lightnings flash from pole to pole,
> Near and more near the thunders roll:
> When, glimmering thro the groaning trees,
> Kirk-Alloway seem'd in a bleeze*,               *blaze
> Thro ilka bore* the beams were glancing,     *every crevice
> And loud resounded mirth and dancing.[12]

All his life he remembered those 'ghosts' that haunted his childhood, but he treasured especially the songs his mother sang as she worked around the house – they were the spark that first kindled the fires of song in him. He loved to listen to his mother's old ballads, unaware that he was storing their words, tunes and rhythms away in his mind for future use. One can only wonder what his child's mind made of the coarse words of one which remained a firm favourite all his life – beloved enough for him to use it in his collection of bawdy songs, *The Merry Muses of Caledonia,* and credit as 'an auld sang o my Mither's'.[13] He cleaned it up in 1792 as *O, Can Ye Labour Lea,* but the last verse came almost straight from his mother's lips:

> O, kissin is the key o' love
>   And clappin is the lock,
> An makin ot's the best thing,
>     That e'er a young thing got![14]

The only school in the neighbourhood had closed almost as soon as William's sons, Robert and Gilbert, started at it, so Burnes joined with four of his neighbours to hire a young man to teach their children. John Murdoch was still not out of his teens himself, but he was obviously a good teacher and a thorough one: as well as reading and writing, he taught the boys to spell, parse sentences, memorize hymns and poems, and learn the meaning of every word in every sentence they read. Oddly enough, Gilbert was the one who struck Murdoch as having the liveliest imagination and Robert seemed singularly slow to learn a tune. 'I attempted to teach them a little church music,' wrote Murdoch years later. 'Here they were left far behind by all the rest of the school. It was long before I could get them to distinguish one tune from another.'[15]

'Left far behind by all the rest of the school . . . long before I could get them to distinguish one tune from another'? Could Robert Burns, the man who gave the world such richness of song, who could handle complex and difficult rhythms with genius, possibly have been tone deaf? The point has been argued by a number of writers, without offering any acceptable explanation. Hans Hecht quotes Keats as being thoroughly puzzled by this 'most unpoetical' poet who sinks his individuality in his creations.[16] Another biographer, Catherine Carswell, believed the melody was there, but Burns' problem was that he just could not sing.[17] Perhaps not, but he could create songs, and one must wonder if James Mackay has not hit on the truth when he suggested that the stubborn young Burns in the schoolroom simply refused to give his best because Murdoch wanted him to sing dull psalms and not the exhilarating Scots folk-songs he heard at home.[18] As a result, in his own words, 'I cost the schoolmaster some thrashings.'[19] In Burns' part of Scotland and mine there is a word *essert,* which means extreme stubbornness, and Robert Burns certainly suffered from that. So did his father. It was (and probably is still) a common complaint, for my father suffered from it too, and so do I. And so, I'm sure, do countless numbers of my fellow countrymen.

William Burnes' high principles and dour determination to do what was right must have caused confrontations with his son, and his mother's temper, difficult to control according to daughter Isabella, could have led to unreported confrontations, but the house at Alloway and later Mount Oliphant, where they farmed from 1766 until 1777, must have held security in spite of the financial troubles which dogged William Burnes' footsteps.

John Murdoch, the teacher, was not exaggerating when he told J.C. Wallace, 'In this mean cottage, of which I myself was at times an inhabitant, I really believe there dwelt a larger portion of content, than in any Palace of Europe.'[20] Around the time of his twenty-seventh birthday, Burns composed a poem which summed up the background in which he grew up: *The Cotter's\* Saturday Night*,[21] although clearly influenced by Gray's *Elegy*, is largely autobiographical as it sets the scene of life at Alloway, Mount Oliphant, and then at Lochlie.

| | |
|---|---|
| November chill blaws loud wi' angry sugh\*; | \*rushing sound |
|   The short'ning winter-day is near a close; | |
| The miry beasts retreating frae the pleugh\*; | \*plough |
|   The black'ning trains o craws\* to their repose: | \*crows |
|   The toil-worn Cotter frae his labor goes, – | |
| This night his weekly moil is at an end, | |
|   Collects his spades, his mattocks, and his hoes, | |
| Hoping the morn in ease and rest to spend, | |
| And weary, o'er the moor, his course does hameward bend. | |

His wife and young children wait to welcome him, 'expectant wee things', just as Robert must have waited at the door for his own father, and his brothers and sisters waited to welcome him when he was old enough to work in the fields. Then they are joined by the older members of the family who had been hired out as servants on other farms, the fate their father had tried so hard to spare them.

| | |
|---|---|
| With joy unfeign'd, brothers and sisters meet, | |
|   And each for other's welfare kindly spiers\*; | \*inquires |
| The social hours, swift-wing'd, unnotic'd fleet; | |
|   Each tells the uncos\* that he sees or hears. | \*unusual news |

\*cotter or cottar = married farmworker who has a cottage as part of his contract of employment

The parents partial eye their hopeful years;
Anticipation forward points the view;
 The mother, wi her needle and her sheers*     *scissors
Gars auld claes* look amaist as weel's the new;  *makes old clothes
The father mixes a' wi admonition due.

They exchange gossip, laugh and enjoy a supper of 'halesome parritch'*, welcome the boyfriend of one of the girls, and then their father reads from the Bible and they sing psalms to the old favourite tunes, *Dundee, Martyrs* and *Elgin*, before they set out for their homes again. Burns may have preferred folk ballads, but if *The Cotter's Saturday Night* paints as accurate a picture of his home life as it seems to, then he cannot have disliked the psalm tunes as much as Mackay has suggested:

They chant their artless notes in simple guise,
 They tune their hearts, by far the noblest aim;
Perhaps *Dundee's* wild-warbling measures rise,
 Or plaintive *Martyrs*, worthy of the name;
 Or noble *Elgin* beets* the heavenward flame,     *fans
The sweetest far of Scotia's holy lays:
 Compar'd with these, Italian trills are tame;
The tickl'd ears no heart-felt raptures raise;
Nae unison hae they, with our Creator's praise.

Robert learnt well from his parents: in their relationship he saw how devotion transcended all the difficulties life could throw at them – contrasts in temperament, values, outlook, day-to-day problems of finance, and coping with the whims of climate and farming. However hard their existence might be, however cheerless and unceasing the toil, nothing could ever come between them. On top of this was Robert's mother's love of love, demonstrated from morning till night in the old ballads she sang, and the art and rhythm of love that these songs imprinted into his receptive mind. His father's upright honesty gave him values to live up to, but the final essential ingredient he needed to turn him into a poet came from his father who no matter how hard things were, ensured that his sons received an education far above that of the average farmer's son in Ayrshire at the time. If the poet's temperament and song-writer's rhythms were inherited from his mother, the tools of the wordsmith came from William Burnes.

*porridge

It was in 1773, or more probably 1774, while he was still only fifteen, that Robert first committed the sin of rhyme (a jocular remark). Burns himself explained in detail how it happened:

You know our country custom of coupling a man and woman together as Partners in the labors of harvest. In my fifteenth autumn, my Partner was a bewitching creature who just counted an autumn less . . . she was a bonie, sweet, sonsie lass. In short, she altogether unwittingly to herself, initiated me in a certain delicious Passion, which in spite of acid Disappointment, gin-horse Prudence and bookworm Philosophy, I hold to be the first of human joys, our dearest pleasure here below . . . I never expressly told her that I loved her. Indeed I did not well know myself, why I liked so much to loiter hehind with her, when returning in the evening from our labors; why the tones of her voice made my heartstrings thrill like an Eolian harp; and particularly why my pulse beat such a furious ratann when I looked and fingered over her hand, to pick out the nettle-stings and thistles.

The girl, like his mother, had a sweet voice and, when she sang a reel tune to which some love-sick small laird's son had composed words, Robert could not resist the challenge of matching, if not bettering it:

I saw no reason why I might not rhyme as well as he, for excepting smearing sheep and casting peats, his father living in the moors, he had no more Schoolcraft than I had.

Thus with me began Love and Poesy.[22]

It was not the best song Burns was ever to write – in fact it has come in for considerable criticism, and the poet himself even admitted it was 'very puerile and silly'. But lyrical imperfections did not matter: the fifteen-year-old Burns was in love with *Handsome Nell* and forever after she melted his heart. 'I remember I composed it in a wild enthusiasm of passion, and to this hour I never recollect it, but my heart melts, and my blood sallies at the remembrance.'[23]

> O once I lov'd a bonie lass,
>   Ay, and I love her still!
> And whilst that virtue warms my breast,
>   I'll love my handsome Nell.

> As bonie lasses I hae seen,
>   And monie full as braw,
> But for a modest gracefu mien
>   The like I never saw.[24]

Burnsians have argued for two centuries over the identity of this girl as well as over the date of the song. When Elizabeth Scott of Wauchope, sent him a long, entertaining poem in Scots dialect, congratulating him on the Kilmarnock Edition, he answered her with a poem in which he described the girl who first 'lighted up my jingle',[25] but he did not give away her name.

We know her only as *Handsome Nell*, the title of the song, and today she is generally accepted as having been Nellie Kilpatrick, daughter of the miller at Purclewan at Dalrymple, who was less than a year younger than Burns. Latest research swings towards another *Handsome Nell*, Helen Blair, who was first suggested as the girl in the cornfield as long ago as 1828 in an anonymous letter to *The Scotsman* newspaper. The Reverend Hamilton Paul, who met *Handsome Nell* in 1811, said Nell had married a Carrick farmer and had a large brood of sons and daughters, a description which does not fit Nellie Kilpatrick but comes close to Helen Blair, who married a man called John Smith and lived at Dailly in Carrick. If *The Scotsman* was right and Helen Blair is *Handsome Nell*, then we have lost a number of other poems which the letter-writer claims Burns wrote to her. Nell may have been in love with Burns, but the farmer for whom she worked as a maid thought little of her suitor from Mount Oliphant. He considered him 'a clever fellow, but a wild scamp.'[26]

William Burnes was a good father and, in spite of his continual financial straits, determined to give his sons as good a start in life as he possibly could. After John Murdoch moved to Ayr, he sent Robert there for lessons, and for a time the boy also attended school at Dalrymple a couple of miles from Mount Oliphant. Robert was well advanced by now in his study of English, but his knowledge of mathematics was poor, so during the summer of 1775, before harvest-time came round, he was sent to Kirkoswald to study under Hugh Rodger, the schoolmaster there, a noted teacher of mathematics and surveying. Kirkoswald offered the great advantage that it lay in Agnes's home country, so the lad could stay with his Brown relations, which would be an economy. No one is sure just how long Robert stayed at Kirkoswald, living at Ballochneil, with his mother's brother, Samuel, and his wife, and attending Dominie Rodgers' school each day.

Kirkoswald may have been convenient, but it had one great drawback, which William Burnes could not have foreseen – it was one of the wildest places in the whole of Ayrshire if not in Scotland. Although the village itself lay several miles inland, the parish ran down to a wild and remote stretch of the Firth of Clyde coast. At that time the whole Ayrshire coast was plagued with smugglers, or free-traders as they were called, who secretly landed silks, tea, tobacco and brandy – especially brandy, much of which was consumed before it had the chance to reach its market. Kirkoswald's coast contained several remote landing places as well as cliffs which were pocked with caves in which the contraband could be stored. Even though the great architect, Robert Adam, had started to build a magnificent castle on the clifftop at Culzean for the 10th Earl of Cassillis three years before Burns came to Kirkoswald, smuggling was still in full swing when he arrived there in 1775.

Robert, out of his father's sight for the first time apart from brief visits to Ayr to study with Dominie Murdoch, savoured the wild life of the village, although he can hardly have participated in it to the extent he suggested. When he came to put his memories of the weeks spent there down on paper, he did not spoil the story in the telling.

> I spent my seventeenth summer on a smuggling coast a good distance from home at a noted school, to learn Mensuration, Surveying, Dialling, &c. in which I made a pretty good progress. But I made greater progress in the knowledge of mankind. The contraband trade was at that time very successful; scenes of swaggering riot and roaring dissipation were as yet new to me; and I was no enemy to social life. Here, though I learned to look unconcernedly on a large tavern-bill, and mix without fear in a drunken squabble.[27]

Robert certainly was not able to afford to join in the roaring dissipation, although no doubt he emulated the smugglers' swagger whenever he could. Along with classmate Willie Niven, from Maybole, who became a lifelong friend, he was able to enjoy a social life such as he had never known before. The blustering life of the village even gave the boy the courage to debate with Dominie Rodger and to backchat the minister. One day the Reverend Mathew Biggar, on his way down the Kirk Brae, met Burns on his way up, and asked where he was going. 'As you see, Sir, I am going heavenwards,' replied the cheeky young Burns and walked on, leaving the minister to contemplate on his own direction of travel.[28]

Young Burns stored up all that he saw and the characters he met for future use in *Tam O' Shanter*. A number of these characters lie in the graveyard of Kirkoswald's old ruined church alongside Burns' own grandparents and great-grandparents: Douglas Graham and his wife, Helen McTaggart (Tam O' Shanter himself, a farmer with smuggling interests, and his scold of a wife, Kate), John Davidson (Souter Johnnie, his ancient, trusty, drouthy* cronie) and Jean Kennedy (Kirkton Jean at whose pub Tam drank from Sunday right through till Monday).

In spite of all the diversions, Robert made pretty good progress with his studies for a time until it all came to an abrupt finish, thanks to a girl.

I went on with a high hand in my Geometry; till the sun enterd Virgo, a month which is always a carnival in my bosom, a charming Fillette who lived next door to the school overset my Trigonometry and set me off in a tangent from the sphere of my studies. I struggled on with my Sines and Co-sines for a few days more; but stepping out to the garden one charming noon, to take the sun's altitude, I met with my Angel,

> 'Like Proserpine gathering flowers,
> Herself a fairer flower'     [Milton, *Paradise Lost*]

It was vain to think of doing any more good at school. The remaining week I staid, I did nothing but craze the faculties of my soul about her, or steal out to meet with her; and the two last nights of my stay in the country, had sleep been a mortal sin, I was innocent.[29]

In spite of this turbulent end to his studies, he claimed that he went home 'considerably improved' in the breadth of his reading, his knowledge of mankind, and with new friends with whom to correspond. Not a breath of what Dominie Rodger had put into his head in the field of mathematics or surveying, so one can only assume he had learnt little of the subjects he had gone to Kirkoswald specially to study.

The 'charming Fillette' was none other than the girl next door, Margaret (Peggy) Thomson, whom he first saw in the garden adjoining the school when he went out to measure the sun's altitude. Peggy was only thirteen at the time,[30] and the question is was this a mere juvenile flirtation or was there physical love between them? The encounter was passionate enough for both Burns and Peggy to be affected by it for years afterwards; therefore, one must accept at the very least, a likelihood that the two tried to share a full sexual relationship. However, one or the

*thirsty

other (probably Peggy) may well have been too inexperienced to carry it through. Robert stated explicitly that if sleep had been a mortal sin, on their last two nights together they were innocent. Whether all that happened was that they lay together, or more likely, they made some blundering juvenile attempt at sexual intercourse, they remained extremely fond of one another ever after.

It was now harvest-time and Robert had to hurry back to Mount Oliphant to help with the corn-cutting, but he did not forget the girl who had upset his studies. The two kept in touch for years afterwards through a fellow scholar at Kirkoswald, Thomas Orr, and Peggy hoped Robert might come back to her; but he did not. Eventually she married a local man, William Nelson, in 1784, and Robert wrote a letter to Orr at that time, which referred to an unidentified girl called 'Peggy', surely Peggy Thomson? By that time Robert Burns was caught up with yet another girl, and he told Orr he was thankful to learn the news. 'I am very glad Peggy is off my hands as I am at present embarrassed enough without her,' he told his former schoolmate.[31]

Thankful as he was to be free of any obligation to Peggy he still remembered her and touchingly sent her a copy of his first book of poems when they were published in 1786 with an inscription which began:

> Once fondly loved and still remember'd dear,
>   Sweet early object of my youthful vows,
> Accept this mark of friendship, warm, sincere
>   (Friendship! 'tis all cold duty now allows.)[32]

'Fondly loved . . . still remember'd dear . . . early object of my youthful vows'. Is there some hidden agenda here? Did he make promises during those two sleepless nights just as he was to make promises to 'Highland Mary' and Jean Armour later? In Kirkoswald Burns had been smitten, and once smitten he could not shake off the fever of love. When the high tides of the Jean Armour and 'Highland Mary' affairs were threatening to sweep him away and he decided to make his escape by emigrating to the West Indies, he went to Kirkoswald to say goodbye to his relatives and called on Peggy.

It is surprising that Peggy Thompson generated little poetry considering the enduring remembrance he had of that chance meeting in the garden behind the school in Kirkoswald. Apart from those lines in the book he sent her, she appears in only one of his songs, *Now Westlin Winds* (also known as *Song Composed in August*).

But, Peggy, dear, the ev'ning's clear,
  Thick flies the skimming swallow;
The sky is blue, the fields in view,
  All fading-green and yellow:
Come let us stray our gladsome way,
  And view the charms of Nature;
The rustling corn, the fruited thorn,
  And ilka* happy creature.              *every

We'll gently walk, and sweetly talk,
  While the silent moon shines clearly
I'll clasp thy waist, and fondly prest,
  Swear how I lo'e thee dearly:
Not vernal show'rs to budding flow'rs,
  Not Autumn to the farmer,
So dear can be as thou to me,
  My fair, my lovely charmer![33]

Mount Oliphant in September 1775, brought Robert back to reality which was bewildering, harsh and incomprehensible to a sixteen-year-old who had just seen the world! A thousand times he must have asked how life could be so easy and carefree at Kirkoswald, yet in his father's house only a few miles away, drab poverty laid its dead hand on everything. Lack of money dominated every day they were in Mount Oliphant, to the point that they could not afford to extricate themselves from the mess when they might legally have done so at the half-way point in their lease. Dr Fergusson generously did not press for the money he had lent William Burnes to take over the farm in the first place, but even so the unimproved land proved a hard bargain.

Fergusson died the year after Robert was in Kirkoswald and a factor took over the running of the estate: he dunned poor Burnes for money owed and made life a misery for all of them. That last year of their lease on Mount Oliphant affected the members of the Burns family in different ways: while Robert simmered over the factor's 'snash'*, Gilbert appeared to accept it all in silence for he never referred to it, and their father's spirit 'was soon irritated, but not easily broken.'[34] None the less his health suffered under the strain and all Agnes and the younger children could do was weep as they watched the change in the poor husband and father.

*sneering abuse

Robert who had his mother's fire in his make-up had to wait to take his revenge, for the episode bit too deeply to be dismissed in a clever little quatrain: it needed more, much more, and it was to take ten years for him to savage the factor in *The Twa Dogs*, a conversation between a poor man's dog and a rich man's dog. He told Dr Moore that the factor 'sat for the picture I have drawn . . . in my Tale of two dogs.'[35] Even then, ten years after the event, he said his indignation boiled over when he recollected the factor and his threatening letters. However, his revenge in *The Twa Dogs* must have felt sweet:

| | |
|---|---|
| I've notic'd, on our laird's court-day* | *rent-day |
| (And monie a time my heart's been wae*). | *sad |
| Poor tenant bodies, scant o cash, | |
| How they maun thole* a factor's snash: | *suffer |
| He'll stamp and threaten, curse and swear | |
| He'll apprehend them, poind their gear; | |
| While they maun stan, wi aspect humble, | |
| An hear it a', and fear an tremble![36] | |

Eventually Dr Fergusson's heirs proved as generous as their father and an instrument of seisin was drawn up in favour of the old doctor's daughters, Elizabeth, Jean, Eleonora, Margaret and Susanne, and Jean's husband, John Hunter; and now Burnes was lent £145 on the security of the still unsold cottage and gardens at Alloway. This allowed him to struggle on until the lease came to an end at last and he was able to take a lease on another farm, nearly twice as large, which should offer him a better living.

Lochlie, sometimes spelt Lochly but usually Lochlea nowadays, lay about 10 miles away from Mount Oliphant, near the village of Tarbolton. At Whitsun in 1777 the family moved there, and settled down to what they hoped would be a contented life and a fair living. Robert was only eighteen at the time of the move, but at Lochlie he had to work as hard as a mature man, and it was at this time that overwork laid the foundations for later ill health that led to his early death. But in 1777 there was no thought of that: he worked hard and played harder for Lochlie had one great advantage in that the farm lay close to both Tarbolton and Mauchline, so it provided him with opportunities to expand his social life. What a change that was from lonely isolated Mount Oliphant where they rarely saw anyone but members of their own family. 'There were no boys of our own age or near it, in the neighbourhood,' Gilbert said. 'My father was for some time almost the only companion we had.'[37]

Robert rejoiced in his new life at Tarbolton, and aired his French, which was remarkably good for a man with so little formal education, when he told Dr Moore of his carefree approach to women and enjoyment. 'My life flowed on in the same tenor till my twenty-third year – *Vive l'amour et vive la bagatelle*, were my sole principles of action,' he wrote.[38] But this wide social life changed him more than he himself probably realized. His brother noted that Robert, who had been 'bashful and awkward' with women in his young days became a different person. 'When he approached manhood, his attachment to their society became very strong, and he was constantly the victim of some fair enslaver,' said Gilbert, who noted also that his brother never chose women who were richer or more socially superior. 'When he selected any . . . to whom he should pay his particular attention, she was instantly invested with a sufficient stock of charms, out of the plentiful stores of his imagination; and there was often a great disparity between his fair captivator, and her attributes.'[39]

Gilbert was not the only member of the family to worry about Robert's waywardness: around the Kirkoswald time he decided to attend a country dancing school to give his manners 'a brush', to the intense annoyance of his father, who went so far as to forbid him to take part in such frivolity. Robert defied his father and went, but later suffered from a troubled conscience, for he said this was a watershed in relations between the two of them. He went so far as to blame this discord for being the cause of his own future wild life.[40]

Burns was right to single out his father as shaping his future wild behaviour and difficult relationships with people. William Burnes expected much of his son even as a child, far too much, so that there was always an uneasy truce between them. William Burnes recognized that his son was brilliant, but failed to see that behind the scholastic ability lay a sensitive, perceptive mind. He saw Robert as unreliable and wayward as the boy grew up. No more could Robert comprehend this narrow man, driven by a high moral sense, who would accept nothing short of perfection, yet he respected and feared his father. Young Burns was kept on such a tight parental rein that the moment he smelt freedom, first at Kirkoswald and later at Irvine and Tarbolton, he broke loose. But events always seemed to go against him and he had to return home to humiliate himself before a disapproving father.

Burns' mother influenced him too, and not just by singing songs and telling him tales which sparked his imagination and interest in folk-songs. Agnes Burnes has always been thought well of, largely, one suspects, because she kept quiet whenever an outsider was within earshot. She reared her children well, but in her own way was as iron-willed as her husband, and her daughter, Isabella, said she had a fiery temper. She was hard-working, but without learning, or any desire for books.

Undoubtedly Robert inherited his mother's more carefree approach to life, but he also grew up with her ability to explode into a rage when something upset him. Perhaps they were too much alike, for it is significant that he rarely mentioned his mother, but confided to Mrs Frances Dunlop all the things a young man might want to say to his mother. Burns could express his literary aspirations and even confess his personal indiscretions to Mrs Dunlop, who became a kind of substitute mother to him.

Burns, as a result of his upbringing and his own hyper-sensitive mind, grew into an insecure man, who hid his distrust of the world behind an aggressive approach to everything in life, even sex. Above all Robert Burns could never cope with rejection or failure, and always remained quick to take offence. In his relationships with the opposite sex he was forceful to the point of belligerence, so that when he wrote of his sexual exploits, he often described them in military terms, for they were battles in which he was either leading a glorious attack, or being routed humiliatingly. But he was always ready to rally his troops for another charge.

William Burnes' 'strong passions' became more forceful as he aged and his health deteriorated: he disapproved of much of his son's behaviour, but that did not stop Robert from continuing assiduously to cultivate his social life. It must be said, however, that Robert never neglected to carry his share of the burden of work on the farm.

At the plough, scythe or reap-hook I feared no competitor . . . I spent the evening in the way after my own heart. A country lad rarely carries on an amour without an assisting confident. I possessed a curiosity, zeal and intrepid dexterity in these matters which recommended me a proper Second in duels of that kind; and I dare say, I felt as much pleasure at being in the secret of half the amours in the parish, as ever did Premier at knowing the intrigues of half the courts of Europe.[41]

Adam Armour and his sister, Jean, would soon be able to vouch for that. Robert's apprenticeship in love was now complete and he was ready to immerse himself in the practice of it.

# CHAPTER THREE

# Silk Purses and Sows' Lugs

But woman, Nature's darling child –
    There all her charms she does compile;
Even there her other works are foil'd
    By the bonie lass o Ballochmyle.

The Lass o' Ballochmyle[1]

As always young Robert's landscape was filled with people wherever he went. He spent much of his free time wandering by the river or in the woods with only his own thoughts or a book (which he took everywhere, even to the dinner table) for company. But of course if there was a human being to be seen, preferably an attractive woman, his heart burst into flame. Towards sunset one evening in the late summer of 1786, while walking beside the River Ayr, he met the sister of a local laird, Wilhelmina Alexander of Ballochmyle. She was far too superior to take notice of him, or to be spoken to, so he walked on, but later he remembered her and invested her with 'a stock of charms,' which led him to write a poem to her, *The Lass o' Ballochmyle*. The *lass* was already thirty and well on the way to becoming the old maid she remained until she died at the age of ninety, but that did not stop Burns, in his usual way, from turning her into a young beauty.

Her look was like the morning's eye,
    Her air like Nature's vernal smile.
Perfection whisper'd, passing by:–
    'Behold the lass o' Ballochmyle!'

But Rab Burns knew Miss Alexander was far above him socially and that he could only gaze at her and think what might have been had she belonged to his own class:

O, had she been a country maid,
    And I the happy country swain,
Tho shelter'd in the lowest shed
    That ever rose on Scotia's plain!

Thro weary winter's wind and rain
  With joy, with rapture, I would toil,
And nightly to my bosom strain
  The bonie lass o' Ballochmyle!

Then Pride might climb the slipp'ry steep,
  Where fame and honours lofty shine;
And thirst of gold might tempt the deep,
  Or downward seek the Indian mine!
Give me the cot below the pine,
  To tend the flocks or till the soil;
And ev'ry day have joys divine
  With the bonie lass o' Ballochmyle.

His first book of poems was about to be published, so she would know
him at least by name: he plucked up courage, therefore, to send the
verses to her with a request that she might permit him to publish them in
his next volume. His letter was quite outrageously over the top: 'Such was
the scene, and such the hour, when in a corner of my Prospect I spyed
one of the finest pieces of Nature's workmanship that ever crowned a
poetic Landskip . . .' and there was more, much more. Hardly
surprisingly, the answer was silence: he felt so desperately snubbed that
he never had time for the Alexanders of Ballochmyle, and even years
afterwards, when he copied the song out for the Glenriddell Manuscript,
he added the note:

Well Mr Burns, & did the Lady give you the desired 'Permission?' No!
She was too fine a Lady to notice so plain a compliment. As to her great
brothers, whom I have since met in life on more 'equal' terms of
respectability, why should I quarrel their want of attention to me? When
Fate swore that their purses should be full, Nature was equally positive
that their heads should be empty. 'Men of their fashion were surely
incapable of being unpolite?' Ye canna mak a silk-purse o' a sow's lug*.[2]

The irony is that Wilhelmina Alexander kept Burns' letter and the poem
and they became treasured possessions in her old age.
  There were to be many 'sows' ears' among both men and women in
Robert Burns' life during the decade after he left Mount Oliphant, and
to be truthful he tried to make silk purses out of quite a number of them.

*ear

But work had to continue as he tried to make ends meet on the farm: Lochlie brought relief, blessed relief – albeit temporary – such as William and Agnes Burnes had never known in all their married days. For Robert it opened up a new life: he was now eighteen and on the verge of manhood. He had grown to his full five feet nine inches in height; in looks he was attractive enough in spite of a broad forehead and coarsish features inherited from his mother, which prevented him from being really handsome. His dark face always had a rather serious look, but glowing – almost melancholy – eyes penetrated the heart of everyone who looked into them. Young Lochlie had a taste for high fashion now: David Sillar, a local lad who fancied himself as a poet, too, and cultivated a friendship with Robert, noted that young Burns tied his brown, curling hair back, the only man in the parish to do so. 'And in the church his plaid, which was of a particular colour, I think fileemot* he wrapped in a particular manner round his shoulders', said Sillar, who was so taken by this newcomer that he went out of his way to get to know him.[3] Burns was well aware that people in the village turned to stare when he passed by.

> My coat and my vest, they are Scotch o the best;
>  O pairs o guid breeks* I hae twa, man,      *trousers
> And stockings and pumps to put on my stumps,
>  And ne'er a wrang steek* in them a', man.    *wrong stitch
>
> My sarks* they are few, but five o them new –    *shirts
>  Twal' hundred*, as white as the snaw, man!    *fine linen
> A ten-shilling hat, a Holland cravat –
>  There are no monie Poets sae braw, man![4]

This description of himself was part of a jibe at Jean and Anne Ronald, daughters of a prosperous farmer at the Bennals farm close to Lochlie, who had proved impervious to his overtures. Burns still felt insecure enough to react sharply to criticism or rejection, even fear of rejection, and it was said that he would fain have offered hand and heart to Anne Ronald, but feared she might refuse him,[5] a view borne out in the poem itself:

> I lo'e her mysel, but darena weel tell,
>  My poverty keeps me in awe, man.

*russet brown, from the French *feuille morte*, meaning dead leaf

And his stubborn, obdurate, silly pride came out in the stanza that followed:

> Yet I wadna\* choose to let her refuse          \*would not
>   Nor hae't\* in her power to say na, man'          \*have it
> For though I be poor, unnoticed, obscure,
>   My stomach's as proud as them a', man.

The Ronalds were not alone in being singled out for the poet's ungallant attention: others suffered his mocking barbs too. He composed a poem on the *Tarbolton Lasses*,[6] in which he mocked several of them – Peggy was too conscious of the fact that her father was a laird, Sophy was an easy conquest in the hay, while Mysie was dour, and Jenny had little sense. Even praise for bonnie Bessy's charms carried a barb.

> There's few sae bonie, nane sae guid,
> In a' King George's dominion:
> If ye should doubt the truth o this,
> It's Bessy's ain opinion!

No wonder then that Tarbolton was suspicious of the arrival of a 'proud stomach' in its midst, and not just the lassies.

The village's weaving trade had suffered badly about the time the Burnes arrived at Lochlie because of the national economic depression due to the American War of Independence. But life went on, with the village awakening each morning and going to bed at night to the tuck of the town drum. Between the drum calls there was a daily routine of weaving, meetings of the Friendly Society, gossip at the bridge, broken on Sundays by kirk attendance, and a gala day when the Coilsfield hounds were out, or the summer cattle fair came round. On the whole it was an unedifying life, as Robert's friend, David Sillar, put it, 'uncontaminated by reading, conversation or reflection.'[7]

All incomers were bound to be looked upon with great suspicion and accepted slowly or not at all, and the Burns family, who arrived with a reputation for pride and poverty, were welcomed without much warmth. Indeed, Robert, with his jaunty dress, versifying and notion for reading books, may have been well received by a few young men of his own age who admired his rebellious spirit, but there were many who never accepted him. Writing more than a century later, a local man, E.H. Letham, quoted an old body in the village as saying of Burns: 'He asked my grandmother to go with him to a dance, but she refused.' Another said, 'My mother and mother-in-law baith shore* beside him, an' nane o' them liked him.' When asked why, she said, 'Oh he was jist that sarcastic a body didna ken what he wad say next.'

As well as the poem ridiculing local girls he produced a few of those mock epitaphs, which hit the mark so painfully. One of his fellow Freemasons, James Humphrey, was given to arguing at great length and displaying his small amount of book learning in front of Burns, who retaliated with a mock epitaph, which it should be said, Humphrey took in remarkably good part – but not every butt of his humour was as equable about it:

> Below thir stanes* lie Jamie's banes*:    *these stones  *bones
> O Death, it's my opinion,
> Thou ne'er took such a bleth'ring* bitch          *chattering
> Into thy dark dominion.[8]

Sometimes the mockery went far further than four lines: John Wilson, the schoolmaster, was an honest enough man, but was paid a pittance for his work, so he had to eke out his teacher's earnings by selling groceries and drugs from his cottage – a very useful service in those days when medical help was beyond the means of most people. When the dominie boasted about his medical expertise one day, Burns warned the parish of the dangers that lay in Wilson's small medical knowledge, and at the same time entertained it by lampooning his quackery. *Death and Dr Hornbook*[9] was a satire, which described how Wilson (Dr Hornbook) met Death as he walked along the road to Willie's Mill, a farm just below the village. Death complained bitterly that there was no trade for 'his awfu' scythe' because the doctor's 'cures' were killing off so many people before he could reach them. Death had fallen on hard times:

> See, here's a scythe, an there's a dart,
> They hae pierc'd monie a gallant heart;
> But Doctor Hornbook wi his art
>     An cursed skill,
> Has made them baith no worth a fart,
>     Damn'd haet* they'll kill!          *damn a thing

This was Burns at his brilliant best as a satirist who needed few words to put his message over. Death cited cases and Wilson's prescribed remedies

*cut corn

– sal-alkali or midge tail droppings and ill-brewed drinks – then reached
his peroration with a vow to nail the doctor 'as dead's a herring' next
time they met. At that point he was interrupted.

> But just as he began to tell,
> The auld kirk-hammer strak\* the bell *struck
> Some wee short hour ayont\* the twal\*, *beyond *twelve
> Which rais'd\* us baith: *roused
> I took the way that pleas'd mysel,
> An sae did *Death*.

Neither Burns nor Death managed to nail Wilson's life or his medical
career. The schoolmaster soldiered on, teaching, selling his potions and
giving free medical advice. He obviously was a man of character, for he
held no grudge against the Poet and when he thought of becoming a
lawyer's clerk in Edinburgh in 1790, he asked Burns for a reference.
Robert advised him strongly against 'the life of an Edinburgh Quill-driver
at twopence a page',[10] and the dominie wisely heeded the advice and
remained a teacher in Tarbolton and later in Glasgow.

Saunders Tait, who fancied himself as a poet too, did not take well to
having a rival in the village, and after Burns apparently wrote some
unflattering verses about him, he had his revenge with a number of
vicious poems after the Lochlie folk fell on hard times. In one, *Burns at
Lochly*, he aped Robert's favourite stanza:

> To Lochly ye came like a clerk,
> And on your back was scarce a sark\*, *shirt
> The dogs did at your buttocks bark,
> But now ye're braw,
> Ye poucht\* the rent ye was so stark\*, *pocketed *mean
> Made payment sma'\*.[11] *small

If Burns did write some scurrilous epitaph or epigram on Tait it is a
pity it has not survived, for he had good reason to dislike this man who
was so envious when a real poet appeared in the parish. Through his
doggerel, Tait ingratiated himself with the Alexanders of Ballochmyle
and was welcomed into their house, while Burns, in spite of his beautiful
*Lass o' Ballochmyle*, was ignored by Wilhelmina Alexander and her
brothers. That must have been hard for young Lochlie to swallow.

In spite of Tait, Robert soon gathered a circle of male companions
around him and built up a busy social life with them rather than among
the Tarbolton women with whom he formed no particularly strong or

lasting associations. David Sillar, and Robert's brother Gilbert were among a small group who helped him to establish a debating society, the Bachelors' Club, in the village, and in 1781 he became a freemason, which gave him introductions to such powerful and useful people as the Mauchline lawyer, Gavin Hamilton, Sir John Whitefoord, and James Dalrymple of Orangefield, who introduced him in turn to the Earl of Glencairn.

In spite of his coolness towards local girls, womankind remained a part of his life too, even within the exclusively masculine walls of the Bachelors' Club for the last of the club's elaborate set of rules ran:

Every man proper for a member of this Society, must have a frank, honest, open heart, above anything dirty or mean; and must be a professed lover of one or more of the female sex. No haughty, self-conceited person, who looks upon himself as superior to the rest of the club, and especially no mean-spirited, worldly mortal, whose only will is to heap up money, shall upon any pretence whatever be admitted. In short, the proper person for this society is a cheerful, honest-hearted lad; who, if he has a friend that is true, and a mistress that is kind, and as much wealth as genteelly to make both ends meet – is just as happy as this world can make him.[12]

Meetings concluded with a toast to the members' mistresses. Among the motions they debated were whether more happiness was derived from love than from friendship, and whether a farmer without prospects should marry a rich girl with neither beauty not conversation or one 'agreeable in person, conversation and behaviour, but without any fortune.' The fine hand of Robert Burns is evident in both.

On the night of Tarbolton races in June 1782, the Society held a dance at which every member had to invite a partner. Again, Robert's passion for dancing, which aroused so much anger in his father, became an issue between the two. Perhaps the old man saw dancing as epitomizing all the traits he feared in his eldest son. Robert was undoubtedly different from the other members of his family, overpassionate in all he did, and becoming obsessed with writing verse – which the old man just could not understand in spite of all the education and reading encouragement he had given the boy.

Dancing seemed to represent the core of their difficult relationship, the kernel of their inability to trust one another. Robert felt deeply enough about this to blame it for being partly responsible for his own future waywardness. 'My father,' he wrote, '. . . was the sport of strong passions: from that instance of rebellion [going to a dancing class when he was sixteen] he took a kind of dislike to me, which, I believe was one cause of that dissipation which marked my future years – I only say Dissipation, comparative with the strictness and sobriety of Presbyterian country life, for through the will-o'-wisp meteors of thoughtless Whim were almost the sole lights of my path.'[13]

It would be wrong to conclude that the Burnes family was disunited: strong bonds of affection always held it together, even William and Robert. While Robert and Gilbert may have been different both in appearance and character, they remained remarkably close to one another.

It is possible from the way some people write about Burns to think he had nothing but girls on his mind all the time, but David Sillar confirms that this was not true. 'We frequently met upon Sundays at church when, between services, instead of going with our friends or the lasses to the inn, we often took a walk in the fields.'[14] Burns would often walk by the river alone, too. So he alternated between sociability and lonely summer Sundays by the River Ayr, or winter walks in the lee of some wood, listening to the sough of the wind high in the trees, or standing on a hilltop just letting the storm engulf him. Here he worked out his own philosophy of life, his responses to family, political and personal problems he saw around him, and to all that he added a deep sense of pride in Scotland. One day he trudged 6 miles to Leglen Wood just to walk where the great thirteenth-century patriot, Sir William Wallace, had once been.

Although he had immersed himself in the masculine domains of the Bachelors' Club and the Freemasons, Robert never really lost his interest in girls. As he said himself at this time 'my heart was compleatly [*sic*] tinder, and was eternally lighted up by some Goddess or other.'[15]

He could certainly pay a girl a compliment:

> Were I a Baron proud and high,
>   And horse and servants waiting ready,
> Then a' 'twad gie* o joy to me                         *give
>   The sharin's* with Montgomerie's Peggy.      *sharing of it

The girl was a housekeeper at Coilsfield House, whom he had noticed and smiled at in church according to Burns' sister. Burns himself sent her *billets doux* and worked himself up into a passion until she told him 'her fortress' belonged to another man, but she offered him 'every alliance, except actual possession.'[16] Isabella spoke of 'an intimacy' between the two, but she was using the word in its original meaning of close acquaintance, and not as a euphemism for sexual intercourse as it is so often used today.

So Robert was no misogynist during these first years at Lochlie even if he was spending more of his time in male company. There probably was no diminution of his sexual urge either. He told Willie Niven on 3 November 1780, 'I have now and then a sweetheart or two, but with as little view of matrimony as ever.'[17] That was not a complete truth. He was now nearly twenty-two and, according to brother Gilbert, was becoming anxious to find a wife.

Eight months later he wrote to Niven again, and this time told a different story, which confirms Gilbert's belief: 'I know you will hardly believe me when I tell you, that by a strange conjuncture of circumstances, I am intirely got rid of all connections with the tender sex . . . though how long I shall continue so, Heaven only knows.'[18]

So there had been a 'Goddess' around between November 1780, and June 1781, and something had happened to bring the relationship to an end.

It is obvious from the poems he wrote at the time he had a few sweethearts among local farmers' daughters. *My Nanie, O* was said by his brother to have been inspired by Agnes Fleming of Doura, who worked at Coldcothill, a neighbouring farm; his sister Isabella named Isabella Steven of Littlehill as the heroine of *O Tibbie, I hae Seen the Day*, but she is also named as Isabella Stein who lived in Tarbolton; and Anne Rankine of Adamhill claimed to be the girl who shared that happy night 'amang the rigs of barley'. But none of these relationships were close enough or long lasting enough to make him vow to forsake love when they were over.

It was just after the Bachelors' Club's first meeting on 11 November 1780, that Burns appears to have met the girl who hurt him enough to make his half-hearted vow of celibacy. Who was she? His sister Isabella told Robert Chambers[19] she was Alison Begbie, who worked as a maid at Cairnhill (known today as Carnell), a mansion beside the Cessnock burn, just a couple of miles from Lochlie. Robert is said to have first seen Alison when he and his father were collecting lime from Cairnhill Lime Kilns to fertilize their land, and he fell in love immediately. Alison was said to be a farmer's daughter from a small farm called Old Place, a mile or so further away from Lochlie. On the strength of Isabella's memory (and we must remember she could only have been a child of about ten at the time) and tradition, Alison Begbie has been enveloped in a great romance as heroine of the song, *The Lass of Cessnock Banks*,[20] which extols the beauties of a girl with whom he is smitten. The song runs to no fewer than fourteen quatrains, every one ending with the line, 'An she has twa sparkling rogueish een.'

> She's sweeter than the morning dawn,
>   When rising Phoebus first is seen,
> And dew-drops twinkle o'er the lawn –
>   An she has twa sparkling, rogueish een*!          *eyes

Burns never identified this girl, except by the letter 'E', and once by 'A' in five letters, which were originally published, and probably lost, by James Currie, who wrote the first biography of the Poet and in the process lost a great many of his manuscript papers. 'E' has been explained away by the fact that the name Alison would often be pronounced Ellison in this part of Ayrshire.

James Mackay carried out considerable detective work among local records in the area where Alison lived, and discovered a competitor for the role of the Bonnie Lass of Cessnock Banks. He suggested that the 'A' and 'E' of the letters were not one, but two girls. In his biography of Burns he wrote, 'I have scoured the registers of [Tarbolton and] *all* the neighbouring parishes without finding a single example of this girl's name before the early nineteenth century.' Following a hunch that the letters were in fact addressed to a girl whose first name really did begin with an 'E', he searched Galston parish registers and found no Begbies, but there were Gebbies, two of whom had daughters called Elizabeth. One of these Elizabeths, born at Pearsland, Galston, on 22 July 1761, married a man called Hugh Brown on 23 November, and Mackay believes they moved to Glasgow. Robert Hartley Cromek, author of *Reliques of Burns*, who is reviled for making up facts and forging documents, visited Glasgow and wrote that *The Lass of Cessnock Banks* (never before published) was sung to him by a lady living in the city, whom the Bard had once 'affectionately admired'.[21] On the basis of this detective work, Mackay believes that at the time of the affair of 1781, Robert was under the spell of *A Sentimental Journey* and *Tristram Shandy*, so he named her after Sterne's heroine, Eliza, rather than by the more common Lizzie or Betty, which would be used in Ayrshire at that time. He believes that the Poet's sister, remembering the romance years later may have distorted the name *Elizabeth Gebbie* into *Alison Begbie*.[22]

Whether addressed to Elizabeth or Alison, four of the letters are formal drafts, and some Burns scholars have cast doubts on their authenticity. It has been suggested that they may have been letters Robert was drafting for other young lovers, as at this time he was acting as a go-between for his friends and their sweethearts. Whether that is what they were or not, the letters were carefully written and certainly lacked the exuberance of his usual correspondence – either young Lochlie was deeply smitten and anxious to make an impression, or he was aping the style of an English writer.

> What you may think of this letter when you see the name that subscribes it I cannot know; & perhaps I ought to make a long Preface of apologies for the freedom I am going to take, but as my heart means no offence but on the contrary is rather too warmly interested in your favor, for that reason I hope you will forgive me when I tell you that I most sincerely & affectionately love you. I am a stranger in these matters Alison, as I assure that you are the first woman to whom I ever made such a declaration so I declare I am at a loss how to proceed.[23]

Robert clearly was aware that this was out of his usual style for making an approach to a girl. In the second letter he refers to the 'serious manner' in which his letters are written, and the third ends with the words:

> When I look over what I have written, I am sensible it is vastly different from the ordinary style of courtship – but I shall make no apology – I know your good nature will excuse what your good sense may see amiss.[24]

At last, in the fourth letter he asked 'E' to marry him, but he even prefaced his proposal with long, rambling thoughts about the importance of a man's honesty and sincerity when he is in love, and the 'foreboding fears' he experiences each time he sits down to write to the woman he loves. At last he comes to the point:

> If you will be so good and so generous as to admit me for your partner, your companion, your bosom friend through life, there is nothing on this side of eternity shall give me greater transport, but I shall never think of purchasing your hand by arts unworthy of a man, and I will add, of a Christian. There is one thing, my dear, which I earnestly request of you, and it is this; that you would soon either put an end to my hopes by a peremptory refusal, or cure me of my fears by a generous consent.[25]

The answer was the peremptory refusal he feared, and it shattered him: 'My heart was so shocked . . . that I can scarcely yet collect my thoughts ,' he told her.

> My imagination had fondly flattered itself with a wish . . . that possibly I might one day call you mine . . . but now I am wretched for the loss of what I really had no right to expect. I must now think no more of you as a mistress, still I presume to ask to be admitted as a friend.[26]

This was when he wrote the second letter to Willie Niven, saying he was finished with women. He probably took 'E's' rejection badly for two reasons: as his brother said, he was anxious to find himself a wife at this time, and 'E' turned him down for another man. Burns always took a girl's rejection very badly.

Three songs have been claimed for Alison Begbie/Elizabeth Gebbie: *The Lass of Cessnock Banks*, *Bonie Peggy Alison*, and *Mary Morison*, a song so beautifully composed that Catherine Carswell has claimed it as coming considerably later in his life. The tombstone of a rival Mary Morison can still be seen in Mauchline Churchyard, but this girl was just twelve or thirteen at the time the song was written, so it seems hardly likely that she was its subject. It was Mary's sister who told the Mauchline minister that the song was written to her sister and the tombstone perpetuates this claim, but the words suggest someone much closer – as close as Alison Begbie, whom Gilbert claims was its heroine:

> O, Mary, canst thou wreck his peace
>   Wha for thy sake wad gladly die?
> Or canst thou break that heart of his
>   Whase only faut is loving thee?
> If love for love thou wilt na gie*,        *give
>   At least be pity to me shown:
> A thought ungentle canna be
>   The thought o Mary Morison.

Mackay adds a final clue to the identity of Alison Begbie. The song, *Farewell to Eliza*, is usually accepted as having been inspired by Elizabeth Barbour or Elizabeth Miller, both of them girls with whom he became acquainted after he moved to Mauchline in 1784, but the Poet himself told Dr Moore that he wrote the poem before 1782, and it certainly ties in with his feelings expressed in the letter to Niven:

Farewell, farewell, Eliza dear,
  The maid that I adore!
A boding voice is in mine ear,
  We part to meet no more!
But the latest throb that leaves my heart,
  While Death stand victor by,
That throb, Eliza, is thy part,
  And thine that latest sigh!

Whether or not rejection of 'E' left Robert as badly or as permanently scarred as all that suggests, it took time for the mortifying experience of rejection to fade, and he was left depressed and confused. He was aware that he had no aim in life – 'I had felt early some stirrings of Ambition,' he told Dr Moore, 'but they were the blind gropings of Homer's Cyclops round the walls of his cave.' He discovered the writings of Laurence Sterne and Henry Mackenzie and both *Tristram Shandy* and *The Man of Feeling* became great favourites. Poetry, too, provided solace, but only temporary comfort.[27]

He still needed some more secure way of life, but it could not be farming at Lochlie in its present form. The first four years at Tarbolton had been better than anything they had known previously, but, to be honest, the farm was not going well in spite of all the effort their father and he and Gilbert were putting into it. Robert and his brother had begun to grow flax on a few acres their father set aside for them, and before the 'E' episode Robert told Willie Niven he had three acres of 'pretty good flax'.[28] *The Glasgow Mercury* reported in January 1783, that Robert's flax seed had earned him a sizeable premium of £3 from the Commissioners for Fisheries, Manufactures and Improvements in Scotland.[29]

Although the textile trade was passing through a very bad phase at that time because of the American War of Independence, the government was offering generous subsidies like that reported in the *Glasgow Mercury*, so it made sense for Robert to learn to dress his own flax ready for the spinner and thus obtain a much better return on his crop.

Irvine was the obvious place to go to learn the trade since it was then the main centre in Ayrshire for flax-dressing, or heckling as it was called, and by good fortune Agnes Burnes had a relation, Alexander Peacock, in the trade there. It must have been about a month after he wrote the letter telling Niven about his rejection by 'E' that he set out from Lochlie to learn the craft of heckling.

Irvine was then the largest town in Ayrshire, a seaport crammed with life, from well-off merchants to the wildest and lowest of humanity such as Robert had never seen, even during his short stays at Ayr when he was a boy. This was Robert's first taste of town life, and he must have found it stimulating, but flax heckling was a dirty, dusty, painful monotonous business, which was a disagreeable contrast to the fresh air life he had known at home.

Almost from the start Irvine proved a disaster on every count. Unfortunately information about Burns' time there is disappointingly scanty, and the story is disjointed because it rests largely on tradition, memories of people who knew him in the town – all written years later – and on his own letter to Dr Moore, in which the sequence of events is garbled and far from complete. He told Moore about the financial problems at home at Lochlie, the rejection by 'E', a serious illness he suffered, and the new friend he made, sea captain, Richard Brown. Of the heckling venture he merely said:

> This turned out a sadly unlucky affair. My Partner was a scoundrel of the first water who made money by the mystery of thieving; and to finish the whole, while we were given a welcoming carousal to the New year, our shop, by the drunken carelessness of my Partner's wife, took fire and was burnt to ashes, and left me like a true Poet, not worth sixpence. I was obliged to give up business.[30]

The heckling shop in which he and Peacock began to work together was in a street called the Glasgow Vennel, and Robert lodged at a house nearby, but the work did not go well. Peacock probably cheated the Poet out of money, so that they split up after working together only for a short time and Robert moved to another site. Several people who lived in Irvine at the time have testified that the heckling shop, which burned down on Hogmanay night in 1781, was not the one in the Glasgow Vennel, but was in the High Street beside a lane called the Grip.

Between the Glasgow Vennel venture and the one that ended in a disastrous fire, Burns passed through nightmare weeks of illness, which he described as his 'hypochondriac complaint': this was not an imagined illness, but a genuine physical disorder brought on by depression, and serious enough for a doctor to have to be called in. For several weeks he lay ill, sleeping badly and unable to work. Alarmed by his son's state, William Burnes came over from Lochlie to see him.

'For three months I was in diseased state of body and mind, scarcely to be envied by the hopeless wretches who have just got their mittimus, "Depart from me, ye Cursed."' Robert said in his autobiographical letter.[31]

He recovered slowly, but even at the end of the year, when he wrote home that he was too busy to come and spend New Year with them at Lochlie, his letter must have alarmed the family desperately unless they were sufficiently familiar with Henry Mackenzie's *Man of Feeling* to realize that a chunk of it had been cribbed from there. He told his father he was sleeping more soundly now, and believed he was improving, but 'by very slow degrees.' The terrible depression of the past months continued to hang over him, and he was still resigned to dying soon:

> I am quite transported at the thought that ere long, perhaps very soon, I shall bid an eternal adieu to all the pains, & uneasiness & desquietudes of this weary life; for I assure you I am heartily tired of it, and, if I do not very much deceive myself I could contentedly & gladly resign it.'[32]

His postscript was enough to terrify any mother: 'My meal is nearly out but I am going to borrow till I get more.' What tortures Agnes Burnes must have suffered to think that her son was short of food especially at this time of year when everybody should have plenty and be happy can only be imagined.

Uncharacteristically, there was no mention of girls during the first part of his flax-dressing time, either in his life or in poetry. His mind was on darker things as can be seen from the titles of some of the poems relating to these days: *Winter: a Dirge*; *To Ruin*; *A Prayer in the Prospect of Death*; *Stanzas, on the same Occasion*; *A Prayer Under the Pressure of Violent Anguish*; *Tho Fickle Fortune has Deceived me*; *O, Raging Fortune's Withering Blast*, and versions of a couple of psalms, the first and ninetieth.

> Why am I loth to leave this earthly scene?
>   Have I so found it full of pleasing charms?
> Some drops of joy, with draughts of ill between;
>   Some gleams of sunshine 'mid the storms?
> Is it departing pangs my soul alarms?
>   Or death's unlovely, dreary, dark abode?
> For guilt, for guilt, my terrors are in arms:
>   I tremble to approach an angry God,
> And justly smart beneath His sin-avenging rod.[33]

It is a mystery why he did not simply pack up and go home after the fire ended the flax-dressing venture, but he didn't: he stayed on until the spring of 1782, perhaps because he didn't have the energy after his illness to get up and go, perhaps he just could not face Lochlie and all its problems, or even because he had made friends at Irvine who were uncritical, comforting company. A man named Robin Cummell (probably Campbell) told later that he regularly met Burns at the Wheatsheaf Inn along with 'Richie Brown, the sailor; Keelivine, the writer (lawyer) and Tammie Struggles frae the Briggate'[34] – who offered him the basis of a much more congenial life than was waiting for him at Lochlie.

Richard Brown, six years older than Robert, had an especially powerful influence over the Poet. Brown was a man with a wealth of knowledge of the world: good fortune, misfortune, adventure, shipwreck, piracy, sexual experience, everything – he had tasted many things that a young poet might envy, so meeting Brown was probably the most important single factor in clearing away the depression of the autumn illness and sense of failure.

Robert had gone to Irvine still a raw youth and there he met Brown who recognized his latent abilities and encouraged them. As a result, while Burns recovered from his illness and the misfortune of the flax-dressing venture, he also increased in maturity and self-confidence. He went to Irvine an adolescent, and returned to Lochlie a man, aware of his own abilities and brimful of the confidence he would need to make something of them. Five years later he was still full of pride about 'Richie' Brown, as he told Dr Moore about their acquaintanceship:

> The principal thing which gave my mind a turn was, I formed a bosom-friendship with a young fellow, the first created being I had ever seen, but a hapless son of misfortune. He was the son of a plain mechanic; but a great Man in the neighbourhood taking him under his patronage gave him a genteel education with a view to bettering his situation in life. The Patron dieing just as he was ready to launch forth into the world, the poor fellow in despair went to sea; where after a variety of good and bad fortune, a little before I was acquainted with him, he had been set ashore by an American Privateer on the wild coast of Connaught, stript of every thing.[35]

Burns overflowed with admiration:

> This gentleman's mind was fraught with courage, independance, Magnanimity, and every noble, manly virtue. I loved him, I admired him, to a degree of enthusiasm; and I strove to imitate him. In some measure I succeeded: I had the pride before, but he taught it to flow in proper channels. His knowledge of the world was vastly superior to mine, and I was all attention to learn.

The mariner was a perfect friend in every way – except one:

> He was the only man I ever saw who was a greater fool than myself when WOMAN was the presiding star; but he spoke of a certain fashionable failing with levity, which hitherto I had regarded with horror. Here his friendship did me a mischief.'

Brown had a successful career afterwards, becoming captain of the West Indiaman *Mary & Jean*, and settling at Port Glasgow with his wife and children, and Burns continued to keep in touch with him at least until 1789. By that time the now respectable sea captain had got wind of the fact that Burns had told people he had been initiated into the art of seduction by Brown, and the captain was not pleased. It was Brown who first suggested Robert should publish his work after he heard the Poet recite some of his verses while they were out walking one Sunday, and when the Kilmarnock Edition was published in 1786, the Poet presented the captain with an inscribed copy.

Sometime around March in 1782, Robert returned home at last full of well-founded apprehension. When his father saw him in Irvine, there had been a modicum of good news: he had at last managed to sell the cottage at Alloway to the Incorporation of Shoemakers in Ayr, who bought it as an investment and let it out as an ale-house, which it remained for a hundred years until it was bought in 1881 by the Burns Monument Trustees. The sale in 1781 gave William Burnes was no more than a blink of sunshine in an exceedingly long storm.

By the time Robert returned a dispute was raging between Burnes and his landlord, David McClure, over how much each should pay towards liming the soil, fencing off the fields and putting up new farm buildings. No written agreement had ever been drawn up between the pair and now McClure was claiming £775 while Burnes maintained that £543 of this should be written off because of improvements he had made to the farm. It was all mind-numbingly complicated and by September 1782, when neither side could agree, the dispute was submitted to arbitration, with Charles Norval of Coilsfield representing Burnes and James Grieve of Boghead as McClure's representative. In the meantime, Burnes was withholding his rent.

The period of waiting while Norval and Grieve negotiated was difficult for all at Lochlie: the harvest that year was so slow to ripen that everyone wondered if it would ever be brought in. Worse, Robert's depressive illness recurred on and off throughout the summer and the health of William Burnes, who had been suffering from tuberculosis for some time, was deteriorating.

At length the arbitrators told Burnes and the landlord that they could not agree, so John Hamilton of Sundrum was called in as referee, and while Hamilton sifted through the complicated accounts, claims and counter-claims, the Burnes family salted away every penny they could, so that if McClure's claim succeeded, they would be able to pay the debt.

Autumn of 1783 produced no better a crop than the previous year, and elsewhere in Scotland ruined crops led to starvation for many people. While the Burnes were not starving they were in dire straits, and William's health was failing alarmingly. He now knew that he was dying.

In August, Hamilton had announced his decision in favour of Burnes. By this time, however, McClure had been caught up in the chain of collapses that followed in the wake of the crash of the Ayr Bank a decade earlier, and was beset by debtors. He took out a writ of sequestration on the stock and crops of Lochlie in an attempt to force Burnes to pay the full amount, a terrible public disgrace for a family as upright as the Burnes of Lochlie. A dying man he might be, but Burnes was stubbornly determined – the word essert again comes to mind – and took his case to the Court of Session in Edinburgh, only to have it thrown out on a technicality. Undaunted, he submitted a new petition, and while this dragged on through the legal process at snail's pace, he clung on to life tenaciously.

At this point Gavin Hamilton, the Mauchline lawyer, who was one of Robert's fellow freemasons in Tarbolton, came on the scene to give advice on how to lessen the blow if the Edinburgh action should go against them. He also offered Robert and Gilbert the lease of Mossgiel farm, which he himself held on lease from the Earl of Loudon, but did not want to farm himself. The rent was a modest £90 a year for 118 acres of good land, situated nearer Mauchline, but only a mile away from Lochlie. Even if the worst happened the Burns family would still be able to stay together.

Soon after New Year 1784, the Mauchline doctor, John Mackenzie, was called in to see William Burnes and the old man told him in detail about his dispute. Mackenzie was impressed and wrote of his patient: 'His appearance certainly made me think him inferior, both in manner and intelligence, to the generality of those in his situation: but before leaving him, I found that I had been led to form a very false conclusion of his mental powers.'[36]

Death was now near, but William Burnes had decided to hold on to see the McClure affair finished, and hold on he did – in body and mind. On 27 January word reached Lochlie from Edinburgh that Burnes had won his case, although it was a Pyrrhic victory, for it had cost him almost every penny of his savings as well as the money he had set aside to pay the landlord.

He could now die content, but for one thing – he had to leave the family in the charge of Robert, and his eldest son appeared poorly suited to guide the fortunes of the family through the future. Robert's health was far from robust, he was subject to moods which changed from black depression to joyful conviviality, and his mind was filled with poetry rather than farming. William would not have chosen Robert to succeed him as head of the house, yet he had no choice – death could no longer be staved off.

Day by day the family waited, with someone sitting at the dying man's bedside every night, waiting for the end. On the night of 12 February, it was the turn of Robert and Isabella to watch: towards morning the old man stirred, drew himself up, and called for Isabella. He told her always to be sure to lead a virtuous life, then paused as if he found it difficult to say what he wanted to tell her. At last he said there was one member of the family about whom he worried: Robert came closer. 'Father, is it me you mean?' he asked.

The old man replied that it was, and Robert turned quickly away to stare at the window, his body shaking and tears running down his cheeks.[37]

William Burnes said no more. A few hours later he died.

His coffin was slung between two ponies and carried in a sad little procession back to Alloway where he had begun his married life so hopefully a quarter of a century before. In the Auld Kirkyard he was laid to rest, and over his grave they carved the words:

> O ye whose cheek the tear of pity stains,
>   Draw near with pious rev'rance and attend!
> Here lie the loving Husband's dear remains,
>   The tender Father, and the gen'rous Friend.
> The pitying Heart that felt for human Woe;
>   The dauntless heart that feared no human Pride;
> The Friend of Man, to vice alone a foe;
>   For ev'n his failings lean'd to Virtue's side.[38]

Only a month later the Burns family moved to Mossgiel, leaving the heartache of the last litigious years at Lochlie behind. Robert had high hopes, which he was not afraid to express, for he was now a man, matured in the hard world of farming and town living. He was close to being a poet of note too, for Lochlie, in spite of all its troughs had been a time of some peaks, of much reading and a little writing – a time of preparation. The rejection by 'E' was in the past, too, and he was almost ready for deep, enduring love: by the time the first harvest on the new farm was safely in, there was a local lass to whom he had an obligation. He had lain with her among the corn and she was pregnant.

CHAPTER FOUR

# Sex and Sensibility

The sky was blue, the wind was still,
　　The moon was shining clearly;
I set her down, wi right good will,
　　Amang the rigs o barley:
I ken't* her heart was a' my ain*;　　　*knew　*own
　　I lov'd her most sincerely;
I kiss'd her owre* and owre again,　　　*over
　　Amang the rigs o barley.


Corn rigs, an barley rigs,
　　An Corn rigs are bonie:
I'll ne'er forget that happy night,
　　Amang the rigs wi Annie.

*The Rigs o Barley*[1]

Events at Lochlie at harvest-time in 1784 must have been very much like those he described in *The Rigs o Barley*, but the girl was Elizabeth Paton, and not the Annie named in the song. The sun was in Virgo, a month which he admitted was always 'carnival time' in his bosom, and Robert Burns felt better, although his depression still stalked him. He still kept in touch with his Tarbolton friends and went over there frequently. One day he met the girl he had got to know a year before when she had been brought in to help his mother out during those last difficult months at Lochlie, and they stole away together to some secret place.

Elizabeth Paton, usually called Lizzie or Betsey, came from Largieside only a mile or so from Lochlie, and she was certainly not the type of woman one would have expected to appeal to a man of Robert's artistic temperament and education. Lizzie was an honest lassie, pleasant enough and with a good trim figure, but, according to the Poet's niece, Isabella Burns Begg, with an exceedingly plain face. She was 'rude and uncultivated to a great degree . . . with a thorough (tho' unwomanly) contempt for every sort of refinement.'[2]

But Lizzie had one quality in her favour: she was devoted to Robert to such a degree that old Mrs Burnes, who had grown fond of her while she worked at the farm, told her son he should do the right thing by the girl and marry her. Robert, although clearly not in love, would have done so, had his brother and sisters not opposed it. 'They thought the faults of her character would soon have disgusted him,' said Isabella,[3] so it was agreed that Robert would acknowledge the child, but would not marry Lizzie. His niece took care to add that he never treated Lizzie badly though, and he did list her charms in a little poem, *My Girl She's Airy.*[4]

Lizzie Paton's pregnancy came as a blow, for here he was, a farmer, head of the household, responsible for his mother and his brothers and sisters, and within months he had let them and himself down. This sense of failure was made doubly painful by bad luck which upset the vow he had made at the time he moved to Mossgiel. 'I entered on this farm with a full resolution, "Come, go to, I will be wise!",' he told Dr Moore. And he did 'go to', but to no avail.

> I read farming books; I calculated crops; I attended markets and in short, in spite of 'The devil, the world and the flesh,' I believe I would have been a wise man, but the first year from unfortunately buying in bad seed, the second from a late harvest, we lost half of both our crops: this overset all my wisdom, and I returned 'Like the dog to his vomit, and the sow that was washed to her wallowing in the mire'.[5]

Burns was understating his farming problems and doing himself less than justice. Those were two disastrous years when the harvest weather was so terrible that crops were lost all over Scotland. However, it was Lizzie's pregnancy rather than Burns' farming methods that was the talk of Mauchline and Tarbolton through the autumn of 1784, and Burns reacted sharply as he always did when he was put under stress. He bragged defiantly to his male friends about his sexual exploits and attacked the kirk and the 'good' of the parish.

By mid-November Lizzie's condition was obvious but not sufficiently apparent for him to want to talk too publicly about it. He told his Kirkoswald friend, Thomas Orr, obliquely that he was 'cursedly taken in with an affair of gallantry' and thus was glad to learn that Peggy Thomson, who had married that year, was off his hands. However, he did not write any details of the Paton affair in the letter, but promised to tell Orr about it when they met.[6]

He was much more forthcoming to his friend, John Rankine of Adamhill, the man whose daughter claimed to be Annie of *The Rigs O Barley*. Rankine soon heard about Mossgiel's predicament and teased him

about it, to which he received a verse reply, well in keeping with the tone
of their friendship – to Burns, Adamhill was:

> . . . rough, rude, ready-witted Rankine,
> The wale\* o cocks for fun an drinkin'.[7]  \*pick

His *Reply to an Announcement by John Rankine* did not sound in the least
contrite, but he did admit the news had come as something of a shock to
him to find 'a whaup's i' the nest!'\* In another *Epistle to John Rankine*[8] he
picked up the bird metaphor again, likening himself to a poacher, who
brings down a partridge with his gun:

> The poor, wee thing was little hurt;
> I straikit it a wee\* for sport,  \*stroked it a little
> Ne'er thinkin they wad fash\* me for't;  \*bother
> But Deil-ma-care!
> Somebody tells the Poacher-Court\*  \*kirk session
> The hale\* affair.  \*whole

The poem was coarse; it was the kind of joke immature young men
(although Rankine was no youth at this time) make to one another, but
which does not seem so funny when repeated in wider company. As
Professor David Daiches commented, 'The fact is that the atmosphere of
male boasting of success in sexual adventures is not very agreeable
outside the climate of youthful male conviviality in which it flourishes.'[9] It
must be said, however, that our generation looks at the Rankine *Epistle*
more seriously than people did in Burns' time, for it attracted no
comment when it appeared in the Kilmarnock Edition in 1786.

The Paton affair caused no more than a momentary ripple in the
community for the very good reason that the reality of life in Scotland in
those days was that an illegitimate child was readily accepted, so that the
harsh judgement and punishment of the Kirk was far worse than the
sinning. Christina Keith in *The Russet Coat* spells out the kirk's cruelty:

> Sunday after Sunday, this sin, above all other sins, was burned into the
> imagination of the people. You hadn't a chance to forget it. It was the thrill
> you waited for, thro' the long drones of the sermon. The Kirk Session
> records – that damning testimony to the eighteenth-century religion – are
> full of it. With the whole mind of Youth thus deliberately polluted by those

---

\*something unpleasant had happened = literally, a curlew is in the nest who should have been its guardians, it was no wonder that adultery figured, openly and prominently, in the talk of the countryside.[10]

As Robert feared in his epistle to John Rankine, someone did betray him to the poacher-court, and the kirk did have its say that winter: Robert appeared in Tarbolton church with Lizzie at his side, and 'pay'd the buttock-hire'. Even there, as he explained in *The Fornicator*, he was defiant:

> Before the Congregation wide
>  I pass'd the muster fairly,
> My handsome Betsey by my side,
>  We gat our ditty rarely;
> But my downcast eye by chance did spy
>  What made my lips to water,
> Those limbs so clean where I, between,
>  Commenc'd a Fornicator.

Lizzie's child, a daughter, was born on 22 May 1785, and was named Elizabeth. For all his coarse, defiant braggadocio while the kirk was snapping at his heels, Robert welcomed his child with touching pleasure – even joy. Of course he wrote a poem to mark the occasion and, while we call the poem *A Poet's Welcome to his Love-Begotten Daughter*,[11] his own more pithy title was *Welcome to a Bastart Wean*:

> Thou's welcome, wean! Mishanter fa'* me,      *mishap befall
> If thoughts o thee, or yet thy mammie,
> Shall ever daunton me or awe me
>  My sweet, wee lady,
> Or if I blush when thou shalt ca' me
>  Tyte or daddie!

Then there was *The Rantin Dog, the Daddie o't*,[12] in which he set a beautiful lullaby onto Lizzie's lips – though some say it was not written for Lizzie Paton's but Jean Armour's child. Whichever, it was a moving little song, displaying a buoyant, irreverent attitude, and suggesting that this would not be the last time Lizzie or Jean, to whichever the poem was addressed, would lie with him:

> O, wha* my babie-clouts* will buy?      *who *linen
> O, wha will tent* me when I cry?      *tend me
> Wha will kiss me where I lie?
>  The rantin dog, the daddie o't!

, And he still cocked a snook at the kirk:

> When I mount the creepie-chair*,        *repentance stool
> Wha will sit beside me there?
> Gie me Rob, I'll seek nae mair*        *no more
> The rantin dog, the daddie o't!

Lizzie Paton made no financial demand on the Poet when her baby was born; she probably knew there was no money to claim. But when the Kilmarnock Edition of his poems was published she did ask for and received a share of the proceeds for the child, who remained with her mother until Robert moved away from the district. Elizabeth was then taken to Mossgiel where the Poet's mother brought her up until Robert's death. Elizabeth went back to her mother's home, and lived there until she married John Bishop, land steward to the Polkemmet estate in West Lothian. Elizabeth died in 1817, some say in childbirth, and is buried in Whitburn churchyard.

The Elizabeth Paton affair was the start of a long-running confrontation between Robert Burns and the kirk, and it brought him face to face with love and a relationship with a woman that he had never experienced before. These, combined with the Lochlie experience and the self-confidence and maturity that Richard Brown's acquaintance had given him, became the catalysts which drove his muse towards 1785–6, his *annus mirabilis*, which produced the poems which appeared in his Kilmarnock volume and many more: they also delved into every aspect of his past life. The most powerful moving force of all, however, was the death of his father, which left him feeling tortured by a sense of failure, but it also broke the bonds which had constrained him all his life. As a result he exploded into song, then rushed into a hectic social round, and he took Lizzie Paton among the rigs of barley and fathered his first child.

The number of poems he begat during this time was enormous, the range staggering, covering all aspects of his past experience and the world in which he was living at that moment. The *annus mirabilis* work extended from descriptions of life among his own people in *The Cotter's Saturday Night*[13] and *Hallowe'en*[14] to *The Vision*,[15] which set his poetic talent against the Scotland in which he lived, and the glorious *Jolly Beggars*[16] cantata.

*The Twa Dogs*,[17] the first poem in the Kilmarnock book, brought the Poet back to the harsh reality he had lived through when his father was treated so shamefully by landlord McClure during the last years at

Lochlie. The poem, a conversation between two dogs, which are worlds apart socially – Caesar a gentleman and Luath a humble 'faithfu' tyke', based on Robert's own dog – seems amiable enough on the surface, but it is a biting satire on how the rich can impose on the poor, all the sharper because it is drawn straight from Burns' own experience.

Also from experience came a touching little poem about an old farming New Year custom which Burns must have practised year by year – going to the stable to greet his horse and give it a handsel* of food first thing on the morning of the first day of the year. *The Auld Farmer's New-year Morning Salutation to his Auld Mare, Maggie*[18] is a simple enough poem on the surface, but it is exquisitely fashioned, and of course it goes deeper, far deeper, than a description of a simple tradition. Horse and farmer are both old and worn out; they have shared a hard life together rather like John Anderson and his wife – in fact the final verse of the *Farmer's New-year Salutation* was likened by Franklyn Bliss Snyder[19] to the second stanzas of *John Anderson my Jo*:

> We've worn to crazy years thegither;
> We'll toyte* about wi ane anither;               *totter
> Wi tentie* care I'll flit* thy tether      *attentive *change
> To some hain'd rig*,                          *protected ridge
> Whare ye may nobly rax* your leather               *stretch
> Wi' sma' fatigue.

Just as the farmer and his Maggie have 'toyted' about together, John Anderson and his wife have climbed the hill with one another: now that they are up in years they will share the future, the mare on some sheltered meadow where she can relax, as John and his wife go into their declining years hand in hand and 'sleep thegither' when they reach the foot of life's hill. Each is a true relationship.

> John Anderson my jo, John,
>   We clamb the hill thegither,
> And monie a cantie day, John,
>   We've had wi ane anither;
> Now we maun totter down, John,
>   And hand in hand we'll go,
> And sleep thegither at the foot,
>   John Anderson my jo!

*gift for New Year

*The Farmer's New-year Salutation* is a remarkable achievement for a Scotsman, even one as great as Robert Burns. Few of us could have succeeded in avoiding the trap of ending the poem on a maudlin, self-pitying note. We are a sentimental race, yet throughout the eighteen 'Standard Habbie'* stanzas the *Auld Farmer's Salutation* never becomes emotional or drifts into a romantic search for the beast's soul. Burns simply describes the custom and the scene in the stable, but while doing so, he builds up a relationship between the two which transcends many a human experience.

As well as the old farmer's horse, a mouse, a mountain daisy and a louse all were subjects for *annus mirabilis* poems – *To a Mouse*,[20] *To a Mountain Daisy*,[21] and *To a Louse*,[22] and even the louse managed to inspire a profound truth.

> O wad some power the giftie gie us
> To see oursels as ithers see us!
> It was frae monie a blunder free us,
>    An foolish notion:
> What airs in dress an gait wad lea'e us,
>    An ev'n devotion!

At this time he sent a number of sparkling verse epistles to his friends: the poet David Sillar, John Lapraik, Willie Simpson, John Rankine, and one to a young man, who was in fact, Andrew Aiken, son of his old friend, Robert Aiken in Ayr. The *Epistle to a Young Friend*[23] is so crammed with sound advice that one wonders, not just how a man in his mid-twenties should have so much sense of the world but could still 'gang agley' from the straight and narrow path. One critic has described the *Epistle* as 'a pot-pourri of all the bourgeois virtues',[24] but surely Burns was setting out his own credo with frank unpretentiousness. He warned Andrew that he would discover mankind a selfish 'unco squad'†, and talked to him of wealth, thrift and religion. In the midst of all that he managed to slip in some good advice which he must later have wished he had taken at times himself:

> But still keep something to yoursel
> Ye scarcely tell to onie:

---

*verse form popular with Burns. The name is derived from a seventeenth-century mock epitaph on Habbie Simpson, the piper of Kilbarchan
†a strange crew

Of course, any advice from Robert Burns would not be complete without a word on sex as practised and experienced by himself:

The sacred lowe* o weel-plac'd love,      *flame
Luxuriantly indulge it;.
But never tempt th' illicit rove,
Tho naething should divulge it:
I waive the quantum o the sin,
The hazard of concealing;
But, och! it hardens a' within,
And petrifies the feeling!

Drink featured, of course, in both *Scotch Drink*[25] and *The Author's Earnest Cry and Prayer*,[26] an appeal to the Scottish Members of Parliament to ease the heavy taxation of whisky.

The kirk was challenged with *The Holy Fair*, a splendid assault on the hypocrisy and double standards, which had turned the solemn act of holy communion into a carnival. It had become the custom for the sacrament Sunday to attract people from far and wide to spend the whole day listening to sermons, but meeting friends, eating and drinking and turning the very kirkyard into a fairground between sermons. Burns' poem was a devastating satire on the hypocrisy of all this. Let David Daiches sum up the poem and the events it was attacking:

Unlike some of his other satirical poems, *The Holy Fair* shows no bitterness towards any of the characters held up for the reader's amusement, only a delighted acceptance of the bustling, crowded variegated scene, and of the different kinds of hypocrisy, narrowness, confusion, enthusiasm, drinking and love-making which are to be found there. The attack on the ministers he disliked is conducted with happy nonchalance.[27]

Here stands a shed to fend* the show'rs,    *fend off
  An screen our countra* gentry;      *country
There Racer Jess, and twa-three whores,
  Are blinkin* at the entry      *nodding
Here sits a raw o tittlin jads*      *gossiping lassies
  Wi heavin breasts and bare neck;
An there a batch of wabster* lads,      *webster
  Blackguardin* frae Kilmarnock,      *up to no good
    For fun this day.

Here some are thinkin on their sins,
  An some upo their claes;
Ane curses feet that fyl'd his shins*,          *soiled his shoes
  Anither sighs an prays:
On this hand sits a chosen swatch*,       *divinely chosen group
  Wi screw'd up, grace-proud faces;
On that a set of chaps, at watch,
  Thrang* winkin on the lasses            *busy
    To chairs that day.

Auld Nick himself had to be in the cast list of the *annus mirabilis*, in the *Address to the Deil*,[28] which was not so much an attack on Auld Clootie himself as a dig at the Calvinistic kirk and superstition. Burns irreverently cuts his fiery adversary down to homely Scottish size: who else would dare to tap the Prince of Darkness on the shoulder metaphorically and say:

Hear me, Auld Hangie, for a wee
An' let poor, damnèd bodies be;

Who else would suggest he should 'tak a thought an men'*? But of course behind this joking irreverence lay a profound criticism of the kirk's views on original sin. The *Address to the Unco Guid*, *Holy Willie's Prayer*, *The Twa Herds* and *The Ordination* were also part of the young poet's attack on the bigotry and hypocrisy within sections of the church in this time. After what he had gone through that year with the church humiliating him over the Paton affair, it is hardly surprising that it featured prominently in his *annus mirabilis* writings.

Sex was included, too, especially in the kirk poems. He told the ministers and elders some home truths which the whole country knew to be true:

How monie* hearts this day converts        *many
  O sinners and o lasses!
Their hearts o stane*, gin right, are gane*   *stone *gone
  As saft* as onie* flesh is:          *soft *any
There's some are fou* of love divine;      *full
  There's some are fou o brandy;
An monie jobs that day begin,
  May end in houghmagandie*        *fornication
    Some ither day.[29]

*mend his ways

He could smile as he read this gibe at the prudery of local kirkmen, especially alongside the licentious rag-tag *Jolly Beggars* crew in Poosie Nansie's: he could roar with laughter as he shared his own peccadilloes with those of John Richmond and others who had just as many sins of their own to atone for. While he could talk so lovingly about his 'bastart wean', he was able to turn his sexual life into coarse bawdry. By 1785 his attitude to sex and his own sexuality had matured, even if some of the ways in which he expressed it had not.

Always a man to give credit where credit was due, the Poet was fulsome in his praise for his Irvine friend, Richard Brown, but he blamed the sailor for introducing him to 'a certain fashionable failing' which hitherto he had regarded with horror: in this respect Brown's friendship did him a mischief, he said. What the 'fashionable failing' was has seemed clear enough to the whole world for two hundred years – except (so far as I know) to one man, Alan Dent, who propounded what he himself calls 'my scandalous suggestion' that Burns was homosexual or at very least bi-sexual.

'Let me recommend a close study of the relationship between these two young men – the sailor twenty-nine (Richard Brown) and the poet twenty-three when they first met – to those itchy-minded modern writers who cannot bear to imagine that the object of their researches is utterly and unexceptionably heterosexual in his love-life. There is certainly something equivocal about Brown's character,' Dent says darkly, but offers nothing more than Burns' autobiographical letter to Dr Moore with the story of Brown's misfortune in losing his benefactor and being forced to go to sea. Burns' description of his 'bosom-friendship' with the young sea Captain as 'the first created being I had ever seen,' words which Dent puts in italics. '*The first created being I had ever seen*' clearly suggests to Dent a closer interest than merely the admiration the Poet said he had for the young sailor. But Burns was enthusiastic – over-enthusiastic even – about anyone he liked, just as he could be over-critical of anyone he disliked. He even used the word 'love' freely in relation to men in real life and in his poetry – Tam o' Shanter 'lo'ed' Souter Johnnie like a brother – but he was not using the word in any sexual sense. Dent, by profession a theatre critic, seemed only to see love in a dramatic, tactile, erotic sense and not as an abstract emotion devoid of sexual content, which it can sometimes be. In November 1789, Burns sent Brown, by then a successful sea captain and a married man, a long letter welcoming him home from a voyage. In it he wrote:

When you & I first met, we were at a green period of human life. The twig would easily take a bent but would as easily return to its former state. You & I not only took a mutual bent; but by the melancholy, tho' strong, influence of being both of the family of the Unfortunate, we were intertwined with one another in our growth towards advanced Age; and blasted be the sacreligious hand that shall attempt to undo the UNION![30]

Dent, having sought deep, dark meaning in this later letter, fastens on a Sunday the two spent together in Eglinton woods, a place associated with the Scottish hero, Sir William Wallace, when Burns said he read some of his poems to his friend, who gave him the idea of seeking to have them published – the first to do so, Burns told us later.

'We shall probably never know by exactly how much Brown broadened Burns' outlook on that unforgotten day long ago in Eglinton Woods,' wrote Dent. 'Or whether the two young men compared notes, or gathered conkers, or brambles, or bluebells, according to the season of the year. Or just read Burns' verses aloud to one another till the sun went down. One might call it, without speculating too far, an afternoon of two fauns instead of one, and leave it at that.'[31]

Burns' conduct up to 1785 and also his behaviour afterwards, seem sufficient answer to Dent's 'scandalous suggestion'. After Irvine, Burns saw himself as mature enough for marriage, even if he did express it in direct and far from sentimental terms, to young John Tennant, just as news of Lizzie Paton's condition was emerging:

To have a woman to lye with when one pleases, without running any risk of the cursed expence of bastards and all the other concomitants of that species of Smuggling – These are solid views of matrimony.[32]

What Richie Brown taught Burns was to be confident in himself and to enjoy sex freely, although, from the state of the Poet's health during the final months of 1781 when he was depressed and seriously ill, it is hardly likely that young Lochlie was able to live the life of a rake any more than he was able to work at his flax heckling.

After Irvine the Poet was always single-minded about what a relationship should be – his belief was to go for full sexual intercourse as soon as possible – and with the degree of passion Robert showed every time he fell for a girl, that meant *now*. Irvine was a watershed in his sexual life, although it took several years for this to emerge clearly.

Up to 1786 Robert Burns' experience with women was strictly circumscribed: he had never even crossed the threshold of the house of anyone more superior than the Mauchline lawyer, Gavin Hamilton, so he knew nothing of fine ladies and their gentility. He had acquired a veneer of education and manners, but this was on the surface and spread so thinly that it could be penetrated easily.

Burns was accustomed to laying his blandishments at the feet of farm or village girls, who no doubt were suspicious of him because he looked superior to other local lads and could write verse to them. They did not expect deference from their menfolk let alone poetic homage: they were accustomed to being courted crudely and openly, for the hayloft or cornfield was the only place where they had any privacy. At Lochlie and Mossgiel, typical of all other farmhouses in Ayrshire, there were eight or nine members of the family plus various ploughmen, herd laddies and servant girls under the same roof, sharing a couple of rooms and an attic.

This was what farm girls were accustomed to; it was what they expected, and that was what they received – until Rab Mossgiel came along. The lasses of Tarbolton and Mauchline were naturally suspicious (scornful too if they were anything like their twentieth-century counterparts) of this man who dressed so grandly, wrote poetry and made love passionately. Every local girl knew about his reputation, and few could have been surprised when they heard of Lizzie Paton's predicament.

Robert took his fatherly duties seriously and when his younger brother, William, left home for England, he sent the young man advice on how to succeed in his career and with women. On women he was crystal clear:

> I am, as you know, a veteran in these campaigns, so let me advise you always to pay your particular assiduities and try for intimacy as soon as you feel the first symptoms of the passion: this is not only best, as making the most of the little entertainment which the sport-abilities of distant addresses always gives, but is the best preservative for one's peace. I need not caution you against guilty amours – they are bad and ruinous everywhere, but in England they are the very devil.[33]

He warned his brother against whoring and lying with bad women, something which had always aroused the strongest antipathy in him. The reason was not just financial although cost did come into it:

> Whoring is a most ruinous expensive species of dissipation . . . Whoring has ninety-nine chances in a hundred to bring on a man the most nauseous & excrutiating diseases to which Human nature is liable . . . All this is independent of the criminality of it.[34]

Robert disapproved of whoring, but he did not dislike whores: he may even have been rather fond of some of those he encountered 'blinkin at entries' around Mauchline, Edinburgh or Dumfries. There was one in particular for whom he had great sympathy, his namesake, Margaret Burns, an Edinburgh 'madame' who fell foul of the authorities in 1789. Burns had known Miss Burns while he was in Edinburgh during the winters of 1786–8, although he had not patronized her – apart from his strong views on harlots, he had no need to purchase sex.

Margaret Burns, or Matthews to give her the name she was born with, had migrated to Edinburgh from Durham, and in the capital she stood out among the 'ladies of the Canongate' as quite a beauty who always dressed in the height of fashion. In the early summer of 1789 Miss Burns opened a brothel in Rose Street, just across the road from the back door of one of the Court of Session judges, Lord Swinton, and in August of that year a protest was lodged:

'Since Whitsunday last,' it thundered, 'she and a Miss Sally Sanderson, who are persons of bad character, have kept a very irregular and disorderly house, into which they admit and entertain licentious and profligate persons of both sexes to the great annoyance of their neighbours and breach of the public peace.'[35]

The women were brought before the bench, by coincidence in front of William Creech, Burns' Edinburgh publisher, who by then had become a solemn, sober Bailie of the City. Creech, a bachelor, was an upright man, but mean, and the Poet had recently had quite a tussle with him over payment of money due on the first Edinburgh Edition of his poems, so Burns was interested in the case both from the point of view of his namesake and Creech's attitude to it. Creech 'banished Miss Burns forth of the city and liberties for ever,' but she appealed to the Court of Session and won her case. She stayed on in the capital, but died only three years later.

The whole city and much of the country watched with amusement, and a London journal published a story that Bailie Creech was 'about to lead the beautiful and accomplished Miss Burns to the hymeneal altar.' Creech was furious and threatened to sue, so a retraction was printed: 'In a former number we noticed the intended marriage between Bailie Creech of Edinburgh and the beautiful Miss Burns of the same place,' it ran. 'We have now the authority of that gentleman to say that the proposed marriage is not to take place, matters having been otherwise arranged to the mutual satisfaction of both parties and the respective friends.'[36] Bailie Creech's response to that was not recorded.

Burns savoured the Margaret Burns furore from Ellisland at Dumfries, where he was living by then, but obviously he had difficulty in keeping up with progress on the case. In February 1790, he sent a letter to

Edinburgh bookseller, Peter Hill, in which, in the middle of inquiring about friends and the weighty matter of Burgh Reform, he suddenly broke off to ask about the Burns scandal:

> How is the fate of my poor Namesake, Mademoiselle Burns, decided? Which of their grave Lordships can lay his hand on his heart and say that he has not taken the advantage of such frailty: nay, if we may judge by near six thousand years experience, can the World do without such frailty? O Man! but for thee & thy selfish appetites & dishonest artifices, that beauteous form, & that once innocent & still ingenuous mind might have shone conspicuous & lovely in the faithful wife and the affectionate mother, and shall the unfortunate sacrifice to thy pleasures have no claim on thy humanity! As for those flinty-bosomed, puritannic Prosecutors of Female Frailty & Persecutors of Female Charms . . .

At that point he broke off to explain that his pen had not carried him away – he had merely stopped to sharpen its point. This he did, and sharpened his words at the same time:

> It is written, 'Thou shalt not take the name of the Lord thy God in vain,' so I shall neither say, G— curse them! nor G— blast them! nor G— damn them! but may Woman curse them! May Woman blast them! May Woman damn them! May her lovely hand inexorably shut the Portal of Rapture to their most earnest Prayers & fondest essays for entrance! And when many years, and much port and great business have delivered them over to Vulture Gouts and Aspen Palsies, *then* may the dear, bewitching Charmer in derision throw open the blissful Gate to tantalize their impotent desires which like ghosts haunt their bosoms when all their powers to give or receive enjoyment, are for ever asleep in the sepulchre of their fathers!!![37]

This was a powerful expression of Robert Burns' feelings on the subject of the attitude of men towards women, and not just towards women of the streets. He repeated much the same sentiments more neatly and in less passionate words, but every bit as pithily, in a little mocking quatrain aimed at Miss Burns' tormentors:

> Cease ye prudes, your envious railing!
> Lovely Burns has charms-confess!
> True it is, she had one failing;
> Had ae woman ever less?[38]

CHAPTER FIVE

# The Mauchline Lady

Hale* to the sex! (ilk guid chiel* says):      *health *fellow
Wi' merry dance on Winter days,
   An we to share in common!
The gust o joy, the balm of woe,
The saul* o life, the heav'n below,          *soul
   Is rapture-giving Woman.

*To the Guidwife of Wauchope House,*
March 1787[1]

Young Rab Mossgiel saw each of his sexual adventures in terms of military campaigns in which he, as commander in chief, was ardently 'pressing on the siege', bent on displaying his victorious banners: all too often he was routed and forced 'to scamper away, without either arms or honors of war, except his bare bayonet & cartridge pouch.'[2] He was a resilient general though, and soon had rallied his forces again for some new campaign.

His attitude to women and an approach to courting which veered towards blunt frontal attack rather than sweet courtly dalliance carried out with finesse, meant that Mauchline women were soon on the lookout for him and taking avoiding action. The young men of the town on the other hand sought him out, and soon he found himself at the head of a pretty wild pack, who included James Smith, a draper in the town, Gavin Hamilton's clerk, John Richmond, William Hunter, the shoemaker, and John Brown, whose nickname was 'Clockie' because he was a clockmaker. Beyond these 'great planets' of Mauchline's little universe lay the lesser constellations of Adam Armour of whore-stanging fame and the younger lads of the town.

Robert's new-found confidence, which set him at the head of his contemporaries, also helped him to make friends among such influential men of the town as Gavin Hamilton and Dr John Mackenzie, the local medical practitioner, who had found the Poet suspicious and withdrawn when he first encountered him at William Burnes' bedside, but had come to admire him. Robert Burns was beginning to make his mark in spite of his reputation as a womanizer.

Mossgiel and his close friends drank at John Dow's pub, the Whitefoord Arms, or 'Johnnie Doo's', as the inn was known: they were not a riotously drunken crowd, but simply young lads enjoying their crude jokes and gossip about women, and Burns, with his gift for making up a humorous satirical verse comment on almost any and every event or human failing, was at the centre of the group. Here the lads set up the Court of Equity, a kind of secret Bachelors' Club, which met 'to search out, report, and discuss the merits and demerits of the many scandals that crop up from time to time in the village.' This mock court, which tried fornicators in the town, was presided over by Burns as 'Perpetual President', with Richmond as 'Clerk of the Court', Smith its 'Procurator Fiscal' and Hunter 'Messenger at Arms'. The joke was all the richer by the fact that the Court's mock judgement on the morals of Mauchline men was conducted by four of the worst reprobates in the parish: Burns had already been hauled before the Kirk Session over Lizzie Paton, Richmond was on the creepie stool for fornication with Jenny Surgeoner, who bore him a son, and the other two, although they escaped the wrath of the Kirk, were as wild as their co-adjudicators.

One of the verse products of the Court of Equity was a bawdy poem, *The Libel Summons*,[3] in which 'Clockie' Brown and John Dow's son, Sandy, were summoned before the court and tried. One of this band of brothers, 'Clockie' or Smith the draper (we are uncertain which) inspired the Bard to another of his mock epitaphs, which could well have related to any of them:

> Lament him, Mauchline husbands a',
>   He aften did assist ye;
> For had ye staid awa',
>   Your wives they ne'er hae missed ye!
>
> Ye Mauchline bairns, as on ye pass
>   To school in bands thegither,
> O, tread ye lightly on his grass
>   Perhaps he was your father!

After the move to Mossgiel, Burns divided his social life between Mauchline and Tarbolton, where he kept in touch with his Lochlie friends and became involved with the Freemasons. He rose to be Depute-Master of St James's Lodge during the summer of 1784, which was to stand him in good stead when he became famous and went to Edinburgh. His Tarbolton interests, including the Lizzie Paton affair, did not stop him from casting around among the girls of Mauchline, even writing verse about them, some of it every bit as scathing as anything inspired by the lassies around Tarbolton.

His heart gave a flutter over a girl called Elizabeth (Bess or Betty) Miller during the early summer of 1785, but that came to a sudden end when Bess's brother married an heiress for her inherited fortune of £500, and Bess put on great airs about her new wealthy connection. Robert, who was always jealous of wealth and loathed empty pride, dropped her – she 'huffed my Bardship,' he wrote, 'and I, in the heat of my resentment resolved to burlesque the whole business.'[4] The burlesque was a poem titled *The Mauchline Wedding*, a description of the preparations for the marriage of Bess's brother and the heiress. If any poem demonstrates Robert Burns rhyming for fun this is it – a fragment composed for reciting to the boys of 'Johnnie Doo's', but never written down, so that when he tried to recall it years later he could not remember how one verse ended, or so he said. Another explanation of this lapse of memory is that he was writing the poem down for a lady admirer and the two lines were so lewd that he dared not repeat them to her. *The Mauchline Wedding* was never finished, but the five stanzas which have survived, are such gems of satire that one can only hope Bess never saw them. She and her sister Nell rose three and a half hours early to get ready, he wrote, but the effort was well worthwhile when they emerged from their front door to enter the carriage which was to take them to church:

> But now the gown wi rustling sound.
>   Its silken pomp displays;
> Sure there's no sin in being vain
>   O siccan* bony claes!                    *such
> Sae jimp* the waist, the tail sae vast –   *neat
>   Trouth, they were bonny Birdies!
> O Mither Eve, ye wad been grave
>   To see their ample hurdies*               *buttocks
>     Sae large that day!!![5]

As the critic, Thomas Crawford, points out, the satire of *The Mauchline Wedding* possesses universality far beyond the vanity of a pair of country girls: 'Despite the quarrel with Bess which set him writing, he produced a distanced but not unsympathetic presentation of the people concerned.' Crawford comments. 'If this is satire, it has a far more tolerant appreciation of the essential humanity of its victims than Swift's, Dryden's, or even Pope's and it lacks the element of condescension to one's class inferiors which mars Suckling's poem (John Suckling's *Ballad upon a Wedding*).'[6]

1. *The earliest known portrait of Robert Burns was painted by Peter Taylor in 1786, soon after his first book of poems was published.*

2. *The cottage at Alloway in which Burns was born, as it looked at the time of his birth.*

3. *At Mount Oliphant farm, Robert wrote his first poem to Nelly Kilpatrick, his partner in the harvest field.*

4. The singing and story-telling of Robert's mother, Agnes Burnes (née Brown), fired his young imagination.

5. Isabella, the Poet's youngest sister (1771–1858), gives us much detail about her brother's early life.

6. *With his brother, Gilbert (1760–1827), Robert took a lease of Mossgiel farm at Mauchline in 1784.*

7. *At Lochlie Robert met Elizabeth Paton, mother of 'Dear-bought Bess', his first child.*

8. *Mauchline bleaching green, where Robert and Jean Armour first met when the Poet's dog ran across some clothes she was laying out on the grass.*

9. *The Back Wynd, Mauchline, where Robert and Jean had their first home after their marriage was regularized.*

*Song*        Tune – Bonie Dundee –            1.

In Mauchline there dwells six proper young Belles,
  The pride of the place and its neighbourhood a';
Their carriage and dress a stranger would guess,
  In Lon'on or Paris they'd gotten it a':
Miss Miller is fine, Miss Markland's divine,
  Miss Smith she has wit and Miss Betty is braw;
There's beauty and fortune to get wi' Miss Morton,
  But Armour's the jewel for me o' them a'! —

Note, Miss Armour is now known by the designation
of Mrs Burns — who has the finest foot & leg &c had the finest arm.
              See the vision - Coila's leg compared with bonie &c.

---

*Song* —

Anna, thy charms my bosom fire,
  And waste my soul with care;
But ah, how bootless to admire,
  When fated to despair!

Yet, in thy presence, lovely Fair,
  To hope may be forgiven;
For sure 'twere impious to despair,
  So much in sight of Heaven!

---

10. The Belles of Mauchline, *which praised the lassies of the town, ended with the line* 'But Armour's the jewel for me o' them a'.' *The second song,* Anna, thy charms, *was written for a jilted friend.*

11. *Mrs Frances Anna Dunlop gave Burns motherly advice in interminably long letters. He wrote more letters to her than to any other person.*

12. The Cotter's Saturday Night *so impressed Mrs Dunlop that she began her long correspondence with the Poet.*

Song. Tune, Ettrick banks.

On Miss W. A.                    Written by Burns.

'Twas ev'n, the dewy fields were green,
    On ev'ry blade the pearls hang,
The Zephyr wanton'd round the bean,
    And bore its fragrant sweets alang;
In ev'ry glen the Mavis sang,
    All nature list'ning seem'd the while;
Except where greenwood Echos rang
    Amang the braes o' Ballochmyle.

With careless step I onward stray'd,
    My heart rejoic'd in Nature's joy,
When, musing in a lonely glade,
    A Maiden fair I chanc'd to spy:
Her look was like the Morning's eye,
    Her air like Nature's vernal smile,
The lilies' hue and roses' die
    Bespoke the Lass o' Ballochmyle.

Fair is a morn in flow'ry May,
    And sweet an ev'n in Autumn mild;
When roving through the garden gay,
    Or wand'ring in the lonely wild;
But Woman, Nature's darling child,
    There all her charms she does compile;
And all her other works are foil'd
    By th' bony Lass o' Ballochmyle.

*13. After seeing Wilhelmina Alexander walking by the River Ayr, Burns wrote* The Lass o' Ballochmyle *to her.*

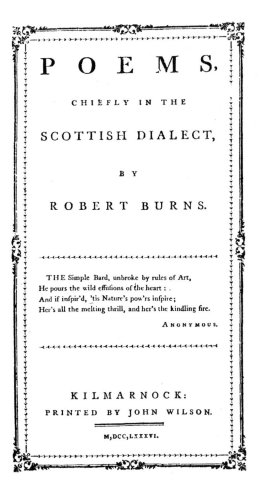

# POEMS,

### CHIEFLY IN THE

## SCOTTISH DIALECT,

### BY

## ROBERT BURNS.

THE Simple Bard, unbroke by rules of Art,
He pours the wild effusions of the heart : .
And if infpir'd, 'tis Nature's pow'rs infpire;
Her's all the melting thrill, and her's the kindling fire.

ANONYMOUS.

## KILMARNOCK:

### PRINTED BY JOHN WILSON.

M,DCC,LXXXVI.

14. *The title page of Burns' first book of poems, called the Kilmarnock Edition because it was printed there.*

15. *A romantic Victorian vision of the meeting with the bonnie lass o' Ballochmyle.*

1786

in the place, to apply to the
Hon:ble Justices to get the said
Woman removed

4. isstly That George Gibson and Elizabeth
Black who haunt and entertain
in their houses such vagrant
persons of suspicious & Bad
Characters, may be laid under
proper restrictions, & obleged to
secure & maintain the peace
& safety of the neighbourhood
under such legall penalties as
to the Hon:ble court shall ap=
pear relevant

2d April Sess. Con. The Session being inform
ed that Jean Armour an unmarried
Woman is said to be with child &
that she has gone off from the
place of ---- to reside elsewhere
The Session think it their duty to
enquire into the truth or false=
hood of this report. But

Jean Armour
with child

16 (above) and 17 (opposite). April 1786 was a bad month for the Armours and for Mauchline Church elders. The minutes of the Kirk Session had no sooner finished recording Adam Armour's 'stanging' of Geordie Gibson's 'jurr' than the elders were on the trail of Jean Armour.

1786

But in the meantime appoint two of their member Viz.<sup>t</sup> James Lamie and William Fisher to speak to the parents on this Subject who it is hoped will be ready to concur with the Session in every thing dutiful & becoming & report

The Session being informed that Mary Borland an unmarried woman is with child order their officer to Summon her to attend ag.<sup>t</sup> Sabbath first

April 9 — James Lamie reports that he spoke to Mary Smith mother to Jean Armour who told him that she did not suspect her Daughter to be with child that she was gone to Paisley to see her friends & would return soon

---

Aug.<sup>t</sup> 6 | Robert Burns John Smith Mary Lindsay
persons absolved | Jean Armour & Agnes Auld appeared before the congregation professing their repentance for the Sin of fornication and they having each appeared two Several Sabbaths formerly were this day rebuked and absolved from the Scandal

18. On 6 August Mauchline Kirk Session minutes reported the last appearance of Burns and Jean Armour before the congregation in Mauchline Church to be rebuked for their sinning. John Smith, Mary Lindsay and Agnes Auld appeared at the same time.

19. *The exchange of Bibles and parting of Robert and Highland Mary Campbell in May, 1786, became a favourite subject for Victorian painters. W.H. Midwood's version is one of the finest.*

20. *The statue of 'Highland Mary' at Dunoon, erected in 1896, looks out across the Firth of Clyde towards the Ayrshire coast.*

21. *The original grave of 'Highland Mary' was in the graveyard of the Old West Kirk at Greenock.*

22. *Baxter's Close, off the Lawnmarket, Edinburgh, by Henry Duguid. On first arriving in the capital in 1786 Burns shared a room and a bed here with his friend John Richmond. He was greatly entertained by city life, especially the ongoings of the ladies of pleasure in the apartment overhead.*

23. *Burns as Edinburgh knew him. This full-length portrait by his friend Alexander Nasmyth was painted in 1828, but is based on drawings made in 1787 when Nasmyth painted a head and shoulders portrait.*

24/25. *Burns was welcomed by the great and the good of the capital. He read his poems (above) in the Duchess of Gordon's drawing room, and at the house of the eccentric judge, Lord Monboddo, he was admired by the judge's daughter, the lovely Bess Burnett.*

Now at the height of his creative year, Robert threw all his prodigious energy into every cause that caught his imagination. Gavin Hamilton, who had been so generous in offering him the lease of Mossgiel was at that time involved in a long-running dispute with the Church, and Burns weighed in to help. Hamilton had already been in dispute with the Kirk Session over the stent, or levy, raised for the poor, which he administered, but during the summer that the Burns family moved to Mossgiel, war broke out again between the two. The trouble this time was that Hamilton was a liberal, one of the New Lights or New Lichts, who were abhorred by the narrow faction of Old Lights or Auld Lichts, whose strict fundamentalism called for total control over parishioners' daily lives.

The Mauchline minister, 'Daddy' Auld, strongly urged on by one of his elders, 'Holy Willie' Fisher, decided to act against those who were doctrinally unsound, a category in which they saw Hamilton. They drew up a list of charges, accusing the lawyer of being absent from church without adequate reason on five Sundays, of setting out on a journey on the Sabbath, of habitually neglecting family prayers, and of writing an abusive letter to the Session on 13 November 1784. Hamilton would not be cowed: he took his case higher, to the Presbytery of Ayr and then to the Synod of Glasgow, at both of which, in the words of the Poet, the Kirk Session came off second best.

Burns, having already skirmished with the Kirk over the Lizzie Paton affair and a poem, *The Twa Herds*, in which he mocked two Auld Licht ministers who were quarrelling over parish boundaries, weighed in to help his friend. This time the poem was *Holy Willie's Prayer*, a devastating satire on the hypocrisy of Auld Licht churchmen. 'Holy Willie' was shown at prayer, confident that God had chosen him as one of His Elect, predestined to salvation. The Old Testament ring which pervades the whole poem led up inexorably to the last smug verse in which Willie expects God to set him and his kin above everyone around him:

> But, Lord, remember me and mine
> Wi' mercies temporal and divine!
> That I for grace and gear may shine,
>     Excell'd by nane,
> And a' the glory shall be Thine –
>     Amen, Amen![7]

The poem set the countryside in uproar; Auld Lichts raged, New Lichts laughed. Burns himself was somewhat appalled by his own daring, so that when the young New Licht minister at Tarbolton, the Reverend John

McMath, asked for a copy of *Holy Willie's Prayer*, he sent with it a long verse 'apology':

> I own 'twas rash, an rather hardy,
> That I, a simple, countra* bardie,        *country
> Shou'd meddle wi' a pack sae sturdy,
>     Wha, if they ken me,
> Can easy, wi a single wordie,
>     Louse* Hell upon me.[8]    *loose

The Poet, fired by the success of *Holy Willie's Prayer*, followed with *The Holy Fair*, then *The Address to the Deil*, *The Ordination* and *The Kirk's Alarm*, all of which were received with acclaim among liberal-thinking members of the community. The Kirk's Auld Licht army was defeated for the timebeing, but it had not yet lost the war. A new campaign was about to open on a battleground chosen by the Kirk, on a subject on which it had already wounded the rhymer from Mossgiel. Burns' own 'holy fair' was on course to end in houghmagandie – and the Kirk was waiting.

By the summer of 1785, his eye caught sight of a new love, although he did not name her in the little verses he entered into his *Common Place Book* that August, giving all the girls of the district fair warning that they were prey for that 'rakish rook' Rab Mossgiel[9]:

> When first I came to Stewart Kyle*    *a division of Ayrshire
>   My mind it was nae steady,
> Where e'er I gaed, where e'er I rade*,    *rode
>   A Mistress still I had ay*:    *always
>
> But when I came roun' by Mauchlin town,
>   Not dreadin' any body,
> My heart was caught before I thought
>   And by a Mauchlin Lady.[10]

The lady was soon to be identified: in a little two-stanza piece, *The Belles of Mauchline*, which mentioned the Millers of *The Mauchline Wedding*, so Robert cannot have been too put out about abandoning proud Bess Miller.

> In Mauchline there dwells six proper young belles,
>   The pride of the place and its neighbourhood a',
> Their carriage and dress, a stranger would guess,
>   In Lon'on or Paris, they'd gotten it a'.

Miss Miller is fine, Miss Markland's divine,
  Miss Smith she has wit, and Miss Betty is braw*,         *splendid
There's beauty and fortune to get wi Miss Morton;
  But Armour's the jewel for me o them a'.[11]

*Armour* was Jean Armour, daughter of James and Mary Armour, the quiet-living parents of Adam of 'stanging' fame. Their daughter, Jean, was a girl of about twenty, some six years younger than her new suitor. Jean's father was a stone-mason who had been involved in some important building work on mansions and bridges in the district, and consequently had done exceedingly well at his trade. He was highly thought of and knew it: comfortably enough off to own a good house in the Cowgate beside the Whiteford Arms and able to afford 10 shillings and 8 pence a year for one of the most expensive pews in Mauchline Kirk.[12] Armour considered himself a cut above most folk in the town socially, and infinitely superior to those struggling Burneses at Mossgiel. Why Jean, the Armours' second child and eldest daughter should bother to respond to Rab Mossgiel's overtures we are unlikely ever to know, but very likely it was his elegant manner and sophistication beside the run of Mauchline 'beaux' that first appealed. She would be intrigued also by his reputation as a poet, for she herself was better educated than most other girls in the parish. As for his reputed sexual reputation, that did not put her off because she herself was a girl of spirit and coquettishness, of which her dour, kirk-going parents did not approve. And, like many another girl before and after her, Jean assuredly thought herself strong-willed enough to be able to resist the Mossgiel poet if he made advances. There is not the slightest doubt that Jean Armour embarked on her affair with Robert Burns with her eyes open.

Robert himself did not think highly of Jean's scholarly abilities. Soon after he married and settled down with her, he told one of his intellectual friends that, apart from the Bible, Jean had scarcely spent five minutes with prose or verse in her life.[13] It must be remembered that he wrote this to fill the time one day when he had been driven from the harvest field – and he was trying to impress an old blue-stocking flame.

Exactly when or how Robert and Jean met belongs to the realm of legend and tradition and, in the words of one of Jean's biographers, 'has been often debated by Burns "experts", those indefatigable diggers in the compost heap of existing Burnsiana.'[14] The various versions differ as to date, some giving it as April 1784, and others 1785, but he certainly had not settled on Jean as the love of his life as late as September 1785. In his

*Common Place Book* at that time he wrote about the old Scots songs and reflected on the 'glorious old bards'. Although he was writing in the third person, he was referring to himself:

> Some of you tell us, with all the charms of verse, that you have been unfortunate in the world, unfortunate in love: he too, has felt all the unfitness of a Poetic heart for the struggle of a busy, bad world; he has felt the loss of his little fortune, the loss of friends, and worse than all, the loss of the woman he adored! Like you, all his consolation was his Muse.[15]

This reflective mood may well have stemmed from a brief recurrence of his old enemy, the depressive illness, but he could hardly have been referring to Lizzie Paton or Bess Miller because he adored neither of them. Since he referred to the source of inspiration for *Montgomerie's Peggy* in his *Common Place Book* at the same time,[16] it seems reasonable to assume that he was harking back to the girl who worked at Coilsfield House, or some earlier charmer. If the Armour liaison had even started by now, it had not yet got far enough under way to drive thoughts of those earlier passions out of his head.

The sequence of events which started the Armour affair, also differs according to who is telling the tale, but Jean's own version, given towards the end of her life, seems quite clear:

> The first time I saw Burns was in Mauchline . . . I was then spreading clothes in a bleach-green along with some other girls, when the poet passed in his way to call on Mr Hamilton. He had a little dog which ran on the clothes, and I scolded, and threw something at the animal. Burns said, 'Lassie, if ye thought ought o' me, ye wadna hurt my dog!' – I thought to mysel – I wadna think much o' you at ony rate!' I saw him afterwards at a dancing-room, and we fell acquainted.[17]

The more usual versions of the first meeting reverse the order of the bleaching green and dance encounters, with Jean first seeing him with his faithful collie at the Race Week dance and telling a girl he was dancing with that he wished he could persuade one of the lassies to like him as well as his dog did. It was some days afterwards that the bleaching green incident took place.

We have no idea of Jean Armour's appearance at the time she met Rab Mossgiel, but tradition and biographers paint a believable picture: she was dark complexioned, with dark eyes and a bewitching smile and had enough of what the Scots call smeddum* to set the Poet's tinder heart ablaze within a very short time. Again if tradition be true, they continued to meet in spite of all the efforts of staid James Armour to prevent his daughter from becoming caught up with the Poet from Mossgiel. Jean was already half promised to a young weaver, Robert Wilson, who was keen on her but had gone off to Paisley to set up his own weaving shop there. Jean and Robert continued to see one another in spite of all Armour's precautions, in part thanks to the convenient window of Jean's bedroom which looked directly on to a window of the Whitefoord Arms, where Robert drank and met his friends. It was all very handy for two young people to fall deeply in love.

This was the start of the saga of Jean Armour, which was to run for the rest of Robert Burns' life, at first turbulently, and then, after they were married, more calmly, for Jean Armour made him a good wife – and Robert Burns, if one allows for his waywardness, was a good husband to her too.

Jean's greatest gift to the Poet was simply to inspire him to write some of his tenderest, most touching songs. When he was planning to emigrate to the West Indies he wrote *Tho' Cruel Fate*; when he married her he rejoiced with *I Hae a Wife o' my Ain*, *My Wife's a Winsome Wee Thing*, *It is na, Jean*, *Thy Bonie Face*, and the two most touching of all, *Of A' The Airts*, written while they were apart, and *O Were I on Parnassus Hill*, the song of a perfectly happy married man. The last song he ever wrote to Jean was *Their Groves o Sweet Myrtle*, a perfectly fashioned little song which he sent to George Thomson in April 1795. It ended with lines that sum up his own life and his love for Jean Armour.

> He wanders as free as the winds of his mountains,
> Save Love's willing fetters – the chains o his Jean.[18]

The prolific year of 1785 ended on a tragic note for the Burns family at Mossgiel when, John, the youngest of the family died on 28 October. He was only sixteen, and the cause of his death is unknown, but he was buried in Mauchline churchyard in a 'second-quality' mortcloth because that was all they could afford. Life resumed at Mossgiel with Robert continuing to spend as little time as possible working on the farm and as much as he could writing verse. He also continued to see Jean in spite of all her father's threats and disapproval, and, inevitably, soon after New

*spirit

Year came round, Jean found herself 'as women wish to be who love their lords.'[19]

Precisely when Jean broke the news of her pregnancy we do not know, but Burns already felt a strong commitment to her in January, even though he may not have known of her condition at the time. In his verse epistle written that month to his friend and former Lochlie neighbour, David Sillar, he said.

> Ye hae your Meg, your dearest part,
>   And I my darling Jean!
>     It warms me, it charms me
>       To mention but her name:
>     It heats me, it beets me,
>       An sets me a' on flame![20]

She had given him the news by 17 February when he wrote to John Richmond, who himself had recently done penance for fornication with Jenny Surgeoner and had fled to Edinburgh. 'I have no news to acquaint you with about Machlin,' he told his friend, 'they are just going on in the old way. I have some very important news with respect to myself, not the most agreable, news that I am sure you cannot guess, but I shall give you the particulars another time.'[21]

Significantly, he added, 'I am extremely happy with Smith; he is all the friend I have now in Machlin . . . If you would act your part as a FRIEND, I am sure neither GOOD nor BAD fortune should estrange or alter me.' Whether this meant the news of Jean's predicament was known at least to some in the town or not, we have no idea: it may only have been that Burns felt himself under pressure from the 'unco guid' of the town because of the previous year's Paton scandal and the Kirk's reaction to the scurrilous poems he was producing about 'Holy Willie' Fisher and his Auld Licht band.

Jean held back from breaking the news to her parents for as long as possible, most probably until the end of March when she could no longer hide her condition, and the blow to James and Mary Armour was severe. Her father swooned from shock and had to be revived with a cordial fetched by his wife. When he recovered he was beside himself with anger: for his Jean to be pregnant was a blow to him as a pillar of the kirk, but to be pregnant by that arrant, blaspheming rogue Burns of Mossgiel was too much to bear. Quite apart from making his favourite daughter pregnant, the stir over the scandalous stanging of Geordie Gibson's jurr by their son, Adam, had just reached its climax in front of the Kirk Session on

6 March, and Rab Burns was involved in that too. Not only had he hidden Adam away at Mossgiel during the hue and cry over the affair, he had spread one of his blasphemous versifications around the town, a profanity which glorified the stanging under the guise of a prayer – and at the same time made his son look silly by describing him as scarcely bigger than a kail-knife. By their example, Burns, Richmond and that clique had encouraged the younger boys, so Armour held the Poet responsible for that stain on his family's good character too.

No wonder Armour said from the beginning that he 'would raither hae seen the Deil himsel comin to the hoose to coort his dochter.'[22] On no account would he accept Burns as a son-in-law, even when Jean produced a piece of paper, which was either a declaration of marriage or some form of promise for the future.

Armour's first thought was not the legality of this document, but how the scandal affected his own reputation and his daughter's. Jean was bundled off to stay with her aunt and uncle in Paisley, a convenient place since Robert Wilson, the weaver who had fancied her earlier, was also there. Armour and his wife may have had hopes that their daughter might persuade Wilson to marry her in spite of her condition; perhaps they just wanted her out of the way of the kirk's wrath, or maybe they just did the first thing that came to mind. 'Daddy' Auld's 'houghmagandie pack' was too quick for them: it picked up the scent within days and on 2 April, less than a month after Adam Armour's case had come before them, Mauchline elders portentously minuted:

> The Session being informed that Jean Armour an unmarried Woman is said to be with child, and that she has gone off from the place of late, to reside elsewhere, the Session think it their duty to enquire into the truth or falsehood of this report.

Two of the elders, 'Holy Willie' Fisher and James Lamie, were instructed 'to speak to the parents on this Subject who it is hoped will be ready to concur with the Session in everything dutiful & becoming & report.'[23]

The holy pair hied round to the Cowgate to find only Mrs Armour at home. She lied nobly for her daughter: a week later Lamie reported to the Session meeting that Mrs Armour had told him 'she did not suspect her daughter to be with child, that she had gone to Paisley to see her friends and would return soon.'[24]

James and Mary Armour now turned their attention to the marriage document which Jean had pushed in front of them after she broke the news. Unfortunately 'that unlucky paper'[25] as Burns called it, has not survived, although this has not stopped the world from arguing over it for two centuries. In the light of what happened subsequently, it seems improbable that the document committed Burns legally to marriage, but it looked binding enough to Armour's ill-educated eye for him to decide to show it to a lawyer as soon as possible. He could not take it to Gavin Hamilton in Mauchline, of course, because Hamilton was a friend of the poet, so he rushed off to Ayr on Friday, 14 April, and asked Robert Aiken to look at it. Of all people, Aiken was the most unsuitable for he also was a friend of Burns. Armour could not have known that Aiken had been an enthusiastic supporter of the young poet for several years: in fact had given Burns such encouragement that the Poet dedicated *The Cotter's Saturday Night* to him – and indeed 'My lov'd, my honour'd, much respected friend'[26] is how he referred to Aiken in the first line of the poem. Burns wrote the *Epistle to a Young Friend* for Aiken's son, around the time of the 'unlucky paper' incident, so there was no ill feeling on the Poet's side over the action Aiken took.

The enraged Armour thrust the document under the lawyer's nose and demanded that he should declare it invalid: he probably asked first for it to be destroyed and, when Aiken refused, ordered the lawyer to delete the names of Robert and Jean from it. Aiken obliged, which seems an unlikely thing for a lawyer to do if the marriage document was legally binding. Aiken surely would never have been tempted to mutilate such an agreement, especially one signed by his friend, Burns. He must have believed it made no difference whether the scrap of paper contained the couple's names or not, so to pacify Armour, he cut the names out of it.

Armour lost no time in passing this news on to the Poet, for only the following day, Saturday 15 April, Robert wrote to tell Hamilton what had happened in Aiken's office the day before:

Old Mr Armour prevailed with him [Aiken] to mutilate that unlucky paper, yesterday. Would you believe it? tho' I had not a hope, nor even a wish, to make her mine after her conduct, yet when he told me, the names were all cut out of the paper, my heart died within me, and he cut my very veins with the news. Perdition seize her falsehood, and perjurious perfidy! but God bless her and forgive my poor, once-dear, misguided girl. She is ill advised,[27]

He ended the letter:

I am indeed a fool, but a knave is an infinitely worse character than any body, I hope, will dare to give the unfortunate Robt Burns.

Robert was in turmoil, unable to think clearly, but not in such confusion as to be unable to turn an exaggerated, elaborate phrase. Even now he was still writing to impress his reader: '*Perdition seize her falsehood, and perjurious perfidy!*' These were the words of a man in a towering rage rather than the depths of despair. He had been defeated by Armour and, as always, took defeat badly. He told Hamilton that Jean had betrayed him by going to Paisley, yet surely he could not have believed her running away was her own idea, and admitted as much when he called her 'my poor, once-dear misguided girl' – note that Jean was *my* poor, misguided girl. His love for her still ran deep, and he realized that she had been ill-advised by her father, but for the moment he could not think beyond the mutilation of the 'unlucky paper' and his anger at this humiliation.

In his confusion and misery, Burns felt a warm affinity to a fellow Ayrshire man, John Arnot of Dalquhatswood, a mysterious character, who appears to have squandered his fortune and earned 'the world's contempt'. Perhaps it was because Arnot was not a close friend – indeed he appears to have been a total stranger – that Burns felt able to use the excuse of inviting Arnot to subscribe to the Kilmarnock Edition of his poems to open his heart and tell the story of the miserable disaster that had resulted from his association with Jean. The letter[28] is full of rebellious, bawdy sexual bravado of the kind he usually reserved for other young men of his own circle: this letter could have been written to Richmond or Smith, as it described in detail his conquest of Jean Armour. The original of the letter has been lost, but Burns thought it worth copying into the book of manuscripts he compiled for Robert Riddell of Glenriddell in 1790–1. This was fortunate since the letter probes deeply into the Poet's state of mind around April 1786. Burns wrote in the introduction to the copy in the Glenriddell Manuscript:

> The story of the letter was this:– I had got deeply in love with a young Fair-One, of which proofs were every day arising more & more to view. I would gladly have covered my Inamorato from the darts of Calumny with the conjugal Shield, nay, had actually made up some sort of Wedlock; but I was at that time deep in the guilt of being unfortunate, for which good & lawful objection, the Lady's friends broke all our measures, & drove me *au desespoir.*[29]

Although he felt certain that this total stranger to whom he was writing was bound to have heard his story already 'with its exaggeration', he launched into it at full tilt – it seems a strange way for an author to persuade a stranger to buy his book, but then Burns was no ordinary author. Before he reached the end of the letter Burns told Arnot, 'There is a pretty large portion of bedlam in the composition of a Poet at any time, but on this occasion, I was nine parts & nine tenths, out of ten, stark staring mad.' By the time he reached the end of this letter from someone he did not even know, Arnot must have agreed.

> I have lost, Sir, that dearest earthly treasure, that greatest blessing here below, that last, best gift which compleated Adam's happiness in the garden of bliss, I have lost – I have lost – my trembling hand refuses its office, the frightened ink recoils up the quill – Tell it not in Gath – I have lost – a – a – WIFE!

Entertainingly, and with an eye to his reader all the time, he told Arnot of the 'damned star' which ensured that whatever he did always failed to prosper. 'I rarely hit where I aim; & if I want any thing, I am almost sure never to find it where I seek it. For instance, if my pen-knife is needed, I pull out twenty things: a plough-wedge, a horse-nail, an old letter or a tattered rhyme, in short, every thing but my pen-knife;' Even in love others were more fortunate:

> My mouth watered deliciously, to see a young fellow, after a few idle, common-place stories from a gentleman in black, strip & go to bed with a young girl & no one durst say black was his eye; while I, for just doing the same thing, only wanting that ceremoney, am made a Sunday's laughing stock, & am abused like a pick-pocket.

He had warmed to his task and proceeded to describe how he took Jean only to be routed by Armour; his sexual encounter became a military campaign in which he, the commander-in-chief, was left with nothing but the equipment under his cloak to fight another day. And one is left re-assured that there will be another day, another battle, before long:

> Whilst I was vigorously pressing on the siege; had carried the counter-scarp, & made a practicable breach behind the curtin in the gorge of the very principal bastion; nay, l having mastered the covered way, I had found means to slip a choice detachment into the very citadel: while I had nothing less in view than displaying my victorious banners on the top of the walls, 'Heaven & Earth, must I remember'! my damned Star wheeled about to the zenith by whose baleful rays

Fortune took the alarm, & pouring in her forces on all quarters, front, flank & rear, I was utterly routed, my baggage lost, my military chest in the hands of the enemy; & your poor devil of a humble servant, commander in chief forsooth, was obliged to scamper away, without either arms or honors of war, except his bare bayonet & cartridge-pouch; nor in all probability had he escaped even with them, had he not made a shift to hide them under the lap of his military coat.

Abandoning the military metaphor he turned his passion into a storm against which advice and reason were powerless. But now he said he had recovered:

A storm naturally overblows itself. My spent passions gradually sank into a lurid calm; & by degrees, I have subsided into the time-settled sorrow of the sable widower, who, wiping away the decent tear, lifts up his grief-worn eye to look – for another wife.

Almost as an afterthought he remembered that, although he was ready to look for another wife, the affair was not yet over – the Kirk had yet to fire off its guns in the Poet's 'campaign' to win Jean Armour:

Already the holy beagles, the houghmagandie pack, begin to snuff the scent; & I expect every moment to see them cast off, & hear them after me in full cry: but as I am an old fox, I shall give them dodging & doubling for it; & by & bye, I intend to earth among the mountains of Jamaica.

But what had he told Arnot at the beginning of his letter? 'A damned Star has always kept my zenith, & sheds its baleful influence, in that emphatic curse of the Prophet, "And behold, whatsoever he doth, it shall not prosper", I rarely hit where I aim; & if I want any thing, I am almost sure never to find it where I seek it.'

The Poet in Mossgiel at that moment was seeking many things apart from Jean Armour, but the star of fortune was just as wily an old fox and was there waiting.

CHAPTER SIX

# St Mary of Argyll

But the sweetest song that cheered me
Was thy voice my gentle Mary,
And thine artless winning smile
That has made this world an Eden,
Bonnie Mary of Argyll.

Victorian music hall song written
at the time when *Highland Mary*
was at her most popular[1]

The strange intimate letter which Burns sent to John Arnot, describing his military campaign to capture Jean Armour and the subsequent rout at the hands of her father, demonstrates just how confused the Poet was in heart and mind by April 1786. But the 'commander-in-chief' was marching manfully on in spite of threats from every quarter: enemies were closing in and farming was all but forgotten as he tried to recapture the high ground of life in Mauchline.

Robert Burns was never defeated for long. When the flax-dressing venture at Irvine fell apart at Hogmanay 1781, he dashed off a defiant little poem:

O, why the deuce should I repine,
  And be an ill foreboder?
I'm twenty-three, and five feet nine,
  I'll go and be a sodger*!                   *soldier

I gat some gear wi meikle* care,             *much
  I held it weel thegither;
But now it's gane – and something mair*:     *more
I'll go and be a sodger![2]

This was one of those spontaneous defiant responses so typical of Burns when 'that damned star' turned against him, showing how irrational he could be at times of stress. He would not have survived a week in an officer's uniform: as an enlisted man he would have been court-martialled within forty-eight hours. He demonstrated his attitude to the army officers one evening in 1793 when he went to join his friend, Maria Riddell, in her box at the theatre in Dumfries, but crept away the moment he saw 'one of these lobster-coated PUPPIES' sitting beside her.[3] In spite of all the military metaphors in his wooing, the soldier's life was not for Burns.

He soon had his guns primed again ready to return to the fray after Armour vanquished him and Jean appeared to desert to the 'enemy' in April 1786. One idea, just as improbable as the notion of joining the army, was to emigrate to the West Indies, where many of his countrymen had settled and made their fortune. This was not the first time he had considered escaping the Kirk's wrath by fleeing abroad or enlisting in the army. In a verse epistle to John Rankine at the time news of Lizzie Paton's pregnancy broke, Burns suggested he might join up and serve the King in the American War, or go and 'herd the buckskin kye . . . in Virginia'*.[4]

The army or emigration, especially to the West Indies, would have been a death sentence in view of his poor health. As Professor DeLancey Ferguson has pointed out: 'The West Indies' climate helped to insure the financial success of a small minority of white immigrants by killing off most of their rivals.'[5] Life in the services would have been no better.

While the Armour saga ground its inevitable course, Robert made plans to emigrate, and by April 1786, all was sufficiently settled for him to tell Arnot of Dalquhatswood that he intended to escape the 'holy beagles' by going 'to earth among the mountains of Jamaica'.[6] That must have brought a quiet smile to Robert's lips as he thought of those Kirk Session meetings on 2 and 9 April when the elders were sniffing at Armour's door to discover the truth about Jean.

Thanks to the influence of some of his Ayr friends, Patrick Douglas of Garallan in Ayrshire was persuaded to help Robert to be obtain a post as book-keeper on the estates owned by his brother, Charles Douglas, at Port Antonio in Jamaica. The salary was to be £30 a year, and Douglas agreed to finance Burns' passage in a brig called the *Nancy* at the beginning of September. The fare was to be repaid out of the Poet's salary over three years.

As his emigration plans became clearer, Burns' thoughts turned to his poetry and he had pangs of regret about leaving behind the huge amount of verse which he had recently written, and, more important,

*herd American cattle in Virginia

abandoning his growing reputation among influential Ayrshire folk who were enjoying reading it – especially the irreverent satirical poems targeted at hypocrites within the Kirk. Robert remembered Richard Brown's suggestion that he should try to have some of his poems published, and he realized that if he didn't publish them before he left for Jamaica, he would never see them in print. It was now or never.

The decision to publish was not taken to raise the fare to the West Indies as has sometimes been suggested, nor was it mere vanity, although he did long for a favourable response from the world to his work as any poet would. As he told Dr Moore:

> I weighed my productions as impartially as in my power; I thought they had merit; and 'twas a delicious idea that I would be called a clever fellow, even though it should never reach my ears a poor Negro-driver, or perhaps a victim of that inhospitable clime gone to the world of Spirits.[7]

Burns evaluated 'how much ground' he occupied both as a man and a poet and felt certain enough of his talents to show himself off to a wider public in a volume of his poems.

> I can truly say that *pauvre Inconnu* [poor unknown] as I then was, I had a pretty nearly as high an idea of myself and my works as I have at this moment . . . I was pretty sure my Poems would meet with some applause; but at the worst, the roar of the Atlantic would deafen the voice of Censure, and the novelty of West Indian scenes make me forget Neglect.[8]

By the day the 'houghmagandie pack' set their two elders on the trail of Jean Armour he had finalized his publishing plan, and on 14 April, the very day that Armour persuaded Aiken to cut the names out of the 'unlucky paper', the proposal for his book was printed and ready for sending to possible subscribers. As any new author would, Burns lost no time in circulating it among all his friends – and to many people he didn't know, like John Arnot of Dalquhatswood who was also rewarded with that magnificent letter about the Armour 'campaign'. The response was immediate and beyond anything he could have hoped for, with all his influential friends in Ayrshire persuading their friends to subscribe. Almost everybody who writes about Burns, refers to his emigration plan, publication of *Poems Chiefly in the Scottish Dialect*, farming progress (or lack of it) and the Jean Armour saga as if they were all separate, self-contained events, quite unconnected. They were not. All were unfolding at the same time, in a great confusion, and at varying speeds. The same people were involved in several strands of his life, some in all of them. Gavin Hamilton was lawyer, landlord, confidant, friend, drummer-up of subscribers; Bob Aiken was his opponent's legal adviser, but Robert's friend, enthusiastic admirer of his poetry, and recommender of the proposed book. Even 'Daddy' Auld, while deploring Robert Burns' blasphemous verse, made no complaint about the satires on the Kirk, and would have said it was charity that drove him to seek out Mossgiel's waywardness and make him atone for his sins. Only James Armour hated Robert Burns with all his heart, and in the burning intensity of his antipathy, would not hear a word in the Poet's favour. In the light of all that, it is hardly surprising that Robert's mind was in a state of turmoil.

By the middle of April yet another strand had been added to the complicated life – one about which (unusual for him) he was most secretive, and which, by its very mystery, was to shape opinion of him for a century and more after his death. Burns was smitten by love again.

He told Arnot in April 1786, he was lifting up his grief-worn eye to look for another wife,[9] and soon he found one, a Highland girl called Mary Campbell. We have always assumed she was called Mary, but James Mackay discovered from a study of Argyll baptismal registers that 'Highland Mary' was in fact Margaret Campbell, daughter of Archibald Campbell, captain of a collier which carried Ayrshire coal to Kintyre, and his wife, Agnes or Anne Campbell. She was baptized at Dunoon on 18 March 1766.[10]

Margaret, or Mary, as she had better be called since that is how she is known in the Burns legend (and in any case Margaret would not fit euphoneously into the poems about Mary), came over to Ayrshire while still in her teens and found work as a byre-maid with Colonel Hugh Montgomerie at Coilsfield House, near Tarbolton. From there she moved to Mauchline around Whitsun 1785, to become nursemaid to Gavin Hamilton's children, but that lasted no more than a few months, probably until Martinmas the same year. We have no evidence that Burns' tinder heart burst into flame while Mary was at Hamilton's house, but he must have seen her there often, and a tradition quoted in Mauchline claims that they met secretly while she was there.[11] It would be surprising if he had not tried to court her, and knowing his attitude to women and in the light of what happened subsequently, it is perfectly possible that he had a relationship with Mary which ran concurrently with the Jean Armour affair. Gavin Hamilton, who was an observant lawyer and privy to Burns' every move, would be aware of what was happening and may have got rid of Mary for that reason. Others said later that Mary Campbell was a very loose woman, and, since she was living in his house and nursing his children, Hamilton would soon get wind of that. For whatever reason, 'Highland Mary' left Hamilton's employ after a very short time and for the next six months either returned to Coilsfield or went to work at Stairaird farm, which is perched on a crag just above the river at the point where the Mauchline burn joins the River Ayr.

Mary was described as 'not a beauty, but decent-looking; slightly pox-marked',[12] but that would not put Robert off, especially if Mary was a bit 'loose' and showed willingness to flirt with him. It would be natural for him to try for sexual intercourse at the first opportunity, so Mary, too, may have been expecting his child by the spring of 1786.

It is ironic that *The Jolly Beggars*, which was based on an incident at Poosie Nansie's in the autumn of 1785, ends with a call for the Poet, sitting there 'between his two Deborahs', to give them a song. The Bard (clearly Burns himself) obliged, and two lines of his song ran:

> And at night, in barn or stable,
> Hug our doxies on the hay.[13]

Did Burns hug two doxies on the hay that winter, or did he take up with Mary only after Jean became pregnant, either early in the new year, or in April 1786, when Armour rejected Burns as a son-in-law and sent his daughter off to Paisley?

If only the answer to that were known it would help to solve the great mystery of 'Highland Mary' – whether she died bearing his child. Unfortunately, Burns for once was very economical with the truth: a man normally open and honest about his life, he said little about Mary Campbell, yet something troubled his conscience about this relationship, and frequently – too frequently to be acceptable to anyone with a searching mind – he suggests in letters and the poems the affair inspired that it happened in his 'very early life'. There are too many misleading clues around the 'Highland Mary' courtship to reject the unpalatable truth that very probably he chased both girls and impregnated each of them within a few weeks – if true, it was not the last time Burns achieved that.

It must be admitted that available evidence might point to the fact that he was not involved with Mary Campbell until after the middle of April, when the declaration he had given Jean was mutilated and in his (and her) view invalidated. In fact it has been suggested that he had a brief flutter with a girl called Elizabeth Barbour after Jean rejected him. By the time he wrote to Arnot sometime in April, he said he had 'subsided into the time-settled sorrow of the sable widower',[14] and was looking for another wife. He would never have written that if he had been besotted with Mary at the time.

On the second Sunday in May 1786, Robert and Mary met beside the River Ayr, or possibly one of the little streams that join it there; they exchanged Bibles and plighted their troth, then Mary returned to Campbeltown, where her parents lived. Robert's Bible is lost, but the little two-volume Bible he gave her is preserved at Burns Monument at Alloway. The books contain religious texts written on the fly-leaf, and for many years the names of Robert and Mary were believed to be inscribed in them, although deliberate attempts had been made to obliterate these. Recently the volumes were submitted to forensic tests, which show they do not contain Mary's name at all, but only Robert's and his address as Mossgaville, the old spelling of Mossgiel.[15] Perhaps he gave Mary a Bible he already had at home rather than a new one as a token of his love.

Burns made little reference to Mary Campbell apart from a few songs and an introductory note to one of these, *My Highland Lassie, O*, when he transcribed it for the Glenriddell Manuscript. This makes it clear that he intended to take Mary with him to the West Indies:

*The Highland Lassie, O.* This was a composition of mine in very early life before I was known at all in the world. My Highland Lassie was a warm-hearted, charming young creature as ever blessed a man with generous love. After a pretty long tract of the most ardent reciprocal attachment, we met by appointment, on the second Sunday of May, in a sequestered spot by the banks of Ayr, where we spent the day in taking farewel, before she should embark for the West Highlands to arrange matters among her friends for our projected change of life.[16]

Burns himself referred to her as 'Highland Mary' only once, in 1792, in a song of that title, about a girl who was 'one of the most interesting passages of my youthful days'.[17]

> But still within my bosom's core
> Shall live my Highland Mary.[18]

Whether Burns ever intended to take Mary with him to Jamaica is open to question, but it does seem odd that a man, who was always so open with his friends, never referred to her accompanying him at the time. In fact only three weeks after the exchange of Bibles and vows Armour returned to Mauchline, throwing Burns into even greater confusion than when he sent his letter to Arnot. Jean was making him miserable, because he still loved her to distraction and hinted darkly that one day she might become his wife. He was so besotted with her that it was as if Mary Campbell had never been. In this state of turmoil he sat down on 12 June to give the news of her return to David Brice, a Mauchline friend who had moved to Glasgow. Words spluttered from his pen in a torrent of misery and joy at having her, if not there with him, at least back in the town:

I have no news to tell you that will give me any pleasure to mention, or you, to hear. Poor, ill-advised, ungrateful Armour came home on Friday last. You have heard all the particulars of that affair; and a black affair it is. What she thinks of her conduct now, I don't know: one thing I know, she has made me compleatly miserable. Never man lov'd, or rather ador'd, a woman more than I did her and, to confess a truth between you and me, I do still love her to destraction after all, tho' I won't tell her so, tho I see her which I don't want to do. My poor dear, unfortunate Jean! How happy have I been in her arms! It is not the losing her that makes me so unhappy; but for *her* sake I feel most severely. I foresee she is on the road to, I am afraid, eternal grief, and those who made so much noise, and showed so much grief, at the thought of her being *my wife*, may, some day, see her connected in such a manner as may give them more real cause of vexation. I am sure I do not wish it: may Almighty God forgive her ingratitude and perjury to me, as I from my very soul forgive her! and may His grace be with her, to bless her in all her future life! I can have no nearer idea of the place of eternal punishment than what I have felt in my own breast on her account. I have tryed often to forget her: I have run into all kinds of dissipation and riot, Mason-meetings, drinking matches, and other mischief, to drive her out of my head, but all in vain: and now for a grand cure, the Ship is on her way home that is to take me out to Jamaica, and then, farewel dear old Scotland, and farewel dear, ungrateful Jean, for never, never will I see you more![19]

Not a word of Mary. In Jean's absence he had been leading a life of dissipation and riot, which could be an oblique reference to his association with Mary Campbell, but the Kirk soon brought all that to a halt. Within a week, Jean was called to 'compear'* in the Kirk on the following Sunday,

*appear for rebuke

but she did not turn up. Instead, she sent a letter to the minister on 13 June, full of contrition, which was duly noted in the Session minutes.

> I am heartily sorry that I have given your Session trouble on my account. I acknowledge that I am with child, and Robert Burns in Mossgiel is the father. I am, with great respect, your most humble servant, Jean Armour.[20]

Robert could not resist calling in at the Cowgate to see how Jean was faring, but as he ought to have expected, he was shown the door by Mrs Armour. He told Richmond all about it:

> I have waited on Armour since her return home, not by – from any the least view of reconciliation, but merely to ask for her health; and – to you I will confess it, from a foolish, hankering fondness – very ill-plac'd indeed. The Mother forbade me the house; nor did Jean shew that penitence might have been expected.[21]

Robert too was summoned before the Kirk Session and admitted his guilt before the elders. 'June 25th, 1786. Compeared Robert Burns and acknowledges himself the father of Jean Armour's child(ren).'[22] One imagines that those kirkmen, who had been humiliated and scourged so often in Mossgiel's poems over recent months, might have taken terrible revenge now that they had him at their mercy, but for all the vengeful reputation these old style Calvinists were reputed to have, they were very forbearing. They remained remarkably calm about it all, and simply ordered him to appear before the minister and congregation on three Sundays, which was no more than would have been the punishment of any other fornicator. He was also allowed to strike a bargain with the minister that thereafter he would be free of Jean Armour or any other girl in his past. He told Richmond this in the letter he wrote on the evening before his first appearance:

> The Priest, I am inform'd will give me a Certificate as a single man, if I comply with the rules of the Church, which for that very reason I intend to do.

The following morning, Sunday 10 July, he added a final jaunty paragraph, which showed the shallowness of his contrition and that his mind was on the publication of his poems, due in a couple of weeks, rather than on repentance:

I am just going to put on Sackcloth & ashes this day. I am indulged so far as to appear in my own seat. *Peccavi Pater, miserere mei.* My book will be ready in a fortnight. If you have any Subscribers return me them by Connell. The Lord stand wi' the righteous. Amen Amen.[23]

The Armours were livid that Burns was indulged by 'Daddy' Auld to such a degree that he did not even have to stand on the cutty stool, but was able to remain at his own place. He told David Brice how hard the Armours had tried to have him forced to stand alongside Jean, and in the course of this letter, repeated the tale of his visit to the Armour's house and that he was going through the formality of appearing in the church in order to obtain the bachelor certificate he wanted before he set off for Jamaica:

I have already appeared publickly in Church, and was indulged in the liberty of standing in my own seat. I do this to get a certificate as a batchelor, which Mr Auld has promised me. I am now fixed to go for the West Indies in October. Jean and her friends insisted much that she should stand along with me in the kirk, but the minister would not allow it, which bred a great trouble I assure you; and I am blamed as the cause of it, tho I am sure I am innocent; but I am very well pleased, for all that, not to have her company.[24]

Two more appearances followed, after the last of which the Session minuted that 'Robert Burns, John Smith, Mary Lindsay, Jean Armour and Agnes Auld, appeared before the congregation professing their repentance for the sin of fornication, and they having each appeared two several Sabbaths formerly were this day rebuked and absolved from the Scandal.'[25]

Throughout the entire spring and summer Robert had responded to his own nagging conscience and the criticism of others in the only way he knew – by retaliating. He never was able to accept criticism or to allow anyone to question his behaviour, and in the Jean Armour/'Highland Mary' affairs he still could not accept that what he had done was wrong. After Jean abandoned him he turned to Mary Campbell and lived a life of 'dissipation and riot'[26] as he admitted to Brice, he had railed against all the Armours, Jean included, and backed down only to show sufficient contrition to mollify the Kirk and obtain that certificate of bachelorhood, which he needed to tidy up his disordered life. It was not a very edifying performance.

But he was now a free man in the Kirk's eyes, free to marry whomsoever he pleased, free to rush off to the West Indies, free to begin a new life. But was he legally free, or was he already not only married but a bigamist? Since before the Reformation Scotland had her own law on irregular marriage, and this continued without change right up to the present century. There were three valid forms:

(i) Marriage *per verba de praesenti*, a declaration by the parties that they took each other as husband and wife. The consent of the parties was sufficient to constitute the marriage, and the presence of an ordained priest, minister, or witnesses was not required.

(ii) Marriage *per verba de futuro subsequente copula* was a promise to marry at some future date followed by sexual intercourse on the faith of that promise. The intercourse was deemed to be the agreement to marry, and understandably the presence of a churchman was not required.

(iii) Marriage by cohabitation with habit and repute. In this case the marriage was constituted by a tacit agreement of the parties to marry, that being presumed from a period of cohabitation with habit and repute that they were husband and wife.

The first two of these forms was only abolished by the Marriage (Scotland) Act of 1939, and marriage by cohabitation and repute still remains a valid method of constituting a marriage in Scotland.

If the 'unlucky piece of paper' Robert gave to Jean was a declaration that they accepted one another as man and wife, then Robert and Jean were married under the law of Scotland. If it was merely a declaration of Robert's love for Jean, then Bob Aiken was perfectly within his rights to humour James Armour by cutting the names out of it. As I have said earlier, it is inconceivable that Aiken, a reputable lawyer, would put his reputation at risk by destroying a legally binding document, so it seems fair to assume that in fact the paper had no validity in law. Nevertheless, something was niggling at the back of Robert's mind all that summer, suggesting that he may have intended by the document to accept Jean as his wife, and only the Armour parents' behaviour, Jean's apparent desertion to Paisley and Aiken's act of vandalism made him accept that he was no longer bound to her in law.

As for Mary Campbell and the exchange of Bibles and whatever words passed between them, this was a case of the tinder heart, probably already glowing, being fuelled by Jean's desertion. He probably did make a promise to marry Mary and take her to the Indies beside the River Ayr that day in May, and would have done so if the success of his *Poems Chiefly in the Scottish Dialect* had not intervened, and Jean's return into his life made him realize that she was the one he really loved. That summer he was in a great confusion, and from remarks he made in letters to his closest friends, it is clear that he still loved Jean Armour to distraction, but also felt some obligation to Mary Campbell, whom he also loved in a way. John Gay had the short-term answer at least to Burns' problem – in the longer term one wonders if he would have been happy with Mary Campbell:

> How happy I could be with either,
> Were t'other dear charmer away![27]

Burns was a cad that July of 1786, for he was even more in love with the idea of becoming a published poet than with any woman. On the 13th of the month his book of poems went to press at Wilson's print-shop in Kilmarnock, and Mauchline buzzed with the news that it would be published before the end of the month just as much as with the scandal of the penance the Poet was due to make in the kirk over Jean Armour's pregnancy.

Armour, smarting over the lenient treatment Mossgiel had received in the kirk, recognized that books meant money, some of which was surely due to his daughter's unborn child. Burns had tried to keep secret his impending departure, but somehow word must have leaked out that the Poet from Mossgiel was planning to disappear beyond the control of Scottish courts of law. Armour acted quickly and persuaded Jean to sign a complaint against the father of her child, and on the strength of this, obtained a writ against the Poet, claiming damages on his daughter's behalf.

Armour thought he was acting with great stealth, but Burns found out about it; he never named his informant but from a letter he wrote to Richmond at the time it is always assumed that it was Jean herself who whispered the warning. He told Richmond:

Would you believe it? Armour has got a warrant to throw me in jail till I find security for an enormous sum. This they keep an entire secret, but I got it by a channel they little dream of . . . I know you will pour execration on her head, but spare the poor, ill-advised Girl for my sake; tho', may all the Furies that rend the injured, enraged Lover's bosom, await the old Harridan, her Mother, until her latest hour! May Hell string the arm of Death to throw the fatal dart, and all the winds of warring elements rouse the infernal flames, to welcome her approach![28]

The embers of love for Jean still glowed warmly in Robert's bosom, although her mother seems to have taken over from James Armour as the black villain of the Cowgate. It sounds as if Robert was nursing more than the wrath of being turned away that day he called on Jean after her return from Paisley. Burnsians like to think it was Jean who tipped him off about the writ, and it may have been: on the other hand, in that same letter Burns told Richmond that James Smith was the only person in Mauchline who knew of his plan to emigrate, so Smith could have picked up the information about Armour's plan from Jean or one of her friends. Could it even have been Gavin Hamilton himself, or Bob Aiken, the Ayr lawyer who dropped the hint? Burns had a lot of friends, who may appear to have been less active than his enemies during July 1786, but they were there ready to help. It would be nice to think Jean Armour was one of them.

Whoever clyped* on Armour's scheme, Robert Burns could afford a smile behind his aspect of solemn repentance as he stood with Jean and the others to be rebuked for the third time in Mauchline Kirk on Sunday morning, 24 July. He had earned his bachelor's certificate, promised by the minister, and knew he was secure from the Armours because he had signed a Deed of Assignment the day before making over everything he owned to his brother, Gilbert, on condition that he took care of Lizzie Paton's daughter:

> Wit ye me to have assigned, disponed, conveyed and made over to, and in favor of, the said Gilbert Burns his Heirs, Executors and Assignees, who are always to be bound in like manner with himself, all and Sundry Goods, Gear, Corns, Cattle, Horses, Nolt, Sheep, Household furniture, and all other moveable effects of whatever kind that I shall leave behind me on my departure from the kingdom . . .[29]

He handed over his share of Mossgiel to Gilbert, and even the copyright and profits from the book of poems about to be published, all on the one condition that he 'hereby binds and oblidges himself to aliment, clothe and educate the child of Elizabeth Paton'. There was not a mention of Jean Armour, who was now so large with his child: the mercenary Armours would get nothing, not a penny.

Yet Jean Armour still haunted him: she was that 'poor, ill-advised girl'

*gave away the information

in the letter to Richmond, and when he wrote to James Smith in Mauchline on 1 August, he was obviously replying to news Smith had sent him of Jean, for he began his letter with a little verse:

> O Jeany, thou hast stolen away my soul!
> In vain I strive against the lov'd idea:
> Thy tender image sallies on my thoughts,
> My firm resolves become an easy prey![30]

His mind was still in turmoil about Jean, swinging from love to total rejection, then back again. 'Against two things however, I am fix'd as Fate,' he told Smith: 'staying at home, and owning her conjugally. The first, by Heaven I will not do! the last, by Hell I will never do!' Then, as he finished the letter he could not resist adding, 'If you see Jean tell her, I will meet her. So help me Heaven in my hour of need!'

The deed was as legal as Armour's writ, properly drawn up on paper, with stamp duty paid, and after being signed at Mossgiel it was lodged with the Sheriff-Clerk in Ayr.[31]

As soon as he had made his last appearance in church Robert vanished so that Armour could not serve his writ. He went to Old Rome, a place now known as Gatehead, on the Kilmarnock-Troon road, where his mother's half-sister, Jean Brown, and her husband James Allan lived, There he could feel reasonably sure that the Armours would not find him, yet he would be conveniently near Kilmarnock when his *Poems Chiefly in the Scottish Dialect* was published on the last day of July. It was from here that he wrote to Richmond on the 30th of the month, telling him about the writ and that he was due to leave for Jamaica within three weeks. Portentously, but perfectly in keeping with his exuberant style when communicating with the Mauchline lads, he told Richmond, 'My hour is now come. You and I will never meet in Britain more.'[32]

Three weeks was a long time in Robert Burns' life – long enough to send his plans agley, and the first weeks of August wrought great changes. By the time he sat down to bring James Smith up to date with his news on Monday the 14th, his plans had altered, but he was in high spirits, as any author would be when he had just handled copies of his first book. He told Smith he planned to ride through Mauchline the following Thursday on his way to Cumnock, but it would have to be very early in order to avoid being seen by the Armours with their writ and ill will. If Smith could be up by seven he would see him.

Burns did not have a care at that moment, apart from Jean Armour who was still on his mind. 'After all Heaven bless the Sex,' he told Smith,

'I feel there is still happiness for me among them.' And he finished off with a little quote from *Venus Preserved* – duly altered by himself!

> O woman, lovely woman sure Heaven design'd you,
> To temper Man, we had been brutes without you.[33]

He had been to see Patrick Douglas, brother of the man for whom he would be working in Jamaica, and there he met some people just back from the West Indies who strongly advised him not to sail to Savannah la Mar in the *Nancy* as he planned, but to wait for another ship which was scheduled to sail from Greenock direct to Port Antonio.

The trip to Cumnock was to deliver books and say his farewells to old friends, among them John Kennedy, factor to the Earl of Dumfries at Dumfries House, and Annie Rankine, the girl who claimed she was the lass among *The Rigs o Barley*. Annie was now wife of the innkeeper there. He also headed into Carrick to say goodbye to friends in his mother's home country. At Kirkoswald he saw Peggy Thomson, the girl who had upset his trigonometry years before, and gave her a copy of his poems inscribed, 'Once fondly lov'd and still remembered dear.' His parting with Peggy and her husband was affecting: in the *Glenriddell Manuscript* he wrote of Peggy, 'When I was taking leave of my Carrick relations, intending to go to the West Indies, when I took farewell of her, neither she nor I could speak a syllable. Her husband escorted me three miles on my road, and we both parted with tears.'[34] At Maybole leave-taking was just as moving, but more jolly. His friend Willie Niven introduced him to 'a worthy knot of lads' including 'spunkie, youthfu' Tammie' and celebrities in the town who made a great fuss of him as a poet.[35] When he left, Niven and his friends gathered half a mile along the Ayr road, to take farewell as was the custom in those days. They jokingly recited some doggerel about their wild carousal at the King's Arms the night before, and the poet, riding an old hired nag called Rosinante, responded with two lines composed on the spot:

> Here comes Burns on Rosinante
> She's damned puir*, but he's damned canty.[36]          *poor

Between Kirkoswald and Maybole there seemed to have been a sea-change, literally a sea change, for Burns was enjoying life as a published poet and was beginning to have second thoughts about the voyage to Jamaica. The *Nancy* was to sail on 1 September, but on 30 August Robert was still at Mossgiel, and on the day the ship left, he wrote to Richmond,

'I am still here in status quo.'[37] The excuse he gave was that he had only had two days' warning of the ship's departure – although he told Smith quite clearly that he was to depart at the beginning of September – and said he was now due to sail in the *Bell* at the end of the month.

Jean's confinement was near, and Robert was worrying about her. 'I have called on her once and again, of late,' he told Richmond, 'as she, at this moment is threatened with the pangs of approaching travail; and I assure you, my dear Friend, I cannot help being anxious, very anxious for her situation. She would gladly now embrace that offer she once rejected, but it shall never more be in her power.' He then scolded Richmond and told him how wrong he had been not to marry Jenny Surgeoner, the girl he had 'ruined', but who still loved him very dearly.

Two days later young Adam Armour walked up to Mossgiel with the news that his sister had given birth to twins, a boy and a girl. Robert dashed off another joyful message to Richmond:

Wish me luck, dear Richmond! Armour has just now brought me a fine boy and girl at one throw. God bless them poor little dears!

> Green grow the rashes, O,
> Green grow the rashes, O,
> A feather bed is no sae saft*,     *not so soft
> As the bosoms o' the lasses, O.
>              RB[38]

That same evening, according to Joseph Train, Robert walked in to the Cowgate to see his children, with a guinea in his pocket and some tea and sugar for their mother. This was 'thought very handsome'.[39] Two days later the twins were baptized Robert and Jean, something neither Armour nor his 'old harridan' of a wife could have been happy about, although they would have been far less pleased if Jean had followed the old Scots custom and named the boy after Robert's father and the girl after her own mother: Jean too must still have felt room in her heart for the man who had wronged her as she nursed her two babies.

In the highest of spirits following the news of the twins' birth, Burns took on a bet with Gavin Hamilton that he could write a poem on any subject Hamilton suggested. The lawyer chose the text of the minister's sermon that morning in church: 'And ye shall go forth and grow up as calves of the stall.' (Malachi iv. 2). The result was the poem *The Calf*, which he sent to his wine merchant friend, Robert Muir, in Kilmarnock two days later. In the accompanying letter he told Muir about Jean:

You will have heard that poor Armour has repaid my amorous mortgages double. A very fine boy and girl have awakened a thousand feelings that thrill, some with tender pleasure and some with foreboding anguish, thro' my soul.[40]

Robert Burns always loved his children – more than he did their mothers a lot of the time, it must be said – and he found boys easier to cope with. 'I am not equal to the task of rearing girls,' he told his friend Mrs Dunlop when Jean was pregnant in the autumn of 1792.[41] With Jean Armour love was a different matter; he cared deeply about both mother and babies, who awoke in him strong fatherly feelings as well as a sense of responsibility. Somehow after 3 September the Jamaica plan seemed less attractive, and before the month was out, it was evident that the *Bell* would sail without him. Nor was he on board the *Roselle*, in which it was then suggested he might travel, when she sailed down the Firth of Clyde in early October. There were now far more attractive prospects for Robert Burns than the West Indies.

On the 26th he poured out a father's feelings to John Kennedy: paternity had aroused within him what he called emotion 'above the trodden clod' as he clasped the woman of his soul to his bosom and he sensed 'the tender yearnings of the heart for the little Angels to whom he has given existence.' He waxed lyrical about fatherhood: 'These, Nature has pour'd in milky streams about the human heart; and the Man who never rouses them into action by the inspiring influences of their proper objects, loses by far the most pleasurable part of his existence.'[42]

He was beginning to waver on emigration, not merely because of the children, but because his book was showing signs of immediate success. He was miserable and wretched about his future, and conscience-stricken about deserting his Armour mites, but was now considering some career other than farming, possibly in the Excise Service, although he realized that his past might go against him. Part of that past included the mysterious 'Highland Mary' Campbell, but for two centuries people have argued over exactly how deeply he was involved with her.

Burns' sister, Isabella, told Chambers that one afternoon during the autumn of 1786 a letter arrived at Mossgiel for Robert. 'He went to the window to open and read it, and she was struck by the look of agony which was the consequence. He went out without uttering a word.'[43]

Mary Campbell was dead.

Fanciful tales were told of her death: some said Burns had indeed asked her to go to Jamaica with him and she died at Greenock while she waited for him to join her, while others claimed she died in childbirth bearing his child. Neither story can be proved or disproved and Burns himself said nothing at the time and very little later. Perhaps his silence provides the best answer to the riddle.

As for intending to take her to the West Indies, it is true he did refer in August to her going home 'to arrange matters among her friends for our projected change of life.'[44] Not *my* change, but *our* change of life. On the other hand, he booked a passage for himself only. Then there is the song *Will Ye Go to the Indies, my Mary*: at the end of October, 1792, about the time of the sixth anniversary of Mary's death, he told George Thomson:

> In my very early years, when I was thinking of going to the West Indies, I took the following farewell of a dear girl . . . You must know that all my earlier love-songs were the breathings of ardent Passion.[45]

Thomson thought little of this song, but by the Poet's own confession it was the breathing of 'ardent Passion':

> We hae plighted our troth, my Mary,
>     In mutual affection to join;
> And curst be the cause that shall part us!
>     The hour and the moment o' time![46]

In another song, *Highland Mary*, sent to Thomson only a fortnight later he again spelt out his grief over Mary's death – grief which had lasted for years after he was married to Jean Armour and settled with their family. In *Highland Mary* he wrote:

> But O! fell Death's untimely frost,
>     That nipt my flower sae early!
> Now green's the sod, and cauld's the clay,
>     That wraps my Highland Mary![47]

Was it grief though, or perhaps conscience that still haunted him every year as the anniversary of her death came round? And had Mary really died in childbirth?

After exchanging Bibles and promises of some sort, Mary Campbell had returned home to Campbeltown where she remained all summer. It has been said that Burns wrote to her there several times, but his letters were destroyed by Mary's father who would not even allow the Poet's name to be mentioned. The two volumes were taken to Canada by Mary's nephew and sold to a group of Scottish-Canadians, who gave them to the trustees of Burns Monument at Alloway where they remain to this day.

Mary returned from Campbeltown to Greenock with her young brother at the beginning of October 1786, to stay with an uncle by marriage, Peter McPherson; the boy took ill with a fever almost the moment they arrived. Mary caught the fever too and died, exactly when no one is sure, but McPherson acquired a burial plot in the West Parish Churchyard on 12 October, presumably to inter the body of his niece.

Whether Mary died of the fever or giving birth to Burns' child we do not know but there may be a clue in the depth of the Poet's anguish – first when he learned of her death and then as the anniversary came round each year. It was at that time in 1789 that he composed the doleful song, *Thou Lingering Star* and sent it to his friend, Mrs Dunlop. A few days later he again poured out his anguish over the loss of Mary: in 'another world' he said, 'should I, with speechless agony of rapture, again recognize my lost, my ever dear MARY, whose bosom was fraught with Truth, Honor, Constancy & LOVE.'[48]

> My Mary! dear departed shade!
>   Where is thy place of heavenly rest?
> See'st thou thy lover lowly laid?
>   Hear'st thou the groans that rend his breast?[49]

Mary was revered by Burnsians from the earliest days, and by the opening of the nineteenth century 'Highland Mary' had well and truly become a legend. As early as 1803 the recently formed Greenock Burns Club, sought permission to put a memorial on her grave, but it remained neglected for many years. It took until 1843 for a memorial stone to be placed over the grave, but when it was erected it was done in style. The *Greenock Telegraph* reported that the grave was surrounded by an iron railing 'entwined with Ayrshire roses and honeysuckle, of which Burns sings in Ye Banks and Braes'. Although visitors came to this shrine to Mary Campbell from many parts of the world the local newspaper was sad to record that it was not held in the reverence due to Burns' 'white rose'.[50]

By the turn of the twentieth century the grave at Greenock had become overgrown as the area around it deteriorated and turned into a slum. Just after the First World War a shipyard alongside the burial ground wanted to expand and, after much argument, it was agreed to demolish the Old West Parish Church and re-inter the bodies in its churchyard in the newer Greenock West Cemetery. On 8 November 1920, this was done, watched by a little knot of dignitaries, who included the Chief Constable, officials of the Town Council, members of the local Burns Club and Ninian McWhannell, President of the Burns Federation. The opening of the grave disturbed more than the bones of Mary Campbell: it released a swarm of demons which set the Burns world in an uproar, and has not settled down even today. Both Hilton Brown in his book *There Was a Lad* and more recently, James Mackay, in his biography, have told the story in detail, yet neither they nor any other writer has managed to dredge the truth from the morass of surmise and doubt that surrounds it. Hilton Brown describes the moment the 'demons' emerged from the sodden ground:

> In the grave was found – the bottom board of an infant's coffin. On this slice of woodwork, sodden with water but perfect and unmistakable in shape, the patient investigators of the Highland Mary mystery fell with a gasp of reverent delight; here at last was Material Object Number Two, and it explained everything. Mary Campbell had had an illegitimate child by Burns; she had died of it – plus or minus the 'malignant fever'; a hundred conundrums were resolved in an instant by this happy discovery. Would God it had been as simple as they thought![51]

In the grave also lay the body of the child who had been in that coffin, so it was reasonable for the onlookers to believe they had solved the riddle of Burns and 'Highland Mary' at a stroke. Everybody knew that if Burns courted a girl sooner or later she would become pregnant with his child and 'Highland Mary' had been no exception. He had been carrying on with her while courting Jean Armour, she had become pregnant at much the same time as Jean did, and it was when she came to him with this news that they exchanged Bibles and he made his vow; in Scots law that may have been as binding as the promise he had made to Jean Armour, and that could make him a bigamist. By asking Mary to go to the West Indies with him it was an escape for him and a solution for her, so it was with that in mind that she returned home to prepare for the journey. It made clear, too, why the Campbells hated Burns so heartily, and was the reason why the Burns family said nothing about Mary. Above all, it explained his anguish when that letter arrived at Mossgiel in late October 1786, and why, as October came round each year he was filled with such remorse that he wrote those sad poems, *Will ye go to the Indies, My Mary*; *Highland Mary*; *My Highland Lassie, O* and *Thou Lingering Star*.

This was surely the solution to the great riddle and it seemed to stun the Burns world for a decade during which there was a great silence, which Hilton Brown for one suggests was 'a sort of conspiracy of silence'.[52] In fact, no one in Greenock or the Burns world appears to have been very curious about the exhumation of Mary or the coffin board. *The Burns Chronicle*, the annual publication of the Burns Federation had nothing to say about it and even the local newspaper, *The Greenock Telegraph*, took little notice of what one would have thought was a newsworthy event. It published a longish article at the beginning of 1921, which revealed that three skulls were lifted from the grave, also some human remains 'black and quite hard', a thigh, some smaller bones and part of a jawbone with four teeth in good state of preservation. The sodden infant's coffin board was found at the bottom of the grave and it did not occur to anyone to have it examined to establish how long it had lain there. In short, a number of people other than Mary and the child had been buried in the grave. All the remains taken from the grave were put into a box and locked away until the following Saturday when the box was re-interred without being re-examined.[53]

In 1930 Catherine Carswell published her *Life of Robert Burns*, in which she stated boldly that the child was Mary's. On 23 October 1786, Burns went to Professor Dugald Stewart's house at Catrine, and there was introduced to Lord Daer, the first aristocrat he had ever met. Carswell's imagination ran riot:

> That same afternoon, while the poet was taking wine with Lord Daer at Catrine, earth was being shovelled over the body of Mary Campbell in Greenock churchyard. The same grave contained her dead baby. Round the grave the men of the Campbells and the Macphersons were cursing the name of Robert Burns as the Armours had never cursed it.[54]

Franklyn Bliss Snyder repeated the bald statement in his *Life of Robert Burns* two years later.[55] Burnsians were not pleased; Carswell's book did not receive so much as a line of review, as it surely deserved, in the *Burns Chronicle*. It must be admitted her biography was romantic and contained a number of unauthenticated scraps of tradition and legend. Snyder's book was a much more authoritative work, but it too found Burns guilty of seducing Mary.

At that moment, however, a minister of the Church of Scotland, Dr Lauchlan Maclean Watt of Glasgow Cathedral, wrote to the *Times Literary Supplement* to declare that in all his thirty-five years as a parish minister of the Kirk, in town or country, when a mother and baby died in childbirth it was the universal custom for both to be buried in the same coffin with the dead child laid on the mother's breast. This tells us no more than that Mary Campbell's child (if there was one) did not die at exactly the same time as its mother. He or she could have died a few days or weeks later and in such circumstances would have been buried in a separate coffin.

As a result of Dr Watt's article in the *Times Literary Supplement* a man named Hendry, who lived in Greenock, came forward to announce that one of his ancestors, a Captain Duncan Hendry, had brought his wife from Campbeltown to Greenock in 1826 and she gave birth to a child early in 1827 who died at the age of only a few weeks. The Hendrys were neighbours of the Macphersons at whose house 'Highland Mary' died, and Macpherson gave the father permission to bury his child in the grave where Mary lay. Hendry corroborated that there was a tradition in the family that an 'auntie' had been buried in 'Highland Mary's' grave. This was even recorded in his family tree.

In view of this Hendry said he was not in the least surprised to learn of a child's coffin board being discovered in 1920 – although it had not occurred to him to mention this at the time or subsequently when Burnsians were angry over Catherine Carswell's slur on the Poet's memory. A letter from ex-Bailie Carmichael, who had been present at the exhumation, confused the whole business further by locating the exact part of the grave in which the board lay, but asserting that three burial plots were moved, although he was unable to say which of them was Mary's. Unfortunately the parish burial registers have vanished. As Hilton Brown wrote, 'All one can say is that if the coffin-board does not prove the Carswell-Snyder theory, the Hendry-Carmichael story does not disprove it . . . the 'Highland Mary' mystery is on the whole darkened by the exhumation rather than clarified.'[56] As to a verdict on whether Burns seduced Mary and she died bearing his child, Brown sums the answer up neatly: 'No jury on earth would convict on the existing evidence; few juries would be left without a strong suspicion of guilt. I do not think one can say more than that – or less.'[57]

Maurice Lindsay, writing in 1954, took a less open-minded view: 'To me, the Hendry story seems to bear all the marks of the spurious legend,' he wrote. 'As to the manner of its presentation, I cannot get rid of my suspicion that the story might never have been produced at all but for the enthusiasm of some local Mariolater (supporter of Highland Mary), who had heard of the Hendry legend, who knew of the need of the Mariolaters for new evidence, and who thus set out first to convince Dr

Maclean Watt, then to deceive the world at large, in the interests of Mary's posthumous reputation.'[58]

If that were so, it would not be the first piece of deception perpetrated to preserve the memory of 'Highland Mary' Campbell and Robert Burns' pure love for her. At the start of the nineteenth century Mary blossomed into the 'white rose' of the Burns story, nurtured by the very mystery of her relationship and her sad, sudden end. She generated far greater interest than dull Jean Armour, who became his stolid, supportive wife and mother of his children, ever did. Reams of prose and verse were poured out in Mary's praise, none shedding any more light on her story.

> O loved by him whom Scotland loves,
>   Long lov'd, and honoured duly
> By all who love the bard who sang
>   So sweetly and so truly!
> In cultured dales his song prevails,
>   Thrills o'er the eagle's aëry –
> Ah! who that strain has caught, nor sighed
>   For BURNS' 'Highland Mary.'[59]

Fortunately the author of those dreary lines and the twenty-one ensuing stanzas in praise of Mary Campbell was 'Anon'; too many others were not. It was all done with the best of intentions: to avoid tarnishing the pious memory of the poet who had written such sublime poetry, and consequently could not be guilty of any sin or misdemeanour.

Thus, Mary became the pure love who was lost to Burns', and no one dared say a word against her. Maurice Lindsay quotes Allan Bayne's nineteenth-century view that Mary Campbell was 'the inspirer of Burns at his best.' This shining knight spoke for many of his period when he said, 'Whoever seeks to defile this ideal maiden deserves the reprobation of all pure-minded men and women.' As Lindsay comments, 'One smiles, in passing, at the Victorian pretence that virginity is woman's "pure" or "ideal" state!'[60] Little better is the slushy ballad, *Bonnie Mary of Argyll*, wailed (seldom sung) from Gretna Green to John o' Groats right up to the present day.

> I have heard the mavis singing its love-song to the morn.
> I have seen the dewdrop clinging to the rose just newly born.

These words have wavered across drawing-rooms and music-hall stages for more than a century; the ballad has disturbed many a Scots night as drunken revellers skail* from the public houses. It must be the worst-mangled, most ill-treated song in the whole history of Scottish song. For that song which her memory has inflicted on Scotland, Mary of Argyll has a lot to answer for.

After Burns' death there were people around, who must have known about Mary and could have set the record straight, yet they said nothing. Burns' Ayrshire friends, among whom she had lived remained silent, and when James Currie came to write the first biography of the Poet in 1800 he could not bring himself to tell what he knew. Obliquely, he spoke of 'Youthful passions . . . the history of which it would be improper to reveal, were it even in one's power.'[61]

His family at Mossgiel was vague and told little of what they knew, although Gilbert did suggest that Mary was the heroine of the song *Sweet Afton*. Eight years after Currie, Robert Cromek, author of *Reliques of Robert Burns*, named Mary Campbell and told the story of the exchange of Bibles and the parting by the River Ayr.

The Mary saga, wrapped in mystery, moved on, growing year by year. But still nothing clarified or cleared Mary's reputation or Burns'; no new information was forthcoming.

Mary Campbell suited the Burns legend very well. Behind the sentimental and sad songs he wrote about her and all the other beautiful songs and poems of Burns which have enhanced Scotland's nationhood and glory, there lurked the awful picture of the Bard as a drunken, debauched womanizer which was quite unacceptable to the Victorians on their high moral ground. Biographers reflected this general attitude for they wanted to see their Bard redeemed by the pure and undefiled love of 'Highland Mary'. The very fact that she was a simple Highland lassie helped his image, and the mystery that enveloped her like Scotch mist made her even more attractive. No one said a bad word about her, and these word pictures were matched by touching paintings and etchings of the romantic parting beside the River Ayr. Victorian artists found a popular subject, filling every gallery and every home with beautiful images of Mary and true love.

It was only at the very end of the nineteenth century, when the centenary of Burns' death came round, that this romantic image was questioned by W.E. Henley. But by then it was too late for the Mariolaters had achieved their ideal and Mary was an azure-eyed 'Beatrice'. Auguste

*disperse

Angellier, the French biographer of Burns, called her '*le plus pure, le plus durable et de beaucoup le plus élevé de ses amours . . . La douce fille des Hautes Terres aux yeux azurés fut sa Béatrice signe du bord du ciel.*' [The purest, most enduring and by far the most exalted of his loves . . . the sweet, blue-eyed Highland girl was his Beatrice, a sign from the brink of heaven.][62]

The Mariolaters fell silent until the opening of Mary's grave in 1920 and the re-opening of the Burns–Mary Campbell controversy. Even now one needs to 'gang warily' when propounding Mary's legend. Forensic science today would enable one to compare a DNA profile of Burns with one of the child found in Mary's grave, and that is what Ian McIntyre, whose biography of Burns was published in 1995, proposed to do. He relates the resulting saga, which extended over several years, when every effort to do this met with refusal, or worse still, prevarication on the part of the authorities who have charge of Burns' good name in Scotland today. There would be no need to exhume the poet's body – a tiny sample from one of several locks of the Poet's hair which exist would suffice. But, no, Burns' reputation is too sacred. He never tried to hide his sexual adventures, so it is fair to assume his reputation could survive the proof of one more illegitimate child – or one fewer.[63]

Is Mary Campbell, therefore, the heavenly heroine of a beautiful love story, or should the Poet's friend Richmond have the last word on her? After all, he must have known her in Mauchline during the latter part of 1785. He told Joseph Train that Mary's character was loose in the extreme. She was, indeed, the mistress of one of the Montgomeries, a relative of Lord Eglinton and the Poet's friends despised her. Richmond claimed that one night he and his friends knew Mary was with Montgomerie in the back room of the Elbow tavern in Mauchline so they took Burns there. 'After waiting long, and when Burns was beginning to ridicule their suspicions, Mary Campbell appeared from one of the rooms, was jeered by the party, in a general way – blushed and retired. Another long interval elapsed and Burns began to rally his spirits, which were much sunk. Montgomerie walked out of the same room. Burns coloured deeply – compressed his lip – and muttered "damn it". After enduring considerable bantering from his friends, he soon gave way to the general hilarity of the evening, and his friends thought he had seen enough of "Highland Mary", but in a few days after, he returned "like the dog to its vomit".'[64]

So was this the true Mary Campbell? Unless some other information comes to light we shall never know.

CHAPTER SEVEN

# 'The Most Valued Friend'

Genius and humour sparkle in the eyes,
Frank independence native ease supplys.
Good sense and manly spirit mark the air,
And mirth and obstinacy too were there.
A peering glance sarcastic wit confest,
The milk of human kindness fill'd the brest.
While pride and parts the features thus control,
Good-nature lurk'd an inmate of the soul.
So the green nut's sweet, milky juice comprest
In a hard shell and acid husk is drest.

Mrs Frances Dunlop of Dunlop's
verse picture of her friend Burns[1]

Success and money changed everything. An arrangement was easily reached with the Armours, who were now beginning to grovel to this new celebrity. Jean's boy, Robert, it was decided, would be handed over as soon as he was weaned to be reared by the Poet's mother at Mossgiel, while baby Jean would remain with her mother in Mauchline. Agnes Burnes, already committed to raising Lizzie Paton's daughter, would now have two infants in her care but she was well practised in coping with babies and did not seem to mind that at all. Agnes' only problem was the mothers: she preferred Lizzie Paton to Jean Armour, probably because Lizzie was a country girl whose ways she understood, but Jean was a townswoman.

Robert Burns was now able to get on with his own life as a farmer, poet and, technically if unenthusiastically, potential emigrant. He was a local hero, with a reputation extending further afield every day. Everybody wanted to read *Poems Chiefly in the Scottish Dialect*, and within weeks, as far away as Galloway, 'even ploughboys and maid-servants would have gladly bestowed the wages . . . if they might but procure the works of Burns.'[2] These were his peers who could easily understand and appreciate what he was saying and the words in which he was expressing himself. Others further up the social scale were showing interest too: when Robert Heron, who was to write the first biography of the Poet, was given a copy he opened it as he undressed for bed and began to read. He didn't close the book until he had read 'every syllable it contained'.[3] Lawyers, doctors and even ministers were soon commending Burns to their friends and, as Robert's fame spread, copies of the Kilmarnock edition began to become scarce.

As Depute-Master of the freemasons at Tarbolton Robert had, as we know, met a number of important people, like Sir William Cunninghame of Robertland and Sir John Whitefoord. Another, even more useful member of the lodge was Professor Dugald Stewart, who divided the year between his Ayrshire home at Catrine Bank, and Edinburgh University, where he was Professor of Moral Philosophy. Dugald Stewart was only a few years older than the Poet and he certainly was not a dry academic: according to Lord Cockburn, he was 'without genius or even originality of talent,'[4] but he enjoyed life and took a great liking to Robert. The up-and-coming poet was welcomed into Stewart's house and other fine houses around Ayrshire.

Catherine Carswell, using a bit of novelist's licence, caught the spirit of his relationship with his betters in the days following publication of the Kilmarnock Edition:

Enthusiastic ladies and gentlemen of Ayrshire the while were bidding the poet to their houses, as much to see how he comported himself as to tell him how much they had enjoyed his poems. He always went – for triumph, curiosity, distraction; and his hosts and hostesses always expressed their surprise at his self-possession and simple dignity. It would seem that some were not a little piqued to observe that he appeared free from embarrassment in their presence. He for his part – though fully sensible of their kind condescension and apt in epistolary expression of the same – found a different piquancy in these drawing-room visits to mansions where he had been long conversant with the byres, the stables, and the situation of the servants' bedroom windows.[5]

If the tales of Alison Begbie and 'Highland Mary' are true, Burns knew the servants' windows of Coilsfield, Cairnhill, Stair House and quite a few other 'big houses' as well. During the Lochlie years, he is also said to have visited the kitchens of Stair with his Tarbolton friend, Davie Sillar, who was then courting the Stair nursemaid, Peggy Orr. One night while Robert was reciting his poems and singing songs to the lovers and the housekeeper, Mary (or Maillie) Crosbie, the mistress of the house, Mrs Catherine Stewart, heard the singing and laughter and sent down to find out what it was all about. On being told that Rab Burns from Mossgiel was the cause of the merriment she invited him up, and so began a long friendship between the two.[6]

Mrs Stewart was one of the first ladies of the local gentry to admire *Poems Chiefly in the Scottish Dialect*, and she invited the Poet to visit her. Her reward was a 'parcel of Songs', which included *The Lass of Ballochmyle*, the song he had recently sent to Miss Alexander in the hope that she would allow him to circulate it at least in manuscript. He had 'no common friend to procure . . . that permission',[7] so perhaps he was looking to the main chance and hoping Mrs Stewart might intercede. Burns knew how to turn a flattering phrase for a fine lady just as surely as he knew how to persuade a country lass into the hay. He laid on the 'obscure bard' and 'high ancestry' line to great and condescending effect:

> One feature of your character I shall ever with grateful pleasure remember, the reception I got when I had the honor of waiting on you at Stair. I am little acquainted with Politeness, but I know a good deal of benevolence of temper & goodness of heart. Surely, did those in exalted stations know how happy they could make some classes of the Inferiors by condescension & affability, they would never stand so high, measuring out with every look the height of their elevation, but condescend as sweetly as did Mrs Stewart of Stair.[8]

Five years later, after she had moved to Afton Lodge a few miles from Stair, he sent her a second 'parcel of songs' with the dedication:

To Mrs General Stewart of Afton

The first person of her sex & rank that patronised his humble lays, this manuscript collection of Poems is presented, with the sincerest emotions of grateful respect by –

The Author[9]

It has been suggested that *Sweet Afton* honoured Mrs Stewart, and the song was certainly among those sent to her in 1791, but Burns himself told Mrs Dunlop that it was inspired by 'a small river, Afton, that falls into Nith near New Cumnock, which has some charming, wild, romantic scenery on its banks.'[10] In spite of his high regard for the lady of Afton Lodge and the ubiquitous Mary asleep by the murmuring stream, which brings 'Highland Mary' to mind, it would appear that the *Sweet Afton*, or *Clear Afton*, as it was first called, has no connection with Afton Lodge and no particular heroine:

> Flow gently, sweet Afton, among thy green braes!
> Flow gently, I'll sing thee a song in thy praise!
> My Mary's asleep by thy murmuring stream
> Flow gently, sweet Afton, disturb not her dream![11]

In those early months after fame struck, Robert was managing very nicely among his 'betters'. Even men of the cloth were showing interest, and before September was out he was invited to stay with the Reverend George Lawrie and his family at Newmilns in north-east Ayrshire. Dr Lawrie, minister of Loudon parish, was one of the moderate New Licht clergy and his manse, a house called St Margaret's Hill, was filled with music, dancing, culture of every kind, and happiness, a very different atmosphere from that which prevailed in the home of old-style ministers such as 'Daddy' Auld back home at Mauchline. Burns was charmed, by Lawrie, his wife, Mary, and their children, Archibald, a student at Edinburgh University, Christine, or Christie as she was known, and Louisa. The girls played the spinet for the poet, the first time he had ever heard the instrument, and he was utterly carried away by the music. He heard Christie play again in Edinburgh some time later and was equally taken by her musicianship. But that night after dinner the minister arranged an impromptu dance in which Robert partnered the girls. He managed to keep his tinder heart under control, but by the time he went to bed he was in love with the whole Lawrie family and everything they stood for. On the windowpane of his bedroom he scratched the words, 'Mrs Lawrie. She's all charms.' That night Robert hardly slept, and in the morning he presented his hosts with a poetic prayer he had composed for them. While the verses spoke highly of the Lawrie girls, 'the beauteous seraph sister-band', it was Mrs Lawrie who seemed to inspire deepest affection:

> She, who her lovely offspring eyes
> With tender hopes and fears
> O, bless her with a mother's joys,
> But spare a mother's tears![12]

Robert was easily won over by an older woman wherever he went, especially when he moved up the social scale. However, at Loudon he also presented the Lawrie girls with a pretty little poem of their own:

> The night was still, and o'er the hill
>   The moon shone on the castle wa',
> The mavis sang, while dew-drops hang
>   Around her on the castle wa':

Sae merrily they danc'd the ring
  Frae e'enin till the cock did craw,
And ay the o'erword* of the spring*        *refrain *dance-tune
  Was: 'Irvine's bairns are bonie a'!'*[13]    *title of a dance-tune

Robert had good reason to be grateful to the Lawries, because Dr Lawrie had been so taken with *Poems Chiefly in the Scottish Dialect* that he immediately sent a copy to Dr Thomas Blacklock, the blind poet in Edinburgh, who could not only judge the work, but had the contacts to introduce it to other people of influence. The day after the Armour twins were born, Blacklock wrote enthusiastically to Dr Lawrie, who passed on the good news to the poet, and it was this, more than anything else that persuaded Burns to postpone emigration. 'A letter from Dr Blacklock to a friend of mine overthrew all my schemes by arousing my poetic ambition,' he told Dr Moore the following year.[14]

Blacklock had asked Dugald Stewart to read Burns' poems to him; this was a good idea because Stewart was an Ayrshire man, so he heard them in the accent for which they were written. Stewart opened up new doors for the Poet. He invited Burns and the Mauchline doctor, John Mackenzie, to come to Catrine Bank on 23 October, to meet Lord Daer, a son of the Earl of Selkirk, and the first member of the real aristocracy Burns had ever met on equal terms. Robert felt he really had arrived in society, and by the time he returned home he had a joyful little poem in his head:

This wot ye all whom it concerns:
I, Rhymer Rab, alias Burns,
  October twenty-third,
A ne'er-to-be-forgotten day,
Sae far I sprackl'd* up the brae,    *struggled laboriously
  I dinner'd wi a Lord.

It was all written tongue in cheek, with just a touch of that proud Burns who wrote *A Man's a Man for a' That*, but there can be no doubting that Robert realized as he was welcomed into Catrine Bank drawing-room that he was being accepted not merely as a poet, but as a man who had 'sprackl'd' a few steps up the ladder of society. There was scope after all for him in Scotland.

To meet good Stewart little pain is,
Or Scotia's sacred Demosthenes*:    *Dr Hugh Blair, another
  Thinks I: 'They are but men!'    eminent Edinburgh man
But 'Burns'! – 'My Lord!' – Good God! I doited*    *stumbled
My knees on ane anither knoited*    *knocked
  As faltering I gaed ben*.    *went through

| | |
|---|---|
| I sidling shelter'd in a neuk*, | *corner |
| An at his Lordship staw* a leuk*, | *stole *glance |
|    Like some portentous omen: | |
| Except good sense and social glee | |
| An (what surpris'd me) modesty | |
|    I marked naught uncommon.[15] | |

By then his mind, if not totally made up, was close to a decision on emigration. On 26 September he told John Kennedy he did not think he would leave until after the harvest. The following day another reason for the delay became clear when he wrote to Richmond with the news: 'I am going perhaps to try a second edition of my book',[16] because *Poems Chiefly in the Scottish Dialect* had proved a success beyond his dreams.

Although the book was priced at three shillings, a sum beyond the reach of his immediate circle, soon only thirteen copies of the 612 Wilson had printed remained unsold. The financial return counted for nothing because Burns had made the money over to his family, but the glory of being recognized as a poet by influential people in high places, was all his own to savour.

The attraction of Jamaica receded during October while he concentrated his energies on trying to persuade Wilson to print a second volume. The canny Kilmarnock printer was reluctant; after all 600 was a fair printing for an unknown local poet and he could see no market for a second book hard on the heels of the first. All Wilson could be persuaded to offer was a second edition provided Robert advanced £27 for the paper and £15 or £16 to cover printing costs. This sum was beyond Robert. 'Farewell hopes of a second edition 'till I grow richer! an epoch, which, I think, will arrive at the payment of the British national debt,' he told Bob Aiken.[17]

Dr Blacklock opened another door, however: if Wilson would not print, why should Burns not go to Edinburgh and try to find a publisher there. The idea appealed greatly, but in the meantime he was enjoying himself well enough where he was: with the prospect of money being available soon, old Armour had not proceeded to enforce his writ, leaving the Poet free to visit his children and Jean without fear. Harvest was over and life was easier at Mossgiel, so he was in a position to accept invitations from friends and all the fine people who wanted to meet him. Emigration remained an option should the worst come to the worst, but it was no longer at the forefront of his mind.

He saw nothing odd about spending time in the drawing-rooms of people like Mrs Stewart of Stair or the Lawries and then returning to the cramped farmhouse and restricted lifestyle at Mossgiel. He may have envied the gracious style of living and financial ease his hosts enjoyed, but he did not see himself as ever being part of it. Burns remained the countryman he always had been and did not aspire to their riches or style. He could have joined the ranks of the literati at least, if not the aristocracy, had he chosen to, but instead he continued to allow everyone to accept him as a simple unlettered ploughman-poet. This was not a pose inspired by inverted snobbery, but simply meant he felt most at home among farming folk where his roots were, and he determined to remain there.

He conducted himself suitably decorously among the gentle and genteel women with whom he was now mixing, especially older women who admired and smothered him with compliments and adulation. If the tinder heart smouldered just a little at times, it was never set alight, and certainly he always held his sexuality on a tight rein. But he had to admit he enjoyed having his ego massaged by older women, as he told them his troubles and tested out his work on them. They in turn were mesmerized by the dark passion which they knew lurked under that coarse country exterior. Robert Burns may not have made overt sexual approaches to these middle-aged and elderly women of quality, but an unspoken sexuality certainly flourished deep within the relationship, so that one senses a frisson of long-forgotten passion passing through their withering bodies when they were with him.

It was during this waiting time that he forged the most important of these platonic 'affairs' with an older woman, a relationship which was to last nearly a decade, and was only broken near the end of his life.

Quite out of the blue a messenger arrived at Mossgiel on 15 November 1786, with a letter, highly praising *Poems Chiefly in the Scottish Dialect*, and requesting six copies. The letter came from a member of the old Scottish aristocracy, whose name was well known and revered by Burns, for Mrs Frances Anna Dunlop of Dunlop was born a Wallace, descended from the great thirteenth-century Scottish patriot, Sir William Wallace. This established an immediate bond between the two, for Wallace had been one of the poet's heroes since childhood.

Mrs Dunlop obviously inherited some of the spirit of her ancestor of whom she was inordinately proud. While still very young she had eloped with John Dunlop of Dunlop, a man twenty-three years older, but they lived happily and she bore him six daughters and seven sons, one of whom inherited the Wallace estate of Craigie at Ayr, and took the Wallace name. Unfortunately this son turned out to be such a wild spendthrift that the Wallace house and lands had to be sold off to pay his debts. Soon after this her husband died and during the months that followed Mrs

Dunlop suffered periods of black depression, so severe, she said, that she felt her 'only refuge would inevitably have been a madhouse or a grave.'[18] At that moment Betty McAdam of Craigengillan, near Dalmellington, who knew about Burns, showed her *The Cotter's Saturday Night*, and Mrs Dunlop was moved greatly by the sentiment of the poem, and especially by the lines about her ancestor:

> O Thou! who pour'd the patriotic tide,
>> That stream'd thro Wallace's undaunted heart,
> Who dar'd to, nobly, stem tyrannic pride,
>> Or nobly die, the second glorious part:[19]

She sent off at once for six copies of Burns' book and invited the poet to call on her at Dunlop House, which lay only about 15 miles away from Mossgiel. Mrs Dunlop was twenty-nine years older than Robert and two years older than his own mother, but a long friendship developed, which turned into a kind of mother-and-son relationship, but quite a different one from the bond between the Poet and his own mother.

Burns' relationship with his parents was never satisfactory and plenty has been written about his father's failure to understand or help Robert's urge to satisfy his creative and poetic longings. Less has been said about the bond between Agnes Burnes and her son: she is always seen as a simple peasant woman without literary abilities or aspirations, but a good mother, who never stood in her son's way. Yet she must often have been as bewildered and hurt by Robert's behaviour as his father was. Neither she nor her son said a word outside the home about their feelings towards each other – which probably speaks volumes for the true relationship when the front door at Mossgiel was shut.

Agnes Burnes could not have approved of Robert's sexual waywardness, yet she took his love children in without comment and raised them as her own, yet her heart must have ached often as she watched helplessly, or heard the tittle-tattle of folk in the parish about her son's way of life. Robert had been unable to unburden himself to his father, and now he found little common ground with his mother. In the circumstances, Mrs Dunlop was invaluable and she became a substitute parent, with whom he was able to build that kind of mother-son relationship which irritated both at times, but held together for years because it was bonded by love.

Robert was able to be open and frank with Mrs Dunlop although that brought disapproval, pique, or reprimands down on his head, and in the end his frankness caused a break between them. The atmosphere in their correspondence could be distinctly frigid at times, but she could also

ROBERT BURNS: *The Tinder Heart*

share a joke with him, telling him just after he married, the story of Lord Bankton, whose fourth wife noticed a napkin was missing from a packet of twelve in the house. 'My dear,' he replied, 'when my last wife was buried, I forgot to draw it out in putting her corpse into the coffin. I shall behave better next time.'[20]

Robert was away from home when Mrs Dunlop's first letter arrived, but as soon as he returned he sat down and wrote to her, regretting that the book was now out of print and the most he could gather together was five copies. His letter began with a long impassioned introduction about her brave-heart ancestor:

> Had you been thoroughly acquainted with me, Madam you could not have touched my darling heart-chord more sweetly, than by noticing my attempts to celebrate your illustrious Ancestor, the SAVIOUR OF HIS COUNTRY – Great Patriot hero! ill-requited Chief!

He told her he had grown up with the lives of Hannibal and Sir William Wallace, and related the story of his Sunday walk to Leglen Wood, where Wallace had hidden, 'with as much devout enthusiasm as ever Pilgrim did to Lorreto,' just to meditate on his hero.

'I recollect (for even then I was a Rhymer) that my heart glowed with a wish to be able to make a Song on him equal to his merits,' Burns told Mrs Dunlop.[21]

Mrs Dunlop moved into Burns' life taking over the mother role and that of literary adviser as well. 'I have been told that Voltaire read all his manuscripts to an old woman and printed nothing but what she would have approved,' she told him. 'I wish you would name me to her office.'[22] Few people could have got away with making such a suggestion and, although Burns ignored the offer, he did continue to answer her letters, and the result was a correspondence lasting nearly a decade during which she wrote 107 letters to him and he sent 79 in return.

From the start Mrs Dunlop simply appointed herself to the 'office' of Voltaire's old woman and began to amend and 'improve' his verse, pointing out faults she found in it, and removing unladylike language to cure him of what she called 'undecency'.[23] Not content with advising on his poetry she pronounced on just about every other aspect of his life as well. She treated him like a wayward son whose love a mother craves, but who cannot be relied upon, and she was quick to express her disapproval of his manners on the five occasions on which he visited her. She was especially censorious about his sexual exploits.

Robert indulged his friend to a remarkable degree as a son would a fussing mother, but by and large he ignored her opinions and advice on his poetry – and he was scolded for that too. From time to time she accused him with justice of not reading her letters. Robert can hardly be blamed for that because her long, ill-composed, opinionated letters were written in a cramped scrawl, which took a lot of time to decipher. The Poet probably enjoyed receiving her letters more than reading them.

She suggested he should not refer to her patriot forebear as 'the unhappy Wallace'. Then, within six weeks of first making his acquaintance, she took up this matter of 'undecency,' which she found so painful. On 30 December she told him:

> I can wish you catch no one thing from Thomson (the poet James Thomson), unless it were the resolution with which he plucked up every one of those luxuriant weeds that will be rising in too rich a soil, and from which I would be glad to see you exempt.[24]

Nothing was too trivial for Mrs Dunlop to comment upon: she raised an eyebrow as she read these lines in *The Twa Dogs*:

> They set them down upon their arse,
> An there began a lang digression
> About the 'lords o the creation'.[25]

'You describe a dog sitting in the only way a dog could sit, or rather two dogs sitting as they could not possibly sit, both on one tail,' she corrected him primly.[26] One can see a flicker of a smile behind her words, however. As Hilton Brown remarked, 'This gem is unfortunately tucked away in a letter of such length and verbosity that Burns may never have reached it.'[27]

Frances Dunlop, like other genteel people, discouraged his use of Scottish language. She told him frankly whenever she thought he had fallen below his best, as in the elegy he wrote following the death of Robert Dundas, Lord President of the Court of Session, and a man with whom Burns was totally out of sympathy politically and in every way. Burns admitted readily that the elegy had not come from his heart. 'Your criticisms and observations on the President's Elegy are just. I am sick of writing where my bosom is not strongly interested,' he told her.[28] He was more explicit to his Edinburgh friend, Alexander Cunningham, adding that he remembered the elegy 'with gnashing of teeth'. He told Cunningham he sent the poem with a letter to Dundas's solicitor son. 'His Solicitorship never took the smallest notice of the Letter, the Poem, or the Poet,' Burns complained.

Burns often did not acknowledge her criticism of his work, and admitted he did not act on it. Once he told her, 'Your criticism, Madam, I understand very well, and could have wished to have pleased you better. You are right in your guesses that I am not very amenable to counsel.' Other poets, he added, might flatter those who had wealth or power, but 'I am determined to flatter no created being, either in prose or verse, so help me God.'[29] Bold words to utter to a patron, but motherly love overcame the annoyance she must have felt about such a highhanded rebuff.

Burns appreciated her interest in his career more than her interference in his verse-making, and meant every word sincerely when he told her early on in their acquaintance:

> Your patronising me, and interesting yourself in my fame and character as a poet, I rejoice in; it exalts me in my own idea; and whether you can or cannot aid me in my subscription (to a new volume of poetry), is a trifle. Has a paltry subscription-bill any charms to the heart of a bard, compared with the patronage of the descendant of the immortal Wallace?[30]

Naturally, he came in for other reprimands, sometimes even when the faults or errors were not his. Once when he sent some books to Mrs Dunlop's mother-in-law, Lady Wallace, they were delivered by mistake to her daughter-in-law, also Lady Wallace and the extravagant wife of the son who had lost a fortune and the family home at Craigie. Mrs Dunlop was furious and told him so.

She found it easier to forgive his social *faux pas* when he visited her at Dunlop House, although these visits must have brought considerable unease to both of them, but at the same time deepening the affection between them. The first of his five visits to Dunlop House in July 1787, was to collect a copy of the long autobiographical letter he had written to Dr Moore. She had sent a copy of the Kilmarnock edition to Moore, who was quite an eminent man of letters at the time, and Moore suggested the poet should write to him. After a long delay Burns did, and he sent her a copy of the letter: Mrs Dunlop was delighted to have put her two literary friends in touch. She told the Poet she read the letter with 'more pleasure than Richardson or Fielding could have afforded me.'[31] We should be grateful to Mrs Dunlop for this introduction because the letter to Moore and the Dunlop correspondence shed more light on Burns' life than almost any of his other correspondence.

Following a second visit to Dunlop House when he spent two days there in February 1788, Robert made a humiliating gaffe, which would have ended any other relationship in his life. The visit itself was a success and Mrs Dunlop's daughters made a great fuss of him: Miss Rachel was busy painting a picture of his muse, Coila, and Miss Keith, happily discussed poetry with him. Robert had promised to lend Mrs Dunlop a particular book, and when he sent it to her, he enclosed a copy of Gray's poetry as a present for Miss Keith, who had told him she had never read the poet. Mrs Dunlop starchily replied that she could not allow her daughter to accept a present from a man who was not a member of the family, and told him she would return it, or at the very most, allow her daughter only to tear out those pages with the poems she liked best. However, their friendship survived this slight – anyone else would have received a biting little satire by return of post and that would have been the end of the association. The relationship between Burns and Mrs Dunlop was truly amazing. Only three months later, in May 1788, he was back at Dunlop for two days, and he saw her again in June the following year when he was in Ayrshire for the marriage of his brother Gilbert. In December 1792, Burns met Mrs Dunlop for the last time when he and Dr James Adair spent four days at her house.

Robert's letters became spasmodic and shorter as worries pressed in on him after he married and took up farming in due course at Ellisland in Dumfriesshire and later joined the Excise Service. During one of his Excise journeys, on 25 June 1794, he admitted: 'I have so long been exceedingly sinful as to neglect the correspondence of the most valued Friend I have on earth.'

It is interesting that when he married Jean Armour he felt he needed to explain to Mrs Dunlop how much their correspondence meant to him, and he raised a fear that time might take her from him – after all she was nearly sixty by now, which was elderly in those days. He wrote:

In this kind of literary, sentimental correspondence, FRIENDSHIP must be my social channel; at the same time I declare to God, You are almost the (only) friend of this Kind I have . . . it would be one of the greatest misfortunes that could befall me, were I to lose it. I really tremble at the idea that days & years are making you older, and that the all-conquering hand of Time may deprive me of a FRIEND whose WORTH I shall ever gratefully revere, and whose loss (should I be so unfortunate) I shall ever inconsolably deplore.[32]

The irony is that he did lose it, but not through death for Mrs Dunlop survived her young friend by nearly twenty years.

Throughout their correspondence, Robert continued to send her poems and she criticized them; he ignored her views but sent her more, and she passed judgement on those. And so it went on. There was plenty of personal gossip and family concern in the letters as well – Robert comforting her on the death of her son-in-law and daughter and the illness of another daughter, paying her the compliment of naming one of his sons Francis Wallace in her honour. On the other hand he offended her by naming another son William Nicol after his teacher friend in Edinburgh, of whom she disapproved.

She sent the Burns children a five pound note from time to time, much to his embarrassment, and she fussed like a mother over his health – to such a degree that she once sent a messenger 20 miles to find out if there was something wrong because she knew he had been ill and was worried about him. She sent some of her poems to comfort him, and Burns, deeply flattered by her solicitude, was gallant in his praise of them.[33] A mother could not have asked more of a son, nor a son of a mother.

One point of dissent was his sexual adventures: she always thoroughly disapproved of these, and his honesty led to much metaphorical finger-wagging. He told her all about Jean and their children, of course, but she was astounded when he announced that he was married. The news came out of the blue in a letter which began without preamble:

My much honoured Friend,
Yours of the 24th June is before me. I found it, as well as another valued friend – MY WIFE – waiting to welcome me to Ayrshire: I met both with the sincerest pleasure.[34]

Anticipating jealousy from this woman who had hitherto been his only confidante, he assured her that their friendship would not suffer.

Mrs Dunlop knew at least a little about 'Highland Mary', too: in 1789, when the third anniversary of Mary's death came round and she was troubling the Poet's conscience, he sent Mrs Dunlop his song *Thou Lingering Star*, and in an accompanying letter asked her opinion of it as he was 'too interested in the subject, to be a Critic'.[35] Five weeks later, when he had been suffering from 'a nervous headache' for weeks past, he was still bowed down under the misery of Mary's memory, and mentioned her name to Mrs Dunlop again, in capital letters – 'my lost, my ever dear MARY' – then quoted four lines from *Thou Lingering Star*.

> My Mary dear departed shade!
>   Where is thy place of heavenly rest?
> See'st thou thy lover lowly laid?
>   Hear'st thou the groans that rend his breast?[36]

126

Mary's shade had not departed, far from it, and unless he had already admitted the affair, Mrs Dunlop must have been very puzzled.

The only woman about whom Burns was economical with the truth to Mrs Dunlop was Agnes McLehose, that is Clarinda, with whom he had an affair in Edinburgh during the Winter of 1787–8. He never identified her to Mrs Dunlop and referred to her only once, in a letter in February 1788, when the association was coming near to its end. In the letter he sent her at the time of the Lord President Dundas elegy, he enclosed two songs. One was *Anna, thy Charms*, written about Anna Stewart, an Edinburgh girl who had jilted his friend Alexander Cunningham, and the other, *Clarinda, Mistress of My Soul*, inspired by Mrs McLehose. 'Tell me what you think of the following?' he asked. 'There, the *bosom* was perhaps a little *interested*.'

She tried to find him a career, with a mother's usual confidence that her child can turn his hand to anything. First she suggested at the beginning of 1787 that he might use the money from his poems to buy an army commission, a nonsensical idea given his allergy to 'lobster-coated puppies'. She did have wit though to warn him not to buy a commission unless he could 'command at least £250 more than the £400 which is the regulated price' – fond hope of Robert Burns finding such a sum even if the military life had been what he hankered after most in life. She was realist enough to add, 'At any rate, the pomp of war is more for poetry than practice, and although warriors may be heroes, peace soldiers are mostly powdered monkeys.'[37] Wisely, he never mentioned the subject again.

She passed on a suggestion from Adam Smith that he should become a Salt Officer, but that came to nothing either. A couple of years later, when she heard that Edinburgh University was about to appoint a Professor of Agriculture, she proposed that Robert should offer himself for the post. Fortunately he had the good sense to realize he would not fit into the academic world any more than the army, so he ignored that too.

Although she did not give any specific help for Burns to be accepted by the Excise service, she used her connections with Robert Graham of Fintry and the wife of the Supervisor General to procure a post and the promotion he wanted, and Robert certainly used her name when it suited him to further his career. Despite all his sneering at patronage he was content to let her use her influence on his behalf, but he warned her when she offered to intercede with Robert Graham, 'I must not seem to know any thing of the matter.'[38]

On farming, too, he felt able to confide in her, although his letters during the Ellisland days, tended to be largely about his poor health and poetry rather than agriculture. But it was to her that he first hinted that Ellisland might be a failure: on 25 March 1789, in the middle of a long letter, he suddenly bared his soul about the farm.

> Mr Miller [Patrick Miller, his landlord], out of real tho' mistaken benevolence, sought me industriously out . . . to give me a lease that would make me comfortable and easy. I was a stranger to country, the farm and the soil, and so ventured on a bargain, that instead of being comfortable, is & will be a very, very hard bargain, if at all practicable. I am sorry to tell you this Madam, but it is a damning truth; though I beg as the world think that I have got a pennyworth of a farm, you will not undeceive them.[39]

Mrs Dunlop was probably the only person to whom Robert felt able to confide such a profoundly disturbing worry.

She did not stop at showing him her own verse, but pushed the scribblings of one of her maids under his nose and expected him to discuss them. Jenny Little, a milkmaid at the house of Mrs Dunlop's daughter, fancied herself as a poet, and Mrs Dunlop persevered in trying to persuade Burns to encourage Jenny's writing. Burns resolutely refused to lie about the milkmaid's verse, which he disliked intensely. Her mistress often slipped a few of Jenny's verses in with her letters to Burns, but he rarely took notice of them.

When Jenny herself wrote to him, he did go so far in September 1789, as to describe her 'part-poetic, part-prosaic' letter as 'a very ingenious, but modest composition.'[40] But Burns admitted he had not yet answered it. The following March, Mrs Dunlop threatened to send him a poem by Jenny on the subject of hope. 'I would rather have . . . another sheet of your prose,' he told her.[41] Robert's lack of tact was staggering – in November, 1790 he belittled verses Jenny had written in praise of Mrs Dunlop's grandson and enclosed a poem of his own which he said had been written 'extempore almost'.[42]

One day in the early spring of 1791, on her way to visit her family at Ecclefechan, the poetic milkmaid turned up on the doorstep at Ellisland to pay her respects. Robert was out, but was expected back shortly, so Jean invited her to wait. The Poet arrived in a dreadful state, having had a fall from his horse in which he had broken an arm. Jean, who was on the point of being delivered of another child, wept, while the Poet sat in a chair all night nursing his painful arm, unable to lie down. Jenny had to leave bitterly disappointed. She reached for her pen to express her feelings:

'Is't true? or does some magic spell
  My wond'ring eyes beguile?
Is this the place where deigns to dwell
  The honour of our isle?

The charming Burns, the Muse's care,
  Of all her sons the pride.
The pleasure oft I've sought to share,
  But been of it denied.'[43]

Mrs Dunlop was not pleased, and this rebuff was probably one of the factors which stirred her to help Jenny Little, now married to John Richmond, a labourer at Loudon Castle, to publish her poems the following year. She badgered the Poet to help find subscribers, but again he was reluctant and told his patron, 'I am glad to hear so good an account of Jenny Little's affairs. I have done next to nothing for her as yet, but I shall now set about & soon fill up my Subscription-bill.'[44] It appears that he never did get round to it.

When he visited Dunlop House towards the end of 1792, Mrs Dunlop produced Jenny's book, published without his support. Burns would hardly look at it. 'Must I read all that?' he asked. For ten weeks she nursed her wrath, then struck:

Methinks I hear you ask me with an air that made me feel as I had got a slap in the face, if you must read all the few lines I had pointed out to your notice in poor Jenny's book. How did I upbraid my own conceited folly at that instant that had ever subjected one of mine to so haughty an imperious critic! I never liked so little in my life as at that moment the man whom at all others I delighted to honour . . . I then felt for Mrs Richmond, for you, and for myself, and not one of the sensations were such as I would wish to cherish in remembrance.[45]

The incident can hardly be blamed for a distinct change in the relationship which soon followed: there were already problems over Robert's political views, which he must have known she would dislike, yet he continued to push his radical opinions at her. Times were very unsettled and only a month before that last visit to Dunlop House in December 1792, she spelt out her fear about the spread of revolutionaries in Scotland.[46] She was extremely sensitive on the subject of the French revolution and threat of war with France because two of her daughters were married to French aristocrat émigrés, yet, with supreme insensitivity, Robert blundered on. He should have been restrained by the fact this his own loyalty was called into question by the Excise Service at that very time, but not a bit of it, Burns reacted as always when challenged by fighting back against the person who had denounced him. Only a month before France was to declare war on Britain, he referred to the French in a letter to Mrs Dunlop as 'that gallant people'. 'My real sentiments of them shall be confined to my correspondence with you,' he added darkly,[47] as if that made any difference.

Ten weeks passed before she replied. ''Tis not enough, my Dr. Sir, never to write improperly but to one: that one cannot wish you as well as I do and encourage it.'[48] He still remained as insensitive as ever to her political beliefs, and in June 1794 he sent her a poem: 'The subject is LIBERTY,' he told her, 'you know, my honoured friend, how dear the theme is to me.'[49] The poem was his *Ode for General Washington's Birthday*, and neither ode nor Burns' sentiments on liberty were to her taste.

Mrs Dunlop replied to this only on 8 September, when she noted that he was 'enthusiastically fond of the theme' of liberty. 'So was I once,' she told him, 'but your Goddess has behaved in such a way as to injure her reputation, and acquire so very bad a name, that I find it no longer fit to acknowledge my favour of her, since her company is not now profuse of bliss nor pregnant with delight; and she is too much attached of late to the society of butchers.'[50] Mrs Dunlop's views had been brought clearly into focus by the execution of the French King, Louis XVI, and Queen Marie Antoinette the year before.

Robert still did not take the hint: he started a letter to his friend on 29 December but did not manage to finish it until 12 January 1795. In this he talked about their mutual friend, Dr Moore's new book, *Journal During a Residence in France*, and (although Moore, too, was fairly radical) this book was not to Burns' political taste:

He has paid me a very pretty compliment, by quoting me, in his last Publication, though I must beg leave to say, that he has not written this last work in his usual happy manner. Entre nous, you know my Politics, & I cannot approve of the honest Doctor's whining over the deserved fate of a certain pair of Personages. What is there in the delivering over a perjured Blockhead & an unprincipled Prostitute into the hands of the hangman, that it should arrest for a moment, attention, in an eventful hour, when, as my friend Roscoe in Liverpool gloriously expresses it –

When the welfare of Millions is hung in the scale
And the balance yet trembles with fate!

But our friend is already indebted to People in power, & still looks forward for his Family, so I can apologise for him; for at bottom I am sure he is a staunch friend to liberty. Thank God, these London trials have given us a little more breath, & I imagine that the time is not far distant when a man may freely blame Billy Pit, without being called an enemy to his Country.[51]

Mrs Dunlop did not answer this tactless, insulting diatribe, which she cannot be blamed for taking as an affront to her family with its French connections and to her friend, Dr Moore, who had been so generous in praising Burns. Robert could not understand why she did not answer this and other letters. 'These many months you have been two packets in my debt,' he wrote a year later when she still ignored him. 'What sin of ignorance I have committed against so highly a valued friend I am utterly at a loss to guess.'[52] Still there was silence from Dunlop House. Finally, on 10 July 1796, when he knew he was dying, he made a final plea to her.[53]

Mrs Dunlop could not let her friend die without reconciliation, and she sent him a guarded, but still disapproving letter. But at least it was recognition of his existence. This was the last letter he read before he died, according to Jessie Lewars, who nursed the Poet in his last days. If Jessie is right, it must have brought comfort to his last hours.

The Burns–Dunlop story did not end on Robert's deathbed. Mrs Dunlop's eldest daughter, Agnes, one of those married to a French émigré, became Jean Armour's closest friend. After the Poet's body was moved from its original grave in St Michael's churchyard in Dumfries to the splendid mausoleum built for him in 1815, Jean made over the original burial plot to her friend. In time Mrs Dunlop's daughter was duly interred in it and there she still lies. Mrs Dunlop would have approved of that.

CHAPTER EIGHT

# *From Greenland to Rapture*

My heart thawed into melting pleasure after being so long frozen up in the Greenland bay of Indifference amid the noise and nonsense of Edin<sup>r</sup>.

The Poet's comment on being captivated by Isabella Lindsay
soon after setting out on his tour of the Borders[1]

The winter spent in Edinburgh in 1786–7 was a spectacular success; but it was a disaster too. He achieved his ambition of publishing a second book of poems and, having left Mauchline an upstart versifier without a copper in his pocket, he left the capital famed from end to end of Scotland. He had mixed with the mighty and was accepted as an equal by them. But, on two other scores he had failed: his creativity had dried up so completely that he produced no new poetry of which he could be proud while he was there, and in the icy, Greenland wastes of the capital he found no love. And Robert Burns always needed love.

By the beginning of November Robert had decided there was no chance of persuading John Wilson in Kilmarnock to oblige with a new edition of his poems, so he wisely made up his mind that the best chance of a second book lay in Edinburgh. He rode off from Mossgiel on a borrowed pony on Monday, 27 November, and arrived in the capital the following day after a truly poetic progress in which he was fêted by farmers who had read and enjoyed the Kilmarnock Edition. He stopped overnight at Covington in Lanarkshire, but managed to get little sleep since his presence led to a long night's carousal in which even the local minister joined. Burns liked him, and his wife, 'a Mr Lang, a dainty body of a clergyman; a glorious good fellow, and with a still more glorious wife.'[2] No wonder Robert arrived in the capital with a headache that lasted a week and was unable to get out of bed the morning after his arrival.

The first woman he met in the city was his landlady, Mrs Carfrae, who possessed all the canniness which has been handed down by Edinburgh landladies until the present day. Robert's Mauchline friend, John

Richmond, was already lodging with Mrs Carfrae in Baxter's Close in the Lawnmarket, at the upper end of the Royal Mile, and he offered to share his room and his bed with Robert. When Mrs Carfrae found she had a second tenant she put Richmond's rent up by sixpence to three shillings a week. So for eighteen pence Robert shared 'a deal table, a sanded floor and a chaff bed'.[3]

Robert soon felt well enough to take in his surroundings, and in case he was not fully aware of them, the garrulous Mrs Carfrae told him all about his neighbours in graphic colour. He described them to John Ballantine, the Ayr banker, in a letter written on the shared deal table on 14 January 1787.

> I have just had a visit from my Landlady, who, is a staid, sober, piously-disposed, sculdudery-abhoring Widow, coming on her grand climacterick. She is at present in sore tribulation respecting some 'Daughters of Belial' who are on the floor immediately above . . . as our floors are low and ill-plaistered, we can easily distinguish our laughter-loving, night-rejoicing neighbors – when they are eating, when they are drinking, when they are singing, when they are &c.

Robert suspected that the worthy Mrs Carfrae considered him 'a rough an' roun' Christian' too, and the sermon she delivered on the whores who sent the plaster flaking off the ceiling, was partly for his benefit:

> We should not be uneasy and envious because the Wicked enjoy the good things of this life; for these base jades who . . . lie up gandygoing with their filthy fellows, drinking the best of wines, and singing abominable songs, they shall one day lie in hell. weeping and wailing and gnashing their teeth over a cup of God's wrath![4]

Burns lost no time in meeting the influential, the literati and the glitterati of the city. He had a letter from James Dalrymple of Orangefield at Monkton to introduce him to the Earl of Glencairn and he was accepted by a wide circle of influential men within a week. Caledonian Hunt members agreed to subscribe a guinea each to the new edition of his poems, and Patrick Miller, brother of the Lord Justice Clerk, sent him ten guineas anonymously – but not anonymously enough to prevent Burns from soon discovering who the benefactor was. Robert was invited to Miller's house to drink a glass of claret with this generous new friend, who was already talking of offering him the lease of 'some farm or other in an estate called Dalswinton which he has lately bought near Dumfries.'

Even at that early stage Robert suspected his future might not lie in farming and expressed a thought that Miller's proposal could prove 'a bargain that may ruin me'.[5]

Dugald Stewart proved as generous as he had been at Catrine Bank in October, and Robert was soon on talking terms with Hugh Blair, minister of the High Kirk of St Giles, William Greenfield, Professor of Rhetoric and minister of St Andrew's Church, and Henry Mackenzie, author of *The Man of Feeling*, who reviewed the Kilmarnock Edition for *The Lounger* with generous praise for the poems and the poet. 'I think I may safely pronounce him a genius of no ordinary rank,' Mackenzie wrote.[6]

The Poet's freemason contacts proved useful, too, so that when he went to a lodge meeting early in January, attended by Francis Charteris, Grand Master for Scotland and 'all the Grand Lodge of Scotland', they called for a toast to 'Caledonia & Caledonia's Bard, brother Burns.'

'I was downright thunderstruck, and trembling in every nerve made the best return in my power,' he told Ballantine. 'Just as I finished, some of the Grand Officers said so loud as I could hear, with a most comforting accent, "Very well indeed!" which set me something to rights again.'[7]

During those first weeks in the capital Burns was mesmerized by the women who now entered his life. A visit to Mrs Stuart's house at Stair was one thing, but now he found himself in drawing-rooms, which glowed with exquisite paintings and furnishings and glittered with the leaders of Scottish society – the beautiful, vivacious Duchess of Gordon outshone all the others, but the Dowager Countess of Glencairn and her daughter, Lady Elizabeth Cunningham ('Lady Betty'), who lived at Coates House just outside the city, entertained him in fine style, and the society beauty, Eliza Burnett, daughter of Lord Monboddo, fussed round him. Alison Cockburn, a stolid woman from the Scottish Borders, who was well known as a hostess and as the author of the song, *The Flowers of the Forest*, was able to judge him as a poet as well as a man. After meeting him for the first time she summed him up:

> The town is at present agog with the ploughman poet, who receives adulation with native dignity, and is the very figure of his profession, strong and coarse, but has a most enthusiastic heart of love. He has seen Dutches Gordon and all the gay world: his favourite for looks and manners is Bess Burnet – no bad judge, indeed.[8]

Every woman in Edinburgh was as anxious to meet Burns as he was to be accepted by them. Not since Bonnie Prince Charlie stormed the city forty-one years earlier had any newcomer to Edinburgh turned women's heads so. 'No doubt he will be at the Hunters' Ball tomorrow, which has made all women and milliners mad. Not a gauze-cap under two guineas – many ten, twelve,' Mrs Cockburn remarked,

In Edinburgh society to be received by the Duchess of Gordon, not once but several times, was the seal of success, for she was beautiful, fascinating and quite a character. This was a combination of qualities that might easily have set Burns' tinder heart alight, but for the fact that she was nearly forty and on the mature side. The Duchess was tempted by Burns too, and admitted to Sir Walter Scott years later that the Bard was the only man whose conversation carried her off her feet. Burns must have heard of Jane Gordon's reputation before he met her because her sister, Betty, was Lady Wallace of Craigie, that heartily disliked daughter-in-law of his new friend, Mrs Dunlop, who blamed Lady Wallace for much of her son's trouble. Jane Gordon and Betty Wallace were daughters of an eccentric, hard-drinking laird from Wigtownshire, who had abandoned his wife and daughters, leaving them to fend for theselves. This they did successfully, but Jane and Betty soon earned the name of being the wildest girls in Edinburgh society – a reputation many thought well deserved after they rode down the High Street on the backs of a couple of pigs one day. This may have been the kind of escapade to endear the Duchess to Robert Burns, but prim Edinburgh society did not know what to make of it. Sir Walter Scott had a low opinion of Jane Gordon, whose 'sole claim to wit,' he said, 'rested upon her brazen impudence and disregard to the feelings of all who were near her.'[9]

Jane was indeed a rough diamond, in speech and her coarse wit, but her warm-heartedness appealed to Burns and he was delighted to attend her drawing-room receptions, where his broad Scottish dialect and wit mingled well with hers. In spite of her high spirits and eccentricities the Duchess of Gordon was a leader of fashion and fun; she stayed up regularly till four in the morning, dancing, gossiping and playing cards long after everyone around her was exhausted and, after five hours sleep, was ready to begin all over again.

Tongues wagged about her: she was reputed to have borne other men's children. She shocked society when the Gordon Highlanders regiment was being raised by rewarding every recruit with a kiss.

Burns was furious when, early in 1789, *The Star* in London printed a scurrilous, snide little verse about the Duchess, which was reprinted in two other newspapers. He wrote a long and angry letter to the newspaper in which he said, 'I never composed a line on the Duchess of Gordon in my life. I have such a sense of what I personally owe to her Grace's benevolent patronage, and such a respect for her exalted character, that I have never yet dared to mention her name in any composition of mine, from a despair of doing justice to my own feelings.'[10] This was duly published along with 'some flattering editorial observation of the very ingenious poet from whose pen it came.'[11]

Burns did not write a poem to the Duchess. He did, however, call on her and the Duke at Gordon Castle, near Fochabers, during his Highland Tour, and in their honour he composed two poems, *Castle Gordon*, and the Jacobite song, *The Young Highland Rover*.

Jane Gordon continued to lead her eccentric life after Burns moved out of her circle. She went to London, where even King George III and Prime Minister Pitt enjoyed her wine and her coarse wit at her house in The Mall, which became a great Tory social centre. She was a master at match-making and succeeded in marrying off three of her daughters to the Dukes of Richmond, Manchester and Bedford. Jane Gordon's final days were sad: she became estranged from her husband and many members of her family, which cost her her social status in society. She led an unsettled, aimless life until her death at Pulteney's Hotel in Piccadilly, London, in 1812.

Robert was no good at hiding his feelings – he didn't even try – and Alison Cockburn quickly noticed that the one woman who had caught his fancy in all Edinburgh that Winter was Eliza Burnett, the younger daughter of an eccentric Judge, Lord Monboddo, who gave 'learned suppers' to which Burns was often invited. The Poet adored his hostess, but from a suitable distance. 'There has not been anything nearly like her in all the combinations of Beauty, Grace and Goodness the great Creator has formed, since Milton's Eve on the first day of her existence,' he told his Ayr friend, Willie Chalmers in a letter with which he enclosed a copy of his poetic *Address to Edinburgh*.[12] The verse of this salute to the Scottish capital reads like a chore he felt he had to face to thank the city for what it had given him, but it was easy to see his heart was not in the task, and it was far from his best verse. However, the reference to Eliza in the Edinburgh poem at least rings sincere, although he had paid more heartfelt compliments to other girls who had taken his fancy:

> Fair Burnet strikes th' adoring eye,
>   Heav'n's beauties on my fancy shine:
> I see the Sire of Love on high,
>   And own His work indeed divine![13]

Mrs Cockburn and Burns both agreed that Eliza Burnett was a beauty, and her portrait confirms this, but she had her critics. Alexander Young,

136

a young lawyer, although admitting she was pretty, found fault: 'She had one great personal defect however, her teeth were much decayed and discoloured, but fortunately she had a very small mouth, and took care not to open it much in mixed company.' On the other hand, Agnes McLehose, who later became Burns' lover in Edinburgh, saw Bess Burnett 'softly speak and sweetly smile'.[14] The Right Honorable Charles Hope was as ungallant as Alexander Young: 'She had very thick, clumsy ancles [sic], which she was at pains to conceal by wearing her petticoats uncommonly long,' he wrote, 'and she was not a good Dancer – but take her in all she is a beautiful creature.'[15] Her critics may well have been right because the lovely Eliza wasted away and died of consumption in 1790. She was only twenty-three. Robert wrote an elegy on her, but this, like the *Address to Edinburgh*, proved hard work, Eliza died on 17 June, but it was only the following January that he sent the incomplete poem to Alexander Cunningham, accompanied by a letter admitting, 'I have these several months been hammering at an elegy on the amiable and accomplished Miss Burnet.'[16] It began:

> Life ne'er exulted in so rich a prize,
>  As Burnet, lovely from her native skies;
> Nor envious Death to trumph'd in a blow,
>  As that which laid th' accomplish'd Burnet low.[17]

It took another year's work before he had the poem polished and ready to send to Mrs Dunlop, but even then the best he could put together was sentimental and ordinary. As he himself remarked, the elegy was 'so exhausted a subject that any new idea on the business is not to be expected.'[18] But at least his regret for Eliza's death was sincere.

> We saw thee shine in youth and beauty's pride,
>  And Virtue's light, that beams beyond the spheres;
> But, like the sun eclips'd at morning tide,
>  Thou left us darkling in a world of tears.[19]

In spite of all the honour and adulation showered on him, Robert soon felt lost and unsettled in this new world. He was acute enough to realize that he was a novelty in the city, a kind of sideshow to entertain the guests in society drawing-rooms and literary salons. The fact that he was a simple country ploughman, who did not pretend to be anything more superior, made him all the greater an attraction. But he knew the great and the good of the capital would tire of him sooner or later, and he confessed to a Kilmarnock friend, Robert Muir, that he was still uncertain of his future, although he told Muir he never thought about what lay ahead for him. The Poet was worried about a career and a settled life. 'I have now neither house nor home that I can call my own, and live on the world at large,' he told Muir. 'I am just a poor wayfaring Pilgrim on the road to Parnassus, thoughtless wanderer and sojourner in a strange land.'[20]

Mauchline was still on his mind, although the Paton business had been settled at the beginning of December and he had no more worries about Lizzie or the child, who was still with his mother at Mossgiel. But he was missing Jean sorely; he confessed this to Gavin Hamilton, although he would not have admitted it to many people:

I feel a miserable blank in my heart, with want of her, and I don't think I shall ever meet with so delicious an armful again. She has her faults, and so have you and I; and so has every body.

> Their tricks an craft hae put me daft,
>   They've taen* me in, an a' that;                                        *taken
> But clear your decks, an here's the Sex!
>   I like the jads for a' that.
>
> For a' that and a' that,
> And twice as muckle's* a' that.[21]                                      *much as

It was difficult enough missing Jean, but to be without a woman at all was impossible. Since there was no hope of getting further than the drawing-rooms of Edinburgh's grand houses, he sought out someone nearer his own social class, and found a farmer's daughter who appealed. He spoke enthusiastically of her to Gavin Hamilton:

I have met with a very pretty girl, a Lothian farmer's daughter, whom I almost persuaded to accompany me to the west country, should I ever return to settle there. By the bye, a Lothian farmer is about an Ayrshire squire of the lower kind; and I had a most delicious ride from Leith to her house yesternight in a hackney-coach, with her brother and two sisters, and brother's wife. We had dined all together at a common friend's house in Leith, and danced, drank, and sang till late enough. The night was dark, the claret had been good, and I thirsty . . .[22]

We have no idea who this 'very pretty girl' was, but then we know virtually nothing about Robert's romances (if there were any) in Edinburgh at this time. Here and there in his correspondence can be found intriguing references to girls, which make it clear that his heart glowed several times that winter. But he encountered no one to match Jean.

He met Christie Lawrie and her brother again in Edinburgh and Christie's harpsichord playing charmed him as much as it had done at Loudon manse. James Mackay suggests that he may have courted Christie for a time, but there is no real evidence of this. The only time he spoke of another flirtation he was as secretive about the girl's identity as he had been about the Lothian farmer's daughter. He told James Dalrymple of Orangefield about 'uncoupling' his heart and fancy for 'a slight chase after a certain Edinburgh Belle,' but the quarry soon escaped:

My devotions proceed no further than a forenoon's walk, a sentimental conversation, now and then a squeeze of the hand or interchanging an oeillade, and when peculiar good humor and sequestered propriety allow –

– 'Brethren, salute one another with a holy kiss.'[23]

Mackay has also suggested that this hand he squeezed was that of Isabella Farquhar, daughter of James Farquhar, who lived at 11 Princes Street, and the Miss Farquhar to whom he inscribed a copy of the first Edinburgh Edition of his poems.[24] He ended by quoting his mother's old song, *Kissin is the key o' love*, but seems not to have got beyond the first line in his pursuit of this particular girl – or any other Edinburgh lass for that matter. West country girls were warmer-hearted and more willing.

Burns savoured Edinburgh life at the lowest end of the social scale every bit as much as he enjoyed the Duchess of Gordon's drawing-room, and from the moment his headache lifted after he arrived, he and Richmond doubtless spent many an evening in city drinking houses. Soon he was to find a quiet corner among the straw every bit as convenient as the rigs of barley back home. The lassies at that end of the social scale showed some of that West Country warmth he missed.

As the novelty of drinking and being fêted by the great and the good wore off, Robert felt he was being patronized, for a number of them urged him to abandon writing in his Ayrshire home tongue and use standard English. They recognized his genius, but warned that he would never achieve the heights to which he aspired as long as he wrote in Scottish dialect. This was a bitter disappointment to the Poet who never saw himself as a writer of Augustan verse to please a London audience. He was what he was and had no intention of abandoning that: thus he found himself gravitating from the houses of the élite to Daniel or

'Dawney' Douglas's tavern down a narrow alleyway called Anchor Close, just off the High street. It was here that the Crochallan Fencibles, one of the city's many drinking clubs, met.

The Crochallan Fencibles, whose name derived from a Gaelic song *Crodh Chaillein* or *Colin's Cattle*, were much to Robert's liking, since most of its members were men like himself: witty, a bit rough, out of harmony with the establishment, and convivial. 'Rattlin', roarin'' Willie Dunbar was 'Colonel' of the Crochallans and Charles Hay, 'famed for law, paunch, whist, claret and worth' the Major and Mustermaster-General. Among the members were William Smellie, a brilliant self-taught man, Peter Hill, the bookseller, the staid Alexander Cunningham, and a jolly farmer called Robert Cleghorn, from Saughton Mills, who had a taste for bawdy songs and ballads – a taste which Burns helped to satisfy. At this boisterous drinking club Burns' bawdy poetry (and a lot composed by others) circulated. Burns sent poems to both Cleghorn and Smellie, but unfortunately Smellie's heirs destroyed all of his correspondence. The book of bawdry in which Burns wrote down any verse that appealed to him, has also been lost and, as a result the collection, *The Merry Muses of Caledonia*, which was published after his death, is far from being simply what Burns wrote and collected. Much of it came from other sources.

Burns loved bawdry almost as much as he loved women, but many apologists for the Bard claim either that he did not write such verse, or that he did not intend it to be published. It is true that he probably did not intend to publish what he calls his 'delicious, secret sugar plumbs',[25] but he did enjoy sharing them with others and lent his book of them out or sent copies of individual songs to his friends. He felt the same about a number of his other poems, which are now freely published in complete works and anthologies. *Holy Willie's Prayer*, *The Jolly Beggars*, *The Poet's Welcome to his Bastart Wean*, *The Court of Equity* and *Why Shouldna Poor Folk Mowe*, for example, all circulated only in manuscript until after his death.

Burns never lost sight of the fact that the visit to Edinburgh was not to eye beautiful women or to talk with the finest minds and drink with the sharpest wits in Scotland: it was to find a publisher for a new edition of his poems, and he was lucky enough to have an introduction from the Earl of Glencairn to William Creech, who had a publishing and bookselling business in the High Street. The Poet lost no time, and was able to tell John Ballantine as early as 13 December 1786 that he had 'nearly agreed' with Creech on the publication and planned to start sending out subscription lists the following week.[26]

Robert had no trouble keeping himself busy during the first months of 1787 while he waited for his new book to appear. He continued his busy social life and kept up his correspondence with his Ayrshire friends, and even took time to tell his life-story in rhyme to Alison Cockburn's niece, Mrs Elizabeth Scott of Wauchope, at Jedburgh. Mrs Scott had sent him a verse epistle questioning whether he could really be no more than the 'canty, witty rhyming ploughman' he claimed to be, and ended her epistle by offering to send him a plaid to keep him warm.[27] He replied in verse, explaining his desire to 'sing a sang' for poor old Scotland, and passing on his views on women as well:

| | |
|---|---|
| Hale to the Sex! (ilk guid chiel* says): | *lad |
| Wi merry dance on winter days, | |
| An' we to share in common! | |
| The gust o joy, the balm of woe, | |
| The saul* o life, the heav'n below, | *soul |
| Is rapture-giving Woman. | |
| Ye surly sumphs*, who hate the name, | *slow-witted creatures |
| Be mindfu of your mither; | |
| She, honest woman, may think shame | |
| That ye're connected with her! | |
| Ye're wae* men, ye're nae* men | *woeful *no |
| That slight the lovely dears; | |
| To shame ye, disclaim ye, | |
| Ilk honest birkie* swears.[28] | *lively fellow |

On his twenty-eighth birthday, which fell on 25 January 1787, he dashed off another piece of light-hearted autobiography, *Rantin, Rovin Robin*, which might have taken Mrs Scott aback by the soothsayer's prophesy of his future sexual adventures:

| | |
|---|---|
| 'Guid faith,' quo she, 'I doubt you gar* | *make |
| The bonie lasses lie aspar*; | *legs apart |
| But twenty fauts*, ye may hae waur* – | *faults *worse |
| So blessins on thee, Robin.'[29] | |

That first winter in Edinburgh produced remarkably little poetry at the time: only that stilted *Address to Edinburgh*, *To a Haggis*, and a few other pieces a bit later. There were the poems to Eliza Burnett, and a couple of others, written for Isabella MacLeod, daughter of the Laird of Raasay, who entertained him by singing or playing at the family house in the Canongate. The first was written to mark the death of her sister and brother-in-law, but the second was more personal: in *To Miss Isabella McLeod*, composed at the beginning of March, 1787, he wrote:

> The crimson blossom charms the bee,
>   The summer sun the swallow:
> So dear this tuneful gift to me
>   From Lovely Isabella.[30]

He tried his hand at a dramatic prologue for the actor William Woods. He also arranged for a headstone to be placed on the unmarked grave of Fergusson, the poet, with a verse inscription written specially for it. The city throbbed with interesting characters beyond the literary and academic people of importance he met in his first weeks there. He had his portrait painted by Peter Taylor, who was a signwriter and coach-painter by trade, and also by Alexander Nasmyth, a landscape artist rather than portraitist. John Beugo produced an engraving for the title page of the first Edinburgh edition of Burns' poems, and on his walks in Pentlands with Nasmyth that spring the artist made a pencil sketch of him under the great Norman arch at Roslin. On this sketch Nasmyth based a portrait completed in 1828. Early in April he began to keep a *Second Common Place Book,* promising in the preface to give his 'amours, rambles, smiles and frowns.' Alas, he did not keep his word.

His second book of poems, known as the first Edinburgh Edition (there was to be a second Edinburgh Edition in 1793), was greatly over-subscribed before it appeared on 17 April. At the same time he agreed to sell the copyright to Creech for a hundred guineas. The publisher did not pay this for another year, and it was March 1789, before Creech finally paid all the money he owed Burns.

Burns needed a break from Edinburgh, and as his strength and spirits burst forth with the new spring of 1787, the longing to escape increased. He now knew where he stood as a poet and a man, but he was also aware that he could never fit comfortably into polite Edinburgh society. Yet he saw no settled future anywhere else. Patrick Miller, who had given him the anonymous present of ten guineas, was still anxious for him to take a lease of one of his farms in Dumfriesshire, but Robert was as unsure as ever about returning to farming.

At that point, Robert Ainslie, one of his wilder young friends in the city, came to his rescue and agreed to accompany him on a trip through the Borders at the end of which he could stop off at Dumfries and view Miller's farms. This was the first of four journeys around Scotland (with a brief foray into England) which Burns was to make that year.

The reason usually given for the tours is found in a patriotic remark he made in a letter to Mrs Dunlop, that he had no greater wish than to make leisurely pilgrimages 'through Caledonia; to sit on the fields of her battles;

to wander on the romantic banks of her rivers; and to muse by the stately tower or venerable ruins, once the honored abodes of her heroes.'[31]

On his various travels he missed Flodden and a number of important places connected with Scotland's history, but he did visit Roxburgh Castle, where James II of Scotland was accidentally killed, he became quite emotional at Bannockburn, he meditated for a while at Culloden, and he became so carried away with Jacobite sentiments at Stirling Castle that he took his diamond stylus and scratched a little verse on a window which ended:

> The injured Stewart line is gone,
> A race outlandish fills their throne:
> An idiot race, to honour lost –
> Who know them best despise them most.[32]

On a later visit to Stirling he went back and smashed the pane of glass, but it was too late for the lines were well known to those in the Scottish establishment who could use them to do him harm.

Escape, first from Edinburgh and then from facing the future, was the primary reason for the journeys, and Dumfries provided a convenient excuse for the first tour to the Borders. But as always, 'that damned star' had other plans for Burns, and just as he was about to leave with Ainslie he met someone who was to change his life.

He was probably unaware of it at the time, but two totally different Edinburgh environments had helped to point him towards his future: the drawing-rooms and the taverns held one common strand for him, music. The society ladies and Crochallan Fencibles sang very different tunes – and words – but that did not matter. What they sang interested Robert just so long as it was Scottish and traditional. Together these two unlikely environments filled his mind with melodies of Scotland, which were to be the catalyst for his poetic future as a song-writer.

Just about the time the Edinburgh Edition appeared Robert was introduced to an Edinburgh engraver and music seller, who was caught up in a publishing plan, which fascinated the Poet. James Johnson came from a country background similar to Robert's, and in Edinburgh he used his talents to introduce a new method of printing music by using pewter plates instead of copper or steel, which were much poorer in quality but considerably cheaper. Johnson had an avid interest in old Scottish songs and planned to publish those he collected using his new plate-making process. Although his collection of a hundred airs was virtually complete and due to be published under the title, *The Scots*

*Musical Museum*, Burns could not resist involving himself in it. On the evening before the Poet and Ainslie were due to set out on the Borders tour, Robert sent Johnson a song for his collection. Burns was truly sorry that he had not been able to involve himself in the project, and told Johnson so:

> Had my acquaintance with you been a little older, I would have asked the favor of your correspondence; as I have met with few people whose company & conversation gave me so much pleasure, because I have met with few whose sentiments are so congenial to my own.[33]

It was not the last the two heard of one another. Burns took up the friendship and song-collecting avidly, and through his tours and for the rest of his life, songs became a consuming passion. What he did was little short of miraculous: he uncovered every air he could find, studied all the songs he heard, and gathered tunes to which he could put words. In a Scotland where music and dancing were immensely popular at every level of society, the scope was enormous, but Burns went further. He got hold of every book of songs or airs he could lay hands on and studied them until he had a huge store of music to which he could add words. While assuring Johnson, sometime possibly in 1791, that he need not fear want of material for his *Museum*, he said:

> I was so lucky lately as to pick up an entire copy of Oswald's Scots Music & I think I shall make glorious work out of it. I want much Anderson's Collection of strathspeys &c. then I think I will [have] all the Music of the country.[34]

The first volume of *The Scots Musical Museum* appeared at the end of May with only a couple of Burns' songs squeezed into it at the last minute, *Green Grow the Rashes, O* and *Young Peggy Blooms Our Boniest Lass*. By October the Poet had taken over the work as editor-in-chief in all but name, and when the second volume was published the following March forty of the hundred songs it contained were his, and he wrote the preface as well. It was from then on that he collected old folk-songs and airs, badgered his friends to supply tunes and went around the country listening for old tunes he had not heard before. He arranged for Stephen Clarke, the organist at the Episcopal church, to help with the musical arrangements, and became the driving force behind the work. Johnson had no qualifications other than his enthusiasm and that withered away and would have died but for Burns' burning passion, which kept the

*Musical Museum* going. Clarke, too, was a terrible trial to the Poet: he was lazy and careless and even managed to lose packets of irreplaceable songs which Burns sent him. In spite of all this Robert beavered away at the task he had set himself and, although it is hard to be precise about exactly how many songs he contributed, more than half of the songs in the third volume, published in 1790, and the fourth volume, published in 1792, were his. He coded his work in the *Museum* with the letters 'R', 'B', or 'X', and 'Z' for old songs which he had re-worked, but this provides a far from accurate indication of his involvement. A number of other songs are believed by experts to be Burns' work and the 'Z' symbol could mean anything from a couple of lines rewritten to a virtually new lyric. Signs and symbols apart, Burns' contribution to *The Scots Musical Museum* went far beyond song-writing. Without him the task would certainly never have got beyond volume two. Indeed the fifth volume only appeared shortly after the Poet's death in 1796, and the sixth and final one was not published until 1803.

James Johnson probably never realized the debt he owed to Burns, but what the Bard owed to this music-seller is incalculable. For Burns working on the *Musical Museum* undoubtedly provided him with the creative spark he needed to sustain his poetry through the years after he accepted Patrick Miller's lease of Ellisland farm in Dumfriesshire and worked in that part of Scotland, first as a farmer and then as an excise man.

The Border Tour lasted from 5 May until 1 June, and took Burns as far south as Newcastle, then across to Carlisle before re-crossing the Border to Dumfries. He enjoyed himself well enough, although at times found the going hard, especially among the wives and daughters who rushed to meet him. But his tinder heart lit up on the very first day when he set eyes on Bob Ainslie's sister, Rachel. She was pronounced 'an angel' even if her ample figure made her, in Burns' words, 'a little of the *embonpoint*'. Robert accompanied the Ainslie family to worship in Duns kirk and managed to seat himself beside Rachel, and when he saw her become restive during the minister's hell-fire sermon on sinners, he took her Bible and wrote a little epigram on the fly-leaf:

> Fair maid, you need not take the hint,
> Nor idle texts pursue:
> 'Twas guilty sinners that he meant
> Not angels such as you![35]

Rachel made such a conquest that when he found her all alone in the house one day he was sorely tempted – but she was his friend's sister and a man, even a man as highly sexed as Robert Burns, had to set a limit somewhere. 'Heavenly Powers who know the weaknesses of human hearts support mine! What happiness must I see only to remind me that I cannot enjoy it!' he recorded in his journal afterwards.[36] Burns had to leave her behind as he and Ainslie continued their journey, and as far as love was concerned, there were no involvements from then on, apart from one romantic interlude at Jedburgh. He enjoyed meeting Mrs Scott of Wauchope, but she was thirty years older and was no temptation. He had painful encounters with the wives and families of some of the men he visited and dined with, and pronounced the daughter of Captain John Rutherford of Mossburnford beautiful, although 'too far gone woman to expose so much of so fine a swelling bosom'. At Eyemouth Betsy Grieve caught his eye and when he called on Miss Clarke, a woman noted for her tea parties, he found her 'a maiden, in the Scotch phrase, "Guid enough but no brent* new"'

Only one woman nearly got the better of him, Nancy Sherriff, who clung to the Poet and his every word with joy for a whole evening while he talked love to her. Next morning she announced that she would ride with him to Dunbar 'by way of making a parade of me as a sweetheart of her among her relations'. He was in for a surprise:

> She mounts an old cart horse as huge and as lean as a house, a rusty old side saddle without girth or stirrup but fastened on with an old pillion girth – herself as fine as hands could make her in cream colored riding clothes, hat & feather, &. I, ashamed of my situation, ride like the devil and almost shake her to pieces on old Jolly (her horse) – get rid of her by refusing to call at her uncle's.[37]

None of this was very gentlemanly or gallant, but it has to be admitted, Burns never liked his women to make the running.

The woman who caught his fancy most during the whole of the journey through the Borders was Isabella Lindsay, daughter of the doctor in Jedburgh, who managed to flirt with him in spite of the fact that she was only three weeks away from being married to someone else. On a walk with a group of ladies beside the River Jed, he tried to flirt with Isabella and took her hand, only to be frustrated by a 'cross-grained, whiggish, ugly, slanderous hag, Miss Lookup with all the poisonous spleen of a disappointed, ancient maid.' Robert spelt out his frustration in his journal:

*brand

146

I hardly refrain from cursing her to her face – May she, for her pains, be curst with eternal desire and damn'd with endless disappointment! Hear me, O Heavens, and give ear, O Earth! may the burden of antiquated Virginity crush her down to the lowest regions of the bottomless pit! for daring to mouth her calumnious slander on one of the finest pieces of the workmanship of Almighty Excellence. Sup at Mr F[air's] vexed that the Miss Lindsays are not of the supper party as they only are wanting – Mrs F[air] & Miss L[ooku]p still improve infernally on my hands.[38]

He relished getting that off his chest, but found even greater satisfaction a couple of days later when he persuaded his host to invite Isabella to join them and heard from Isabella's own lips the scurrilous stories Miss Lookup had been spreading about him. Robert presented her with a copy of the Beugo engraving and left her and Jedburgh with the thought: 'Peace dwell in thy bosom, uninterrupted except by the tumultuous throbbings of rapturous Love! That love-kindling eye must beam on another, not me; that graceful form must bless another's arms, not mine!'[39]

Across the Border in England he recorded only one encounter with the opposite sex in his journal, and that was when he met a couple of girls on the way from Longtown, where he had enjoyed the hiring-day fair and was 'a little cut with the bottle', to Carlisle. It appears that he made the first overture to the girls, but when one of them offered to take him across the Border to Gretna Green and marry him, he was sober enough to realize that a quick departure was called for. He arranged to meet her in Carlisle and there gave her 'a brush of caressing and a bottle of cyder', and left her.

At Carlisle on the evening of 1 June, he sat down and wrote to his Edinburgh friend, Willie Nicol, to tell him all about the journey through the Borders. He was in such high spirits (both natural and alcoholic) that he wrote his letter in broad Scottish dialect, and practically all he remembered to talk about was his mare, Jenny Geddes, and the girls he had met, especially the 'twa dink quines . . . ane o' them a sonsie, fine, fodgel lass, baith braw and bonie; the tither was a clean-shankit, straught, tight, weel-far'd winch, as blythe's a lintwhite on a flowrie thorn.*'[40] Rachel Ainslie and Isabella Lindsay were well remembered.

*two neat girls, one of them a buxom, fine, plump lass, both well turned out and beautiful; the other was a clean-limbed, straight, tight, good-looking girl, as happy as a linnet on a flowering thorn.

Thus Robert rode back into Scotland, a single man, with that certificate of bachelorhood which he had obtained a year before still in his pocket to prove it, and on his way to look at his future as a farmer. In Dumfries he discovered he was a celebrity, and was accorded the freedom of the town and fêted by friends he already had there. Unfortunately his pleasure was dampened by a letter he found waiting for him, with bad news from Edinburgh – another girl was pregnant.

The letter, said to have been dated 26 May, has never been seen, but from what William Wallace wrote in the centenary edition of Burns' *Life and Works* in 1896, the letter came from a Mrs Hog, who said she had been asked to write it on behalf of the girl, an Edinburgh domestic servant called Meg Cameron, who didn't know how to write. The girl was 'in trouble', precisely what trouble Mrs Hog did not specify, but with Robert's past record, that was not hard to guess. She had asked Mrs Hog to tell Burns she was:

> . . . out of quarters, without friends, my situation at present is really deplorable. I beg for God's sake, you will write and let me know how I am to do. You can write to any person you can trust to get me a place to stay in till such time as you come to town yourself.[41]

Mrs Hog was probably the wife of James Hog, whose name was jotted down in pencil at the end of the Poet's *Border Journal*. He was a shoemaker, who lived in Buchanan's Land at the head of the Canongate. Burns' first thought was for the girl and he sent a letter to her at once. He then wrote to his travelling companion, Bob Ainslie, asking him to go and see the girl and give her any help she needed. 'My first welcome to this place was the inclosed letter. I am very sorry for it, but what is done is done,' he wrote to Ainslie, then gave explicit, but strange instructions:

> Please call at the James Hog mentioned, and send for the wench and give her ten or twelve shillings, but don't for Heaven's sake meddle with her as a piece. I insist on this, on your honor; and advise her out to some country friends. You may perhaps not like the business, but I just tax your friendship thus far. Call for God sake, lest the poor soul be starving.[42]

He asked Ainslie to retrieve the letter, 'by way of token' was his explanation, but it sounds more like a canny move in case there should be trouble. He had not signed the letter to the girl anyway, probably for the same reason. It was a wise move, for she did take out a writ against him the following month.

'*Don't for Heaven's sake meddle with her as a piece. I insist on this, on your honor*: the words are chilling (but not as chilling as others he was to write to Ainslie later), and presumably were meant as a black joke, for he surely could never have thought his friend might meddle with this pregnant girl? Even so, and allowing for the fact that it was said in a private letter not intended to be seen by anyone else, its appalling bad taste can hardly be ignored as most writers on Burns have done over the years.

The only excuse can be that Ainslie was his closest friend – closer than close to him. They had been in many scrapes together, they understood one another, and they had been sharing a similar bawdy sense of humour for months. The other difficulty with such a remark is that it comes from a man from whom we expect wisdom, albeit often homespun, with wise truths that have guided our lives, and instead we find cheap bawdiness. Today it is not seen in the context of the times, when bawdry was an important element of male social life. It is read only in the context of Burns' collected letters, cheek by jowl with serious correspondence which touches the base of human existence. Robert Burns was speaking the truth when he said he was a humble ploughman – for all he learned of life at Kirkoswald, Irvine, or during the winter in Edinburgh, he was not a man of the world. This is the reason he valued Bob Ainslie, seven years younger than himself, as the only person to whom he could 'talk nonsense without forfeiting some degree of his esteem'.[43] In this letter and some of his others to Ainslie he was pushing that to the limit.

When he had time to think the matter through, Burns doubted whether he could be the father of this child, but unfortunately only part of the letter expressing those doubts to Ainslie has survived:

> . . . the Devil's Day-book only April 14 or fifteen so cannot yet have increased her growth much. I begin, from that, and some other circumstances to suspect foul play; and to tell the truth I w. . .[44]

Burns was saying he had not had intercourse with Meg Cameron before 14 or 15 April, yet here was a letter, dated 26 May, saying that she had lost her home and her job. If true, and Robert was always honest in such matters, it was far too soon for her condition to show. However, he accepted his guilt in a joyful letter, only a month later, when replying to a confession from Ainslie that he too had made a girl pregnant.

> Give you joy, give you joy, My dear brother! may your child be as strong a man as Samson, as wise a man as Solomon, & as honest a man as his father. I have double health & spirits at the news. Welcome, Sir, to the society, the venerable Society, of FATHERS!!![45]

Almost as a throw-away thought he told Ainslie:

> Peggy will bring a gallant half-Highlander – and I shall get a farm and keep them all about my hand, and breed them in the fear of the Lord and an oakstick, and I shall be the happiest man upon earth.

Meg's writ was served on him after he returned to Edinburgh in the autumn, but he admitted his guilt and the matter was duly settled. That was the last anyone heard of Meg or the Poet's 'gallant half-Highlander'. He used the back of the legal document to jot down a couple of verses of an old bawdy song which he had probably heard sung somewhere, which shows how seriously he took Meg's writ.

While the Meg Cameron business was at the forefront of his mind, he spent little time looking at Miller's farms but agreed to return again in August. He then rode home into Mauchline, even more unsettled and undecided than when he had left the town: he was so low he was even thinking of Jamaica again. He described his return to Mrs Dunlop as '*éclatant*', but the truth was that he could not bear to go straight back to Mossgiel and face the old life, which had been all but forgotten, and the family who were still wallowing in the poverty which he left behind nearly seven months before. That night he stayed at Johnnie Dow's in Mauchline.

Whatever Robert thought, the return was '*éclatant*' as far as Mauchline folk were concerned. He had left the parish a 'ne'er-do-well rhymer' and now returned Caledonia's Bard, but he bridled at all their fawning: he told Willie Nicol, 'The damn'd servility of my plebeian brethren, who perhaps formerly eyed me askance . . . have nearly put me out of conceit altogether with my species.'[46]

The morning after his return he called at the Armours' house to see his daughter, he told Nicol, and their 'mean servile compliance' disgusted him. Armour, who had warmed a modicum last year when he saw the prospect of some money from the Kilmarnock Edition, now grovelled before the celebrity who was father of his grandchildren. Jean was thrown at him and, had he not cared so deeply about her in his heart, he would have fled in disgust. As it was, he took her to a quiet corner, and she lay with him as joyously as she had done two harvest-times ago.

Next Mossgiel had to be faced. Catherine Carswell sums up the situation there with a woman's eye. 'Beneath the pride of mother, brothers and sisters, their reliance upon the famous one set them right with the world,' she wrote. 'Gavin Hamilton must be paid; Gilbert must be disembarrassed; William must be found a good place; the womenfolk must be enabled to make a suitable show in church with silk dresses and cloaks.'

If he could not satisfy all the other expectations of life in Mauchline at least he could satisfy that last need. Within a fortnight he was off again, first to Glasgow and then on another pilgrimage to the West Highlands. In Glasgow he stopped to send home some silk, enough to make a bonnet and cloak for his mother and each of his sisters, and a gown for his mother and his youngest sister. Isabella remembered years later how she had been sent to Ayr for more than a week to help with the making up of the material, and by the time she returned to Mossgiel, Robert was home again, and asked her to put on her dress so that he might see how smart she looked in it.[47]

Indeed some things in Mauchline were no different from fashionable Edinburgh.

CHAPTER NINE

# *The Passionate Pilgrim*

Where, braving angry winter's storms.
  The lofty Ochils rise,
Far in their shade my Peggy's charms
  First blest my wondering eyes:
As one who by some savage stream
  A lonely gem surveys,
Astonish'd doubly, marks its beam
  With art's most polish'd blaze.

Song written to Margaret Chalmers
after meeting her at Harvieston, Dollar

Robert could hardly wait to escape from Mauchline where people, who had accepted him a year ago as wild Rab Mossgiel who wrote verse, now eyed him as warily as if he were some superior being who was no longer one of them. He had to kill the time between now and August when he was trysted to meet Patrick Miller again at Dalswinton. So sometime during the second half of June he made a brief tour to the West Highlands, a journey about which he wrote so little that it has been suggested it was a sad, sentimental pilgrimage to 'Highland Mary's' home country, and that he even made a pilgrimage to her graveside in Greenock.

The real reason may have been much less romantic: we know that George Grierson, a Glasgow friend, was with him during part of his travels, so it seems reasonable to guess that when the Poet went to Glasgow (where he bought the silk for his mother's and sisters' cloaks and gowns) he met Grierson and told him about his restiveness, therefore the two decided to go off to Inveraray, so Robert could collect the money due from the Duke of Argyll for subscription copies of the Edinburgh Edition. Even if they were unable to obtain the money, it would have done the Poet no harm to meet yet another member of the Scottish aristocracy, so the journey may have been undertaken virtually on an impulse. Unfortunately Burns arrived at Inveraray to find that the Duke was entertaining a castleful of guests and had no time to spare for this poet who had arrived unannounced.

In the village, the inn was also packed with overflow guests from the Duke's party, so there was no room there either. If the plan was to collect subscriptions for the Edinburgh Edition the disappointment was a double one, and in his frustration or anger at this apparent slight from his 'betters' Burns took his diamond stylus and scratched two ill-tempered little verses on one of the windows of the inn:

> Whoe'er he be that sojourns here,
>   I pity much his case,
> Unless he come to wait upon
>   The lord their god, 'His Grace'.

> There's naething here but Highland pride,
>   And Highland scab and hunger:
> If Providence has sent me here,
>   Twas surely in an anger.[1]

Apart from the Inveraray disappointment, Robert enjoyed the West Highland trip. It may not have been a 'Highland Mary' pilgrimage, but it did provide female company with whom to flirt in a mild way, and an abundance of bowls of hot punch over which to put the world to rights long into the night. 'Our dancing was none of the French or English insipid formal movements,' he told his friend James Smith, 'the ladies sung Scotch songs like angels, at intervals; then we flew at *Bab at the Bowster, Tullochgorum, Loch Erroch side,* &c. like midges sporting in the mottie* sun, or craws† prognosticating a storm on a hairst§ day.' They danced till the ladies retired at three in the morning, then drank till six, when they went out and made devotions to the sun as it rose over Ben Lomond. No wonder he was in such high spirits that, when a Highlander rode past him later in the day, Burns raced him down Loch Lomondside until the man's horse 'threw his rider's breekless a—e in a clipt hedge', and Burns fell too, but fortunately escaped with nothing more serious than a few cuts and bruises.[2]

His return to Mauchline was an anti-climax again and, though Robert felt certain that the farm question would be resolved soon, his personal life, especially finding a wife, was still in pieces. The best he could tell Smith in the same letter was:

---

*dust-speckled, †crows, §harvest

I have yet fixed on nothing with respect to the serious business of life. I am, just as usual, a rhyming, mason-making, raking, aimless, idle fellow. However, I shall somewhere have a farm soon. I was going to say, a wife too; but that must never be my blessed lot. I am but a younger son of the house of Parnassus, and, like other younger sons of great families, I may intrigue, if I choose to run all risks, but must not marry.[3]

Jean was no longer even a prospect, he told Smith. 'My heart no more glows with feverish rapture. I have no paradisical evening interviews stolen from the restless cares and prying inhabitants of this weary world.' Jean must have been making it hard for him to see her, but he was still on her mind.

Through the days that followed he finished off his long autobiographical letter to Dr Moore, then called on Mrs Dunlop to discuss it with her before sending if off. He then returned to Edinburgh, where he immediately arranged yet another pilgrimage, to the North this time. On 25 August 1787 he set out, accompanied by William Nicol, a man fifteen years older, and travelling in a carriage at Willie's insistence instead of riding on horseback.

Nicol was a crusty old Latin teacher, full of opinions, ill-tempered and so huffy that Burns once said in a letter to another friend: 'I would send my compliments to Mr Nicol, but he would be hurt if he knew that I wrote to any body and not to him.'[4] Nicol had one redeeming feature in Burns' book in that he loved a convivial evening, and they had spent many together in Edinburgh. On the journey through the Highlands he proved a much less agreeable companion than Ainslie and all the way to Inverness, across to Aberdeen and south again by way of a visit to Robert's Burnes relations in Kincardine and Angus, he huffed and puffed and spoilt the Poet's enjoyment at key moments. When Burns went to visit important people, Nicol often stayed behind and then, just as Burns was beginning to enjoy himself, he was hurried on by the irascible man. Several times he prevented Robert from cementing contacts which might have been useful in the future. But that was Nicol and Robert Burns could not change him: Burns cursed him but forgave him in the end.

At Blair Atholl the Poet was very well received by the Duke of Atholl's family. But here he had to leave because Nicol who had stayed behind at the inn as usual would not accept an invitation the family sent, asking him to join them for dinner. The reason was probably that Nicol was an uncompromising Jacobite, while the Duke of Atholl's branch of the Murray family had been pro-King George at the time of the Forty-Five Rising. It was a great pity Burns had to rush away since Henry Dundas, a politician so powerful that he was known as 'the uncrowned king of Scotland', was due to arrive shortly and his patronage could have made Burns' future more secure.

They continued the journey by Inverness and Culloden and came to Gordon Castle, near Fochabers, where Burns again met his friends from the previous winter in Edinburgh, the Duke and Duchess of Gordon. Nicol again stayed behind at the inn and when the Duke of Gordon discovered this and sent Burns back to fetch him the crusty old Latin master simply refused to come. Another opportunity had been missed, and Robert was in bad spirits as he and Nicol drove on along the coast. He was still smarting over Nicol's behaviour a month later when he wrote to the Duke's librarian, James Hoy:

> May that obstinate Son of Latin Prose be curst to Scotch-mile periods, and damn'd to seven-league paragraphs; while Declension & Conjugation, Gender, Number and Time, under the ragged banners of Dissonance and Disarrangement eternally rank against him in hostile array!!!!!![5]

Robert was charmed, as ever, by the women he met, but treated them with the greatest of care and behaved with decorum. He knew they belonged to that lofty stratum of society to which he had no wish ever to belong, and therefore were not worth so much as a flutter of his heart. The Murray girls begged him to stay on at Blair Atholl while at Kilravock he enjoyed listening to Miss Rose of Kildrummie singing folk-songs which he tucked away in his mind for later use. But as far as love was concerned his twenty-two days in the Highlands had been poor value. He had, however, met the fiddler Neil Gow and collected a number of songs and tunes which would be useful in the future. As he told Patrick Miller: 'My journey through the Highlands was perfectly inspiring; and I hope I have laid in a good stock of new poetical ideas from it.'[6]

Burns had missed his appointment with Patrick Miller at the end of August, to look at Dalswinton estate. He really had no excuse, so he gave none. The letter, and some poems enclosed with it, were designed to keep Miller happy for the moment for Robert could not face up to his future yet. Jean Armour must have known that she was pregnant again as a result of Robert's return to Mauchline in June, but he made no effort to contact or comfort her either. And yet his heart told him he had to settle his future soon.

It was then that he made the last of his four 'pilgrimages' with the clear objective to settle some unfinished business in his love life. The woman he wanted to see was Margaret (Peggy) Chalmers, a friend since Mauchline days, whom he had been wooing sedately during the early part of the year. Peggy Chalmers had the great advantage over Jean Armour or any other country girl he had courted previously because she was a cultured woman, superior both socially and intellectually. Though she was above his social class she was not too far up the scale: her father had owned a small estate and later been a farmer.

Peggy was born at Fingland in Kirkcudbright, around 1763, but her father ran into financial difficulties, which forced him to sell his estate and take Braehead Farm just a mile or two from Mauchline. It is most likely that Peggy was at Braehead while Robert was in Mossgiel. Her mother was a sister of Gavin Hamilton's step-mother, so Robert must have known her well through his friendship with the Hamiltons. The Hamiltons were socially above the Burns of Mossgiel and it probably never occurred to Robert to consider even a flirtation with Peggy in the Mauchline days. But when they met again in Edinburgh, away from their roots, and he was a celebrity in the city, things were different. They must have met often in Edinburgh the previous winter, because Peggy was also in the city, playing and singing to old, blind Dr Blacklock, who was a close contact of the Poet.

Peggy would be all too well aware of his reputation as a womanizer, so he had to go very warily if he wanted to court her. Peggy Chalmers was now living at Harvieston, near Dollar, and Robert's 'pilgrimage' of the autumn of 1787 was to try to persuade her to become his wife.

It was a last desperate attempt which followed an overture of some kind that he had made during their time together in Edinburgh. A draft letter, written in the early days of 1787, and beginning only: 'My Dear Country woman', was almost certainly addressed to her. 'My Dear Country woman' meant the addressee came from Ayrshire, and a reference to his 'black story *at home*' showed she must have been conversant with the details of the Paton/Armour affairs. The letter also referred to the girl's piano-playing which he had heard in Edinburgh, so everything points to Peggy as his 'dear country woman.'

By the beginning of 1787 Lizzie Paton had settled her claim against him, 'Highland Mary' was dead, Jean Armour was quiescent, and he had a certificate in his pocket to prove he was a bachelor. Robert was free to love again, and he had fallen for this woman to whom he sent the long 'Countrywoman' letter. Clearly he was hoping she would respond to him, but feared rejection:

I know you will laugh at it, when I tell you that your Piano and you together have play'd the deuce somehow, about my heart. I was once a zealous Devotee to your Sex, but you know the black story at home. My breast has been widowed these many months, and I thought myself proof against the fascinating witchcraft; but I am afraid you will 'feelingly convince me what I am.' I say afraid, because I am not sure what is the matter with me. I have one miserable bad symptom, when you whisper, or look kindly at another, it gives me a draught of damnation. I have a kind of wayward wish to be with you ten minutes by yourself; though, what I would say, Heaven above knows, for I am sure, I know not. I have no formed design in all this; but just in the nakedness of my heart write you down a mere matter-of-fact story. You may perhaps give yourself airs of distance on this, and that will completely cure me; but I wish you would not: just let us meet if you please in the old, beaten way of friendship.[7]

Peggy – if the 'Countrywoman' letter was to her – did not encourage him, and in a letter to his friend James Smith shortly after the West Highland tour, he said with his customary hyperbole, 'I may intrigue, if I choose to run all risks, but must not marry.'[8]

In that same letter, however, he confided to Smith that he still had one hope for a marriage partner, but thanks to James Currie, we can only guess that Peggy was the person he meant. When Currie published the letter he replaced the woman's name with four asterisks, and the original of the letter has vanished. Certainly Peggy Chalmers would fit the description in the Smith letter as a 'distant acquaintance' of James since he had a draper's shop in the town at the time Peggy was living nearby and she would be a customer, and thus known to him if only at a distance. Burns told Smith:

I have only ****. This last is one of your distant acquaintances, has a fine figure, and elegant manners; and in the train of some great folks whom you know, has seen the politest quarters in Europe. I do like her a good deal; but what piques me is her conduct at the commencement of our acquaintance. I frequently visited her when I was in —, and after passing regularly the intermediate degrees between the distant formal bow and the familiar grasp round the waist, I ventured in my careless way to talk of friendship in rather ambiguous terms; and after her return to —, I wrote to her in the same style. Miss, construing my words farther I suppose than even I intended, flew off in a tangent of female dignity and reserve, like a mounting lark in an April morning, and wrote me an answer which measured me out very completely what an immense way I had to travel before I could reach the climate of her favour.[9]

But Burns was an old campaigner and counter-attacked with success:

> I am an old hawk at the sport; and wrote her such a cool, deliberate, prudent reply as brought my bird from her aerial towerings, pop, down at my foot like corporal Trim's hat.[10]

When he returned to Edinburgh in September 1787 his first objective was to settle with Creech, but he now came to realize just what a wily creature his publisher was, and how hard it was going to be to squeeze any money out of him. This made it all the more urgent for Robert to face up to the future, which he still hoped Peggy Chalmers might share. It was important for him to try once more to persuade Peggy to marry him.

He had a good excuse for calling at Harvieston to see her, because it lay conveniently on the road to Ochtertyre, near Crieff, where Sir William Murray had invited him to stay when they met at Blair Atholl a few months earlier. Sir William was a cousin of Robert Graham of Fintry, who had just become a Commissioner of the Scottish Board of Excise, and therefore could help Robert towards a career in the Excise Service if he chose that course instead of farming. The visit could thus be worthwhile on several counts, and the sooner he made it the better.

During the first days of October, Robert set out. Wisely, he avoided Nicol as his travelling companion this time, although by pure chance he encountered Nicol in Stirling at the very start of the journey, and they spent an evening together, drinking and singing, 'thoughtless of to-morrow'. This was when Robert smashed the window pane with that embarrassing scratched verse about the Stuarts. Nicol went his own way afterwards, and left Robert to his *amour*.

Burns chose James McKittrick Adair as his companion on this fourth tour. He was the son of an Ayr doctor and a relation of Mrs Dunlop, who had been introduced to him through Dr Lawrie, the Loudon minister. As a member of the professional class in Peggy Chalmers's home country, Adair was the ideal choice, since he knew Ayrshire well and could put her at her ease by talking about people she knew. Adair was a doctor himself and practised in the Pleasance in Edinburgh, but later moved to Harrogate, where he spent the rest of his life. The visit to Harvieston was much more successful for Adair than for Burns: he fell in love with Charlotte Hamilton, a half-sister of Gavin Hamilton, and they were married two years later.

On the morning after the merry evening with Nicol, the doctor and Burns rode 'through the romantic vale of Devon' to Harvieston, where they spent eight blissful days. Adair told Currie[11] they had spent about ten days at Harvieston, but they were there for only eight. For both, these were the eight happiest days of their lives. Fortunately, Adair remembered everything that happened clearly enough to pass it on to Currie, for Robert kept no journal – probably all that mattered to him was written on his tinder heart:

> We made excursions to various parts of the surrounding scenery, inferior to none in Scotland in beauty, sublimity, and romantic interest; particularly Castle Campbell, the ancient seat of the family of Argyll; and the famous cataract of the Devon called the Caldron-linn; and the Rumbling Bridge, a single broad arch, thrown by the devil, if tradition is to be believed, across the river, at the height of about one hundred feet above its bed.

Adair expected such scenery to inspire great poetry from the Bard, but was sorely disappointed: the ladies from Harvieston felt equally let down:

> I was surprised that none of these scenes should have called forth an exertion of Burns's Muse. But I doubt if he had much taste for the picturesque. I well remember that the ladies at Harvieston, who accompanied us on this jaunt, expressed their disappointment at his not expressing in more glowing and fervid language, his impressions of the Caldron Linn scene, certainly highly sublime, and somewhat horrible.[12]

They did not know Burns well, or they would have realized that the Poet's landscapes were always filled with people, and at Caldron Linn that day there was only one person in his line of vision. Why did he not write a poem to Peggy there and then? Perhaps his emotions were running too high, and his thoughts were in turmoil as he tried to pluck up courage to propose to Peggy again.

He did ask her to marry him before he left Harvieston, only to be turned down. We are told the reason she gave was that she was already engaged to Lewis Hay, a young man with considerably better prospects than the wayward poet, but she could hardly have been committed to Hay so soon since they were not married until more than a year later.

The truth was more likely that Peggy was aware that, while she was intelligent enough to talk to Burns about intellectual matters, she was not a deep-thinking scholarly type; neither was she a peasant who could understand or live with that underlying humble farming mentality of which he was justly proud. Peggy Chalmers wanted more from life, and Lewis Hay could offer it. Hay was already a clerk in Sir William Forbes' banking house in Edinburgh, and about the time he married Peggy, he became a partner in the business. It was a wise choice for Peggy perhaps, but a heart-breaking one for Robert, for she was one of only two women in his life who was intellectually suited to him and sufficiently attractive for him to fall in love with. The other, Maria Riddell, was already married and not available. However, it has to be admitted, the match with Peggy would only have ended in disaster because she would not have been able to put up with the kind of wayward life that Jean Armour tolerated. Peggy was a lady, and could never have suffered being treated like a humble tenant farmer's wife.

None the less, her refusal hurt at the time and remained a lingering regret: the Poet never mentioned this proposal to anyone, and we know of it only because Peggy herself told the poet Thomas Campbell years later that Burns had asked her to marry him. She must have turned him down with enormous tact and grace because they remained friends for years afterwards.

After his return to Edinburgh, Robert wrote to Peggy, enclosing a copy of the first volume of *The Scots Musical Museum* about which he had no doubt talked enthusiastically at Harvieston, and promising to compose a song for Charlotte if he could 'hit on some glorious old Scotch air'.[13] Eventually he did write his song for her; it was *The Banks of the Devon*, the river that runs through Clackmannanshire, but the opening verse (like the rest of the song) could have been written for his Peggy:

> How pleasant the banks of the clear winding Devon,
>   With green spreading bushes and flow'rs blooming fair!
> But the boniest flow'r on the banks of the Devon
>   Was once a sweet bud on the braes of the Ayr.[14]

He also wrote some verses on a blank page in the book, verses no doubt devoted to Peggy, for he mentioned that Dr Blacklock had approved them, although he himself was not yet satisfied with them. The language of this letter showed he still hankered after Peggy, for in telling him that he had been trying to persuade one of the Chalmers' Edinburgh friends, Miss Erskine Nimmo, to visit Harvieston, he said:

My rhetoric seems quite to have lost its effect on the lovely half of mankind . . . I look on the sex with something like the admiration with which I regard the starry sky in a frosty December night . . . I am charmed with the wild but graceful eccentricity of their motions, and – wish them good night. I mean this with respect to a certain passion *dont j'ai eu l'honneur d'être un misérable esclave*: as for friendship, you and Charlotte have given me pleasure, permanent pleasure, 'which the world cannot give, nor take away' I hope; and which will outlast the heavens and the earth.

A few weeks later he sent Peggy a couple of poems, the first, *Where Braving Angry Winter's Storms*, was about the wild scenery in the Ochil hills around Harvieston, but once again the landscape contained a figure – for on the wild Ochils Peggy's charms blest his 'wondering eye'. The second song, *My Peggy's Charms*, was pure love. These were not the best songs Robert was to write, but the sentiment certainly was sincere and in case she thought differently, he spelt out to her that 'the poetic compliments I pay cannot be misunderstood.'[15]

> I love my Peggy's angel air,
> Her face so truly heavenly fair,
> Her native grace so void of art:
> But I adore my Peggy's heart.[16]

Peggy was unwilling to allow these songs to be published in spite of protests from the Poet that they complimented her almost solely on her mental charms rather than her physical ones. He told her at the same time that she possessed wit, understanding and worth 'much above par', and couldn't resist adding. 'This is a cursed flat way of telling you these truths.'[17] However, he did respect her wishes, and *My Peggy's Charms* did not appear until six years after his death.

Burns never forgot Peggy Chalmers and what might have been: he sent her the friendliest of letters, often confiding his worries and fears, and one depressing day in September 1788, when harvesting was rained off at his farm in Dumfriesshire, he sat down and wrote her a long letter in which he told her:

When I think I have met with you, and have lived more of a real life with you in eight days, than I can do with almost any body I meet with in eight years – when I think on the improbability of meeting you in this world again – I could sit down and cry like a child![18]

He ended this letter by telling her he had married Jean Armour, but to the last he did not forget Peggy. On 12 July 1796, only a fortnight before his death, Burns sent Thomson his last letter, enclosing with it the song *Fairest Maid on Devon Banks*. The Harvieston visit was not forgotten even then:

> Full well thou know'st I love thee dear –
> Couldst thou to malice lend an ear
> O, did not Love exclaim: – 'Forbear,
>     Nor use a faithful lover so!'
>
> Then come, thou fairest of the fair,
> Those wonted smiles, O, let me share,
> And by thy beauteous self I swear
>     No love but thine my heart shall know!

The chorus of the song harked back to those eight blissfully happy days with Charlotte and Peggy:

> Fairest maid on Devon banks,
>     Crystal Devon, winding Devon,
> Wilt thou lay that frown aside,
>     And smile as thou wert wont to do?

After the rejection at Harvieston in the autumn of 1787, Burns and Adair continued their tour, with the Poet successfully hiding his injured feelings from the people he met. At Ochtertyre they stayed with Sir William Murray, whose wife, Lady Augusta, set the Poet's Jacobite spirit in motion for she was the daughter of the Earl of Cromartie, who had been tried and sentenced to death for taking part in the Forty-Five rising, but was later pardoned. Sir William's cousin, Euphemia, also gave Burns' heart a boost, for she was a pretty eighteen-year-old, and he wrote a song to her. *Blythe Was She* praised her beauty – after all she was known locally as the Flower of Strathmore – but Phemie Murray responded in the same high-handed way as the Bonnie Lass of Ballochmyle had done, by ignoring the compliment. Burns sent the song to George Thomson in 1794: she would never have become immortal otherwise.

> The Evening sun was ne'er sae sweet
>     As was the blink o Phemie's e'e.[19]

On the return journey to Edinburgh, the travellers called on John Ramsay at another place called Ochtertyre at Kincardine-in-Menteith, then stopped off at Clackmannan Tower to meet old Mrs Bruce of Clackmannan, a woman of over ninety but still full of vigour. She corrected them when they remarked that they believed she was descended from the family of Robert Bruce. It was the other way round, she told them: 'Bruce was sprung from her family.' Although semi-paralysed, Mrs Bruce 'knighted' the pair with the Hero King's sword which she had in her possession. She had a better right to do this than 'some people', she said as she dubbed them.[20] At Dunfermline Peggy was forgotten for the moment when the pair went into the Abbey church, and Adair mounted the cutty stool while Burns harangued him from the pulpit in words which, Adair said, 'parodied from that which had been delivered to himself in Ayrshire, where he had, as he assured me, once been one of the seven who mounted the seat of shame together.' That was Burns making the most of his sinning to show off to a male friend – for only five people were brought to the repentance stool the day he and Jean appeared in Mauchline church.

Burns now returned to Edinburgh to all the old problems concerning a career and Creech. He and Adair arrived back on 20 October and five days later he wrote to Richmond, temporarily back in Mauchline at the time, to tell him he had just learned that his daughter, Jean, had died; this was a sad personal blow. It was a strangely off-hand letter, out of character for this man who loved his children so much, glossing lightly over what had obviously been a tragic accident, yet asking anxiously what was happening at the Armours. He wrote:

By the way, I hear I am a girl out of pocket and by careless, murdering mischance too, which has provoked me and vexed me a good deal. I beg you will write me by post immediately on receipt of this, and let me know the news of Armour's family if the world begin to talk of Jean's appearance any way.[21]

Even allowing for the fact that Burns was writing to the one friend with whom he always enjoyed a rough, masculine friendship, this seems a very callous way to refer to the death of his child. He said he was vexed, but vexed about what? The child's death or the 'careless, murdering mischance'? Perhaps it was both? Burns, a brilliant wordsmith, was rarely ambiguous in anything he wrote, yet this letter is open to various interpretations. The same day he sat down and wrote a long letter to the Reverend John Skinner in Aberdeenshire about another matter and made no reference to his child's death. Even allowing for the fact that he was ill at the time, and that he had Creech's money and the farm in Dumfriesshire on his mind, it is hard to forgive him the casualness of his tone.

Most biographers quote the letter without comment. Maurice Lindsay suggests that grief at baby Jean's loss was 'uneasily concealed behind the nonchalant manner of expressing it.' James Mackay says, 'The casual reference to the death of baby Jean is sometimes taken out of context by Burns' detractors to show him in a callous light, but the full quotation shows that, far from making light of the little girl's death, Robert was sorely vexed by the news.' Both of these interpretations make too light of Burns' response: however kindly one tries to look on it, this letter was not one on which he could have looked back with pride. One of the Poet's most recent biographers, Ian McIntyre, while admitting the comment was made 'altogether too casually', suggests that Burns' spirits were constantly rising and falling at this time, which may give a clue to his behaviour.[22]

It is true, Burns' return to Edinburgh in the autumn of 1787 was very different from his arrival a year before: the great and the powerful no longer rushed to meet him; it was no coup for fine women to have him in their drawing-rooms, and Burns was well aware of this change. He had to move on, but where and how? In his indecision he wavered and his spirits ebbed and flowed like the tide at Leith. When caught off-guard in these changes of mood he could say or write things that would have been better left unsaid. The remark about being a girl out of pocket was one, just as the warning to Ainslie not to meddle with Meg Cameron 'as a piece' was another.

In the capital, Robert moved into the house of William Cruikshank, a Latin master and colleague of Nicol's. The house was in St James's Square in the New Town and was quite the most comfortable home he ever had in the city. Here he continued his struggle to obtain satisfaction from Creech, and to make his mind up about the farm. It was at this time that he found a new interest, or more accurately, became utterly engrossed in an old one, that of folk-song.

At Cruikshank's house he got down to the work of finding, fashioning and refurbishing old songs, and writing new words of his own to old tunes, thus beginning what was to become a second career as a poet. Everyone who could was roped in to help, even the schoolmaster's twelve-year-old daughter, Jean, who played and sang the tunes over to him. Jean was rewarded with a dedication in verse in a book the Poet gave to her and a song of her very own, *A Rose-Bud by My Early Walk*, one of his most exquisite songs, and one which is still as fresh today as the day he composed it for the 'rose-bud' who sang to him two hundred years ago.

> So thou, dear bird, young Jeany fair,
> On trembling string or vocal air,
> Shall sweetly pay the tender care
>     That tents* thy early morning!                    *guards

So thou, sweet rose-bud, young and gay,
Shall beauteous blaze upon the day,
And bless the parent's evening ray
That watch'd thy early morning.[23]

During that winter of 1787–8 collecting songs for James Johnson and singing them over with little Jeany Cruikshank filled every spare moment, but Robert had to break off to ride down to Dumfries to look at the farms Patrick Miller was offering him on Dalswinton estate. It is not known exactly when this journey was made, but one letter to Peggy Chalmers, written on 21 October, said he was due to go to Dumfries on Thursday or Friday,'[24] and another, written about 1 December, said, 'I have been at Dumfries, and at one visit more shall be decided about a farm in that country.' He still had doubts, but hoped that his brother, Gilbert, might help him to make up his mind. If the farming venture in Dumfries failed, he told Peggy he would return to Mossgiel and join his brother to farm there. The trip had really settled nothing, and at the back of his mind the Excise Service beckoned.

At last on 24 November he wrote to Mrs Dunlop to inform her that he intended to return to Ayrshire in eight or ten days and hoped to call at Dunlop House on his way. This trip was probably planned to give him an opportunity to discuss the Dumfries farming project with his brother. However, on 4 December, the day he should have been riding to the west, he was still in Edinburgh, in the drawing-room of a house in Alison Square taking tea with Miss Erskine Nimmo, a rather tart, spinsterish friend of Peggy Chalmers.

Among the guests was someone quite different altogether: Agnes McLehose, a vivacious little woman, rather plump around the bosom, but with a pert little retroussé nose, lustrous eyes, and a smile that displayed pretty white teeth – an improvement on Bess Burnett's smile. Her dancing golden curls caught his attention, for he always thought golden locks were a sign of amorousness. When she spoke she revealed herself as flirtatious, but with a witty mind and conversation that displayed more than the usual education and culture than Robert had come to expect among the creatures he encountered at Edinburgh tea parties. She was refined, but in no way did she make Burns feel she was out of his class. There was more: Mrs McLehose loved poetry, particularly the poetry of her fellow guest, and as Robert Burns looked into her beckoning eyes his tinder heart burst into flame. 'That damned star', which had so often overturned his plans, was shining again, and Robert was smitten. Gilbert, Patrick Miller, Mrs Dunlop and even Peggy Chalmers were all forgotten: the only person he could see was Agnes McLehose.

CHAPTER TEN

# *Clarinda, Mistress of my Soul*

O, what a fool I am in love! – what an extravagant prodigal of affection! Why are your sex called the tender sex, when I never have met with one who can repay me in passion! They are either not so rich in love as I am, or they are niggards where I am lavish.

Letter to Nancy McLehose, 21 January, 1788[1]

As he sipped tea with Agnes McLehose in Miss Nimmo's drawing-room, Robert Burns had no idea that it had all been arranged by Mrs McLehose who had been scheming for ages to persuade her friend to invite Robert to Alison Square so that they might meet. 'Miss Nimmo can tell you how earnestly I had long pressed her to make us acquainted,' she admitted to Burns boldly only a few days after first meeting him. 'I had a presentiment that we should derive pleasure from the society of each other.'[2]

Agnes, or Nancy as she was usually called, had a habit of striving for what she wanted and usually getting it, though it seldom seemed to bring her lasting happiness. She was nine months older than the Poet,[3] and was the daughter of an eminent Glasgow surgeon, Andrew Craig, and his wife Christian McLaurin, who had died when Nancy was only nine. Nancy grew into such a pretty girl that, at the age of only fifteen, she was the toast of the Hodge Podge Club, a Glasgow gentlemen's drinking club, which is perhaps one reason why her father chose to send her away to a finishing school in Edinburgh to polish up her writing and social manners. As well as the Hodge Podge members, Nancy caught the eye of a young Glasgow lawyer, James McLehose, who fell so utterly in love with her that one day when he heard she was due to travel to Edinburgh, he booked every other seat in the coach so that he could have her to himself for the whole ten-hour journey. His plan succeeded, and she was his wife by the time she was eighteen and had borne him three children before she was twenty-four. By that time, however, his wild lifestyle and beatings had driven her to seek a separation.

Nancy's father died in 1782 after a long illness which drained away most of his money, leaving her dependent on charity from the physicians' and lawyers' professional bodies in the city. She collected her two surviving children, who had been living with her husband's mother, and took herself off to Edinburgh with them, and there she found a good ally in her cousin, William Craig. Her cousin was a very successful young lawyer, who was later to become an eminent judge with the title Lord Craig, but in those early days in Edinburgh he helped her out financially and with comfort and advice. Craig also provided Nancy with introductions to men of letters in the capital, for, like her, he was interested in literature. It is hard to imagine how Burns did not manage, during his first winter in Edinburgh, to fall in with this young woman who was trying so desperately to become a part of the Edinburgh literary scene.

Nancy had only one other relative in the city who was of any importance, John McLaurin, a cousin of her mother. He, too, was a lawyer, but the exact opposite of William Craig in character, as Nancy soon discovered when she contacted him soon after her arrival in the city. McLaurin was a dour-faced, narrow-minded man, thoroughly disapproving of young women separated from their husbands, living alone, and trying to push their way into Edinburgh society. McLaurin, soon to become a Senator of the College of Justice with the title Lord Dreghorn, did not appear to approve of women very much at all, and cut Nancy dead when he met her in the street. Perhaps he thought she would fall into wicked ways or even prostitution, for he had a great hatred of whores.

A few years later Burns had a brush with him on this very topic: Lord Dreghorn was the judge who rejected the appeal of the Poet's prostitute namesake, Margaret Burns, when she was ordered to leave the city in 1789. Robert was then prompted to write the little satirical verse beginning:

> Cease ye prudes, your envious railing!
> Lovely Burns has charms – confess![4]

Although that was in the future, when Burns and Nancy met McLaurin was already known as a killjoy and prude, and the two must often have laughed at his narrow-mindedness.

After Miss Nimmo's tea party Nancy positively threw herself at the Poet, with an invitation to visit her at her house only two days later, on Thursday, 6 December. He was not free, so she sent another invitation for Saturday, the 8th. This time he accepted at once, telling her he too had been disappointed to miss the Thursday meeting. 'I had set no small store by my tea-drinking tonight, and have not often been so disappointed,' he told her. 'Saturday evening I shall embrace the opportunity with the greatest pleasure.' He was due to leave town in a week and regretted that he had made her acquaintance so late, but he enclosed a poem, a 'bagatelle . . . a tolerable off-hand *jeu d'esprit*', and would willingly send more should she be interested.[5]

Saturday could not come soon enough for Robert had found a woman (Peggy Chalmers apart perhaps) such as he had not encountered since he first set foot in Edinburgh a year before, and for poor, lonely Nancy this was a chance to adore the poet everybody was talking about. It was an enormous social coup for her, and she savoured it, which made her disappointment harder to bear when Saturday evening came and, instead of bringing the Poet to her house in Potterrow, a letter arrived to tell her he had met with an accident and could not come. What had happened was that in the early hours of the morning, on the way home from a night's dining and drinking with a party which included the ubiquitous Miss Nimmo, Burns had fallen as he got out of a coach. He blamed the drunken driver of the coach for the mishap in one letter, but it looks much more likely that Burns had been drinking, or perhaps both poet and coachman were the worse for wear. Whoever was at fault, Robert dislocated his kneecap and when he should have been enjoying Nancy's company in the intimacy of her house on Saturday evening, he was sitting at Cruikshank's in St James's Square, resting his painful leg on a cushion.

The letter Nancy opened was no casual apology for a cancelled invitation. It began by saying straight out that he had never met anyone in his life whom he had been more anxious to see again: he was intoxicated with the idea of being with her, but here he sat, unable to stir from his chair.

> If I don't see you again, I shall not rest in my grave for chagrin. I was vexed to the soul I had not seen you sooner; I determined to cultivate your friendship with the enthusiasm of Religion, but thus has Fortune ever served me. I cannot bear the idea of leaving Edinburgh without seeing you . . .
>
> I am strangely taken with some people; nor am I often mistaken. You are a stranger to me: but I am an odd being: some yet unnamed feelings; things not principles, but better than whims, carry me farther than boasted reason ever did a Philosopher.[6]

Nancy was devastated, and sat down to reply at once. 'If my sympathy, my friendship, can alleviate your pain, be assured you possess them,' she told him. Nancy was determined he should not leave town without her seeing him again however, and seized on the word *stranger*, which was the barrier that kept them apart. Perhaps she had her second cousin, sour-faced McLaurin, in mind as she told Robert:

I am determined to see you; and am ready to exclaim with Yorick, 'Tut! are we not all relations?' We are indeed, strangers in one sense – but of near kin in many respects . . . If I were your sister, I would call and see you; but 'tis a censorious world this, and (in this sense) you and I are not of the world. Adieu. Keep up your heart, you will soon get well, and we shall meet. Farewell . . . God bless you.

She thanked him for sending his verses: 'Your lines were truly poetical: give me all you can.' She also responded with some of her own: 'Read the enclosed, which I scrawled just after reading yours. Be sincere; and own that, whatever merit it has, it has not a line resembling poetry. Pardon any little freedoms I take with you: if they entertain a heavy hour, they have all the merit I intended.[7]

The following Wednesday, 12 December, Burns replied, gushing with praise for her poetic ability: 'Your Friendship, Madam! by Heavens, I was never proud before. Your lines, I maintain it, are Poetry, and good Poetry; mine, were indeed partly fiction, and partly a friendship which had I been so blest as to have met with you *in time*, might have led me – God of love knows where.'[8]

When she answered on Sunday morning, the 16th, she had begun to flirt dangerously even as she rebuked him for being so familiar: it was a half-hearted reprimand, which could not deceive a man as experienced as Robert Burns – and it certainly would not put him off. 'When I meet you, I must chide you for writing in your romantic style. Do you remember that she whom you address is a married woman? Or, Jacob-like, would you wait seven years, and even then, perhaps be disappointed, as he was? No; I know you better: you have too much of the impetuosity which generally accompanies noble minds.' Neither could she resist a jealous little barb against Robert's grand female friends for not helping him. 'Were I the Duchess of Gordon, you should be possessed of that independence which every generous mind pants after; but I fear she is "no Duchess at the heart".'[9]

His reply was both arch and teasing, yet behind its light tone lurked deadly seriousness about his love for Nancy. He showed compassion for her plight and, though he admitted his heart might have strayed into love, it had done so for the best of reasons, therefore should be forgiven. His leg was improving very slowly, and he still was unable to put his foot to the ground, so he had time to ramble on at great length:

> 'Pay my addresses to a married woman!' I started as if I had seen the ghost of him I had injured . . . I cannot positively say, Madam, whether my heart might not have gone astray a little; but I can declare, upon the honour of a poet, that the vagrant has wandered unknown to me . . . To meet with an unfortunate woman, amiable and young; deserted and widowed by those who were bound by every tie of Duty, Nature and Gratitude, to protect, comfort and cherish her; add to all, when she is perhaps one of the first of Lovely Forms and Noble minds . . . should a vague infant-idea, the natural child of Imagination, thoughtlessly peep over the fence – were you, my Friend, to sit in judgement . . . you could not, my Dear Madam, condemn the hapless wretch to 'death without benefit of Clergy?'[10]

Without so much as a second meeting their relationship had crossed the frontier from flirtation into the dangerous territory of love. Nancy's next letter is missing, but in it she suggested they abandon the formal 'Sir' and 'Madam' of their earlier correspondence and adopt classical names which would conceal their identity if ever the letters were seen. The letter appeared in a work published about the middle of the nineteenth century:

> I have proposed to myself a more pastoral name for you, although it be not much in keeping with the shrillness of the Ettrick Pipe. What say you to *Sylvander*? I feel somewhat less restraint when I subscribe myself CLARINDA.[11]

Robert agreed: in the next day's letter he called her Clarinda for the first time.[12] Nancy McLehose was a new experience for Burns, for here was a woman with a mind as well as a quality which other clever women he had met lacked. Even Peggy Chalmers lacked an ability to flirt with him in verse. In his letter of 20 December[13] he let slip that he was writing this 'scrawl' to her because he had nothing else to do, and Nancy retaliated with some verses, every one ending, 'you'd nothing else to do.'

> When first you saw 'Clarinda's' Charms,
> When rapture in your bosom grew!
> Her heart was shut to Love's alarms,
> But then – you'd nothing else to do.[14]

A delighted Robert responded with ten clever little four-line verses in the same metre, each ending with the word 'do' and the last finishing, 'I'll write, whatever I have to do.'[15]

There was no stopping him now his heart was on fire. 'I do love you if possible still better for having so fine a taste and turn for Poesy . . . but you may erase the word, and put esteem, respect, or any other tame Dutch expression you please in its place.' He did not hide from his past sexual reputation: 'I believe there is no holding converse or carrying on correspondence with an amiable woman, much less a gloriously-amiable, fine woman, without some mixture of that delicious Passion, whose most devoted Slave I have, more than once, had the honor of being.'

At the end of the letter he resorted once more to the irresistible military metaphor: 'I may take a fort by storm, but never by siege.'[16]

By New Year, he was in such a fever of passion that he had to tell someone about the conquest, and fortunately his old friend from Irvine, the sea captain, Richard Brown, reappeared on the scene to make an understanding and safe confidant:

Almighty Love still 'reigns and revels' in my bosom. and I am at this moment ready to hang myself for a young Edinburgh Widow, who has wit and beauty more murderously fatal than the assassinating stiletto of the Sicilian Banditti, or the poisoned arrow of the savage African.

If there had been any doubt hitherto, Burns made the sexual side of his desire for Clarinda crystal clear to Brown:

My Highland durk, that used to hang beside my crutches, I have gravely removed into a neighbouring closet, the key of which I cannot command, in case of spring-tide paroxysms.[17]

Locking the closet was not his wish, and if he had his way it would soon be open. Clarinda was receiving much the same message without it being spoken, and she now began to hide behind her honour and religion. Nancy McLehose always became depressed at this time of year when she had to sit alone, separated from husband and with scarcely enough money to keep herself and her children, while the rich world around her was filled with enjoyment. But this year she had serious matters to ponder as she sat alone at home, nursing her misery. On New Year's Day, 1788, she sent Robert a letter on the subject of love and

171

friendship, setting both against the background of her own deep religious convictions. 'My heart was formed for love,' she told him, 'and I desire to devote it to Him who is the source of love! Yes: we shall surely meet in an "unknown state of being", where there will be full scope for every kind, heartfelt affection – love without alloy, and without end.'[18] Love in the afterlife was not what Robert Burns wanted to hear at all, but fortunately she was begging him only two days later, to try to visit her if his leg had mended sufficiently.[19] She enclosed another poem, which had resulted from her deep, dark thoughts on love over the festive season:

> Talk not of Love! It gives me pain –
> For Love has been my foe;
> He bound me in an iron chain!
> And plunged me deep in woe!
>
> But Friendship's pure and lasting joys
> My heart was formed to prove –
> The worthy object be of those,
> But never talk of Love!
>
> The 'Hand of Friendship' I accept –
> May Honour be our guard!
> Virtue our intercourse direct,
> Her smiles our dear reward.[20]

Burns was delighted to tell Clarinda that his limb was 'vastly better', though he still needed crutches, but he was shortly going to dine at the house next door, and as soon as he was able to travel further, Clarinda's would be the first house he would visit.[21] His compliments on her poem were fulsome, but not the most tactful. He praised her use of language as 'beyond any woman of my acquaintance except one whom I wish I knew,' (probably Peggy Chalmers) and told her, 'Your last verses to me have so delighted me, that I have got an excellent old Scots air that suits the measure, and you shall see them in print in the "*Scots Musical Museum*".'[22] In due course Clarinda's song did appear with some amendments and an extra verse by Burns, set to the tune *Banks of Spey*:

> Talk not of love, it gives me pain,
>   For love has been my foe;
> He bound me with an iron chain,
>   And plung'd me deep in woe.

But friendship's pure and lasting joys,
  My heart was form'd to prove;
There, welcome win and wear the prize,
  But never talk of love.

Your friendship much can make me blest,
  Oh why that bliss destroy!
Why urge the only one request
  You know I will deny!

Your thought, if love must harbour there,
  Conceal it in that thought;
Nor cause me from my bosom tear
  The very friend I sought.[23]

The following day, Friday, 4 January, he was able to be taken to Potterrow in a sedan chair for only his second meeting with Clarinda, and on the morning following the visit he wrote ecstatically, managing to quote from the Bible and the poet, James Thomson, which should have satisfied Nancy on religious and literary levels:

Some days, some nights, nay some *hours*, like the 'ten righteous persons in Sodom', save the rest of the vapid, tiresome, miserable months and years of life. One of these *hours*, my dear Clarinda blest me with yesternight

'One well spent hour,
In such a tender circumstance for Friends,
Is better than an age of common time.'
Thomson[24]

As mobility returned, Burns clearly had one aim in mind, that of full-blown love and sexual intercourse with Clarinda as was his goal with every woman who appealed to him, but with Nancy McLehose it was not as easy as that: religion and reputation always intervened. Her situation in Edinburgh was always precarious since her husband paid her no money, and she was dependent on her cousin for financial support and on her friends for comfort in her loneliness. It is not known whether Burns ever did manage to have sexual intercourse with Nancy or not but the evidence suggests that he never managed to take her to bed.

In an attempt to break down her resistance Robert tried to make her

173

jealous during the first half of January. He had already mentioned another woman on 2 January, and when she passed his house on the 10th of the month without looking up to his window, he referred in a letter to two other women, one of them Jean Armour for whom Clarinda had no grounds for jealousy, and the other Peggy Chalmers:

> I told you I had but one Male friend. I have but two female. I should have a third, but she is surrounded by the blandishments of Flattery and Courtship. Her I register in my heart's core – by Peggy Chalmers. Miss Nimmo can tell you how divine she is. She is worthy of a place in the same bosom with my Clarinda. That is the highest compliment I can pay her.[25]

Clarinda showed not the slightest jealousy, or else was extremely cunning in concealing it. 'I am proud of being compared to Miss Chalmers,' she replied off-handedly. 'I have heard how amiable she is. She cannot be more so than Miss Nimmo: why do ye not register her also?'[26]

The position might have been very different had Clarinda really been a widow, but James McLehose was inconveniently alive and well, first in London and then in Jamaica. Robert referred to her several times as a widow, but Nancy herself never forgot her status was deserted wife. She was prepared to indulge in a vicarious sexual relationship on paper or even verbally when they were alone together: perhaps she'd even allow some fondling; however, full physical love was barred – but only just. On Sunday, 13 January, she confessed: 'I will not deny it, Sylvander, last night was one of the most exquisite I ever experienced . . . But, though our enjoyment did not lead beyond the limits of virtue, yet today's reflections have not been altogether unmixed with regret.'[27]

And again a fortnight later:

> For many years, have I sought for a male friend, endowed with sentiments like yours; one who could love me with tenderness, yet unmixed with selfishness; who could be my friend, companion, protector, and who would die sooner than injure me. I sought – but I sought in vain! Heaven has I hope sent me this blessing in my Sylvander. Whatever weaknesses may cleave to Clarinda, her heart is not to blame: whatever it may have been by nature, it is unsullied by art. If she dare dispose of it – last night can leave you at no loss to guess the man.[28]

*'last night can leave you at no loss to guess the man'* . . . Sylvander and Clarinda had reached something so close to sexual intercourse on that night, which must have left Burns in agony. But always she held back. She made it worse on this occasion by sending him a little poem she had composed some years earlier, while out walking on Bruntsfield Links, *To a Blackbird Singing in a Tree*:

> Go on, sweet bird, and soothe my care,
> Thy cheerful notes will hush despair;
> Thy tuneful warbling, void of art,
> Thrill sweetly through my aching heart.
> Now choose thy mate, and fondly love,
> And all the charming transport prove;
> Those sweet emotions all enjoy,
> Let Love and Song thy hours employ;
> Whilst I, a love-lorn exile, live,
> And rapture nor receive nor give.
> Go on, sweet bird, and soothe my care
> Thy cheerful notes will hush despair.[29]

Burns took her poem and, in his own words, pruned its wings a little, and in due course it also appeared in *The Scots Musical Museum*. No wonder Clarinda's lover was driven nearly to distraction.

Throughout January he felt desperately low, suffering from his old 'hypochondria' as troubles gathered around him. The only light that shone brightly in a very dark world was Clarinda. His leg was mending, it is true, but complete mobility was returning only very slowly and he felt far from well. He was producing very little verse other than songs and that wretched elegy to Lord President Dundas, which cost a lot of creative effort and won him little thanks. The songs were occupying him more and more, and the second volume of Johnson's *Scots Musical Museum* was about to appear with around forty of his songs in it. But there were no 'big' poems any more . . . no *Cotter's Saturday Night*, no *Twa Dogs*, no *Jolly Beggars*; not even a satire on the hypocrites in the Kirk. Burns had lost much of his creativity, which is hardly surprising given the turmoil his heart was in and the many problems which were turning him mad with worry. Edinburgh life had lost its sparkle, with Creech proving as wily as ever and his application to join the Excise Service causing problems. The news from Mauchline was worse than ever too.

Gilbert was in ever-deepening financial trouble at Mossgiel and Jean Armour, now more than six months pregnant, had been thrown out by her father. Robert wrote to Ayr to arrange for Gilbert to be given a few pounds if needed, but realized that because of these problems he would have to return to Ayrshire as soon as his health allowed. All his efforts to open the door into the Excise Service at last brought him a painful interview with a Mrs Stewart, a friend of Miss Nimmo, who questioned him like a child and cross-examined him on the inscription he had scratched on the window in Stirling the previous summer. He told Clarinda he was so angry he almost gave up the Excise idea altogether. 'Why will Great people not only deafen us with their fastidious pomp, but they must also be so very dictatorially wise?' he raged.[30]

Robert's health began to break down during the latter half of January as a result of all his problems. On the evening of the 20th he got paper and pen out to write to Clarinda, but couldn't. 'The impertinence of fools has joined with a return of an old indisposition, to make me good for nothing today,' he began, but after a few lines, he broke off, 'I can no more, Clarinda: I can scarce hold up my head: but I am happy you don't know it, you would be uneasy.' By morning he felt well enough to continue although he still had 'a horrid languor' in his spirits. He needed comfort and asked anxiously if he could depend on her friendship for life.[31]

Once more he turned to his old friends whom he had neglected of late: he wrote to Mrs Dunlop for the first time in two months. It was a short letter – probably as much as he felt able to write – in which he poured out his troubles.

'After six weeks' confinement, I am beginning to walk across the room. They have been six horrible weeks, anguish and low spirits made me unfit to read, write, or think.' He resorted to the favourite military metaphor and told her he had wished a hundred times that he could resign life as an officer resigns a commission. 'Though I do want bravery for the warfare of life, I could wish, like some other soldiers, to have as much fortitude or cunning as to dissemble or conceal my cowardice,' he told her. He intended to leave Edinburgh as soon as he was able, probably about the middle of the following week, he said, and he hoped to call at Dunlop House on his way back to Mauchline.[32]

He also wrote to Peggy Chalmers the following day, in much better spirits again, telling her he had quarrelled with Creech, but had the promise of immediate settlement. But Creech was to renege on his promise once again. Although he had been in such low spirits only a day before, Robert was in full flow again: 'God have mercy on me! a poor damned, incautious, duped, unfortunate fool! The sport, the miserable victim, of rebellious pride; hypochondriac imagination, agonizing sensibility, and bedlam passions!'[33] He told her he had had a hair's breadth escape in love lately, too, but 'got off heart-whole, "waur fleyd* than hurt."'

He had not escaped as lightly as he thought: he was still as passionately in love as ever, still hoping that one of these nights Clarinda would allow him into her bed, but Clarinda always said, 'Talk not of love'. Robert obeyed, which speaks volumes for the depth of his love for her. She also begged him not to breathe a word about their correspondence to a living soul, or to do anything to give their secret assignations away. She lived in fear that he might be seen and begged him not to take a sedan chair and to come late. 'A chair is so uncommon a thing in our neighbourhood, it is apt to raise speculation; but they are all asleep by ten,' she warned him. That was of little comfort to him if he was allowed to stay late but barred from sharing her bed. Every visit ended in an agony of frustration. He released his feelings one night in February by seducing another Edinburgh servant girl, Jenny Clow, with the inevitable consequences – that he fathered yet another illegitimate child. Fortunately, Clarinda was to know nothing of that for some time.

On 7 February he told John Richmond in Mauchline of his utter frustration with Edinburgh. 'Every thing going on as usual – houses building, bucks strutting, ladies flaring, blackguards skulking, whores leering, &c. in the old way.' But Ayrshire was no better: he had seen John Smith, another of the old Mauchline crew lately, and his news had not been good. 'I have heard melancholy enough accounts of Jean: 'tis an unlucky affair,' he told Richmond.[34] The need to return to the West was becoming more urgent than ever, yet he was hemmed in by his slow recovery and Clarinda's coyness. More and more she began to parade her religious convictions before him. They were made more inconvenient by being both deep and sincere, but he patiently listened to them and responded with his own views. One of her closest friends, and indeed a father-confessor to her, was her minister, the Reverend John Kemp, of the Tolbooth Church, where she worshipped regularly. Kemp was fifteen years older than Nancy, but he ruled her moral life and that of other women in his congregation with that brand of Calvinism that Robert thought he had left behind in Mauchline. Burns did not like Kemp, and with good cause, for the Tolbooth Kirk minister was a hypocrite. His personal life appeared godly enough in 1788, but he had three wives (two of them earls' daughters) and became involved in a huge scandal when

*more frightened

Sir James Colquhoun cited him in a divorce action. Kemp was only saved from disgrace because both he and Sir James died just before the action came to court. In Burns' more aggressive days, a couple of years before the Clarinda affair, Kemp would have been the subject of a well-deserved holy satire, which would have entertained Edinburgh where he was not a favourite among the great or the good.

As the affair with Clarinda became more passionate, the barrier of religion was lowered constantly – always by Nancy – and Burns responded with comments on what he called 'your darling topic.'[35] Dr Kemp remained an avenging angel, hovering in the background. On Sunday, 3 February, Clarinda excelled herself, sending Robert screeds on a sermon she had just heard Kemp deliver on the text: 'Let me live the life of the righteous, and my latter end be like His.' It might have been delivered specially for Nancy: she commented to Robert that it contained her principles, and the foundation of all her immortal hopes, 'elegantly delivered'. The point of the sermon was brought home more sharply by a chance meeting with her mother's sober-sided cousin, Lord Dreghorn, who passed her on his way to the High Kirk of St Giles. He was dressed in his new judge's robes and he cut her dead because of her friendship with Burns. Nancy was convinced that the minister was right to keep her from straying on to wicked paths.

Little more than a week after this sermon, Kemp sent Clarinda a letter, which unfortunately has been lost, but its gist was to reprove her for her behaviour and warn her to break off contact with Burns. Nancy blamed Miss Nimmo for betraying her, but in the light of her own little 'confessional' talks with Kemp and that apt sermon on the righteous life, it could well have been Clarinda herself who let the secret slip out. She sent the letter to Burns, who was so furious he kept a group of friends with whom he was about to dine, waiting while he replied:

My Dearest Clarinda,

I make a numerous dinner party wait me while I read yours and write this. Do not require that I should cease to love you, to adore you in my soul – 'tis to me impossible – your peace and happiness are to me dearer than my soul. Name the terms on which you wish to see me, to correspond with me, and you have them – I must love, pine, mourn and adore in secret – this you must not deny me.

. . . I have not patience to read the puritanic scrawl – Vile Sophistry! – Ye heavens! thou God of nature! thou Redeemer of mankind! ye look down with approving eyes on a passion inspired by the purest flame, and guarded by truth, delicacy and honour: but the half-inch soul of an unfeeling, cold-blooded, pitiful presbyterian bigot, cannot forgive any thing above his dungeon bosom and foggy head.

Farewell! I'll be with you to-morrow evening – and be at rest in your mind – I will be yours in the way you think most to your happiness! I dare not proceed – I love, and will love you, and will with joyous confidence approach the throne of the Almighty Judge of men, with your dear idea, and will despise the scum of sentiment and the mist of sophistry.

Sylvander[36]

But he did read Kemp's letter, and sat down at midnight 'while preparing for a sleepless night' to write her a second letter:

I have read over your friend's haughty, dictatorial letter: you are only answerable to your God, in such a manner. Who gave any fellow-creature of yours (a fellow-creature incapable of being your judge because not your Peer) a right to catechize, scold, undervalue, abuse and insult, wantonly and inhumanly, to insult you thus? . . . but though it were possible you could be still dearer to me – I would not even kiss your hand, at the expence of your conscience.[37]

Kemp's kind made Burns sick of Edinburgh; he was tired, too, of dunning and pestering Creech to no avail, anxious to decide between the farm or the Excise, and still worried about his future in general to the point that he felt he was good for nothing.

Even his poetry was suffering and when Mrs Dunlop criticized that albatross of an elegy of Lord President Dundas he exploded. 'I am sick of writing where my bosom is not strongly interested,' he replied. 'Tell me what you think of the following?' There, the *bosom* was perhaps a little interested. The poem he enclosed was *Clarinda, Mistress of my Soul*, which he had sent to Nancy a couple of weeks earlier with a little note saying he had carried it about in his pocket and thumbed it over all day:

> Clarinda, mistress of my soul,
> The measur'd time is run!
> The wretch beneath the dreary pole
> So marks his latest sun.

179

To what dark cave of frozen night
Shall poor Sylvander hie,
Depriv'd of thee, his life and light,
The sun of all his joy?

We part – but, by these precious drops
That fill thy lovely eyes,
No other light shall guide my steps
Till thy bright beams arise!

She, the fair sun of all her sex,
Has blest my glorious day;
And shall a glimmering planet fix
My worship to its ray?[38]

He told Mrs Dunlop that he was now due to leave Edinburgh on Saturday, 16 February, and once again said he hoped to call on her on his way to the West. He loved Clarinda as deeply as ever, so, as his time with her in Edinburgh grew short, letters flew between Potterrow and St James's Square. On the 14th, the day after his midnight fulminations against Dr Kemp, he sent her two letters. 'Clarinda,' he told her, 'matters are grown very serious with us; then seriously hear me . . . :'

I met you, my dear Clarinda, by far the first of womankind, at least to me; I esteemed, I lov'd you at first sight, both of which attachments you have done me the honor to return; the longer I am acquainted with you, the more innate, amiableness and worth I discover in you . . . I esteem you, I love you, as a friend; I admire you, I love you, as a Woman, beyond any one in all the circle of Creation: I know I shall continue to esteem you, to love you; to pray for you – nay to pray for *myself* for *your* sake . . .[39]

The following day he promised: 'I am yours, Clarinda, for life', and reassured her he would be with her about eight o'clock, 'probably for the last time till I return to Edinburgh.' At the same time he advised her to admit nothing to Kemp or 'the other gentleman' (possibly cousin William Craig), who were still trying to discover more details of her romance. 'As to their jealousy and spying, I despise them,' he ended.[40]

On the 17th he was still in the capital and said in a letter to Peggy Chalmers that he was due to depart the following morning. He had decided against farming, and had settled for the Excise Service. He said, 'It is immediate bread, and though poor in comparison of the last eighteen months of my existence, 'tis luxury in comparison of all my preceding life: besides, the commissioners are some of them my acquaintances, and all of them my firm friends.'[41] On Monday morning, 18 February he left Edinburgh for Glasgow on his way to Mauchline. In his luggage were 'twa wee sarkies',* a present from Clarinda for Jean Armour's little son at Mossgiel. Clarinda felt she could behave generously towards the woman she considered no rival for the Poet's affections.

*two little shirts

CHAPTER ELEVEN

# *Farthing Taper . . . Meridian Sun*

The wives drew up their coats did kilt,
And through the streets so clean did stilt,
Some at the door fell wi' a pelt
    Maist broke their leg,
To see the Hen, poor wanton jilt!
    Lay her fourth egg.

A scurrilous poem by Burns' enemy, Saunders Tait,
on the birth of Jean Armour's second set of twins[1]

When he stepped down from the coach in Glasgow that Monday evening
Robert found a most agreeable surprise awaiting him – there at the Black
Bull Inn was Captain Richard Brown, his old friend from Irvine and the
flax-dressing days. The reunion was as joyful as it was unexpected. Robert
knew Brown's ship was in Greenock at the time, preparing to leave for
the West Indies, and he had written from Edinburgh on Friday, 15
February, to apologize for not having time to come to Greenock, but
suggested a meeting in Glasgow on Tuesday, or somewhere in the West
during the fortnight he expected to stay there. Brown did better: he
travelled to Glasgow to wait for his friend.

Burns' young brother, William, was there also, and the three settled
down to a night's carousal, but first Robert had to send off a hurried note
to his Clarinda. The letter dated 'Glasgow, Monday even: 9 o'clock', told
her that, unlike Newtonian Philosophy, in which the nearer objects were
the stronger was the attractive force, 'every milestone that marked my
progress from Clarinda, awakened a keener pang of attachment to her.'
He was still troubled about those Edinburgh curmudgeons who had been
sniffing out the affair between them, and tried to comfort her. 'How do
you feel, my Love? Is your heart ill at ease? I fear it. God forbid that these
Persecutors should harass that Peace which is more precious to me than
my own.' He told her he had just met Captain Brown and his brother,

and was off to spend the evening with them: 'Adieu, Clarinda! I am just going to propose your health by way of grace drink.'[2]

He had missed the post, so he wrapped his note in a dozen sheets of blank paper and sent it as a parcel by a carriage which was about to leave.

The evening's reunion was just the start of a triumphal progress, meeting old friends, drinking and reminiscing with them all the way to Mauchline where he arrived after fighting his way 'thro' Paisley and Kilmarnock against those old powerful foes of mine, the Devil, the World, and the Flesh.'[3] Two much-enjoyed days were spent at Dunlop House as well, where he met Mrs Dunlop and her daughters, one of whom was painting a picture of his muse, Coila, and the other who talked poetry to him. The first opportunity he had to dash off another letter to Clarinda was at Kilmarnock on Friday, the 22nd, just as he was about to set out on the last leg of the journey home. 'In about two hours I shall present your "twa wee sarkies" to the little fellow,' he told her. He assured Nancy she was ever present with him, and looked forward to that happy hour when he would be with her again: this would be in two weeks after he had spent some time at Mauchline and visited Dumfries.[4]

But he was not at Mossgiel in a couple of hours to hand over Clarinda's present to his son. In another letter, written the following day, the 23rd, he informed Clarinda, 'I have just now, My ever dearest Madam, delivered your kind present to my sweet, little Bobbie, who I find a very fine fellow.'[5] On the 24th he wrote to Richard Brown and he stated quite clearly that he arrived at his brother's *only yesterday*. He may have stayed over at Kilmarnock that night, we do not know, but it is much more likely that he called in at Tarbolton Mill, where Jean, in the last stages of her pregnancy, was living with his very good friends, William Muir and his wife, and spent the night there. Was Burns for once being economical with the truth when he said to Clarinda in the letter written on the 23rd:

Now for a little news that will please you. I, this morning as I came home, called on a certain woman. I am disgusted with her; I cannot endure her! I, while my heart smote me for the prophanity [sic], tried to compare her with my Clarinda: 'twas setting the expiring glimmer of a farthing taper beside the cloudless glory of the meridian sun. Here was tasteless insipidity, vulgarity of soul, and mercenary fawning; there, polished good sense, heaven-born genius, and the most generous, the most delicate, the most tender Passion. I have done with her, and she with me.[6]

If, as he told Clarinda, he had called on 'a certain woman' that very morning on his way home, he could hardly have had time to find Jean so totally disagreeable as to trigger this intemperate outburst. It is understandable that the kitchen of Tarbolton Mill might appear a poor enough place after Edinburgh drawing-rooms; Jean may have fawned sickeningly in her joy and relief at having him home with her; the Muirs may have appeared rough enough, too, after Clarinda's fine manners; but he hardly had time to make a judgement as absolute as the one he passed on to Clarinda. It could not be that he himself felt superior, for even in Edinburgh, he had remained proud of his peasant origins. Nor had he acquired much of a social veneer, otherwise he would not have made the gaffes of etiquette for which Mrs Dunlop criticized him after he visited her. Yet here he was, repelled by Jean Armour, within an hour or two of meeting her again.

This all may have been largely 'talk' for Clarinda's benefit because Nancy McLehose was clinging to him in spite of the fact that she was not free to marry him and certainly had no intention of compromising herself by giving him the sexual gratification he craved. Robert was still deeply upset by the fact that Dr Kemp continued to pester Nancy, and on his arrival at Mossgiel had found a letter waiting to tell him of a visit which someone unnamed, but probably Kemp, had made to Potterrow on Tuesday, 19 February:

> Mr — [probably Kemp] has just left me, after half an hour's most pathetic conversation . . . I expressed my thanks for his call, but he told me, it 'was merely to hide the change in his friendship from the world.' Think how I was mortified: I was, indeed; and affected so, as hardly to restrain tears. He did not name you; but spoke in terms that showed plainly he knew.[7]

Rage and frustration at this mistreatment of Clarinda probably helped to drive Burns to write that 'farthing taper' letter, but there is really no excuse for the way he treated Jean. Yet, while behaving so badly towards Armour in one way, he was doing the right thing by her in another. He took her back to Mauchline, reconciled her with her mother, and found her somewhere of her own to live while she awaited her confinement, which was due early in March. Tradition has it that he rented an upstairs room and kitchen for Jean in a house belonging to his friend, John Mackenzie, the Mauchline doctor, but more likely he took only a single apartment in the house, which was situated in the Back Wynd just over the road from Nance Tinnock's pub. Back Wynd is now known as Castle Street and the house where Jean settled is a Burns Museum. It was a clever move to take accommodation in the doctor's house in Mauchline since that brought Jean close to her family and friends, and it meant she could have all the medical attention she would need when her time came. He bought her a mahogany bed, and gave her enough money to buy whatever she required.

Burns, with so much to arrange, had little time to write to Clarinda as often as he had promised, let alone to be sure to say what she would want to hear in his letters. Before he had even reached Mossgiel Nancy was seated at her desk in Edinburgh, reprimanding him: 'I wish you had given me a hint, my dear Sylvander, that you were to write me only once in a week,' she scolded.[8] Absence made Clarinda more demanding, yet Robert was finding it impossible to keep up with the promises he had made so easily in Edinburgh when he had little else to do but write love notes to her or spend time with her in secret. In Mauchline many matters were pressing in on him, and consequently he did not write a single letter to Nancy between 23 February and 2 March. She was not pleased. On 5 March, she told him tartly, 'I fear, Sylvander, you overvalue my generosity; for, believe me, it will be some time ere I can cordially forgive you the pain your silence has caused me!'[9]

He told Clarinda in his letter of 23 February that he intended to leave for Dumfries to look at Patrick Miller's farms the following day – but had no hopes for taking one. ''Tis merely out of Compliment to Mr Miller,' he wrote, 'for I know the Excise must be my lot.'[10] But he did not leave Mauchline as planned, and there is no record of any reason for his delay; it seems likely that it was simply because he was fully occupied with making arrangements for Jean – but he could not tell Nancy McLehose that.

In his heart he was not keen to return to farming after a year living the life of a celebrated poet in Edinburgh. He also felt uneasy about his own judgement on farming matters: hitherto he had always had his father and brother behind him to back up decisions. So he asked John Tennant of Glenconner, an experienced farmer and a very old family friend, to accompany him when he rode off to Dumfries to look at Ellisland Farm on the Dalswinton estate just a few miles north of Dumfries. Ellisland was set in lovely countryside, beside the River Nith just across the water from Dalswinton itself. It stood high, giving beautiful vistas across Nithsdale, and although it was still only the end of February, it must have looked deceptively beautiful as he and Tennant walked over its land. Glenconner thought it a fine farm in spite of the fact that the soil was exhausted and very stony, and it did not even have a farmhouse where Burns could live. Tennant was of the opinion that it could be a good bargain. Robert's farmer's mind was doubtful, but his poet's eye urged the canny mind to see the best in it. Any doubts he had were dispelled by John Tennant as they discussed the matter while they rode back to Ayrshire, and by the time they reached Cumnock on the way home, Robert had virtually decided he could succeed as a farmer. At Cumnock he wrote to the neglected Nancy McLehose to tell her about it. 'I am thinking my farming scheme will yet hold,' he wrote, but asked her to keep quiet about it for the time being.[11]

Much of the following day was occupied in letter-writing for there was much to be settled. First he contacted Patrick Miller, enclosing a document giving Tennant's opinion of Ellisland, and setting out Burns' own ideas about the state of the farm and the conditions under which he might lease it. He suggested that as the land was so exhausted, the tenancy might run from Martinmas (the end of November) at an initial rent of £50 for three years with additions thereafter. 'I shall be in Edinburgh the beginning of next week, when I shall wait on you,' he told Miller.[12]

His next letter was to his old Edinburgh landlord, William Cruikshank, for he could not resist passing the news of Ellisland on to him, despite all the secrecy he had spoken of in Nancy's letter the day before. He had not quite made up his mind yet between the Excise and farming, but soon would he said. 'I have the two plans of life before me; I shall balance them to the best of my judgement; and fix on the most eligible.' He confirmed that he would be in Edinburgh the following week, although his 'unlucky knee' was worse, probably as a result of all the walking around Ellisland.[13]

He sent a third letter later that day, to Robert Ainslie, although he had told Cruikshank he did not intend to write to Ainslie until tomorrow. By now his mind was pretty well made up to return to farming. The first paragraph was very similar to what he had written to Cruikshank, but he appeared rather more confident about the farm. 'On the whole, if I find Mr Miller in the same favourable disposition as when I saw him last, I shall in all probability turn farmer,' he said.

Suddenly the letter turned to the subject of Jean, and Burns let himself go to this friend with whom he had shared many secrets in the past. It was an extraordinary outpouring even to a raunchy young friend who had been a bosom companion on many sexual adventures:

I have been through sore tribulation and under much buffeting of the Wicked One since I came to this country. Jean I found banished, like a martyr – forlorn destitute and friendless: All for the good old cause. I have reconciled her to her fate, and I have reconciled her to her mother. I have taken her a room. I have taken her to my arms. I have given her a mahogany bed. I have given her a guinea, and I have f—d her till she rejoiced with joy unspeakable and full of glory. But, as I always am on every occasion, I have been prudent and cautious to an astonishing degree. I swore her privately and solemnly never to attempt any claim on me as a husband, even though anybody should persuade her she had such a claim (which she had not), neither during my life nor after my death. She did all this like a good girl, and I took the opportunity of some dry horse-litter, and gave her such a thundering scalade* that electrified the very marrow of her bones. Oh, what a peacemaker is a guid weel-willy pintle! It is the mediator, the guarantee, the umpire, the bond of union, the solemn league and covenant, the plenipotentiary, the Aaron's rod, the Jacob's staff, the prophet Elisha's pot of oil, the Ahasuerus' Sceptre, the sword of mercy, the philosopher's stone, the Horn of Plenty, and Tree of Life between Man and Woman.[14]

For two centuries Burnsians have not known what to make of this incredible outburst, or have simply pretended it never happened. Hans Hecht speaks for all by summing it up as revealing 'such downright, elementary, unsurpassable vulgarity that one can understand the editors who have covered the greater part of it with the mantle of brotherly love.'[15] Any writer on Burns will say 'Amen' to the comment of Ian McIntyre in his *Dirt and Deity; A Life of Robert Burns*: 'There is no period in his short life when it is so hard to read Burns as in those early spring months of 1788.' A second 'Amen to that' will follow McIntyre's judgement: 'Nor is there a time at which it is so difficult to observe his behaviour with any degree of sympathy.'[16]

DeLancey Ferguson offered the explanation that 'it is more than possible that he [Burns] was talking brazenly for Ainslie's edification',[17] but of course neither Ferguson nor anyone else believed that excused him. Immature bragging, as it has also been called, is not sufficient excuse either.

Perhaps a perceptive woman ought to be allowed a comment on this vulgar bravado. In her *Life of Burns*, Catherine Carswell suggests that Robert was reacting to Clarinda's reproaches and nagging about his negligence in the usual aggressive manner he adopted in response to any criticism. On his return from Dumfries on 2 or 3 March, he received her

*attack (corruption of escalade)

187

letter of 22 February, in which she chastized him for not writing, and peremptorily told him, 'I have ever found my highest demands of kindness accomplished: nay, even my fondest wishes, not gratified only, but anticipated! To what, then, can I attribute your not writing me one line since Monday?' This was the talk of grand women in the rarefied atmosphere of Edinburgh drawing-rooms, and Robert had been accustomed in recent days to the down-to-earth, passive docility of country women. Comparison between the two and Clarinda's bleating caused a violent revulsion in the Poet, or so Carswell believed.

'Next day he wrote, not to Clarinda, but to Ainslie, asking him to tell the lady that he had written to her four times and that she was the only person to whom he had written at all,' wrote Mrs Carswell. 'His mood led him to add, for Ainslie's information, an account of that same meeting with Jean which he had formerly described to Clarinda in more seemly but less truthful terms . . . If Ainslie were to give Mrs McLehose some gentle indications of reality, so much the better for all concerned.' Ainslie had moved in immediately to comfort Nancy after Robert left, and it is interesting that she told Robert on 5 March that 'Mr Ainslie called just now to tell me he had heared [*sic*] from you,'[18] – presumably the notorious letter written two days previously, but how much of its contents did he reveal to her?

Ignoring all the blind eyes that have been turned to the horse-litter incident over the years, and taking full account of the excuses, sympathy, or just plain disgust which his vulgarity has generated, the letter still makes one's blood run cold. Factually, it is accurate about the care he took to find somewhere for Jean to live, to furnish the apartment, give her money and reconcile her with her mother, so there is no reason to doubt the truth of the remainder – the horse-litter scalade, the extraction of a promise never to lay claim on him as her husband, and the sexual intercourse all happened. Jean was once again carrying twins, neither of whom survived, and some people have blamed this on the sexual intercourse. We are uncertain exactly when or where the episode took place, or if indeed every act he spoke of happened at the same time – he may have telescoped the events of several days together, just as he talked of settling Jean in the house, buying her a bed, making peace with Mrs Armour and giving her money sound as if they all happened together. This seems to me the most likely explanation of the letter – Burns was simply giving his friend a graphic account of all the events which happened over several days. He is unlikely to have written the letter to Clarinda if he had made his peace with Jean. It reads like an immediate reaction when he first met the tearful girl on his arrival home.

The most likely location was Tarbolton Mill since there would be no horse-litter to hand in Mauchline, so one must conclude that it took place immediately after his arrival or very soon thereafter. It is possible to reconstruct the scene: they went to the stable to discuss matters in private since there would not be a lot of privacy in a small farmhouse. Jean must have been frantic and wept and begged him to stand by her and help her, which would be enough to send the unsure, insecure Burns into a rage. He always reacted furiously whenever he was put on the defensive, and he threw the first thing that came to hand at her, which was the horse-litter. Dry dung never injured anyone, as anybody brought up on a farm can confirm, but it would have terrified Jean into promising never to lay claim to him as her husband. Then he made his peace in the only way he knew (apart from writing a poem) by offering sexual satisfaction. Some women with whom I have discussed this letter have expressed an opinion that Jean may have been a willing party to the sexual intercourse, which was the sealing of the peace between them.

Why did Jean accept this brutality so meekly? We must remember that women of the lower classes in those times were brought up to accept what any man, or life itself, threw at them, literally or figuratively. Jean's condition, a few weeks away from childbirth, terrified, and without friends or money, would make her doubly docile.

The most apparently callous aspect of the whole business was the effect that sexual intercourse, so close to confinement, might have had on the unborn children. Although medical opinion does not recommend sexual penetration during the weeks prior to confinement, there is not necessarily any medical risk in it other than that it might cause the woman's waters to break and thus make her go into premature labour. It could possibly be an unpleasant experience for a mother-to-be, but it need not necessarily be so, and it need not harm her.

Jean told John McDiarmid in Dumfries in 1825 that the second set of twins, both girls, were born on 3 March, in which case sex on the day Robert arrived at Tarbolton Mill places the intercourse roughly eleven days before her confinement. But the most recent research suggests that the twins were not born until about a week later, on 9 or 10 March, making the time lapse nearer to three weeks.[19]

Robert never mentioned his two little daughters who were born around this time, a silence which suggests that their deaths upset him considerably. On Sunday, the 3rd, when Jean was supposed to be giving birth, he was writing letters to Miller, Cruikshank, and that terrible one to Ainslie. Those he wrote in the days which followed give not the slightest indication that Jean had been delivered of her twins, and one indeed suggests the opposite.

On Wednesday 6 March, the morning after some 'savage hospitality' at a friend's house the previous evening left him 'sick – headache – low spirits – miserable – fasting, except for a draught of water or small beer', he wrote to Clarinda.[20] He wrote again the following day, when he also sent letters to Mrs Dunlop, Robert Muir in Kilmarnock, Gavin Hamilton, Willie Nicol and Richard Brown. Apart from the one to Nicol and his sea captain friend, these were not pleasant letters to write: he had to grovel to Mrs Dunlop about a social *faux pas* he had made by sending the present of a book to her daughter, which she would not allow her to accept. Then he had to tell Gavin Hamilton most reluctantly that he could not commit himself to stand guarantor for his brother in respect of a large sum of money, and he had to ask Muir about collecting some subscription money due for copies of the Edinburgh Edition of his poems. He informed Willie Nicol in Edinburgh that his mind was made up about the farm: 'If my offer to the Proprietor is accepted, I shall commence Farmer at Whitsunday . . . Poesy must be set aside for some time: my mind has been vitiated with idleness, and it will take a good deal of effort to habituate it to the routine of business.' He was due to leave for Edinburgh the following Monday, the 11th, but was uncertain how long he might remain in the capital. There was not a mention of the birth of the twins as one might have expected in a letter to his old companion of the Highland Tour, had they been born.

Sylvander and Clarinda were still bickering like children about how often each had written. In his Wednesday letter he pointed out that he had received only three from her against the five or six he had sent. He called a truce, but Nancy in the meantime stirred him up again by accusing him of overvaluing her generosity. 'I hope I can make every reasonable allowance for the hurry of business and dissipation,' she said self-righteously. 'Yet, had I been ever so engrossed, I should have found one hour out of the twenty-four to write you. No more of it: I accept your apologies; but am hurt that any should have been necessary betwixt us on such a tender occasion.' It made little difference to his temper that she went on to approve of his farming scheme as opposed to the Excise, which she had never felt good enough as a career for her Sylvander.[21]

In his reply, written with all those other letters on Thursday, 7 March, he snapped back:

Your future views are fix'd, and your mind in a settled routine. Could not you, my ever dearest Madam, make a little allowance for a man, after long absence, paying a short visit to a Country full of friends, relations, and early intimates? Cannot you guess, my Clarinda, what thoughts, what cares, what anxious forebodings, hopes and fears, must crowd the breast of the man of keen sensibility, when no less is on the tapis than his aim, his employment, his very existence thro' future life?[22]

This was not an apology, he told her, but a defence of himself. Robert was stung by Nancy's petulance, but he had not told her all: in fact he had said nothing to her of what really was *on the tapis*, if we interpret the last letter he wrote that day correctly. When he wrote to Richard Brown, still at Greenock waiting to sail, he used a very different tone in a letter larded with appropriate nautical metaphors:

I found Jean – with her cargo very well laid in; but unfortunately moor'd almost at the mercy of the wind and tide: I have towed her into convenient harbour where she may lie snug till she unload; and have taken the command myself – not ostensibly, but for a time, in secret. – I am gratified by your kind enquiries after her; as after all, I may say with Othello –

'Excellent wretch!
Perdition catch my soul but I do love thee!'[23]

This reveals much more than that Jean had not yet unloaded her cargo. '*I . . . have taken the command myself – not ostensibly, but for a time, in secret.*' Surely this can mean only one thing? Robert Burns had made up his mind to accept as his wife this girl whom he had continued to love in spite of all the other dear charmers who had flitted in and out of his life over the past two years, and especially Clarinda, the one who was still hoping to keep him at her beck and call.

Why had he taken this unexpected action? W.E. Henley, in the edition of Burns' poems published to mark the centenary of the Poet's death in 1896, claimed that old Mrs Armour would only be reconciled to her daughter on condition that Robert married her, and certainly Mary Armour would be reluctant to allow him to resume any contact with her daughter on any other condition.[24] But there were other reasons as simple as they were complex.

Again, it is worth looking at what a woman has to say on the subject, and Mrs Carswell speaks volumes on it:

He had rung down the curtain upon youth's 'bewitching levity,' and held it quite possible that he had also made his exit as a poet. With sublime realism he would let youth and poetry and pleasure go, and

191

would contest to his last fibre for what remained and was worth them all – his 'intrinsic dignity' as a man. To maintain this in the behaviour of life was the fundamental article of his creed, the single matter in which free will had the advantage over fickle fortune. By this in a world of prose he would stand. For this he would face the most odious realities – even those which were imposed, not by nature, but by the society in which he found himself.

To begin with, he would make public acknowledgment of his marriage with Jean Armour and take her as his wife . . . half mad with material worries, he had considered of this matter, seeing it as a sacrifice, yet finding no way out of it, as things were, but by the violation of his essential honesty and pride. For long, under the spell of success and his disgust with the Armours, he had felt free from Jean, except as regards financial and paternal responsibilities. But a further turn of the wheel now indicated her establishment as due alike to his manhood and to her nature. She was a woman clearly capable of happiness, and she was the only woman whose happiness was in his power.[25]

Mrs Carswell saw it also as making amends for failing Mary Campbell, a failure which never ceased to torture him, although it was only partly his fault. Mary and Jean belonged to his class and 'in turning from them to a woman of another class he would turn from himself.'

On a practical level, too, Robert realized that if he was returning to farming he needed a level-headed, active woman to help him. On farms in those days as well as the present women did much more than keep house: they also ran the dairy, attended to the poultry and assisted with outside work as necessary. A good healthy wife was an asset, even if she was seldom cherished as such a support ought to be. Clarinda would never make a farmer's wife even if the absent Mr McLehose were translated to that higher world and Nancy became available as a wife for the Poet. Despite his treatment of Jean Robert still cared deeply for her, as he demonstrated in hints in letters from time to time during his stay in Edinburgh, even when he was mad with love for Clarinda. In those few days while he was back in Mauchline, he realized that Ellisland would be impossible without her. 'Whether Clarinda guessed it or not,' said Carswell, 'there could be no Ellisland without a wife sooner or later, preferably sooner, and a working wife at that. If so, who but Jean?'

He was honest to the point of ungallantry when he wrote, several months after his marriage, to Peggy Chalmers, the girl who had turned him down, and whom he still respected and cared for:

Shortly after my last return to Ayrshire, I married 'my Jean.' This was not in consequence of the attachment of romance perhaps; but I had a long and much-loved fellow creature's happiness or misery in my determination, and I durst not trifle with so important a deposit. Nor have I any cause to repent it. If I have not got polite tattle, modish manners, and fashionable dress, I am not sickened and disgusted with the multiform curse of boarding-school affectation; and I have got the handsomest figure, the sweetest temper, the soundest constitution, and the kindest heart in the country.

What is more, he told Peggy, Jean believed him '*le plus bel esprit, et le plus honnête homme* in the universe'.[26]

Clarinda herself may unwittingly have driven him into the arms of Jean by her nagging and complaining, which he found just too much to cope with on top of the many other, more urgent matters on his mind. She was patronizingly cloying about little Robert and dismissive of Jean, telling Sylvander in one letter: 'I hope you have not forgotten to kiss the little cherub for me. Give him fifty, and think Clarinda blessing him all the while. I pity his mother sincerely, and wish a certain affair happily over.'[27] Catherine Carswell put her finger on the reason for that letter to Ainslie, and it may well have been that same annoyance that gave Robert the prod he needed to make up his mind to marry Jean.

His reasons overall were the need of a wife, pique at Clarinda's behaviour, compassion for Jean's situation, and love – love had remained a continuing thread through all the years of his association with Jean Armour, but not that brand of romantic, hands-off love that Clarinda was offering. Jean's love may have been earthy and ill-expressed, but it was profound, while his was a deep affection lit up by passions whenever he was with her. Now he acted on impulse as he did in all important things in his life: he needed a wife, and the ever-faithful Jean was there, waiting to bring him the stability and resolution he knew he would require as a farmer. Suddenly he realized that knowledge of literature was not what he needed, but the practical help and affection that Jean Armour had in abundance, and he took it. What he told the Dunlops about not 'dallying' with her happiness and misery was rationalization of a practical decision. Burns was doing the right thing, for the wrong reasons, but the important thing is that his action was based on love.

Marriage, however, lay somewhere in the future as Jean awaited her confinement during those early days of March. While she herself gave 3 March as the date, James Mackay gives '9 March or even as late as the following day' as the more probable date for her confinement. Mackay unearthed proof to support this in the Mauchline Burials Register, which are preserved at the Scottish Register House in Edinburgh: 'Page 304, headed "Burials 1788", has two identical entries of "Jean Armour's Child, unbaptised", one on 10 March and the other of 22 March.' No charge was made, which was the custom in the case of a still-born baby, or one who had not been baptized. Mackay added, 'Putting this matter in perspective, it should be noted that this page [of the Burial Register] records nineteen burials between 11 February and 11 May, and of these no fewer than seven were of unbaptized new-born infants.'[28]

It would appear, therefore, that one of Jean's daughters was still-born, and the other survived a few days, but was not baptized. In Scotland it was the custom for a child to be baptized as soon as possible after birth, and the only explanation possible is that Jean, grieving for her dead child and organizing its burial, was unable to arrange for the surviving baby to be christened. Robert was not there to stand by her, as he certainly would have done had he still been in Mauchline. He left for Edinburgh on Monday, 10 March, and the tragedy is that the babies must have been born only hours after his departure.

The 'scalade' with horse-litter and sexual intercourse so close to the twins' birth has been sugggested as a possibility for their deaths, but Professor J.A. Raeburn, currently Professor of Clinical Genetics at the University of Nottingham, offers another possibility. Professor Raeburn has had a major interest in the genetic disorder cystic fibrosis for three decades. In the course of this work, he has studied the family trees of Burns and Jean Armour and, so far as is possible, of the Poet's other offspring. Robert Burns and Jean Armour had nine children in all, two sets of twins born before their marriage was regularized (three of whom died at birth or in early infancy probably from some kind of respiratory infection), and five born after they were married. Two of these five legitimate children, Elizabeth and Maxwell, died as young children. All the children born to other women (with the exception of 'Highland Mary's' baby, if indeed she ever had a child by the Poet) lived beyond infancy.

Professor Raeburn has conjectured that Robert and Jean might both have been carriers of the cystic fibrosis gene, and, if so, their children would have been at quite high risk of having a double dose of the cystic fibrosis gene. In the eighteenth century this would have been fatal at a very young age, but the carriers themselves would be totally healthy. Professor Raeburn regarded this as a good story to illustrate his lectures until one day a member of his audience, a woman who had a son with cystic fibrosis, approached him and said that her father was descended from Robert Burns' family and that with an affected son she was a known cystic fibrosis carrier. Could it be that her gene derived from Burns' side of the family?

Clearly much more evidence would be needed to substantiate or refute such a theory, but it could be done. A sample of Burns family descendants could be compared with a 'controlled' sample from the population at large, or genetic material from the Poet – a preserved hair plus its roots for example – could be tested. Professor Raeburn believes that the first form of test could be achieved by using a computerized register of Burns' living descendants which exists in Arbroath. In the course of his researches he hopes one day to be able to follow up this interesting theory for the explanation of the deaths of several of Jean Armour's children at such an early age.

After Burns left Mauchline on 10 March 1788, unaware of the tragedy that was unfolding around Jean, he collected money due to him for copies of the Edinburgh Edition, then rode to Glasgow to pick up some books from Dunlop and Wilson's bookshop in Trongate for Clarinda. He was back in Edinburgh by Wednesday morning, 12 March. Although consumed by anger against Creech and greatly preoccupied with his farming arrangements, he sat down and wrote to Clarinda immediately. He saw her that evening and the following day, when he also met Patrick Miller to agree final details of the Ellisland lease.

He was to take the farm from June 1788, on a 76-year lease (with breaks each nineteen years) at £50 a year for the first three years and £70 thereafter. Miller was to pay £300 towards the farmhouse which Burns was to build. As he told Peggy Chalmers on 14 March:

Yesternight I compleated [*sic*] a bargain with Mr Miller, of Dalswinton, for the farm of Ellisland, on the banks of the Nith, between five and six miles above Dumfries. I begin at Whitsunday to build a house, drive lime, &c. and heaven be my help! for it will take a strong effort to bring my mind into the routine of business, I have discharged all the army of my former pursuits, fancies and pleasures; a motley host![29]

The will to succeed was there just as it had been at Mossgiel when he and his brother took that farm over.

Robert was still writing to Clarinda as frequently as ever, but somehow the passion had waned: he had not told her of his decision about Jean of course – to do so would be even more difficult than telling Mrs Dunlop, which he was to find hard enough. He was not being exactly honest with Nancy, telling her in his letter of Friday evening, 14 March: 'The first thing I did was to thank the Divine Disposer of events, that he has had such happiness in store for me as the connexion I have with you.' They had discussed the fact that he would have to leave Edinburgh, and, using a mixture of the second and third persons as he sometimes did in his letters to Clarinda, he reassured her that they would keep in touch:

> I have my dearest partner of my soul; Clarinda and I will make out our pilgrimage together. Wherever I am, I shall constantly let her know how I go on . . . what adventures I meet with. Will it please you, my love, to get, every week or, at least, every fortnight, a packet, two or three sheets, full of remarks, nonsense, news, rhymes and old songs?[30]

Robert never learnt for here he was again making promises he must have known he could never keep.

While he was considering farming, he had not dropped his application to be accepted for the Excise Service and, after he took the lease on Ellisland, he did not withdraw his application, but now considered it merely as a back-up in case the farm should fail. Clarinda, of course, in her snobbish, ladylike way did not approve of the Excise as a career for the Poet, in spite of the fact that the brother of her close friend, Miss Nimmo, was in the service. When Robert told her at the beginning of March that he was seriously thinking of opting for farming in preference to the Excise, she told him: 'I am happy that the farming scheme promises so well. There's no fickleness, my dear Sir, in changing for the better. I never liked the Excise for you; and feel a sensible pleasure in the hope of your becoming a sober, industrious farmer . . . The distance is the only thing I regret.'[31]

Originally Robert was to undertake his course of instruction for the Excise in Edinburgh, and on Monday, 14 March, he received an order to start. That same week, probably because he was such a celebrity, he was invited to dine with some important officials of the Excise, and with one of the Commissioners – in all probability Robert Graham of Fintry, who had been instrumental in securing a position in the Service for him. He decided that with all the preparations for taking over his farm, and the decision to marry Jean Armour (although he said nothing of that to anyone yet), it would make sense for him to be instructed on the Excise duties in Ayrshire, so he made good use of all the influence Graham of Fintry could exercise to ensure that this might be arranged.

During that week he was so busy he neglected poor Nancy. Therefore, he sent her a pair of wine glasses accompanied by some *Verses to Clarinda* by way of atonement.

> Fair Empress of the Poet's soul
>  And Queen of Poetesses,
> Clarinda, take this little boon,
>  This humble pair of glasses:
>
> And fill them up with generous juice,
>  As generous as your mind;
> And pledge them to the generous toast,
>  'The whole of human kind!'
>
> 'To those who love us!' second fill:
>  But not to those whom *we* love,
> Lest we love those who love not us!
>  A third – 'To thee and me, love!'[32]

On the same day, Monday, 17 March, he managed to meet her in spite of the fact that he had told her he would be too busy to visit Potterrow. They walked together that evening, and the following morning he told her, 'I thank you for all the happiness you bestowed on me yesterday. The walk – delightful; the evening – rapture. Do not be uneasy today, Clarinda; forgive me. I am in rather better spirits today, though I had but an indifferent night: care, anxiety, sat on my spirits.' He closed with the words, 'The Father of Mercies be with you, Clarinda! and every good thing attend you!'[33]

The wine glasses and poem turned out to be a farewell present, for then the correspondence virtually ended. By the time he left Edinburgh to return to Mauchline on 20 March, he still had not told Nancy about his marriage plans, and she probably learned nothing of them until Robert gave the news to Ainslie two months later. He kept the deaths of his babies to himself, too, which must have been difficult because he was always open-hearted about his children. On 20 March he told Richard Brown that the Creech affair 'with watching, fatigue, and a load of Care almost too heavy for my shoulders, have in some degree actually fever'd me.'[34] The 'load of Care' was probably the sad news from Mauchline.

Clarinda's biographer, Raymond Lamont Brown,[35] believes Nancy and Burns exchanged a few letters over the next year, but none of these can be traced now. However, we do know something of relations between them through Robert's drafts of his correspondence with Ainslie, who moved into Clarinda's life as soon as Robert moved out. Thus she was kept well informed of what was happening to the Poet. Unfortunately Ainslie's side of the correspondence does not exist, because he asked for his letters back after Burns' death and destroyed them.

It was very likely Ainslie who told the Poet that Jenny Clow, the servant girl he turned to when Clarinda was goading him on and then holding back, was pregnant. There is an intriguing aside in a letter to Ainslie on 30 June, a response to receiving first news of Jenny's pregnancy. 'I am vexed at that affair of the girl', Burns told his friend, but refused to say more because Ainslie was likely to move and he did not want to make further comment in a letter which might fall into the wrong hands.[36] Jenny Clow bore Robert a son towards the end of the year, who was named Robert Burns after his father. Although the Poet offered to take the child, she refused, but later took out a writ against him for the baby's maintenance. Burns asked Ainslie to find Jenny when he decided to come to town in four or five weeks to settle the matter.

What Ainslie knew, Clarinda also knew, so she must have been well aware of Robert's 'unfaithfulness' during their winter of love. Burns was already in trouble with Clarinda over a lawsuit involving Willie Nicol, and now the Jenny Clow affair was a terrible insult to her womanhood: she was affronted that, while he had been visiting her almost daily and calling her his ever-dear Clarinda, he could shamelessly take a servant girl to bed. But, worst of all, marrying Jean Armour made her so bitter that even a year after the event she warned Ainslie she did not want to see Burns while he was in Edinburgh sorting out the Clow business.

She forbade Robert to correspond again until he admitted his guilt, presumably over the Armour affair, but probably over Jenny Clow as well. He angrily refused. 'I have already told you, and I again aver it, that at the period of time alluded to, I was not under the smallest moral tie to Mrs B—.' he wrote. 'Was I to blame, Madam, in being the distracted victim of Charms which . . . no man ever approached with impunity? Had I seen the least glimmering of hope that these Charms could ever have been mine . . . but these are unavailing words.' He ended with a little piece of gallantry Clarinda must have found hard to resist: 'When I have regained your good opinion, perhaps I may venture to solicit your friendship; but be that as it may, the first of her Sex I ever knew, shall always be the object of my warmest good wishes.'[37]

They corresponded once or twice during the remainder of the Poet's life and Nancy's unhappy existence after the Edinburgh affair, but they met only once. Nancy's troubles mounted during 1788, with one of her sons dying, and the surgeons and lawyers in Glasgow cancelling her allowances because they had learned that her husband was doing well in the West Indies. It took letters from her cousin, Lord Craig to persuade McLehose to send her £50, and promise to pay for his son's education, but that was all the money she ever received from him and needless to say he reneged on the promise to fund his son's schooling. McLehose asked Nancy to join him in the West Indies, but she hesitated, the memories of his ill-treatment were still too vivid for her to trust him, and so she remained in Edinburgh for a further two years.

In 1790 Robert sent her a letter with a little poem, which began:

> Thine am I, my faithful Fair,
> Thine my lovely Nancy!
> Ev'ry pulse along my veins,
> Ev'ry roving fancy![38]

Some years later, when the poem was sent to George Thomson as a song for the *Select Collection of Original Scottish Airs*, Robert asked Thomson to change the name Nancy to Chloris, after Jean Lorimer, who was then his current charmer.

Clarinda kept in touch with the Poet, but remained bitter enough to tell him she intended to preserve his letters 'with a view, sooner or later, to expose them on the pillory of derision and rack of criticism.'[39] It gave her satisfaction towards the end of 1791 to write and tell him Jenny Clow was in poverty and dying, alone and without the necessities for life. She challenged him to help:

> In circumstances so distressing, to whom can she so naturally look for aid as to the father of her child, the man for whose sake she has suffered many a sad and anxious night, shut from the world, with no other companions than guilt and solitude. You have now an opportunity to evince you indeed possess those fine feelings you have delineated, so as to claim the just admiration of your country.[40]

Burns replied at once:

> Mrs M— tells me a tale of the poor girl's distress that makes my very heart weep blood. I . . . beg you, for Heaven's sake, to send a porter to the poor woman – Mrs M., it seems, knows where she is to be found – with five shillings in my name; and, as I shall be in Edinburgh on Tuesday first . . . make the poor wench leave a line for me . . . at Mr Mackay's White Hart Inn, Grassmarket . . . I would have taken my boy from her long ago, but she would never consent.[41]

In this same letter Burns also said, 'I shall do myself the very great pleasure to call for you when I come to town, and repay you the sum your goodness shall have advanced.' Nancy had by now made up her mind to join her husband in Jamaica, after going down to Leith to talk to a sea captain who had met James McLehose and assured her that he was a reformed character who wanted his wife back with him. On the strength of this assurance she made up her mind to return to him.

Did Burns ride all the way to Edinburgh to help Jenny Clow or to say farewell to Nancy McLehose before she sailed away for ever? He was indeed worried about the wisdom of Nancy's decision to rejoin McLehose and told her, 'I pray God my fears may be groundless.'

In Edinburgh he no doubt saw the dying mother of his child, and he called at Nancy McLehose's house at Potterrow, where the initial welcome may have been cool, but the visit turned into an evening as torrid as any during that winter of shared passion. She gave him a lock of her hair, which he had set in a ring, and in the weeks prior to her departure, he showered her with poems and letters in which she became his Clarinda again.

There was a *Lament for Mary, Queen of Scots*, with an accompanying letter likening the tragic queen's misfortune to their own; there were sad songs to mark her sailing away from him forever – *Thou Gloomy December* and *Behold the Hour, the Boat, Arrive*. And there was *Ae Fond Kiss*, that exquisite little song, which made all the suffering and heartache of the Sylvander-Clarinda affair worthwhile. *Ae Fond Kiss*, a gem among all Burns' songs, was worth all the others that derived from their relationship put together. It is so simple in its theme of parting and is expressed in language as plain as it is beautiful.

> Ae\* fond kiss, and then we sever!             \*one
> Ae farewell, and then forever!
> Deep in heart-wrung tears I'll pledge thee,
> Warring sighs and groans I'll wage thee.
> Who shall say that Fortune grieves him
> While the star of hope she leaves him?
> Me, nae cheerfu twinkle lights me,
> Dark despair around benights me.
>
> I'll ne'er blame my partial fancy:
> Naething could resist my Nancy!
> But to see her was to love her
> Love but her, and love for ever.
> Had we never lov'd sae kindly,
> Had we never lov'd sae blindly,
> Never met – or never parted –
> We had ne'er been broken-hearted.

Fare-thee-weel, thou first and fairest!
Fare-thee-weel, thou best and dearest!
Thine be ilka* joy and treasure,                    *every
Peace, Enjoyment, Love and Pleasure!
Ae fond kiss, and then we sever!
Ae fareweel, alas, for ever!
Deep in heart-wrung tears I'll pledge thee,
Warring sighs and groans I'll wage thee.[42]

On Robert's thirty-third birthday, 25 January 1792, Nancy sat down to tell him she was due to sail for Jamaica in exactly a week, and to give him 'the last advice of her, who could have lived or died with you!' He was to keep God's commandments, laugh no more at holy things or holy men, and re-read her letters and follow the religious tenets they contained. He must not write to her in Jamaica until she told him he could do so with safety – Nancy's fear of her husband's jealousy was well-founded on past experience.[43]

Clarinda sailed for Jamaica in the ship *Roselle* – by one of those ironies of fate, the very same ship in which Robert Burns should have sailed six years earlier. Up to the last moment she had qualms about the wisdom of going, especially when she received a letter from her husband, only the day before she sailed, urging her not to come because of the danger of yellow fever and slave riots. She arrived at Kingston, ill after a stormy voyage, to find no husband at the quay to meet her. He turned up three hours later, reeking of brandy, and created a scene because she had not heeded his advice to remain in Scotland. There was worse to come when she found he had taken a coloured mistress, whom he had no intention of giving up. Nancy stayed only a few weeks and arrived back in Edinburgh in early August with only £21 in her purse.[44]

Unaware of her return, Burns had been trying to get in touch with Clarinda through her friend, Mary Peacock in Edinburgh, in order to send her a copy of the fourth volume of *The Scots Musical Museum*, which had just been published. He wrote to Mary three times, but heard nothing for months. Eventually when Mary sent the news that Nancy was home again, the letter arrived while Robert was away in Ayrshire. Unfortunately it fell down behind a chest of drawers and was found only months later when the chest was moved. He wrote to Nancy, enclosing the book and asking her to write, but warned her that he wanted no more religious harangues:

But first, hear me! – No cold language, no prudential documents – I despise Advice & scorn Controul [*sic*]. . . If you send me a page

201

baptised in the font of sanctimonious Prudence – By Heaven, Earth & Hell, I will tear it into atoms![45]

He sent only one more letter to his Clarinda (for she remained Clarinda always), and never saw her again. He found corresponding with her difficult now. 'When I take up the pen, Recollection ruins me. Ah! my ever dearest Clarinda! – Clarinda? – What a host of Memory's tenderest offspring crown on my fancy at that sound!' He still cared enough for Nancy to name her when his friends called for a toast to a married lady, but he simply called her 'Mrs Mack' then. Her real name had never passed his lips even to the most intimate friends, he told her. Sitting alone at an inn in Castle Douglas now, he raised his wine glass to her with a 'most ardent wish for your happiness.'

'I have been rhyming little of late,' he told her, but the two pieces he enclosed were miserable scraps, both epitaphs to his association with Maria Riddell, another love which had gone wrong:

> How cold is that bosom which Folly once fired!
>   How pale is that cheek where the rouge lately glisten'd!
> How silent that tongue which the echoes oft tired!
>   How dull is that ear which to flatt'ry so listen'd![46]

They were never in touch again. What a pity he had not left his love for Clarinda to die with *Ae Fond Kiss*:

> Had we never lov'd sae kindly,
> Had we never lov'd sae blindly,
> Never met – or never parted –
> We had ne'er been broken-hearted.

CHAPTER TWELVE

# *A Wife o' My Ain*

I hae a wife o my ain,
  I'll partake wi naebody;
I'll take cuckold frae nane,
  I'll gie cuckold to naebody.

A song written by Burns on his
marriage to Jean Armour[1]

The stay in Edinburgh during the winter of 1787–8 had been brief and in retrospect not particularly happy. Burns had failed to wring a penny-piece out of Creech and he had left Clarinda behind with her memories and a pair of drinking glasses by which to remember their passionate time together. He had managed to persuade the Excise authorities to allow him to undergo his period of instruction for entry into the Service in Ayrshire instead of Edinburgh, under James Findlay, the Tarbolton Excise officer, who was a personal friend. Findlay was married to Jean Markland, whom the Poet described as 'divine' in his poem, *The Belles of Mauchline*. It was said that Burns first introduced Findlay to Jean Markland.

Robert was under no illusion about the Edinburgh friends he was leaving behind. He admitted as much to William Dunbar, one of his freemason and Crochallan Fencibles companions:

The time is approaching when I shall return to my shades; and I am afraid my numerous Edinburgh friendships are of so tender a construction that they will not bear carriage with me.[2]

A return to Mauchline was particularly convenient since it brought the Poet back to Jean Armour and nearer to the farm in Dumfriesshire which he had agreed to lease from the end of May. Even so, it robbed him of so much time and strength that he was left with little creative energy for writing poetry. He was due to start his course of instruction with Findlay in April so he snatched time for a short visit to Dumfriesshire at the end of March to start making arrangements for taking over Ellisland. He was an 'entire stranger' to this part of the country so he visited William Stewart, factor at Closeburn estate, to ask for help in finding a couple of men to assist on the farm during the summer.[3] As time was desperately short, Robert stayed only a couple of nights in Dumfriesshire before returning to Mauchline on Sunday, 31 March.

He may not have had time for profound poetical thoughts, but on the long rides over 'joyless muirs, between Galloway and Ayrshire' his mind and muse turned to good friends from the past and to old psalms and song tunes, which were always comforting. In his thoughts he was able to see a glimmer of spring – and perhaps hope – as he set some words to an old tune for a Crochallan Fencibles friend, Robert Cleghorn, who was particularly fond of singing. He added more words to it later to turn it into a Jacobite song, *The Chevalier's Lament*. But at that time, all Cleghorn received was these few lines:

> The small birds rejoice in the green leaves returning,
> The murmuring streamlet winds clear thro the vale,
> The primroses blow in the dews of the morning,
> And wild scatter'd cowslips bedeck the green dale:
> But what can give pleasure, or what can seem fair,
> When the lingering moments are number'd by care?
> No flow'rs gaily springing, nor birds sweetly singing,
> Can soothe the sad bosom of joyless despair![4]

His joy was shallow and the verse turned to such despair that he added the comment in his letter to Cleghorn: 'I am so harrassed with Care and Anxiety about this farming project of mine that my Muse has degenerated into the veriest prose-wench that ever picked cinders, or followed a Tinker.'[5]

There was no time for writing 'big' or deep poems any more. A few songs were the most he could manage, and, as he told William Dunbar, 'Most of all, I am, earnestly busy to bring about a revolution in my own mind', in order to overcome the effects of what he referred to as his 'late scenes of idleness and dissipation'.[6]

Preparation for a career in the Excise, should the need arise, was one of these disciplines he was facing: marriage was the other. We have no idea exacly when, or how, the marriage of Robert and Jean became regularized, but it was probably in early April just after he began his Excise training. The only hint came in a letter to Peggy Chalmers, written early in April 1788, in which he said: 'I am going on a great deal progressive in *mon grand bût* [my great goal], the sober science of life. I have lately made some sacrifices for which, were I *viva voce* with you to paint the situation and recount the circumstances, you would applaud me.'[7] This might simply refer to his career, but it has the sound of something much deeper, probably marriage, which of course Peggy would have approved of.

There are a number of traditional stories about the form the marriage took and where. The Ayrshire historian, Joseph Train, believed that Robert and Jean were married in Gavin Hamilton's office by a Justice of the Peace, John Farquhar-Gray of Gilmilnscroft, with Gavin Hamilton as a witness. Train, born in 1779, may have heard this discussed by his father, who was employed by Farquhar-Gray at Gilmilnscroft at the time. Another strong story originated with a Mrs Alexander, who was the daughter of Burns' friends Jenny Surgeoner and John Richmond. She believed the marriage took place in John Ronald's public house in Main Street (now Loudon Street).

John Taylor Gibb, writing in the *Burns Chronicle* in 1896, quoted another traditional location – the upstairs room of Hugh Morton's inn, just a few yards along the road from the house in which Jean was living, and the place where Burns and Jean first met at a dance on the night of Mauchline races in 1785. This inn stood beside the Church and Gavin Hamilton's house, usually called the Castle, but an old man named Gunnyon, who told the story to Gibb, called the house The Priory. Gunnyon said:

> There used to be a thoroughfare between the Churchyard and The Priory, . . . by which one could, in a step or two, pop out of The Priory into the public house . . . By this way, Burns went and came when he wrote the famous notes of the sermon preached by 'the Calf'.[8] And by this way stepped Gavin Hamilton when he acted as a witness to Burns' irregular marriage by the J.P., the Laird of Gilmilnscroft.[9]

This brings us back to Farquhar-Gray as the man who took the oaths, which regularized the marriage, with Gavin Hamilton as a witness, and leaves only the location in doubt. It may well be that the declaration was made in Hamilton's house, and then the party 'popped out of The Priory into the public house' afterwards.

The 'marriage' was not a wedding ceremony uniting two unmarried people, but a solemn admission that they had been married by an exchange of vows two years earlier, so that, whatever its legal status, Robert and Jean considered the piece of paper, which Armour senior mutilated, proof of marriage. All the business of obtaining the bachelor's certificate from the minister had been a sham. No wonder the Kirk was far from pleased when it learned that Burns was making an honest woman of Jean Armour at last. Towards the end of June, Robert wrote to his friend James Smith and told him he had informed 'Daddy' Auld of his marriage:

> I have waited on Mr Auld about my Marriage affair, & stated that I was legally fined for an irregular marriage by a Justice of the Peace. He says, if I bring an attestation of this by the two witnesseas, there shall be no more litigation about it. As soon as this comes to hand, please write to me in the way of familiar Epistle that, 'Such things are.'. . . Mrs Burns joins in kindest Compliments to you along with, my dear friend,
>
> yours most truly
>
> Robert Burns[10]

The matter came before Mauchline Kirk Session in August 1788, when the elders recorded their acceptance of it in a minute, which was far from cordial:

> Compeared Robert Burns with Jean Armour, his alledged [*sic*] spouse. They both acknowledged their irregular marriage and their sorrow for that irregularity and desiring that the Session will take such steps as may seem to them proper in order to the solemn confirmation of the said marriage.
>
> The Session taking this affair under their consideration agree that they both be rebuked for their acknowledged irregularity, and that they be taken solemnly engaged to adhere faithfully to one another as husband and wife all the days of their life.
>
> In regard the Session have a tittle [*sic*] in Law to some fine for behoof of the Poor, they agree to refer to Mr Burns his own generosity.
>
> The above sentence was accordingly executed, and the Session absolved the said parties from any scandal on this account

> William Auld
> Moderator                                 Robert Burns
>                                                   Jean Armour

Mr Burns gave a guinea note for behoof of the poor.[11]

26. Burns' namesake, Edinburgh lady of pleasure, Margaret Burns. The illustration is from John Kay's series of Original Portraits and Caricature Etchings.

*Cease ye prudes, your envious*
*    railing!*
*Lovely Burns has charms – confess!*
*True it is, she had one failing;*
*Had ae woman ever less?*

27. Margaret Chalmers, to whom he is said to have proposed in 1787.

28. Eliza (Bess) Burnett, daughter of Lord Monboddo, wrote poetry and was admired by Burns.

29. *Silhouette of Agnes (Nancy) McLehose by John Miers.*

*I cannot delay thanking you for the Pacquet of Saturday — twice have I read it with close attention — Some parts of it did "beguile me of my tears"! with desdemona, I felt 'twas' pitifull 'twas' wondrous pitifull." — When I reach'd the Paragraph where Lord Glencairn is mention'd, I burst out into tears —! 'twas' that delightfull swell of the Heart which arises from a combination of the most pleasurable feelings! —. nothing is so binding to a generous mind as placing confidence in it — I have ever felt it; you seem to have known this feature in my character, Intuitively — & therefore intrusted me with all your faults & follies — the discription of your first Love scene — delighted me! it recalled the Idea of some tender circumstances, which happened myself at the same period of life, only, mine, did not go so far. — perhaps, in return, I'll tell you the Particulars when we meet — Ah! my friend our early Love-emotions are surely the most exquisite — in riper years, we may acquire more knowledge, Sentiment & c. but — none of these can yield such rapture as the "dear delusions of heart throbbing youth! — like yours, Mine was a Rural Scene too, which adds much to the tender meeting — but — no more of these recollections. —*

30. *When the Poet told Clarinda about his first love and gave her his views of Calvinism, she replied in a latter, dated 7 January 1788, that the tale of his love had delighted her, but she was unhappy about his critical opinions on Calvinism.*

*Dumfries 27th Dec: 1791*

*21*

*I have yours, my ever dearest Nancy, this moment — I have just ten minutes before the Post goes, & these I shall employ in sending you some songs I have just been composing to different tunes for the Collection of Songs, of which you have three volumes — & of which you shall have the fourth. —*

*Song — Tune, Rory Dall's port*

*Ae fond kiss, & then we sever;
Ae farewel, & then for ever!
Deep in heart-wrung tears I'll pledge thee
Warring sighs & groans I'll wage thee. —*

*Who shall say that Fortune grieves him
While the star of hope she leaves him?
Me, nae chearful twinkle lights me;
Dark despair around benights me. —*

*I'll ne'er blame my partial fancy,
Naething could resist my Nancy:
But to see her, was to love her;
Love but her, & love for ever. —*

31.
Ae fond kiss, & then we sever;
Ae farewell, & then for ever!
Deep in heart - wrung tears I'll pledge thee,
Warring sighs & groans I'll wage thee.

The hauntingly beautiful song, Ae Fond Kiss, *marked the end of the affair with Clarinda.*

Aug.t 5 Also Comp.ared Robert Burns with Jean Armour
his alledged Spouse They both Acknowledge their irregular
marriage and their sorrow for that irregularity And
Desiring that the Session will take such Steps as may
seem to them proper in order to the Solemn Confirmation
of the said marriage

The Session taking this affair under their Consideration
Agree that they both be rebuked for this Acknowledged
irregularity and that they be taken solemnly engaged
to adhere faithfully to one another as husband and
wife all the days of their life

In regard the Session have a little in Law to
some fine for behoof of the poor They Agree to refer
to Mr Burns his own generosity

The above Sentence was Accordingly executed and
the Session Absolved the said parties from any
Scandal on this acco.t

     William Auld mod.r   Rob.t Burns
                 Jean Armour

Mr Burns gave a guinea note for behoof of the poor
9 Aug.t Intimation was made from the tent that the Seats in
the Area of the Church be sett upon monday first for behoof of
the poor

32. *Mauchline Kirk Session minutes of 5 August 1788 noted that Robert and Jean had acknowledged their irregular marriage and that Robert had given a guinea to the poor of the parish.*

33. *Jean Armour at the age of 65, with grandchild, Sarah, daughter of James Glencairn Burns.*

*34. Song-collector George Thomson persuaded Burns to contribute dozens of songs for his* Select Collection of Original Scottish Airs.

*35. Edinburgh engraver James Johnson had just begun work on his* Select Scottish Airs *when he met the Poet. Detail from* The Inauguration of Robert Burns as Poet Laureate at the Lodge Canongate Kilwinning, Edinburgh, in 1787, *by William Stewart Watson.*

The Rosebud — to its own tune —
Composed by Mr Burns on Miss Cruikshank, Edin.
& the Music by Mr Sillar a gentleman in Irvine Ayrshire —

A Rose-bud by my early walk,
Adown a corn-inclosed bawk,
Sae gently bent its thorny stalk,
    All on a dewy morning . —

Ere twice the shades of dawn are fled,
In a' its crimson glory spread,
And dropping, rich, the dewy head,
    It scents the early morning —

Within the bush her covert nest
A little linnet fondly blest
The chilly dew sat on her breast
    Sae early in the morning. —

She soon shall see her tender brood
The pride the pleasure of the wood
Amang the fresh green leaves bedew'd
    Awauk the early morning. —

*36.* A Rosebud by my Early Walk *was written for 12-year-old Jeany Cruikshank, daughter of his Edinburgh friend, William Cruikshank.*

37. *Lieutenant-Colonel James Glencairn Burns (1793–1865), fourth son, was with the East India Company. He married twice and had one daughter by each marriage.*

38. *Colonel William Nicol Burns (1791–1872), third son, joined the East India Company, and married Catherine Crone, but had no children.*

39. *Robert and Jean's eldest son, Robert (1786–1857), held a post in the Stamp Office in London. He married Anne Sherwood and had one daughter, Eliza.*

40. *Elizabeth, usually known as Betty (1791–1873), daughter of the Poet and Dumfries barmaid, Ann Park, was brought up by Jean as one of her own family. Betty became Mrs John Thomson.*

41. *Jean Armour (1767–1834) bore the Poet two sets of twins before they acknowledged their marriage.*

42. *Red chalk drawing by Archibald Skirving, made shortly after the Poet's death. Sir Walter Scott described this as 'the only good portrait of Burns'.*

43. *At Ellisland, beside the River Nith, near Dumfries, Burns returned to farming in 1788, but soon he began to work for the Excise.*

44. *One of the first people to welcome the Poet into his home in Dumfriesshire was Robert Riddell of Glenriddell. Burns spent much time at Friar's Carse or in a little hermitage in the grounds, where he composed his poetry.*

45. *Maria Riddell was perhaps the most beautiful and certainly the most intellectually able of all Burns' female acquaintances.*

The Rights of Woman —
Spoken by Miss Fontenelle on her benefit —

While Europe's eye is fixed on mighty things,
The fate of Empires, & the fall of Kings;
While quacks of state must each produce his plan,
And even children lisp The Rights of Man;
Amid this mighty fuss, just let me mention,
The Rights of Woman merit some attention. —

First, in the sexes' intermixed connection,
One sacred Right of Woman is, Protection —
The tender flower that lifts its head, elate
Helpless, must fall before the blasts of Fate
Sunk on the earth, defaced its lovely form,
Unless your shelter ward th' impending storm. —

Our second Right — but needless here is caution,
To keep that Right inviolate's the fashion. —
Each man of sense has it so full before him
He'd die before he'd wrong it — 'tis Decorum —
There was indeed, in far less polished days,
A time when rough, rude man had naughty ways;
Would swagger, swear, get drunk, kick up a riot,
Nay even thus invade a lady's quiet. —

                                                        Now

46. The Rights of Woman, *an address written for the popular actress Louisa Fontenelle on her benefit night at the Dumfries theatre on 26 November 1792.*

47. *Louisa Fontenelle was greatly admired by Burns, who wrote a prologue for her as well as the address (opposite).*

49. *For Jessy Lewars, who nursed him in his last illness, Robert wrote* O Wert thou in the Cauld Blast.

48. *Jean Lorimer, Burns' 'Chloris', inspired a couple of dozen songs, the best-known of which is* The Lassie wi' the Lintwhite Locks.

50. *Robert and Jean's last home was in Mill Hole Brae, Dumfries, now called Burns Street and a museum.*

51. *The room in which the Poet died on 21 July 1796.*

52. *The last portrait, a miniature in water colour on ivory, painted by Alexander Reid at the end of 1795. Burns said of it, 'He has hit the best likeness of me ever taken'.*

Madam

    I have written you so often without rec.g any answer, that I would not trouble you again but for the circumstances in which I am. — An illness which has long hung about me in all probability will speedily send me beyond that bourne whence no traveller returns. — Your friendship with which for many years you honored me was a friendship dearest to my soul. — Your conversation & especially your correspondence were at once highly entertaining & instructive. — With what pleasure did I use to break up the seal! The remembrance yet adds one pulse more to my poor palpitating heart!

            Farewell!!!

July 10th 1796

                        Robert Burns

*53. The last letter he wrote to Mrs Dunlop, on 10 July 1796, ended, 'Your conversation and especially your correspondence were at once highly entertaining and instructive. With what pleasure did I use to break up the seal! The remembrance yet adds one pulse more to my poor palpitating heart! Farewell!!!'*

Just to show defiance of the Kirk's outspoken words, Burns did two things: he sent off to Glasgow the day before the Session met for 15 yards (13½ metres) of black silk, similar to that he had bought for his mother and sisters, to make a gown and petticoat for Jean,[12] and he wrote a little song out of sheer joy that she was his. His wife would look smarter than any other in the kirk on Sunday, and the whole of Mauchline would know she was his: *I Hae a Wife o My Ain* he exulted:

> I hae a wife o my ain,
>   I'll partake wi naebody;
> I'll take cuckold frae nane,
>   I'll gie cuckold to naebody.
>
> I hae a penny to spend,
>   There – thanks to naebody.
> I hae naething to lend,
>   I'll borrow frae naebody.
>
> I am naebody's lord,
>   I'll be slave to naebody.
> I'll hae a guid braid sword,
>   I'll tak dunts* frae naebody.          *blows
>
> I'll be merry and free,
>   I'll be sad for naebody;
> Naebody cares for me,
>   I care for naebody.[13]

By the time this final act of abasement to the Kirk authorities was over, the whole world knew Burns had acknowledged Jean as his wife. As early as 28 April, he gave the news to his old Mauchline draper friend, James Smith, now living in Linlithgow, in a letter ordering a printed shawl, 'my first present to her since I have *irrevocably* called her mine.' The shawl was to be of the best quality and, touchingly, Robert told Smith he wanted him to supply it because he was an old and trusty friend of both himself and Jean. The marriage was still a secret, so he ended the letter: 'Mrs Burns ('tis only her private designation) begs her best Compliments to you.'[14]

A month later he wrote more openly to Ainslie, speaking of, 'Mrs Burns . . . which title I now avow to the World.' He gave Ainslie another clue to the reason for his decision. 'I am truly pleased with this last affair [the marriage]; it has indeed added to my anxieties for Futurity but it has given a stability to my mind & resolutions, unknown before.'[15]

Only in relaying the information to James Johnson of *The Scots Musical Museum*, did he show a spark of the old wayward Robert Burns. While asking Johnson to help him to squeeze his money out of Creech he wrote:

> I am so enamoured with a certain girl's prolific twin-bearing merit, that I have given her a legal title to the best blood in my body; and so farewell Rakery![16]

Robert found it so much harder to break the news to strait-laced old Mother-Confessor Dunlop that even when writing to her as late as 29 June, he could not bring himself to mention marriage, although it was clearly on his mind as he talked to her at length about fine ladies and social divisions. Two days later he steeled himself to confess to Mrs Dunlop's son, Andrew, that he did not know how to tell his mother about his changed state. Andrew would be the best person for her to hear the news from – apart from Robert, of course who felt unable to face her with it.

Needless to say, Mrs Dunlop was upset that Burns had given her the news 'second-hand'. On 4 June she sent a long motherly harangue, beginning with a long reprimand which opened:

> I don't remember whether it is Solomon or Lord Chesterfield that says, 'Go to the ant and learn wisdom.' Instead of torturing your philosophy for the solution of an easy question, let me refer you to the Mouse or the Mountain Daisey [*sic*], to the Cotter or the Farmer's Auld Mare, to things animate and things inanimate . . .

After much more huffing and puffing she came to the point:

> I am told in a letter that you have been a month married. I am unwilling to believe so important an era of your life has past, and you have considered me as so very little concerned in what concerned you most as never to give me the most distant hint of your wishing such a change.

It was a real motherly roasting, blending reprimand with hurt in massive quantities, but, having delivered her rebuke, the tone turned to touching maternal care:

> Allow me, however, married or unmarried, to wish you joy, which I

assure you I do most sincerely in every situation in which yourself or Providence can put you.[17]

She begged Robert to continue to write to her, and with her next letter enclosed a bank draft for five pounds as a 'luckpenny' to mark his new state of life. Robert protested, but accepted the gift gracefully.

Unfortunately, because Robert was travelling so much between Mauchline and Ellisland at this time their letters often crossed and he had not seen her reprimand of 4 June before he plucked up courage to write to her on the 13th to give the news of his married state himself: 'I am indeed A HUSBAND,' he said, with the explanation he gave to the Dunlops and the great and the good for his decision – 'that I had a once, & still much-lov'd fellow-creature's happiness or misery among my hands, and I could not dally with such a matter.'[18] He extolled Jean's virtues to Mrs Dunlop at length:

The most placid of good nature and sweetness of disposition; a warm heart, gratefully devoted with its powers to love one; vigorous health & sprightly chearfulness [*sic*], set off to the best advantage by a more than common handsome figure; these, I think, in a woman, may make a tolerable good wife, though she should never have read a page but The Scriptures of the Old & New Testament, nor have 'danced in a brighter Assembly than a Penny-pay Wedding'.[19]

Andrew Dunlop handled the passing on of the news very tactfully, amusingly and in a matter of fact way. As Mrs Dunlop put it to Burns: 'Andrew tells me he hears you have got on shackles,' she added at the end of a long letter to Robert, together with her son's further comment, 'Don't I think you must be like all our great geniuses a little crackt? Spite of which he sincerely wishes you happy.'

Mrs Dunlop, having recovered from her initial pique, wished the Poet happiness: 'I sit down . . . to give you joy,' she crooned, then launched into a long harangue, praising his decision, but questioning him about it as only a mother would; she wanted to know if Jean would make a good housewife, and raised the fear that he might not settle to marriage. How well she knew him: 'If report has not done you great injury, you have indulged in a freedom of life that poisons a man's mind for a husband, by leading him to measure his ideas of every woman by the standard of the very worst among whom he has connected himself.' Mrs Dunlop knew full well that Robert had 'connected himself' to a motley variety of females in his day. He was questioned closely on his sexual relationship with Jean:

Whether your wife was or is only now become the mother of your children – [is] a point in which I anxiously wish myself to be satisfied. I feel all the indelicacy of my doing so; yet cannot help putting the question. I believe all your motives of action are noble and generous, but would be glad to exchange surmise for certainty . . . Tell me, therefore, I beg you, what prevented your marriage long ago, and on what side the demurs came that are now removed. . . . O Burns! since I have so far overleapt decorum as to touch upon this subject let me go one step further, and tell you where I tremble for your peace. You say there is a heavy atmosphere about your soul that shews painful objects larger than life. You have tryed [*sic*] your influence and found it too powerful with a young innocent girl, who sacrificed everything valuable to convince you of her affection. Set a guard over your heart, lest the jaundiced eye of jealousie should one day view this proof through that magnifying medium, and blast that confidence in your wife which she so implicitly reposed in you, and which is the only bond of conjugal tranquillity.

It is incredible that Burns, who would not have allowed any other person to make such a suggestion to him, accepted this from Mrs Dunlop, and a couple of months later confessed the whole saga of his relationship with Jean to her:

Mrs Burns, Madam is the identical woman who was the mother of twice twins to me in seventeen months. When she first found herself, 'As women wish to be who love their lords,' as I lov'd her near to distraction, I took some previous steps to a private marriage. Her Parents . . . not only forbade me her company and their house, but . . . got a warrant to incarcerate me in jail till I should find security in my about-to-be Paternal relation.

While protesting that he was under no obligation to Jean (although it is clear from the manner in which he formalized his marriage that in his heart he really believed differently), Burns explained to Mrs Dunlop, as he had told her son, that he could not trifle with Jean's happiness. And he gave a forthright and unanswerable reply to the old lady's suggestion that a wife would be a tie to his literary life and muse:

Circumstanced as I am, I could never have got a female partner for life who could have entered into my favorite [*sic*] studies, relished my favorite Authors, &c. without entailing on me at the same time, expensive living, fantastic caprice, apish affectation, with the other blessed, Boarding-school acquirements which (*pardonnez moi, Madame!*) are some times to be found among females of the upper ranks, but almost universally pervade the Misses of the Would-be gentry.[20]

Robert managed to set up house with Jean in her room in Mauchline as if their marriage had taken place in the most conventional manner, and he went off like a dutiful husband to be instructed in the Excise procedures by James Findlay at Tarbolton. In Mauchline the marriage remained an ill-kept secret, which leaked out in the oddest ways even to close friends. Hamilton's daughter, Jacobina, recalled that the first she heard of it was one morning when Burns and the Ayr lawyer, Robert Aiken, were breakfasting at her father's house, and Mrs Hamilton apologized to Aiken for not having an egg to boil for him. The Poet said that if she cared to send across to Mrs Burns she might have some.[21] Jacobina was thunderstruck; she had no idea that Jean Armour had become 'Mrs Burns'.

During May, Robert continued with preparations for taking over Ellisland at the end of the month, and to get ready for the time when he and Jean would be living there as man and wife. He sent off to his mother's brother, Samuel Brown, the man with whom he had stayed at Kirkoswald while learning surveying years before, to ask if the fowling season had started on Ailsa Craig, the rock in the Firth of Clyde noted for its seabird life and, if so, to ask him to send him three or four stones of feathers, presumably to stuff mattresses and pillows for the matrimonial bed. Brown was a shady character involved in the smuggling trade, so Robert could not resist telling his uncle of his sexual and farming projects in slightly coarse smuggling terms:

> Since I saw you last . . . I engaged in the smuggling Trade and God knows if ever any poor man experienced better returns – two for one. But as freight and Delivery has turned out so D—nd Dear I am thinking about takeing [*sic*] out a Licence and beginning in a Fair trade. I have taken a Farm on the Banks of Nith and in imitation of the old Patriarchs get Men servants and Maid Servants – Flocks and herds and beget sons and Daughters.[22]

One can only wonder what the old man made of that unless he had remained in close touch with the family at Mossgiel.

Although Burns took over his Ellisland lease officially on 25 May, he did not move to the farm until 11 June, and even then he had no house to which he could bring Jean, so she had to remain at home in Ayrshire. Jean was not well versed in farming work for she had been brought up in the town and knew nothing of milking cows, making butter and cheese, or all the other jobs expected of a farmer's wife. Robert arranged for her to go to Mossgiel, to learn these things from his mother and sisters, but it is unlikely that she went to live at the farm. Robert would want to keep his independence, and it is very unlikely that Jean would want to give up her rooms in the Back Causeway: however small these may have been, it was preferable to cramming into the little farmhouse at Mossgiel with all the Burns family. Tradition in Mauchline claims that she remained at the house in the Back Causeway.

The first letter Burns wrote from Ellisland was to Mrs Dunlop, but it showed none of the high spirits or hope one might have expected from a man embarking on a new career. Robert was acutely aware of the work that lay ahead on the farm, of his isolation as he lived there alone, and the pain of separation from Jean and all his friends. He opened his letter with some lines from Goldsmith slightly altered to suit his purpose better:

> 'Where'er I roam, whatever realms I see,
> My heart untravell'd, fondly turns to thee;
> Still to my Friend it turns with ceaseless pain,
> And drags at each remove a lengthen'd chain.'

This is the second day, my honored Friend, that I have been on my farm. A solitary Inmate of an old, smoky 'SPENCE'*; far from every Object I love or by whom I am belov'd, nor any acquaintance older than yesterday except Jenny Geddes the old mare I ride on; while uncuth Cares and novel Plans hourly unsult my awkward Ignorance & bashful Inexperience.[23]

In the dark smoke-filled room he remembered past misfortunes and disappointments, and it was in this letter and in that black mood that he chose to inform Mrs Dunlop of his marriage, not realizing she already knew. Apart from being away from Jean, there was plenty to feel miserable about as he looked across the bare, boulder-strewn, tired land of Ellisland, which he had to plough and sweeten if it was to yield a crop the following year. He also had to build a house in which he and Jean could live. He was now impatient to have his wife beside him, but

---

*inner apartment, used as a bedroom or for storage

through the whole of that summer he had to be content with a week or ten days at Ellisland followed by a few days at Mauchline with his wife. During this separation Burns created some of his loveliest songs for Jean, who was constantly in his thoughts as he worked on the farm, sat in his rain-swept miserable hovel, or made the long ride home to visit her. Jean looked forward to being with him too, and would walk along the Dumfries road to meet him when he was due. He would hoist her on to the back of his saddle and she would ride pillion, the pair in blissful unity, all the way to Mauchline. No wonder *Of A' The Airts the Wind can Blaw* was not a song of despair at being parted: how could it be since Burns said it was written during the honeymoon? Through all its sense of longing, *Of A' The Airts* shines with hope – with certainty even – that they would soon be together for always:

> Of a' the airts* the wind can blaw*     *directions *blow
>   I dearly like the west,
> For there the bonie lassie lives,
>   The lassie I lo'e best.
> There wild woods grow, and rivers row
>   And monie a hill between,
> But day and night my fancy's flight
>   Is ever wi my Jean.
>
> I see her in the dewy flowers –
>   I see her sweet and fair.
> I hear her in the tunefu birds –
>   I hear her charm the air.
> There's not a bonie flower that springs
>   By fountain, shaw,* or green,     *wood
> There's not a bonie bird that sings,
>   But minds me o my Jean.[24]

The house he described to Mrs Dunlop stood on the southern edge of the farm, under the shadow of the Isle Tower, and was little better than a shack. It was occupied by the former leaseholder of the farm, David Cullie and his wife, and was not even wind- or water-tight. He told Peggy Chalmers about its comfortlessness one harvest-day in September when rain had driven him in from the cornfield where he had been slaving at the back-breaking work of binding sheaves behind the reapers. 'This hovel that I shelter in . . . is pervious to every blast that blows, and every shower that falls; and I am preserved from being chilled to death by being suffocated with smoke.'[25]

It was from this strange new land 'unknown to rhyme' in which he now found himself, that he sent a verse epistle to his Kilmarnock friend Hugh Parker, describing the misery of sheltering in the Cullies' hovel:

| | |
|---|---|
| Here, ambush'd by the chimla* cheek | *chimney |
| Hid in an atmosphere of reek*, | *smoke |
| O hear a wheel thrum* i' the neuk*, | *throb *corner |
| I hear it – for in vain I leuk*: | *look |
| The red peat gleams, a fiery kernel | |
| Embuskèd by a fog infernal. | |
| Here, for my wonted rhyming raptures, | |
| I sit and count my sins by chapters; | |
| For life and spunk like ither Christians, | |
| I'm dwindled down to mere existence: | |
| Wi nae converse but Gallowa' bodies, | |
| Wi nae kend* face but Jenny Geddes.[26] | * known |

All through that summer and autumn his spirits soared and plummeted with every change of the weather, with each ache or pain, and with the coming and going of friends, or the slightest whiff of good or bad fortune. His feelings about the farm wavered and he missed Jean more and more as time passed. On the day after he sent his first letter to Mrs Dunlop he began once again to reflect on his changed life and marriage in his *Second Common Place Book*:

This is now the third day I have been in this country. Lord, – what is man! what a bustling little bundle of passion, appetites, ideas, fancies! and what a capricious kind of existence he has here! If legendary stories be true, there is, indeed, an elsewhere . . . I am such a coward in life, so tired of the service, that I would almost at any time with Milton's Adam,

'. . . gladly lay me in my Mother's lap,
And be at peace,'

but a wife and children – in poetics, 'the fair partner of my soul, and the little dear pledges of our mutual love' – these bind me to struggle with the stream, till some chopping squall overset the silly vessel, or, in the listless return of years, its own craziness drive it a wreck. Farewell now to those giddy follies, those varnished vices, which though half sanctified by the bewitching levity of Wit and Humour, are at best but thriftless idling with the precious current of existence . . .

In his loneliness and hopelessness he turned his thoughts even more deeply than ever into his marriage, and betrayed just a trace of regret that the cost of marriage to Jean had been the loss of Clarinda for that winter in Edinburgh had not faded from his mind:

Wedlock, the circumstance that buckles me hardest to care, if virtue and religion were to be anything with me but mere names – was what in a few seasons I must have resolved on; in the present case it was unavoidably necessary. Humanity, generosity, honest vanity of character, justice to my own happiness for after life, so far as it could depend (which it surely will a great deal) on internal peace – all these joined their warmest suffrages, their most powerful solicitations, with a rooted attachment, to urge the step I have taken. Nor have I any reason to rue it. I can fancy how, but have never seen where, I could have made it better. Come then, let me return to my favourite motto, that glorious passage of Young

> 'On Reason build Resolve –
> That column of true majesty in man.'

It was all very different from the 'once, & still much-lov'd fellow-creature's happiness or misery among my hands,' of which he had spoken to the Dunlops. Nor were these the thoughts of the song-writer who stood on the high, windswept hill-land of Ellisland and gazed north-westwards until he could discern the peak of Corsincon hill in the parish of New Cumnock: from there his thoughts moved on to Mauchline only a couple of parishes farther away, and to the girl who was soon to share all this with him. The exquisite little song, *O Were I on Parnassus Hill*, speaks more eloquently than all the words of explanation or rationalization that he poured into his correspondence and *The Common Place Book* about his real, deep, inner feelings about Jean Armour. And Jean was well aware of that:

> O, were I on Parnassus hill,
> Or had o' Helicon my fill,
> That I might catch poetic skill
>   To sing how dear I love thee!
> But Nith maun* be my Muse's well,                    *must
> My Muse maun be thy bonie sel,
> On Corsincon I'll glow'r and spell,
>   And write how dear I love thee.

Then come, sweet Muse, inspire my lay!
For a' the lee-lang* simmer's day                    *live-long
I couldna sing, I couldna say,
    How much, how dear I love thee.
I see thee dancing o'er the green,
Thy waist sae jimp*, thy limbs sae clean,            *slender
Thy tempting lips, thy roguish een* –                *eyes
    By Heav'n and Earth I love thee![27]

It is evident from this song that life was not all misery during that lonely, uncomfortable summer and autumn in the Cullies' hovel at the Isle. There were worries other than farming, of course, especially Jenny Clow's pregnancy about which Ainslie wrote to inform him towards the end of June. But Robert faced up to that as he did to the farming problems which beset him, treating all of them as part of that great military campaign which he saw as his battle through life.

Now out marched the battalions of military metaphors to be paraded before Ainslie as he explained how he was going to take a more serious view of life:

I have all along, hitherto, in the warfare of life, been bred to arms among the light-horse – the piquet-guards of fancy; a kind of Hussars and Highlanders of the *Brain*; but I am firmly resolved to *sell out* of these giddy battalions, who have no ideas of a battle but fighting the foe, or of a siege but storming the town. Cost what it will, I am determined to buy in among the grave squadrons of heavy-armed thought, or the artillery corps of plodding contrivance.[28]

Robert did not have to 'buy in' among the grave squadrons of folk around Dumfries, for they soon sought him out. He never could resist fighting alongside the dashing Hussars and Highlanders rather than the grave squadrons. He had been welcomed as a celebrity when he stopped off at Dumfries on his Borders Tour the previous year, and now he was accepted into every level of society in the town and surrounding county. Within days of his arrival he had been introduced to the neighbouring landowner, Captain Robert Riddell of Glenriddell, whose estate of Friar's Carse lay beside Ellisland Farm. In spite of the social gap between the two men, they became firm friends immediately, helped by a common interest in music. Riddell was retired from the Army on half-pay and had just inherited the estate from his father, so he had ample money and time to indulge his interests as an antiquarian and amateur musician. Like Burns, Captain Riddell collected tunes, but he also composed original airs, and some years later published his own *Collection of Scotch, Galwegian and Border Tunes for Violin and Pianoforte*. Robert used some of Riddell's airs for his own songs. Just inside the Friar's Carse boundary Riddell had built a little classical summer house, and he gave Burns a key to it so that the Poet could retire there to think or write whenever he wished – this was a great improvement on the Cullies' hovel as a place to create poetry. Burns rewarded him with a little set of *Verses in Friar's Carse Hermitage*. Later these were expanded into a longer poem for his friend Riddell, and his wife, Elizabeth.

The Friar's Carse hermitage provided Burns with a refuge from the misery and loneliness that surrounded him during these early months on his farm. So too did the company of men like William Stewart, the factor at Closeburn estate, who had been so helpful during his early visits before he moved into Ellisland. Burns and Stewart both enjoyed bawdy songs and one evening early in July, the Poet sat down and wrote a letter to his friend, enclosing three bawdy songs, which later appeared in *The Merry Muses of Caledonia*.

Life at Ellisland may not always have been as drab as the Poet painted it during the summer of 1788, but it was far from pleasant. Even during the earliest days, Burns realized that in the short term and without more cash, Ellisland would not provide for a wife and family. More capital would be required for the farm, but any money he had was already tied up in his brother's financial disaster at Mossgiel. Even before Jean joined him, Robert took the first step towards finding himself an Excise post to augment the Ellisland income, and made full use of his friendship with Graham of Fintry to do so. Burns has been much criticized by every generation for indulging in patronage, and it has to be admitted that he used it expertly. The editors of the centenary edition of his Life and Works in 1896 went as far as to say, 'It must be admitted that the flattery of a patron he scarcely knew and owed little as yet . . . is absurd.'[29] Seen against the background of eighteenth-century business practices, what Burns did was perfectly acceptable.

When he completed his course of instruction at Tarbolton and was granted his Excise commission this did not automatically give him entry into the Service. He now had to be placed on a list to await a vacancy, a process which could take months, even years. When it came through, the appointment might be to a Division 100 miles away. Robert needed an appointment now, and it had to be close enough to Ellisland to allow him to run the farm alongside the Excise work. At that moment, the officer covering the Division in which Ellisland lay, was Leonard Smith, who also rented a farm close by, but had come into an inheritance and was (in

Burns' eyes) 'quite opulent'. The plan was a simple one: Smith should be removed from his post and his position given to Burns.

The man who could achieve this for him was Robert Graham of Fintry, and the Poet sat down and wrote a flattering verse epistle to Fintry, dated, 'Ellisland, 8 September, 1788,' although he had been working on it for weeks before. As early as 2 August he sent a draft of part of the poem – 'the first crude thoughts' he called them – to Mrs Dunlop, composed as he 'jogged through the wild hills of New Cumnock' on his way home to Mauchline. 'I intend inserting them or something like them in an epistle I am going to write to the Gentleman on whose friendship my excise hopes depend – Mr Graham of Fintry, one of the worthiest and most accomplished Gentlemen, not only of this Country, but I will dare to say it, of this Age.'[30] Certainly his flattery of his patron was over-fulsome by our standards but it would not have raised an eyebrow in 1788.

On 5 September he completed the Epistle and sent a copy to Mrs Dunlop for her approval, but without waiting for her reply, he sent it off to Graham with a letter requesting him to do everything in his power to oust Smith, pass over any waiting candidates, and appoint Burns to the post. It was a long, grovelling letter, opening with much flattery, but quickly moving to the nub of the favour:

Your Honorable Board, sometime ago, gave me my Excise Commission; which I regard as my sheet anchor in life. My farm . . . tho' I think it will in time be a saving bargain, yet does by no means promise to be such a Pennyworth as I was taught to expect. It is in the last stage of worn-out poverty, and will take some time before it pay the rent. I might have had Cash to supply the deficiencies of these hungry years, but I have a young brother who is supporting my aged mother, another still much younger brother and three sisters, on the farm in Ayr-shire; and it took all my surplus, over what I thought necessary for my farming capital, to save not only the comfort but the very existence of that fireside family-circle from impending destruction . . . and rather than abstract my money from my brother, a circumstance which would ruin him, I will resign the farm and enter immediately into the service of your HONOURS . . .

There is one way by which I might be enabled to extricate myself from this embarrassment, a scheme which I hope and am certain is in your power to effectuate. I live here, Sir, in the very centre of a country Excise-Division; the present Officer lately lived on a farm which he rented in my nearest neighbourhood, and as the gentleman, owing to some legacies, is quite opulent, a removal could do him no manner of injury; and on a month's warning, to give me a little time to look again over my Instructions, I would not be afraid to enter on business. . . . It would suit me to enter on it beginning of next Summer; but I shall be in Edinburgh to wait upon you about the affair, sometime in the ensuing winter.[31]

Burns admitted he shuddered at his own 'Hardiesse' at asking this favour, but could see no other way out. The Excise post would have the great advantage of allowing more time for his poetry-writing, and, just to prove his point, he sent Graham the highly polished verse epistle of which by now he felt quite proud.

He did not send this request to Graham of Fintry on an impulse: he had considered it deeply, and discussed it with Jean. In a letter written on 12 September he said: 'I have written my long-thought-on letter to Mr Graham.' And he made the point that he was delighted to be able to think about creating poetry again.[32]

Graham did not take exception to Burns' outright request for preferment, replying by return of post to assure Robert of his continued patronage. He could not dismiss Leonard Smith just to make way for the Poet, but clearly gave hope that he would eventually find a position in the area. Robert was immensely grateful, and his response, written while he was stricken with influenza in the middle of harvest-time, assured Graham that he would be able to weather the first twelve months. But he continued to write to Fintry in the hope that something might be found for him sooner:

> I was thinking that as I am only a little more than five miles from Dumfries, I might perhaps officiate here, if any of these Officers could be removed with more propriety than Mr Smith; but besides the monstrous inconvenience of it to me, I could not bear to injure a poor fellow by outing him to make way for myself: to a wealthy Son of good-fortune like Smith the injury is imaginary, where the propriety of your rules admit.[33]

While Robert awaited Fintry's intervention to find him an Excise place, he continued with his farming and the building of a house. Towards the end of harvest-time, he received an unexpected offer, which was too good to keep from Jean. On 14 October he sent her a letter:

> You must get ready for Nithsdale as fast as possible, for I have an offer

of a house in the very neighbourhood with some furniture in it, all of which I shall have the use of for nothing till my own house be got ready; and I am determined to remove you from Ayrshire immediately, as I am suffering by not being on the farm myself.[34]

By great good luck, Robert had become friendly with David Newall, a Dumfries lawyer who had a summer house close to Ellisland, so when Newall's family returned to the town for the winter he offered to lend the house to the Poet until such time as the Ellisland farmhouse would be ready.

Although Robert wrote off so urgently on 14 October, warning Jean to prepare to join him, it took several weeks for arrangements to be completed. Robert was frequently in Ayrshire during this time, transporting furniture and other possessions to Dumfries, and it was not until 7 December that he and Jean were settled together in Newall's house. It seems strange that when Jean came from Ayrshire, she did not bring their son, Robert Junior, now past his second birthday, but he was left behind at Mossgiel until the following summer.

The farmhouse was still not finished by the time Burns had agreed to vacate Newall's house in the spring of 1789, and through the first months of the new year Robert badgered the stonemason, Thomas Boyd, to push ahead with it. At the beginning of February, Robert wrote with wry irony: 'I see at last, dear Sir, some signs of your executing my house within the current year.'[35] A month later, on returning from a visit to Edinburgh, he told Boyd, 'I . . . was a good deal surprised at finding my house still lying like Babylon in the prophecies of Isiah [*sic*].'[36] In Chapter 13 of the Book of Isaiah, it was prophesied that Babylon would be destroyed and left empty of people like Sodom and Gomorrah. In spite of ridicule and Biblical imprecations, Boyd continued at his slow pace, and it was mid-April or later before the new house was ready. Years later, Jean's young cousin, Elizabeth Smith, who had come from Mauchline to help out as a maid at Ellisland, described the ritual of the family's entry into the farmhouse to Robert Chambers:

Burns made her (Elizabeth) take the Family Bible and a bowl of salt, and placing the one upon the other, carry them to the new house, and walk into it before anyone else. This was the old *freit* appropriate to the taking possession of a new house, the object being to secure good-luck for all who should tenant it. He himself, with his wife on his arm, followed the bearer of the Bible and salt, and so entered upon the possession of his home.[37]

The spring work on the farm, clearing stones, ploughing, liming and planting, was well under way by the time Robert and Jean settled down together as husband and wife in their own home, both of them working extremely hard to make it a success. They had two men and two women working for them, but even so both had to work hard, Robert taking his turn at ploughing and sowing and Jean taking charge of much of the dairy work.

William Clark was their ploughman that first spring and he remembered Jean as a 'good and prudent housewife', who kept everything about the farmhouse neat and tidy and was well-liked by all the servants.[38] The food she gave them was wholesome and there was plenty of it, the only difference between family and servants being that Jean and Robert and their family ate together in the little parlour while the hired men and women took their meals in the kitchen. Sir Samuel Egerton Brydges, who visited Ellisland once, described Jean as humble and plain, but accustomed enough to welcoming visitors to produce the whisky bottle for them without being asked . . .

Robert was a good master, who worked alongside his men in the fields, and treated them well, although he could be 'gey guldersome* for a wee while' if anything annoyed him. But afterwards he put his annoyance aside and the matter was forgotten. They had nine or ten milking cows, some young cattle, four horses and a few pet sheep, of which the Poet was extremely fond.

No sooner was the first season's seed brearded† than Burns was again questioning his prospects as a farmer. He prodded Graham of Fintry's memory on 13 May by informing his patron that he had called on the local Collector, John Mitchell with a letter Fintry had sent previously, but Mitchell had been too busy to say more than that Burns should call again at a quieter time. Robert had too much pride to push the matter further then: 'As I don't wish to degrade myself to a hungry rook gaping for a morsel, I shall just give him a hint of my wishes,' he told Graham.[39]

Fintry took the hint, and by the end of July, Collector Mitchell had met Burns again and, as Robert told Graham, agreed that removing Smith 'will be productive of at least no disadvantage to the Revenue', and may likewise be done without any detriment to him. He was, he said, ready to give up the farm.

'Should the Honorable Board think so, and should they deem it

*shout a lot
†green shoots showing through the soil

eligible to appoint me to officiate in his present place, I am then at the top of my wishes,' Robert added.[40] On 19 August he was able to tell Mrs Dunlop that 'the Board have been so obliging as to fix me in the Division in which I live; and I suppose I shall begin doing duty at the commencement of next month.'[41] By October his name was on the list of Excise officers in the district, followed by the words 'Never tryed – a Poet'. Later, someone had added, 'Turns out well.' It was 27 October before Burns was officially sworn into the Service at Dumfries Quarter Sessions of Peace, in the Dumfries first Itinerancy district. He was paid a salary of £50 a year and half of any fines he collected and for this he had to cover 200 miles a week, checking on all kinds of articles, not just tobacco and alcohol, but dozens of other items, from bricks to salt, which were all subject to tax. It was a highly complicated business, often with several different rates applying to the varying qualities of the same product – paper alone was subject to seventy-eight different rates of duty according to size, type and quality. It was also exacting work, which had to be carried out and reported on meticulously day by day, with everything subject to regular checks by his superiors.

While Robert continued to supervise the outside work on the farm in spite of being away for long periods on his Excise rounds, Jean gave him loyal and uncomplaining support at Ellisland. She was well into her third pregnancy by the time she moved into her house in the spring of 1789, and Robert's mother and sisters came down from Mossgiel to help with her confinement. They brought little Robert with them, the first time the child had lived with both of his parents. Jean's new child, another son, was born on 18 August, and was named Francis Wallace in honour of Mrs Dunlop.

The following autumn the combined farm and Excise work placed an exhausting burden on the Poet's already fragile health, in spite of the fact that Jean, as well as looking after her baby, Francis, and little Robert, was coping uncomplainingly with milking the cows, churning butter and making cheese. By New Year though, Robert confessed to his brother, Gilbert, 'My nerves are in a damnable State. I feel that horrid hypochondria pervading every atom of both my body and Soul.' The farm, he admitted was a ruinous affair, but he was still defiant, 'Let it go to hell! I'll fight it out and be off with it.'[42]

In the summer of 1790 he was transferred to the Dumfries Third (or Tobacco) Division, which offered the great advantage of reducing the long distances he had been riding across the countryside throughout the previous winter, but the work still involved long days and hard work.[43] Life was continuing to push him to the very edge, so close that he was deeply worried about his health and no doubt so was Jean. During the winter he had a fall, not from his horse, but with his horse, he was careful to tell Mrs Dunlop:

I have been a cripple some time, & . . . this is the first day my arm & hand have been able to serve me in writing . . . I am now getting better, & am able to rhyme a little, which implies some tolerable ease; as I cannot think that the most poetic genius is able to compose on the rack.[44]

He had scarcely recovered from this fall when he received that surprise visit from Mrs Dunlop's protegée, Janet Little, the milkmaid poet whose work had been thrust at him so often by her mistress. He had suffered a second fall in which he had broken his arm and arrived home in no mood to receive a lady poet, no matter how good she might be – and Robert knew that this particular one was worthless. Jean, in the very last stages of pregnancy, wept, and Jenny was left to return to Mrs Dunlop with another sad tale of a rebuff by Poet Burns.

Robert was at the end of his tether: he knew he had to rid himself of the burden of Ellisland, and fortunately Miller was willing to buy back the lease in order to sell the farm, which was on the opposite side of the River Nith and isolated from the rest of his estate. In October 1791, he wrote to Peter Hill in Edinburgh to say that the lease was sold. All he had to do was sell off his stock and crops and he and Jean would be free to leave farming for the more secure world of the Excise Service.

Jean accepted all this as she had suffered all through their life apart and together. She always took first place in her husband's heart, but second place in his life. Her position is well illustrated by the letter the Poet dashed off to Mrs Dunlop when their son, Francis, was born:

More luck still! About two hours ago I welcomed home your little Godson. He is a fine squalling fellow with a pipe that makes the room ring. His mother as usual. *Zelucco* I have not thoroughly read so as to give a critique on it.[45]

Poor Jean was just 'as usual,' and there was no need to say more – four words crammed between joy at the new child and an opinion on *Zelucco*, a new novel by Dr John Moore, the man to whom Mrs Dunlop had introduced the Poet a couple of years earlier. 'The casual reference to Jean,' wrote James Mackay, 'leaves us with the uneasy feeling that Jean was, by now, of little account. The dozen songs associated with her were compositions of the courtship and honeymoon period; after the spate of "much-loved fellow creature" confessions to correspondents in 1788 Jean virtually disappeared from Robert's letters, beyond the occasional perfunctory reference to "my Rib" or "my Goodwife" or "Mrs B" in the closing salutation. She was an infinitely better wife than he ever appreciated or deserved; but beyond the strictly domestic duties of a wife, mother and dairywoman, Jean played no part in Robert's life, intellectually or socially.'[46]

These circumstances fitted in well with Burns' view of womankind as given to his brother, William, about the same time. 'Women have a kind of sturdy sufferance which qualifies them to endure beyond, much beyond the common run of Men; but perhaps part of that fortitude is owing to their short-sightedness, as they are by no means famous for seeing remote consequences in all their real importance.'[47]

Robert Burns, however, was by no means far-sighted when it came to anticipating the consequences of any of his actions. He could show an incredible failure to understand women despite the crucial part they played in his life and creativity, especially those who were closest and dearest to him, and on whom he depended most. Fortunately, Jean Armour was a loyal and patient woman who expected nothing, and she was not disappointed.

# CHAPTER THIRTEEN

# *Whittling Cherry-Stones*

The man who had written a volume of masterpieces in six months, during the remainder of his life rarely found courage for any more sustained effort than a song . . . but it is not the less typical of his loss of moral courage that he should have given up all larger ventures, nor the less melancholy that a man who first attacked literature with a hand that seemed capable of moving mountains, should have spent his later years in whittling cherry-stones.

Robert Louis Stevenson on
Robert Burns' song-writing[1]

Burns was right when he said that some of his Edinburgh 'friends' would soon forget him, but he continued to be remembered and admired by many others, who kept in touch with him throughout his life. But his time in Edinburgh did set him on the road to his future life's work as a song-writer. By meeting James Johnson and hearing songs in drawing-rooms and pubs, sung by fashionable ladies and wild Crochallan Fencibles, the interest in folk-song which had always absorbed him suddenly became his life's work.

Not only did he enjoy the folk-music, he found that he had a genius for handling it sensitively to revive folk-songs which otherwise would have been lost and to create new songs matched to old tunes. He gave Scotland a gift of song such as she had never known, and to this day Burns' name means song to the Scots more than anything else.

During the first years in Dumfriesshire this interest grew into an obsession into which he poured the same sort of energy and effort as had made 1785, his annus mirabilis, so productive. His legacy of song was little appreciated at the time and was belittled even a century later by men like Robert Louis Stevenson who ought to have known better, but it has proved his enduring gift, not just to Scotland but to the world. Today he is better known and loved for his songs than for any of his other poetry.

Burns' life always followed the pattern of the seasons. Unremitting hard work on the farm and the Ayrshire climate had already so damaged his health that a blanket of depression fell over him each year as the days shortened and became darker. His physical health and spirits sank to their lowest in winter and were only warmed back to life as spring returned. By autumn he reaped his creative harvest: 'I am in song', he was able to cry at this time of year, but it was a brief song with wavering notes, which died away again as winter once again approached.

Throughout that first lonely summer and autumn at Ellisland without Jean, and then on the long rides he had to make through the countryside to carry out his Excise work in subsequent years, Burns always had a song in his mind. Song-writing became the passion that carried forward his career as a poet. The gentle rhythm of the horse's movements, the calm of the country which left him to his own thoughts, suited his way of working perfectly. He was not a poet who set down draft after draft of a poem, polishing it until he was satisfied with it. A poem generally remained in his head until it was virtually complete, then he set it down on paper.

Whenever he tried to work at a piece, as in the *Epitaph on the Death of Sir James Hunter Blair*, the *Epistle to Robert Graham of Fintry*, or the ill-starred chore of an epitaph *On the Death of Lord President Dundas*, it always turned flat and lifeless. As he admitted to his friend Alexander Cunningham, in March, 1791, 'I have two or three times in my life composed from the wish, rather than from the impulse, but I never succeeded to any purpose.'[2] Burns' best poetry was immediate and moved straight from emotion to the words he put on the page.

In song-writing this proved a great advantage, for he was a passionate man, always moved by emotion, so this 'immediate' form of composing suited him well, especially in songs where he was moving from the music to words.

Burns was unaware of it at the time, but from earliest childhood he had been working towards song-writing. His mother's singing of old ballads, the telling of country tales, and all the stories of folk heroes, such as Bruce and Wallace, became the tools of his trade, and his vivid mind added its own emotional dimension.

His meeting James Johnson in Edinburgh brought his song-writing into focus, and created virtually a new career as a poet, which drove him compulsively for the rest of his life. Even during his tours of the Borders and especially on his journeys through the Highlands, his listening ear at all times was tuned to old songs and airs. His greatest piece of good fortune was to meet Neil Gow, the great fiddle composer in Perthshire, and hear him play. Many of Gow's tunes were stored away in Burns' mind for later use in his songs.

The Poet was less lucky when he reached the north-east of Scotland because he passed within a few miles of the home of the Reverend John Skinner, one of Scotland's finest song-writers, without realizing he lived nearby. Skinner was author of *Tullochgorum*, which Burns considered 'the best Scotch Song ever Scotland saw', and other songs he admired greatly. There was some consolation, however, in the fact that he encountered Skinner's son in Aberdeen; Robert would readily have turned back but for Willie Nicol, who was forever hurrying him on during the Highland Tour. Young Skinner told his father he had met Robert Burns, and that the Poet had been collecting 'auld Scotch sangs he had not before heard of, and likewise the tunes that he might get them set to music.'[3] As a result John Skinner sent the Poet a rhyming epistle, and the two corresponded afterwards.

In September 1792, just weeks after the fourth volume of Johnson's *Musical Museum* appeared, Burns received a letter, asking if he would help with yet another Scottish song collection. The moving spirit behind this project was George Thomson, a Fife schoolmaster's son only a couple of years older than Burns, who worked as a clerk with the Board of Trustees for the Encouragement of Art and Manufacture in Scotland. His great passion was music, both as a player and a listener. Thomson played in the orchestra of the St Cecilia concerts in Edinburgh, and enjoyed listening to traditional Scottish songs, but his gentle ear was often offended by the unrefined coarseness of the words or the music. As we know this was a time when every pressure was being put on people in all walks of life in Scotland to repress their Scottishness and adopt English ways, speech and manners. Unlike Burns, the turning of Scottish folk-songs into tame anglicized ballads was exactly what the educated, refined Thomson applauded.

After hearing the Italian Pietro Urbani sing some of these ballads, Thomson conceived a plan to publish his own collection set to refined accompaniments by the leading composers of the day. As De Lancey Ferguson describes it, the publication was to be 'a sort of Golden Treasury of Scots music.'[4] Alexander Cunningham gave him an introduction to Robert Burns, and at the beginning of September he sent off a letter to the Poet with an outline of what he had in mind.

The idea, he told Robert, was to gather together a hundred of the best Scottish airs and have these arranged by Haydn's pupil, Ignaz Joseph Pleyel, and the words refined into English which would grace concert platforms and drawing-rooms of the South. He did not, however, tell Burns all that; he simply told him: 'It is superfluous to assure you that I have no intention to displace any of the sterling old Songs: those only will be removed which appear quite silly or absolutely indecent.'

Burns wrote back appreciatively the moment he received Thomson's letter, promising to support the plan, 'with all the small portion of abilities I have, strained to their utmost exertion by the impulse of Enthusiasm.'[5] He was quite definite on two points however: he would not accept payment for his work, and the Scottish language must not be excluded. 'If you are for English verses, there is, on my part, an end of the matter,' he told Thomson.

In a postscript to the letter he told Thomson he had his reasons for not wanting his involvement to be too obvious, but did not specify what these reasons were; maybe he did not want to offend Johnson or he may have been anxious that his Excise superiors should not know too much about the project. Needless to say, Thomson was happy to agree to everything. It suited him to have the credit for the work and he could keep his money in his pocket – as for the question of English songs, he believed no doubt that he could deal with that in each song as the collection was put together.

It was a repeat of the *Musical Museum* saga all over again: Pleyel and Thomson's other supporters withdrew for various reasons and Robert was left to carry the burden of keeping Thomson, whose judgment and taste were extremely poor, on course. Within a month the Poet's first doubts showed as he warned Thomson, 'Let me tell you, that you are too fastidious in your ideas of Songs & ballads.'[6]

The first volume of Thomson's *Select Collection of Original Scottish Airs* appeared in June 1793, and Thomson was so pleased with it that he sent Robert a copy accompanied by a five pound note and a warm letter of thanks. Burns was delighted with the book, but was hurt to be offered money, although he did not send it back since returning it 'would savour of bombast affectation.'[7] The truth was that the money arrived at a time when war with France was reducing imports and thus affecting the Poet's Excise income. Burns promised to redouble his efforts in the future progress of Thomson's work.

Although the next volume of Thomson's *Original Scottish Airs* did not appear until after the Poet's death, Burns continued to work all his life to supply Thomson with songs and to find old tunes and songs which he could refurbish, or to take old airs without words and add lyrics to them. Throughout their collaboration, Thomson continually interfered with what Burns sent him, damaging and diluting the Bard's work by constantly refining and anglicizing it. Sadly, Burns was mesmerized by this educated man. He did not realise that his own self-taught knowledge of Scottish song was far purer and ran far deeper than all Thomson had learnt from books or visiting Italian singers.

When Burns set down his thoughts on old Scottish songs in his *Common Place Book* as early as the autumn of 1785, long before he ever met Johnson or Thomson, or was even known as more than a local rhyme-maker around Kyle, he was already demonstrating the profundity of his knowledge of the subject:

There is a certain irregularity in the old Scotch Songs, a redundancy of syllables with respect to that exactness of Accent & measure that the English Poetry requires, but which glides in, most melodiously with the respective tunes to which they are set.

Even this early Burns had the ability to analyse the old ballads and compare them with the songs then appearing in modern collections, which sounded 'trite and lamely methodical' alongside the 'heart-moving melody' of the old ones.

There is a degree of wild irregularity in many of the compositions & Fragments which are daily sung to them by my compeers, the common people – a certain happy arrangement of old Scotch syllables, & yet, very frequently, nothing, not even *like* rhyme, or sameness of jingle at the ends of the lines. This has made me sometimes imagine that perhaps it might be possible for a Scotch Poet, with a nice, judicious ear, to set compositions to many of our more favourite airs, particularly that class of them mentioned above, independent of rhyme altogether.

There is a noble Sublimity, a heart-melting tenderness in some of these ancient fragments, which show them to be the work of a masterly hand; and it has often given me many a heartake [*sic*] to reflect that such glorious old Bards – Bards, who, very probably, owed all their talents to native genius, and the meltings of Love with such fine strokes of Nature, and, O mortifying to a Bard's vanity their very names are buried mongst the wreck of things which were.

He longed to be set alongside these nameless bards, although he confessed to them that he was 'far inferiour to your flights, yet eyes your path, and with trembling wing would sometimes soar after you.'

Some of you tell us, with all the charms of Verse, that you have been unfortunate in the world – unfortunate in love; he too has felt all the unfitness of a poetic heart for the struggle of the busy, bad World; he has felt the loss of his little fortune, the loss of friends, and worse than all, the loss of the Woman he adored! Like you, all his consolation was his Muse – She taught him in rustic measures to complain – happy, could he have done it with your strength of imagination, and flow of Verse!

Besides revealing Robert's deep understanding of folk-song, to which he was eventually to devote his life, this entry in the *Common Place Book* demonstrated that, as always, Robert Burns' heart was tinder. Chronologically, the entry came between Lizzie Paton's child and his meeting with Jean Armour, while he was burning with love for Montgomerie's Peggy.

As time went by he extended his knowledge of folk-song, but with Johnson and even more with Thomson, he was far too modest. Burns argued his case point by point in each song where there was a difference of opinion, but Thomson usually ignored him and continued to alter the songs. One of the worst examples of this occurred in the song *Scots Wha Hae*. Burns was moved to tears when he heard the old air *Hey Tutti Taitie*, the tune traditionally believed to have been the march played as Bruce led his men on to the field of battle at Bannockburn in 1314. Burns was also equally affected by the trials of the supporters of reform, the Friends of the People, which took place during the summer of 1793. He fused the old tune to the idea of freedom and the result was the powerful song of liberty, *Scots Wha Hae*. The song began as a cry for freedom by Sir William Wallace and Robert the Bruce, but in its last verses turned into a cry against the trials of the dissident reformers, Thomas Muir and Thomas Fyshe Palmer:

> Scots, wha hae wi Wallace bled,
> Scots, wham Bruce has aften led,
> Welcome to your gory bed
> > Or to victorie!

The last two verses were written with the trials of 1793 very much in mind:

> By Oppression's woes and pains,
> By your sons in servile chains,
> We will drain your dearest veins,
> > But they shall be free!

> Lay the proud usurpers low!
> Tyrants fall in every foe!
> Liberty's in every blow!
> > Let us do, or die![8]

Burns was far too modest in the preface to his letter when he sent the song to Thomson:

> You know that my pretensions to musical taste, are merely a few of Nature's instincts, untaught & untutored by art. For this reason, many musical compositions, particularly where much of the merit lies in Counterpoint, however they may transport & ravish the ears of you, Connoisseurs, affect my simple lug no otherwise than merely as melodious Din. On the other hand, by way of amends, I am delighted with many little melodies, which the learned Musician despises as silly & insipid.[9]

Thomson, having been handed such a self-deprecating opinion of Burns' musical ability, took the liberty of suggesting another tune, which meant ruining the last line by having to extend every fourth line thus: 'But they shall be, *shall be* free.' Burns eventually agreed. After his death this change was discovered and the words restored to their original tune.

Thomson not only vandalized Burns' work, but was so jealous of their association that he endeavoured to ensure that the Poet's work did not appear elsewhere. Burns often suggested that if a song should prove unsuitable for his collection, he should return it so that it might be passed on to Johnson for the *Musical Museum*. Thomson sent nothing back just to prevent Johnson from using it. After Burns' death Thomson inked out comments in the Poet's letters, which he thought might make him look foolish, and he tried to hide the fact that Burns had not given him the copyright to his work.

Thomson was generous with presents and quickly responded when Burns wrote to ask for some payment as he was dying. After the Poet's death, he was a driving force behind the plan to set up a memorial to the Bard in Edinburgh, but he did commit one mean act which is hard to forgive. He wrote an obituary of the Poet, which appeared not only in the Edinburgh and Glasgow newspapers, but was copied by others throughout the country. In this he wrote:

> The public, to whose amusement he has so largely contributed, will learn with regret that his extraordinary endowments were accompanied with frailties which rendered them useless to himself and his family. The last months of his short life were spent in sickness and indigence; and his widow, with five infant children and in the hourly expectation of a sixth, is now left without any resource but what she may hope from the regard due to the memory of her husband.[10]

It was a terrible libel on Burns, and poor reward for all the selfless work Robert Burns had put into his project.

Thomson should have known that what he was writing about Burns was nonsense: although he never met the Bard, Burns sent him no fewer than fifty-seven letters over four years – such was the depth of the Poet's involvement in the *Select Collection of Original Scottish Airs*. In these letters he did much more than demonstrate how he never let up in his search for old airs, and ballads wherever he went: he showed how he altered the tempo to fit his words and refined the words to fit the tune. In short, his letters to Thomson display what a complete song craftsman he was. He revealed to Thomson much of his personal life in his letters, too, and Thomson ought to have known Burns better than to write such an obituary.

Burns, of course, knew far more about folk-song than his editors in Edinburgh: indeed, more about it than probably any man in Scotland. When Thomson objected to the air *The Quaker's Wife*, for example, the Poet was able to tell him that an old Highland gentleman and antiquarian had assured him it was a fine old Gaelic air. When the Highland soldiers of Breadalbane's Fencibles were stationed in Dumfries, he discovered from one of them that he had heard his mother sing Gaelic songs both to the tune *Robin Adair*, which had been giving him much trouble, and to *Gramachree*. Wherever he went his ear was attuned to any singer or instrument he heard, and he talked to people, whatever their social background: as a result he picked up hundreds of old airs, and often the story behind them. The encounter with the Highland soldiers was probably no more than a chance meeting in a public house in Dumfries, but it added to the Poet's store of folk-music knowledge, and that was all that mattered to Robert Burns.

Burns' songs encompassed much more than the subject of love and he wrote on every theme from politics to topical events in the district, such as the 'Whistle' drinking contest between three local lairds in which the prize was a whistle, which went to the last man who remained sober enough to blow it. *The Whistle* was a long, meandering ballad, but was intended to be sung.

Although he never claimed it for himself, Burns put his own stamp of genius on that song which has become the universal song of parting: *Auld Lang Syne* is known throughout the world and is sung from Burns Night to New Year's Eve and at many, many other gatherings in between.

> Should auld acquaintance be forgot,
>     And never brought to mind?
> Should auld acquaintance be forgot,
>     And auld lang syne?*            *long time ago

*Auld Lang Syne* is about love: not physical love between man and woman but that deep affection which unites humankind to humankind. This song does not talk of love in general, but through remembered acquaintance it penetrates the heart. *Auld Lang Syne* is as simple as it is beautiful, and speaks for all people and all times.

> We twa hae run about the braes,
>   And pou'd* the gowans* fine,      *pulled *ox-eyed daisy
> But we've wander'd monie a weary fit,*                *foot
>   Sin* auld lang syne!                                *since
>
> We twa hae paidl'd* in the burn                    *paddled
> Frae morning sun till dine,*                    *dinner time
> But seas between us braid hae roar'd
>   Sin auld lang syne.

Even at the end, when a hand is extended and a toast drunk to those days long gone, the song does not turn into something sentimental but encapsulates enduring affection.

> And there's a hand my trusty fiere,*              *comrade
>   And gie's a hand o thine,
> And we'll tak a right guid-willie waught,*          *drink
>   For auld lang syne.
>
> For auld lang syne, my dear,
>   For auld lang syne,
> We'u tak a cup o kindness yet,
>   For auld lang syne![11]

All through life, love was a mainspring of Burns' inspiration for song-writing, and he was master of the love song. This does not mean he made love to every woman whose name is attached to one of his ballads, although he confessed that being in love helped. Once he told Thomson:

Do you think that the sober, gin-horse routine of existence could inspire a man with life, & love, & joy – could fire him with enthusiasm, or melt him with pathos equal to the genius of your book? No! No!!! Whenever I want to be more than ordinary in song . . . do you imagine I fast & pray for the celestial emanation? *Tout au contraire*! I have a glorious recipe . . . I put myself in a regimen of admiring a fine woman; & in proportion to the adorability of her charms . . . you are delighted with my verses.[12]

Many of the women who were the subjects of his songs were no more than girls, some of them very young indeed. Jeany Cruikshank, the daughter of his Edinburgh schoolmaster friend, William Cruikshank, was only twelve when she was playing and singing his songs; she was rewarded twice over, with *To Miss Cruikshank* and the lovely *Rosebud by my Early Walk*.

Jean Jaffray, the daughter of the minister at Ruthwell in Dumfriesshire, was no more than fifteen when he wrote *The Blue-eyed Lassie*, telling her he had fallen in love with her 'lovely een o bonie blue'. The McMurdo girls from Drumlanrig, Jean and Phillis, were a little older, but one can only wonder how their hearts must have turned over when this respectable married man sent a song to them – especially Jean when she received *Bonie Jean*, accompanied by a letter in which he told her he thought he had hit off 'a pretty likeness' of her.[13]

> O Jeanie fair, I lo'e thee dear.
>   O canst thou think to fancy me?
> Or wilt thou leave thy mammie's cot,
>   And learn to tent* the farms wi me?[14]          *look after

Jean Jaffray and Jean McMurdo are proof that it must not be assumed that in every song in which a 'Jean' appears it refers to Jean Armour. There were others, Jean Ronald of the Bennals, Mauchline Belle Jean Markland and, of course, Jean Lorimer, his Chloris, inspirer of a number of songs. There were many Jessies, Janes and Jennies too – just names which fitted nicely into the ballads he set to old tunes.

Robert enjoyed sharing a bawdy poem with William Stewart, the Closeburn factor, who helped him to make arrangements for taking over Ellisland. But Stewart's teenage daughter was given her very own song, *Lovely Polly Stewart*.

> O lovely Polly Stewart,
>   O charming Polly Stewart,
> There's ne'er a flower that blooms in May,
>   That's half so fair as thou art!

Burns prayed that Polly might find a husband with a loyal and true heart:

| May he whase arms shall fauld* thy charms | *fold |
| Possess a leal* and true heart! | *loyal |
| To him be given to ken* the heaven | *know |
| He grasps in Polly Stewart.[15] | |

Alas, Burns was as unreliable at predicting other people's lives as he was at foreseeing his own. Polly married her cousin, who gave her three sons, then became caught up in some trouble and ran away and left her. She contracted what was described as 'a quasi-matrimonial alliance' with a farmer, George Welsh, a great-uncle of Jane Welsh Carlyle, but left him to follow a Swiss soldier called Fleitz, with whom she wandered around Europe until she died in 1847.[16]

Through the various phases of Burns' life there were many others, like these young girls, who did not light up the Poet's tinder heart. They were paid the compliment, however, of becoming the heroine of one of his songs.

In the early Ayrshire days it was, of course, genuine love that spurred him to poetry, and his heart was then always on fire for some girl. At this time he was not yet aware of his mission to rescue folk-song and it was his heart that was leading him on to write verse and set it to tunes he knew. In the Mount Oliphant and Lochlie days there were many charmers who inspired him: among them Nelly Kilpatrick (*My Handsome Nell*), Peggy Thomson (*My Peggy's Charms*), Agnes Fleming, (*My Nanie O*), and Anne Rankine, of *The Rigs o' Barley*:

> I'll ne'er forget that happy night,
> Amang the rigs wi Annie.[17]

Wilhelmina Alexander was different: he saw her only fleetingly as she walked by the river, and boldly sent *The Lass o' Ballochmyle* to her. He was, of course bitterly upset when she ignored both him and his poem.

In Tarbolton and Mauchline there were 'belles' galore to inspire him, not always to the most gracious thoughts of love, but at least to verse. The Ronalds of the Bennals were so fine that he did not dare tell the girls of the family he loved them for fear of rebuff:

| Yet I wadna choose to let her refuse | |
| Nor hae't* in her power to say na, man: | *have it |
| For though I be poor, unnoticed, obscure, | |
| My stomach's as proud as them a' man.[18] | |

Love continued to reign during the Mauchline period of his life. The

235

shadowy Alison Begbie inspired a number of fine songs, *The Lass of Cessnock Banks*, *Bonie Peggy Alison* and possibly *Mary Morison* and *Farewell to Eliza* as well. Love was certainly the catalyst now, for it was at this point that Jean Armour and 'Highland Mary' Campbell came into his life, and they both remained a source of inspiration for songs all his life.

Another Ayrshire lass, Lesley Baillie, the daughter of Robert Baillie of Mayfield, inspired him, but only much later, when he met her and her sister in Dumfries as they travelled south to England in 1792. In a letter to Mrs Dunlop, written from Annan on 22 August, he told how he took his horse, 'tho' God knows I could ill spare the time,' he said, and rode 14 or 15 miles along the road with them. He never saw Lesley again, but on the ride home he composed a ballad to her, *Saw Ye Bonie Lesley*, and nearly a year later he sent her another song, *Blythe Hae I been on Yon Hill.*

At about the same time he sent the same song to Deborah Duff Davies, a Welsh relation of Robert Riddell, with a letter telling her: 'I am a great deal luckier than most poets. When I sing Miss Davies or Miss Lesley Baillie, I have only to feign the passion – the charms are real,'[19] a revealing comment on his ability to imagine himself in love with any woman on the slightest pretext.

Although Miss Duff Davies was far too well bred for his heart ever to aspire to loving her, he did admire her great beauty and wrote several poems to her, including one of his simplest and most exquisite little songs, *Bonie Wee Thing*.

> Bonie wee thing, cannie* wee thing,      *gentle and kind
> Lovely wee thing, wert thou mine,
> I wad wear thee to my bosom
> Lest my jewel it should tine*.[20]          *lose

Beautiful though the words are, it is the music to which they are set that makes *Bonie Wee Thing* a gem. Thomas Crawford observes in his study of Burns' songs: 'When one considers *"Bonie Wee Thing"*, it is nothing less than criminal to ignore the music . . . When sung to the traditional tune [recorded in a primitive form as early as 1627 . . .] it conveys an almost agonised mingling of protective tenderness with the conviction of absolute unattainability.'[21]

Edinburgh and the Scottish tours spawned their quota of songs in praise of women and love, for it was during this time that Burns gathered much of the raw materials which formed the basis of his future song-writing. On the tours his compliments were not always well received. Euphemia Murray of Lintrose, who was also staying at Ochtertyre in

Clackmannanshire while Burns was visiting, was not at all overwhelmed by his song in her honour, *Blythe Was She*:

> Her looks were like a flow'r in May,
>  Her smile was like a simmer* morn:        *summer
> She tripped by the banks of Earn,
>  As light's a bird upon a thorn.
>
> Her bonie face it was as meek
>  As onie* lamb upon a lea.        *any
> The evening sun was ne'er sae sweet
>  As was the blink o Phemie's e'e.[22]

Perhaps Phemie thought the words too rough and unsophisticated to describe a girl like herself, an eighteen-year-old who was admired by her peers as 'the Flower of Strathearn'. Maybe it was simply that the Poet himself appeared too unsophisticated to her. She may have found his raw sexuality unattractive. Or possibly, as the Editor of the bi-centenary edition of *Burns' Complete Works* suggests, she just objected to the phallic metaphor of the title of the air to which the song was sung – *Andro and his Cutty\* Gun*.[23] For whatever reason, Euphemia Murray did not appreciate the honour Burns had bestowed on her.

More appreciative, but still cautious, were Margaret Chalmers and Charlotte Hamilton whom he met on this same tour. He and James Adair, who accompanied him, both fell in love: Burns with Peggy Chalmers and Adair with Charlotte. Burns was rejected, but Charlotte, the half sister of Gavin Hamilton, eventually married Adair. He wrote the rather tame *Banks of the Devon* to Charlotte, but for Peggy there were three songs, which clearly came from somewhere close to the heart. Peggy was reluctant to allow *My Peggy's Charms* to be published, perhaps because it came too near the truth:

> I love my Peggy's angel air,
> Her face so truly heavenly fair,
> Her native grace so void of art:
> But I adore my Peggy's heart.[24]

*Where Braving Angry Winter's Storms* spoke poetically of tearing Peggy from Burns' soul. *Fairest Maid on Devon Banks*, sent to Thomson at the

*short

very end of his life, showed that the memory of Peggy continued to haunt him in spite of his happy marriage to Jean:

> Then come, thou fairest of the fair,
> Those wonted smiles, O, let me share,
> And by thy beauteous self I swear
>     No love but thine my heart shall know![25]

It was in Dumfriesshire that Burns came into his own and a number of women inspired him there, including his Jean. Marriage suited Burns remarkably well all things considered, and in spite of the way in which he often took Jean for granted, he realized the value of the woman he had beside him. While writing to the recently married Alexander Cunningham, 10 September 1792, he set out his views on the subject:

Marriage, we are told, is appointed by God and I shall never quarrel with any of HIS Institutions. I am a Husband of older standing than you, & I shall give you my ideas of the Conjugal State (*En passant*, you know I am no Latin [scholar], is not 'Conjugal' derived from *Jugum* a yoke?) Well then, the scale of Good-wife ship I divide into ten parts. Good Nature, four; Good-Sense, two; Wit, one; Personal Charms, viz, a sweet face, eloquent eyes, fine limbs, graceful carriage (I would add a fine waist too, but that is so soon spoilt you know) all these, one; as for the other qualities belonging to, or attending on, a Wife, such as fortune, connections, education, (I mean education extraordinary) family-blood, &c. divide the two remaining degrees among them as you please; only remember that all these minor properties must be expressed by *fractions*, for there is not any one of them in the aforesaid scale, entitled to the dignity of an *integer*.[26]

That was all very well, but Jean, for all her lack of education – or perhaps because of it – brought another important quality, a fund of old tunes and a simple ability to hum them over to him so that he could get the 'feel' of the lyric which suited them best. On 2 July 1793, Burns sent Thomson the song *There was a Lass & she was Fair*, with a note saying that Stephen Clarke had taken it down 'from Mrs Burns' wood-note wild', and that Clarke had taught it to 'some young ladies of the first fashion here.'[27] *The Posie*, too, was composed to fit into a West of Scotland air which Jean first sang to him. He added new words, which described the flowers he gathered for the girl he loved and, although the girl in the song was called May, he was surely thinking of his Jean.[28]

Jean inspired many songs, either directly, or simply by being there with him which prompted him to express his feelings of love. She is never named as the heroine of *The Mauchline Lady*, one of his very early pieces, but the song can surely refer to no one else.

| | |
|---|---|
| When I first came to Stewart Kyle*, | *part of Ayrshire |
|   My mind it was na steady: | |
| Where'er I gaed*, where'er I rade*, | *went *rode |
|   A mistress still I had ay*. | *always |

But when I cam roun' by Mauchline toun,
  Not dreadin anybody,
My heart was caught before I thought,
  And by a Mauchline lady.[29]

Jean provided a thread which ran through his song-writing life: from the savage pain of separation in *Of A' the Airts the Wind can Blaw* to the joy of being united at last in *O, Were I on Parnassus Hill*, joy which surpassed the riches of kings and princes because 'I reign in Jeanie's bosom.'[30] *I hae a Wife o' my Ain* is a gloriously simple, direct cry of jubilation, which becomes even more magnificent when it is sung.

Others women reigned in his bosom in Dumfries during those last few years that were left to him: Ann Park, Maria Riddell, Jean Lorimer and Jessie Lewars. But much of his song-writing had little to do with being in love with any of them. J.C. Dick, who wrote one of the earliest definitive works on Burns' songs, divided the love songs into Personal and General. What Dick meant was that some of the Bard's love songs derived from personal experience, from his own loves, but the majority were impersonal, with no girl involved. It has to be admitted that many of this second category were every bit as good, if not better, than the personal ones. These 'impersonal' songs, such as *A Rosebud by my Early Walk* for little Jeany Cruikshank, and *Bonie Wee Thing* join his more general songs of love to produce a staggering range of folk-songs. Often the words are put into the mouth of a young girl or a mature woman, and they range from *I'm O'er Young to Marry Yet* to *John Anderson, My Jo*.

Robert Louis Stevenson, and others who dismissed this as mere whittling of cherry-stones, failed to understand the importance of the task Burns set himself, and the magnificence of his consequent achievement. The richness of love in Burns' life and in his song-writing is a legacy which has enriched not only Scotland but the whole world.

# CHAPTER FOURTEEN

# My Spirits Fled!

His altered appearance excited much silent sympathy; and the evening being beautiful, and the sun shining brightly through the casement, Miss Craig was afraid the light might be too much for him and rose with the view of letting down the window-blinds. Burns immediately guessed what she meant; and, regarding the young lady with a look of great benignity, said: 'Thank you, my dear, for your kind attention; but oh, let him shine; he will not shine for long for me.'

Incident during a visit by the dying
Poet to Ruthwell Manse[1]

Farm-stock sales were always convivial occasions, with plenty of whisky supplied by the vendor, but the one at Ellisland at the end of August 1791, turned out to be truly homeric and probably the happiest day Robert Burns spent on his farm. He had wisely sent Jean and the children back to Ayrshire out of the way until it was all over. The roup, as locals in the Burns' Country call an auction of this kind, attracted plenty of bidders who competed so fiercely that all of Poet's crops fetched a guinea an acre on average above their value. When the auctioneer laid down his hammer the fun began as Robert told his friend, Thomas Sloan a week later:

Such a scene of drunkenness was hardly ever seen in this country. After the roup was over, about thirty people engaged in a battle, every man for his own hand, & fought it out for three hours. Nor was the scene much better in the house. No fighting, indeed, but folks lieing [sic] drunk on the floor, & decanting, untill [sic] both my dogs got so drunk by attending them that they could not stand. You will easily guess how I enjoyed the scene as I was no farther over than you used to see me.[2]

Although he gave up the lease in September, Patrick Miller allowed Robert and his family to stay on in the house until early November when they moved into Dumfries, to a flat in the Wee Vennel (now Bank Street) rented from Captain John Hamilton of Allershaw. The final departure from Ellisland was unhappy, however, for the buyer of the farm refused to pay Burns for the farm manure, yet Robert was forced to compensate him for the poor state of some of the fences and outbuildings on the farm. The Poet had scratched verses and names on the windows of the house, and as they left, he ordered Jean's young brother, Adam, who was helping with the removal, to smash these panes. Adam did his work well; he did not leave a single window unbroken.

The move to Dumfries did not bring happiness, and Catherine Carswell's view is a severe one. Jean, she said, blamed her husband for what she calls the Ellisland fiasco.

'A man's failure is doubled when he fails under the eyes of his wife,' Mrs Carswell wrote.

> Jean was not backward in blaming her husband for the Ellisland fiasco . . . Jean was not a shrew; but for a time there was wifely scolding in the new home, which consisted of four upstair rooms in the Wee Vennel, and after all no place to be found for her nice little cow. For Robert's writing-table and bookshelves, instead of the pleasant parlour commanding the Nith, there was a mere closet wedged between the two front living-rooms. Happily he was undisturbed by the noise of children . . . But the accusing face of his spouse as she cooked in the small back kitchen was destructive of a poet's peace.[3]

Certainly the flat in the Wee Vennel was cramped and a big change from the farmhouse at Ellisland: there was neither space nor fresh air of the country to enjoy. But neither was there the unending, back-breaking drudgery of farm work for little recompense. Jean certainly missed her 'nice little cow' which she had brought from Ellisland to supply the family with milk, but had to let go because there was nowhere in the Wee Vennel for it to graze. There may also have been a little feeling on that score on the part of Robert, who had had to part with his pet sheep of which he had become so fond. But Jean was not born to farming and had lived in the town all of her life, so she could manage without the country. As for failure, no doubt both had their views on that, but Jean was not the kind of person who would have given Ellisland too much thought. Robert's feelings were a mixture of relief and failure, but most of all the whole episode fuelled his rebellious, reactionary thoughts and increased his depression. He complained to Robert Ainslie in November 1791, that he could not even enjoy bawdy songs any more:

Can you minister to a mind diseased? Can you, amid the horrors of penitence, regret, remorse, head-ache, nausea, and all the rest of the d——d hounds of hell, that beset a poor wretch, who has been guilty of the sin of drunkenness – can you speak peace to a troubled soul?

*Misérable perdu* that I am! I have tried every thing that used to amuse me, but in vain . . . and there is none to pity me. My wife scolds me! my business torments me, and my sins come staring me in the face, every one telling a more bitter tale than his fellow.[4]

He had attempted to write *Elibanks and Elibraes* but the stanzas, 'fell unenjoyed and unfinished'. Then he came upon an old letter of Ainslie's and he began to breathe again. This was the first letter he had written to his old travelling and bawdy song-singing friend for two years, but it cheered him up. The depression referred to in this letter may have been largely the result of the previous night's overindulgence, but it sounds like something that ran deeper. Jean would have every right to scold him for sitting around in a morose mood in their small apartment. In her description of life in the Wee Vennel, given years later, the Poet was often under her feet in the cramped space:

Burns was not an early riser, excepting when he had anything particular to do in the way of his profession. Even tho' he had dined out, he never lay after nine o'clock. The family breakfasted at nine. If he lay long in bed awake he was always reading. At all meals he had a book beside him, on the table. He did his work in the forenoon, and was seldom engaged professionally in the evening. Dined at two o'clock when he dined at home. Was fond of plain things, and hated tarts, pies and puddings. When at home in the evening, he employed his time in writing and reading, with the children playing about him. Their prattle never disturbed him.[5]

Mrs Carswell takes the Poet's feelings further, and suggests that Burns felt he had to escape from Dumfries and the family if only for a few days. He decided to spend a week in Edinburgh where he could see Ainslie and say a last farewell to Clarinda, who at that time was making arrangements to sail to Jamaica. It was about this time, the end of November 1791, that Nancy McLehose wrote to tell him that Jenny Clow, who had borne his child two years ago, was dying in poverty. He had, therefore, a genuine reason for going to Edinburgh to sort out the care of his son. We do not know whether he saw Jenny Clow in the capital, but we know he did spend one last passionate evening at Potterrow, which warmed up his feelings for his Clarinda.

If Jean was behaving in a strange manner after the move into Dumfries, perhaps she had every excuse. Mrs Carswell may have sensed this with womanly intuition, for the farm had not been Jean's only worry during the 1790–1 period. During the summer of 1790, about the time he transferred to the Excise Service in Dumfries, Burns often stayed overnight at the Globe Inn in the High Street in Dumfries, which was run by William Hyslop and his wife, Meg. Their barmaid was a relative of the family, Ann Park, a girl barely out of her teens, and before long the inevitable happened and Ann was pregnant. As Burns broke this news to Jean, she replied that so too was she. The two conceptions must have occurred within a fortnight of one another.

Robert confessed his adultery with Ann Park freely, indeed exulted in it, and then composed what he considered to be one of his very best love songs, defiant against every power of this world (and the next) that might come between him and Ann. The song begins gently enough:

> Yestreen I had a pint o wine,
>   A place where body saw na;
> Yestreen lay on this breast o mine
>   The gowden* locks of Anna.            *golden

Spurred on by that beautiful opening, he exulted in his sexual intercourse with Ann:

> Ye Monarchs take the East and West
>   Frae Indus to Savannah:
> Gie me within my straining grasp
>   The melting form of Anna!
>
> There I'll despise Imperial charms,
>   An Empress or Sultana,
> While dying* raptures in her arms,            *climactic
>   I give and take wi Anna!

And in the postscript he hurls defiance at religious and temporal authority – he will go back to his Ann:

> The Kirk an State may join, an tell
>   To do sic* things I maunna*:          * such *must not
> The Kirk an State may gae to Hell,
>   And I'll go tae my Anna.

> She is the sunshine o my e'e,
>  To live but* her I canna:                           *without
> Had I on earth but wishes three,
>  The first should be my Anna.[6]

We know remarkably little about Ann Park other than that she came from Edinburgh and bore Burns a daughter, but that has not stopped two centuries of speculation on her life and character. Adultery was hard to justify, but some have tried it: without any facts to support him, Chambers, for example, blamed the Poet's lapse on the fact that Jean was away in Ayrshire that summer visiting her family. But that omitted to take account of the fact that she herself conceived within a fortnight of Ann's pregnancy so she could not have been away for long at the key time. Nineteenth-century biographers took their cue from Allan Cunningham, who said of Ann: 'She was accounted beautiful by the customers, when wine made them tolerant in matters of taste.'[7]

Ann may have been a flirt as legend around Dumfries claims, she may have been a trifle loose in her morals, or even have whored regularly with the customers, but that hardly excuses Burns for being unfaithful to his wife. Certainly Ann's relatives at the Globe Inn accepted her pregnancy with equanimity and simply sent her home to Edinburgh to have her baby there. Jean's visit to Ayrshire to be with her family that autumn might well have been to give her space to think things out. She appears to the world as compliant and even complacent, but it must have caused her terrible heartache to discover that, at the very moment she herself was again with child, her husband had made the barmaid at the Globe Inn pregnant too.

In the twentieth century Burns' infidelity is accepted with remarkable calm. Hecht says that, 'Burns' passionate temperament succumbed to Ann's charms and to the opportunity that had offered itself.'[8] Catherine Carswell believes, 'she was neither vicious not venal. She was merely a hearty, gay and lavish Scottish barmaid, self-forgetting and inducing self-forgetfulness.'[9] Hilton Brown said much the same: 'the girl was willing and coarsely attractive, Burns was willing and completely unfastidious.'[10]

Ann gave birth to a daughter on 31 March 1791, who was named Elizabeth after Ann's mother.[11] Jean was delivered of another son on 9 April, and he was named William Nicol after Burns' Edinburgh schoolmaster friend and Highland Tour companion. This was around the time that Burns was nursing his broken arm so for Jean the joy of the birth of her son must have been doubly marred.

It is strange that the three daughters that Burns fathered, all to different mothers, Lizzie Paton's 'dear bought Bess', Ann Park's child, and Jean Armour's child born in 1792, were all named Elizabeth. Just as the Poet's mother had taken the Paton child in and reared her at Mossgiel, Jean took Ann Park's Elizabeth and reared her as one of her own family. If Jean was upset at the time of her husband's lapse, she was resigned enough by the time little Betty Park came to the Wee Vennel, for all she said was, 'Oor Rab should hae had twa wives.'

Hecht's charitable verdict is:

> We are less struck by Burns' moral lapse than by the wonderful behaviour of Jean, who in her understanding kindness took the child, apparently without a word of reproach, and brought it up with her own children . . . No better proof can be given of the amiable and good natured disposition which Burns valued and praised as being among the great virtues of Jean, than her courageous acceptance of what could not be altered.[12]

It is sometimes suggested that Ann Park was Burns' only infidelity after he took Jean for his wife, but his tinder heart did flare into flame with other women during the rest of his life in Dumfries. By and large, however, he appears to have been discreet.

The move into Dumfries gave a great fillip to the Poet's social life, although he already had a large circle of friends in the town. Robert Riddell of Glenriddell had provided not only social contacts, but had given great stimulus to Burns as a poet, partly through his own interest in music, but also by introducing him to the man who was to inspire him to his greatest single poetical work, one of the great narrative poems of all time, *Tam O' Shanter*. It all came about through a meeting with Captain Francis Grose, a large, fat, extremely jolly man, with wide experience of the world, and a host of influential friends. Grose could eat, drink and tell entertaining stories; he was a man exactly after Burns' heart. Captain Grose had already completed a six-volume work on *The Antiquities of England and Wales*, and in the summer of 1789, he came to stay with the Riddells while collecting material for a similar work on the antiquities of Scotland. Burns and the Captain enjoyed each other's company, and the Poet wrote an entertaining poem to mark his visit.

| | |
|---|---|
| Hear, Land o Cakes*, and brither Scots | *land of oatcakes |
| Frae Maidenkirk to Johnnie Groat's, | |
| If there's a hole in a' your coats, | |
|    I rede* you tent* it: | *advise *look to |
| A chield's* amang you takin notes, | *lad/fellow |
|    And faith he'll prent* it.[13] | *print |

Burns suggested a number of places in Ayrshire which Grose ought to draw for his *Antiquities of Scotland*, among them the old ruined church at Alloway, which had fired Robert's imagination as a child. Grose agreed but on condition that Burns would write a story to accompany his drawing.

The following June Burns sent Grose three witch stories, followed some months later with one of them in Scots verse. 'Should you think it worthy a place in your Scots Antiquities, it will lengthen not a little the altitude of my Muse's pride,' he told Grose.[14] Grose liked the poem, and the illustration of Alloway Auld Kirk and the long narrative poem, *Tam O' Shanter*, appeared in the second volume of the *Antiquities*.

About the time Burns moved to Dumfries, he was introduced to Captain Riddell's brother, Walter, and his young wife, Maria, who had come to stay at Friar's Carse. The Poet's tinder heart burst into flame once more. Maria was beautiful, she was witty, she was vivacious, and she wrote poetry – not the kind of nonsense that Jenny Little and other women kept pushing in front of him all through his life, but verses 'always correct, and often elegant . . . very much beyond the common run of the Lady Poetesses of the day'[15] in the words of the Poet.

Maria was only nineteen, but she had already been married for more than a year and had a daughter; a second daughter was born towards the end of 1792, the year Burns came into her life. Although still so very young, Maria had seen much of life. She was born Maria Banks Woodley on 4 November 1772, into a family with a colourful international background. Her father, William Woodley, owned plantations in the West Indies and later became Governor of the Leeward Islands. Her mother, Frances Payne, was the daughter of Abraham Payne of St Kitts. Maria appears to have grown up in England, and by the time she was taken out to the West Indies by her parents in 1788 she was a cultured girl of fifteen, who had already developed a taste for writing poetry. She was the kind of girl to be noticed not just because of her beauty, but for her high spirits and intellect.

On the voyage Maria was fascinated by Madeira and by the flying fish and exotic birds around the West Indies, and she wrote a diary and made sketches which she later compiled into a book, *Voyages to the Madeira and Leeward Caribbee Islands; with Sketches of the Natural History of these Islands*. On board the ship was a young widower, Walter Riddell, who had inherited a fortune from his wife who died only a year after marrying him. Walter swept Maria off her feet, and before she was nineteen she had become his wife. They moved back to Britain where he bought an estate near Dumfries which he renamed Woodley Park in Maria's honour.

Although Riddell does not appear to have paid the money due for Woodley Park, and had to hand it back to its owner, he started to make extensive improvements to the house and grounds, during which time he and Maria stayed at Friar's Carse with Robert Riddell and his wife, Elizabeth.

Life must have been uncomfortable for Maria and her husband living at Friar's Carse because Elizabeth Riddell disliked her brother-in-law; indeed, Captain Riddell's wife seems to have disliked many of her husband's friends and relations, even the jolly Captain Grose, and probably Burns as well.[16] She may also have cared little for her pert, verse-writing sister-in-law, especially after Burns met Maria at Friar's Carse and they were clearly attracted to one another.

Elizabeth's opinion of Maria and Burns would certainly not be improved after she foolishly agreed to accompany them on a visit to the leadmines at Wanlockhead. It was January, and they had to set out hours before dawn to ride close on 15 miles to Sanquhar, from where a postchaise took them on to Wanlockhead. Whatever the silent Elizabeth thought, Maria loved it all: the magnificent scenery on the precipitous road 'joined to the interesting remarks and fascinating conversation of our friend Burns, not only beguiled the tediousness of the road, but likewise made us forget its danger.'[17] Eventually they reached a dark, narrow cavern. 'This we entered, each of us holding a taper and bidding Adieu for some hours at least to the fair light of day. The roof is so low, that we were obliged to stoop almost double, wading up to the mid leg in clay and water; and the stalactital fluid continually dropping from the rock upon our heads, contributed to wet us completely thro'.' They walked a mile underground until Burns became claustrophobic and could go no further, but Maria insisted on going down one of the shafts before they returned to the surface, her gloves torn to ribbons by the rock. 'This you will say was a crazy scheme – assailing the Gnomes in their subterranean abodes!' she told her mother afterwards. In her dry drawing-room at Friar's Carse, Elizabeth would have agreed.

When Maria asked Burns to help her find a publisher for her *Voyages to Madeira and the Leewards*, he gave her an enthusiastic letter of introduction to William Smellie, who had printed his Edinburgh Edition. Although Smellie (in Burns' own words) cared nothing 'for the herd of animals called "Young Ladies",' Robert felt certain he would be as impressed by her writing as her outspoken views.[18] He was right, for Smellie loved Maria's work and arranged for it to be published. He enjoyed a kind of fatherly flirtatious correspondence with her from then on, although he was past fifty and she was only turned twenty.

The tone of Burns' own correspondence with Maria quickly became familiar too, and as early as February 1792, he began a letter to her: 'My Dearest Friend'. Maria had been ill, which is hardly surprising considering the rigours of the recent Wanlockhead and Edinburgh visits. He ended the same letter: 'God grant that you may live at least while I live, for were I to lose you it would leave a Vacuum in my enjoyments that nothing could fill up.'[19]

Burns and Maria already had secrets. He told her in reply to a letter she sent him from Edinburgh, which has not survived:

> As to your very excellent epistle from a certain Capital of a certain Empire, I shall answer it in its own way sometime next week; as also settle all matters as to little Miss. Your goodness there is just like your kindness in everything else.[20]

This mysterious reference to Maria helping to *'settle all matters as to little Miss'* was never referred to again, but the most likely explanation is that he had asked Maria to make some arrangements about Ann Park's child while she was in Edinburgh, and she willingly obliged. Certainly the two felt close enough for Robert to ask such a favour.

Robert's career was going well at this time, with promotion to Dumfries Third or Port Division, which he told Maria was worth £70 a year plus a further £15 to £20 of perquisites. It was about this time that he was involved in capturing the smuggling ship *Rosamond*, and subsequently bought four of her carronades and sent them off to France as a gesture of sympathy with the revolutionaries. They got no further than Dover, where they were seized. This and other indiscreet remarks from Robert's unguarded tongue, led to an inquiry into Burns' loyalty before the year was out, but this came out in favour of the Poet.

However, 1792 was not all taken up with coping with a growing family in a small apartment, chasing smugglers, or fending off accusations of disloyalty. The fourth volume of Johnson's *Musical Museum* was published, Burns began work with Thomson on his *Select Scottish Airs*, he was made an honorary member of the Royal Company of Archers in Edinburgh, and towards the end of the year, on 21 November, Jean presented him with their seventh child, a daughter, who was named Elizabeth Riddell in honour of the wife of his friend Robert Riddell. He would probably much rather have named the child Maria, for he was now closer than ever to Walter Riddell and his wife, who had settled into Woodley Park and welcomed Burns into their home or to their box in the Dumfries theatre.

In spite of constant ill health, Burns settled well into his Excise job, was promoted, and provided well for Jean and the children. But his family was growing and he needed more space. Captain Hamilton offered them a fine two-storey house in Mill Hole Brae, a house that was much grander than the street name suggests. Life in Mill Hole Brae (today called Burns Street) was 'genteel', the Poet's son told Chambers.

> They always had a maid-servant, and sat in their parlour. That apartment, together with two bedrooms, was well furnished and carpeted; and when good company assembled, which was often the case, the hospitable board which they surrounded was of a patrician mahogany . . . he possibly was as much envied by some of his neighbours, as he has since been pitied by the general body of his countrymen.[21]

On 18 February 1793, the third edition of Burns' poems, known as the Second Edinburgh Edition, was published by Creech. Although the Edinburgh publisher had bought the copyright of the first volume of poems he published in the capital, the new work was enlarged with a number of new poems by Burns, including *Tam O' Shanter*, but Creech refused to pay the Poet another penny. All Burns received for this edition was a paltry few copies of the work.

Social life at Mill Hole Brae was greatly improved, but Burns enjoyed visiting Friar's Carse and Woodley Park, and he remained as infatuated as ever with Maria. Maria's letters to Burns have disappeared, while his to her tend to be quite short, apologizing for not being able to meet her, to thank her for a copy of her book, to send her a pair of French gloves which he had seized as part of his Excise duties, or to enclose a song or poem. Once he even wrote to ask if she would allow one of her poems to be offered to Thomson for inclusion in the *Select Scottish Airs*. On another occasion he altered the opening of one of his own songs to substitute Maria's name for the original heroine. Thus

> Farewell, thou stream that winding flows
> Around Eliza's dwelling . . .[22]

became:

> The last time I came o'er the moor,
> And left Maria's dwelling.[23]

But it did not please him. 'On reading over this song, I see it is but a cold, inanimate composition,' he wrote. 'It will be absolutely necessary for me to get in love, else I shall never be able to make a line worth reading on the subject.'

Burns was already more than a little in love with this woman who could fire his intellect as well as his heart, who could be compared in intellect only with Peggy Chalmers; certainly Clarinda's mind did not compare with Maria's, and Mrs Dunlop's relationship was on another plane altogether. Mrs Dunlop was intelligent, but she was older and a mother-figure rather than someone with whom to fall in love. Maria soon became 'thou first and fairest of critics', and he came close to revealing his real feeling of love for her. When her birthday came round in November 1793, he sent her a couple of verses in which winter complains to Jove about having been given the worst part of the year – a sentiment which Burns would have endorsed for himself:

> Now, Jove, for once be mighty civil:
> To counterbalance all this evil
> Give me, and I've no more to say,
> Give me Maria's natal day!
> That brilliant gift will so enrich me,
> Spring, Summer, Autumn, cannot match me.'
> ''Tis done!' says Jove; so ends my story,
> And Winter once rejoiced in glory.[24]

At the end of the year he sent Maria a couple of ill-paired songs, *Passion's Cry*, which had originally been written for Clarinda, and *Scots Wha Hae*, but linked them neatly with an accompanying letter which said, 'So much for my two favorite topics, Love & Liberty.'[25]

The tone of his letters is full of teasing affection, daringly close to love, which Maria was too intelligent a woman to fail to understand – and yet there was an uneasiness present. During December 1793, when, after telling her teasingly that she was capricious, he suddenly wrote;

> Could any thing estrange me from a Friend such as you? No! Tomorrow, I shall have the honor of waiting on you. Farewell, thou first of Friends & most accomplished of Women; even with all thy little caprices!!![26]

Nevertheless, as Hilton Brown put it, 'a very pleasant little affair was developing until, only days later he had to face exactly the estrangement he feared and had to sit down and write what has become known as the "Letter from Hell" '.[27]

At the time (and after) not a single person involved mentioned this letter or the incident to which it referred. Currie printed the letter in his biography shortly after Burns' death, but he certainly cut part of it out, as the line of asterisks towards the end indicates, and he may even have altered it as he did with many of the Poet's other letters. Currie did not even say to whom the letter was written: his simple Mrs R**** could have referred to Maria or Elizabeth Riddell, and for a long time it was assumed that the apology was made to Maria. However, the reference in it to 'your husband who insisted on my drinking more than I chose', makes it clear that the letter went to Elizabeth, his hostess, since Maria's husband was in the West Indies at the time. The letter began:

Madam,

I daresay this is the first epistle you ever received from this nether world. I write you from the regions of Hell, amid the horrors of the damned. The time and manner of my leaving your earth I do not exactly know, as I took my departure in the heat of the fever of intoxication, contracted at your too hospitable mansion; but, on my arrival here, I was fairly tried, and sentenced to endure the purgatorial tortures of this infernal confine for the space of ninety-nine years, eleven months, and twenty-nine days, and all on account of the impropriety of my conduct yesternight under your roof. Here am I, laid on a bed of pityless furze, with my aching head reclined on a pillow of everpiercing thorn, while an infernal tormentor, wrinkled and old, and cruel, his name, I think is *Recollection*, with a whip of scorpions, forbids peace or rest to approach me, and keeps anguish eternally awake. Still, Madam, if I could in any measure be reinstated in the good opinon of the fair circle whom my conduct last night so much injured, I think it would be an alleviation to my torments. For this reason I trouble you with this letter.

The 'Letter from Hell' was a long apology for an incident that took place around New Year 1794, and has become known as the 'Rape of the Sabines'. We do not know the details, or even where it happened, but the generally accepted story is that it occurred at the end of a particularly jolly and alcoholic dinner at Friar's Carse. After the ladies withdrew, the gentlemen remained at the table drinking port, and someone suggested they should play a trick on the women by bursting into the room and pretending to seize them as the Romans had carried off the Sabine women. Each man was assigned a 'victim', with Burns given Maria Riddell as his 'Sabine'.

Burns, who had drunk no more than any of the other hard-drinking men at the table but carried it less well, entered into the spirit of the joke

251

with total commitment, and the result was a scene which ended in him being ordered out of the house. Since everybody remained silent ever after, we have no idea who else was involved, but Mrs Carswell, with fanciful (but very plausible) Carswell licence, has envisaged a darker scenario. She suggests that Robert was set up by the 'gentry' and the army officers then stationed in the town, who were well aware that Burns hated them and their 'lobster' coats and who wanted to embarrass him. All the men raced to the drawing-room door, Burns leading the charge – to him it was just the kind of fun that 'might have cropped up as easily at an Ellisland Hallowe'en, a Tarbolton penny bridal or an Irvine Hogmanay.' He grabbed his 'victim' and probably kissed her, only to discover that all the other men had stopped at the door and the poet/Exciseman in Carswell's words 'was stupified to find himself alone.'

A couple of the ladies realized what had happened and tried to intercede on Burns' behalf, but the staid Elizabeth Riddell would have none of it. Neither her husband nor any of the male guests uttered a word of support, and Burns was ordered out of the house. Robert continued his letter, writing expansively and furiously:

> To the men of the company I will make no apology. Your husband, who insisted on my drinking more than I chose, had no right to blame me, and the other gentlemen were partakers of my guilt. But to you, Madam, I have much to apologize. Your good opinion I valued as one of the greatest acquisitions I had made on earth, and I was truly a beast to forfeit it. There was a Miss I—, too, a woman of fine sense, gentle and unassuming manners – do make, on my part, a miserable damned wretch's best apology to her. A Mrs G—, a charming woman, did me the honour to be prejudiced in my favour; this makes me hope that I have not outraged her beyond all forgiveness. To all the other ladies please present my humblest contrition for my conduct, and my petition for their gracious pardon. O, all ye powers of decency and decorum! whisper to them that my errors, though great, were involuntary – that an intoxicated man is the vilest of beasts – that it was not in my nature to be brutal to any one – that to be rude to a woman, when in my senses, was impossible with me – but

> \* \* \* \* \*

> Regret! Remorse! Shame! ye three hell-hounds that ever dog my steps and bay at my heels, spare me! spare me!

> Forgive the offences and pity the perdition of, Madam,
>
> Your humble slave.

The situation called for a short, contrite, grovelling note, but Burns, when he put pen to paper after sobering up, could not stop himself from writing at great length, a half contrite, half hysterical defence, and in language which would not have had the slightest effect on Elizabeth Riddell anyway. Her husband comes out of the affair badly, for he must have realized that Burns was right; he, as host, was as much to blame, but did not have the courage to say so. Riddell was a good man at heart, but perhaps for the sake of peace at home, he accepted that Burns must be struck off his list of friends.

Maria was placed in a very difficult position, since she was in the care of her brother-in-law while her husband was away; she too had to cut herself off from Burns. As far as Friar's Carse was concerned, the breach was final, but towards the end of Robert's life he was reconciled with Maria.

When he received no answer to his letter, Burns' contrition turned into anger and spiteful hatred, which focussed mainly on Maria. Elizabeth Riddell meant little to him, she was merely the wife of one of his closest friends and hostess when he visited Friar's Carse and they could never have had much in common. Naming his daughter after her was a compliment to her husband rather than to her. Burns respected Robert Riddell and they had been good friends. In his heart, he hoped they might be reconciled as time healed Elizabeth Riddell's injured feelings, so he said little against the laird of Friar's Carse.

Maria was another matter. His feelings for her were strong and, when she took the side of the 'enemy' he was deeply wounded and angry. He still cared about Maria as future events showed, in spite of the terrible things he said about her. He returned a book to her soon after the event with a note which said:

> I saw you once since I was at Woodley park; & that once froze the very life-blood of my heart. Your reception of me was such that a wretch, meeting the eye of his Judge, about to pronounce Sentence of death on him, could only have envied my feelings & situation. But I hate the theme; & never more shall write or speak of it.[28]

He also sent back her *Common Place Book* and tried again to win her over, by professing to 'admire, esteem, prize and adore'[29] her, and he sent her an epigram on a remark by Lord Buchan that 'women ought to be flattered grossly, or not spoken to at all.' It flattered Maria fulsomely:

> Maria, all my thought and dream,
>   Inspires my vocal shell:
> The more I praise my lovely theme,
>   The more the truth I tell.[30]

Flattery and talk of books were to no avail. Maria would not dare allow herself to be reconciled because of her family. So it was that Burns turned from flattery to plain abuse in poems like the *Monody on a Lady Famed for her Caprice, From Esopus to Maria,* and those appalling *Lines Pinned on Mrs Walter Riddell's Carriage*:

> If you rattle along like your mistress's tongue,
>   Your speed will out-rival the dart;
> But, a fly for your load, you'll break down on the road,
>   If your stuff be as rotten's her heart.[31]

He sent the lines to Patrick Miller with a suggestion that they should be printed in *The Morning Chronicle*, but Miller wisely ignored them. However, one thing is sure, in a small town like Dumfries, Maria was shown them by someone.

Burns sent the *Lines Pinned on Maria's Carriage* and the *Monody* to Clarinda during the summer of 1794 with a letter as libellous as the verses themselves. The subject, he said, 'is a woman of fashion in this country, with whom, at one period, I was well acquainted. By some scandalous conduct to me, & two or three other gentlemen here . . . she steered so far to the north of my good opinion, that I have made her the theme of several illnatured things.'[32] The *Monody* began:

> How cold is that bosom which Folly once fired!
>   How pale is that cheek where the rouge lately glisten'd!
> How silent that tongue which the echoes oft tired!
>   How dull is that ear which to flatt'ry so listen'd!

And it ended with a chilling epitaph:

> Here lies, now a prey to insulting neglect,
>   What once was a butterfly, gay in life's beam:
> Want only of wisdom denied her respect,
>   Want only of goodness denied her esteem.[33]

Burns was not content simply with slandering Maria, but turned on her husband too and wrote a mock epitaph which was even nastier than the

*Lines Pinned to Maria's Carriage.* It called him vile, a miscreant and a man with a poisoned heart.

In his heart Burns must have hoped for a reconciliation, but as usual 'that damned star' that so often changed the course of his life, intervened. Robert Riddell died unexpectedly in April 1794, leaving Burns so distraught that he sat down immediately and wrote 'a small heart-felt tribute to the memory of the man I loved.'[34] The *Sonnet on the Death of Robert Riddell* appeared in the *Dumfries Weekly Journal.* Even more touchingly, Burns was said to have crept secretly to the little hermitage, which he had enjoyed so much during his first days at Ellisland, and scratched four lines, which expressed his deep feelings:

> To Riddell, much lamented man,
>   This ivied cot was dear;
> Wand'rer, dost value matchless worth?
> This ivied cot revere.[35]

Burns asked for the return of the book of the Glenriddell Manuscripts, which was duly done; his immediate reaction was to insert that nasty little epigram pinned on Maria's carriage in it. Time healed eventually, helped no doubt by the fact that Maria was away from Dumfries for a while during 1794. After she returned first to Tinwald House and then to Halleaths, near Lochmaben, when her husband had been forced to give up Woodley Park, they began to correspond again. By 1795 they were sending one another poems, and she lent Burns a book while he sent the artist Reid's miniature of himself for her to look at. The old teasing note returned: 'I cannot help laughing at your friend's conceit of my picture,' he told her, 'and I suspect you are playing off on me some of that fashionable wit, called HUMBUG.'[36]

Maria comforted him in the autumn when his daughter, Jean's beloved little Elizabeth, died and he was so distressed and ill that he was quite unable to compose for a while. 'I am much correspondence in your debt,' he told her and promised to repay it. 'That you, my friend, may never experience such a loss as mine, sincerely prays RB,' he ended the letter.[37] The relationship may not have been quite on the same plane as before the break, but Robert and Maria were able to give pleasure and comfort to one another again.

Those few weeks at Elizabeth's death apart, Burns hardly ever stopped writing; it was almost as if he realized time was running out and he still had many songs to write for Johnson and Thomson. But the autumn of 1794 was bleak, with ill health, an unsettled life during which he was drinking more than usual and had no Maria. He needed comfort and found it with Jean Lorimer, 'the lassie wi the lint-white locks.'

Jean had just turned twenty-one that autumn, but Burns had known her ever since he first came to Dumfriesshire. Her father farmed not far from Ellisland. She was a lively girl with vivid blonde hair, and Burns was not the only person attracted to her; the hearts of half his Excise colleagues also fluttered for her, but Jean was wooed by a 'ne'er-do-well' from the English side of the Border, whom she married. However, he abandoned her after only a few weeks when he fled from his creditors.

The very first song Robert wrote for the fourth volume of Johnson's *Musical Museum* (published in August 1792) was one he had written for an Excise colleague who was smitten by Jean. *Craigieburn Wood,* named after Jean's birthplace at Moffat, shows how easily he could dash off a song even when he himself was not the person in love:

> Beyond thee, dearie, beyond thee, dearie,
>   And O, to be lying beyond thee!
> O, sweetly, soundly, weel may he sleep
>   That's laid in the bed beyond thee![38]

But Jean did not lie with Gillespie in spite of all Burns' literary efforts. The Bard persevered on his colleague's behalf even after Gillespie left the district, although it would appear that Jean's bedroom door might not have been too tightly shut against the Exciseman had he had the spirit to push it open. Robert sent Gillespie a letter, probably in 1791, enclosing *Craigieburn Wood* and telling him, 'Last night when she and I were a few minutes by ourselves after tea, she says to me, "I wonder, Mr Burns, what pet Mr Gillespie has taken at this country, that he does not come and see his friends again?"'[39] By then the 'great rivals' for Jean's hand, according to the Poet, were his other Excise colleagues, John Lewars and James Thomson.

Burns wrote some twenty-four poems and songs to Jean Lorimer, whom he often called Chloris in his poems. But like Polly Stewart, that other Dumfriesshire heroine of Burns' song, Jean Lorimer never enjoyed a heroic life. After being abandoned by her husband she lived with her father, and when he fell on hard times she went to Edinburgh and lived out her life begging until someone set her up in a housekeeping job. She died in Edinburgh in 1831.

Was Robert Burns in love with Jean Lorimer? James Hogg said as much after meeting her around 1816.

'She said Burns came to Craigieburn all night every time his business called him to Moffat', Hogg wrote . . . 'her feelings were the feelings of a woman, and, though, a ruined one, I loved her for them. She had a lock of his hair keeping in a box. She was then a widow apparently approaching to forty, though she might be younger. She was the ruin of a fine woman, of a fair complexion, and well-made. I heard by her voice that she had once sung well.'[40]

Burns is less explicit, but there are clues in his letters to George Thomson, especially in two long letters written in September and October 1794, when their relationship was at its warmest. Asking Thomson to be sure to include *Craigieburn Wood* in his collection, Burns wrote:

The lady on whom it was made is one of the finest women in Scotland; & in fact (*entre nous*) is in a manner to me what Sterne's Eliza was to him – a Mistress, or Friend, or what you will, in the guileless simplicity of Platonic love. (Now don't put any of your squinting construction on this, or have any clishmaclaiver* about it among our acquaintants) I assure you that to my lovely Friend you are indebted for many of your best songs of mine.[41]

For once, it seems, Burns was using an expression he did not mean for platonic love was not within his ken, unless the woman was utterly unattainable, or an elderly lady like Mrs Dunlop. And, remembering the advice Burns gave to his brother to 'try for intimacy as soon as you feel the first symptoms of passion,'[42] it seems hardly likely that he would have ignored it himself. It seems highly probable that Hogg was right and Robert was in love with Chloris, although there is no evidence as to when their relationship started or when it finished.

> Lassie wi the lint-white locks,
>   Bonnie lassie, artless lassie,
> Wilt thou wi me tent* the flocks-          *tend
>   Wilt thou be my dearie, O?[43]

In November 1794, Burns asked Thomson to send a copy of the *Select Scottish Airs* to Chloris, telling him, 'The Lady is not a little proud that she

*gossip

257

is to make so distinguished a figure in your Collection, & I am not a little proud that I have it in my power to please her so much.'[44]

Burns wrote a great variety of verse for Chloris, not his best, but some heart-felt and delightful songs. In addition to *The Lassie wi the Lint-white Locks*, there were *Ah, Chloris*, the jaunty little *Whistle an I'll Come to You, my Lad*, and *Sae Flaxen were her Ringlets*, whose title identifies the heroine:

> Then, dearest Chloris, wilt thou rove
>     By wimpling burn and leafy shaw*,                    *wood
> And hear my vows o truth and love,
>     And say thou lo'es me best of a'?[45]

A great many of Burns' songs were, as I have mentioned, written as he rode around the countryside on his Excise rounds, but none bears the hallmarks of this style of composing more clearly than one gorgeous little piece he composed to Chloris. It is easy to picture him, approaching Chloris's farm, humming a tune and the words of *I'll Ay Ca' in by Yon Toun* forming within his head as he rode along. He would probably sing it over to her, and write down afterwards in the peace of his study:

> I'll ay ca'* in by yon toun*                         *call *farmstead
>     And by yon garden green again!
> I'll ay ca' in by yon toun,
>     And see my bonie Jean again.
>
> There's nane shall ken, there's nane can guess
>     What brings me back the gate again,
> But she, my fairest faithfu lass,
>     And stow'nlins* we sall meet again.                    *secretly
>
> She'll wander by the aiken* tree,                         *oak
>     When trystin* time draws near again;                 *meeting
> And where her lovely form I see,
>     O haith*! she's doubly dear again.[46]          *exclamation, 'Oh'

'I have been out in the country taking dinner with a friend, where I met with the lady whom I mentioned in the second page of this odds-&-ends of a letter,' he told Thomson on 19 October 1794. 'As usual I got into song; & returning home I composed the following – The Lovers morning salute to his Mistress.' The song was *Sleep'st Thou*, which contained two lines which suggest that the mistress was Chloris:

> When frae my Chloris parted,
> Sad, cheerless, broken-hearted,[47]

In spite of all this complicated life in relation to women, and his political views which caused ripples among his male friends, Burns managed to please his Excise masters. By the end of 1794, when the Supervisor in Dumfries, Alexander Findlater, became ill, Burns was appointed Acting Supervisor for four months. This involved checking the work of the local gaugers and their records, which was meticulous and difficult, but he carried virtually all of it out perfectly despite his poor health at the time. Had his health not broken down, Burns could easily have been on the way to promotion in the Service.

Robert continued to have financial difficulties because of the French Wars, and this clouded his mind. He did some stupid things at this time, but none more silly than write those letters to Mrs Dunlop, which ended their friendship. The only tiny ray of sunshine in this bleak midwinter scene was the return of Maria to him, but she was no longer close to the town and etiquette did not permit them to meet.

At the beginning of the year, while he was doing Findlater's work, there was a very real danger of the French invading. Robert set aside his former pro-French opinions and threw himself wholeheartedly into the formation of a group of Volunteers to defend the area in the event of invasion. He paraded and marched with them and wrote a rousing song for them, *Does Haughty Gaul Invasion Threat?* But all this work and strain took such a terrible toll on his health that he complained to Maria during the spring of 1795, 'I am so ill as to be scarce able to hold this miserable pen to this miserable paper.'[48] But he struggled on to compose, telling her some weeks later that he had not been able to leave his bed that day, yet the muses 'have not quite forsaken me.' And for proof that neither love nor poetry had abandoned him he signed the letter with a flourish – *'L'amour, toujours l'amour!'* and enclosed some lines of verse.

He struggled on with his Excise duties and his work with the Volunteers as well as writing when he felt able. He was well aware of how seriously ill he was becoming, for he told his Edinburgh farmer friend, Robert Cleghorn, he had been suffering from rheumatic fever which 'brought me to the borders of the grave.'[49]

On the last day of January 1796, he made yet another attempt to be reconciled with Mrs Dunlop, but again was ignored. From then on he was constantly ill; his temples and his eyeballs ached and his heart became more irregular. He realized time was short, but continued to try to write. He apologized to Johnson for not having sent him many songs recently, but promised more. 'In the meantime let us finish what we have so well begun,' he told Johnson.[50]

Maria Riddell, who had been away, now felt sufficiently reconciled to invite him to join her party at the King's birthday ball in Dumfries at the beginning of June, but he felt unable to accept. 'I am in such miserable health as to be utterly incapable of shewing my loyalty in any way,' he told her, quoting Hamlet, 'Man delights me not, nor woman either.'[51]

Dr William Maxwell, who was attending him, was alarmed by the deterioration in Robert's condition, and suggested that sea-bathing might be beneficial, so on 3 July the Poet, scarcely able to stand, travelled nine miles along the coast to Brow-on-Solway, where there was a well which was reputed to have medicinal properties. Each day, as ordered by Maxwell, he waded manfully out into the Solway Firth until the water reached up to his armpits, but it had no effect, although at first he did try to believe it was helping. On the fourth day at Brow he wrote to Alexander Cunningham to thank him for some complimentary remarks the literary circle in Edinburgh had made about him:

Alas! my friend, I fear the voice of the Bard will soon be heard among you no more! For these eight or ten months I have been ailing, sometimes bedfast & sometimes not; but these last three months I have been tortured with an excruciating rheumatism, which has reduced me to nearly the last stage. You actually would not know me if you saw me. Pale, emaciated, & so feeble as occasionally to need help from my chair – My spirits fled! fled![52]

Brow was a death sentence, and the only advantage of the stay there was that it brought him closer to where Maria was living, so she was able to invite him to meet her. On the day he wrote to Cunningham, Maria sent her carriage to fetch Robert and they spent some hours together. His greeting shattered her, 'Well, Madam, have you any commands for the other world,' he said as he took her hand. He could scarcely eat anything, but was able to talk freely with this woman who had continued to mean so much to him in spite of the break in their friendship. He spoke anxiously about his family and about his reputation, telling Maria he was afraid his many indiscretions would enable people to attack him using 'every scrap of his writing' against him. They continued this conversation the following day, but as he lifted himself painfully into the carriage to leave, both must have realized that this was their final parting.

Two days later, on the 10th, he sat down and bravely wrote a last farewell to Mrs Dunlop. 'Madam,' he began:

I have written you so often without receiving any answer, that I would not trouble you again but for the circumstances in which I am. An illness which has long hung about me in all probability will speedily send me beyond that bourne whence no traveller returns. Your friendship with which for many years you honored me was a friendship dearest to my soul. Your conversation & especially your correspondence were at once highly entertaining & instructive. With what pleasure did I use to break up the seal! The remembrance yet adds one pulse more to my poor palpitating heart!

Farewell!!!

Robert Burns[53]

He had talked to Maria at length about Jean and the children, and in his last letter to Cunningham on 7 July he asked his friend to use his influence with the Excise authorities to ensure that his salary would not be reduced further. Jean was again pregnant and due to be delivered soon, and the worry of what would happen to her and the children if he died became an obsession as his health deteriorated. By the time he wrote to Mrs Dunlop he was desperate, and sent letters to Gilbert at Mossgiel and to James Armour in Mauchline, both on the same day:

Dear Brother

It will be no very pleasing news to you to be told that I am dangerously ill, & not likely to get better. An inveterate rheumatism has reduced me to such a state of debility, & my appetite is gone, so that I can scarce stand on my legs . . . God help my wife & children, if I am taken from their head! They will be poor indeed. I have contracted one or two serious debts, partly from my illness these many months & partly from too much thoughtlessness as to expense when I came to town that will cut in too much on the little I leave them in your hands. Remember me to my Mother.

Yours

R. Burns[54]

The letter to James Armour contained a note of hysteria and helplessness and it must have cost him a lot to pen such words to the 'auld enemy':

For Heaven's sake & as you value the welfare of your daughter, & my wife, do, my dearest Sir, write to Fife to Mrs Armour [Jean's mother was on a visit there at the time] to come if possible. My wife thinks she can yet reckon upon a fortnight. The medical people order me, as I value my existence, to fly to seabathing & country quarters, so it is ten thousand chances to one that I shall not be within a dozen miles of her when her hour comes. What a situation for her, poor girl, without a single friend by her on such a serious moment.[55]

Burns meant 'friend' in the way the Scots use the word to mean 'relation', for Jean had support from outside the family. Jessy Lewars, the daughter of John Lewars, the Excise Supervisor at Dumfries and sister of his colleague, another John Lewars, had come in to help her during July, and the Burns children were taken to the Lewars' house to be out of the way. But Burns wanted a relative with Jean when her time came. A week later, after he returned to Dumfries, he wrote to Armour again, pleading for Jean's mother to come at once, and this time he told his father-in-law, 'My medical friends would almost persuade me that I am better, but I think and feel that my strength is so gone that the disorder will prove fatal to me.'[56]

Burns had referred to being in debt in his letter to his brother, but he did not in fact owe serious amounts to anybody – it was only in his own mind that the debtor's prison loomed. When he received a letter to say that the bill from a local outfitter for his volunteer uniform was overdue he panicked and wrote off at once to his cousin, James Burness in Montrose to ask for £10. 'A rascal of a Haberdasher to whom I owe a considerable bill taking it into his head that I am dying, has commenced a process against me & will infallibly put my emaciated body into jail,' he told his cousin.[57] He sent a similar letter to George Thomson, asking for £5, and both men responded immediately. In fact, the tailor's bill was just over £7.

Soon after Robert returned to Mill Hole Brae his condition worsened, and Jean and Jessy Lewars watched helplessly as he drifted in and out of consciousness. On 21 July he heart gave out at last and word was whispered round the streets of Dumfries that the Bard was dead.

Jean sat at home for four days grieving for the man she had loved to distraction, and worried about the future – hers and that of her children. A very grand funeral was arranged for the 25th of the month, with everybody who mattered in the town present – everybody except Jean. As the splendid cortège made its way from the Town hall to St Michael's kirkyard, the unpaid Volunteer uniform hat and sword crowning the coffin, Jean was giving birth to another son in the house on the brow of the hill at Mill Hole Brae. Burns had intended this fourth son to be named Alexander Cunningham after his Edinburgh friend, but instead they named him Maxwell after the doctor who attended Robert and Jean during those last days.

# CHAPTER FIFTEEN

# The Rights of Woman

The frailties that cast their shade over the splendour of superior merit are more conspicuously glaring than where they are the attendants of mere mediocrity. It is only on the gem we are disturbed to see the dust; the pebble may be soiled, and we do not regard it.

'Memoir concerning Burns' written by Maria
Riddell for the *Dumfries Journal*[1]

The three volleys fired by Volunteer colleagues over the coffin as Robert Burns was lowered into his grave were also a salute for the birth of his new child, the last fruit of the love which had followed him all the way from that first encounter with Jean Armour on the bleaching green at Mauchline. Marriage had proved no easier for Jean than courting, but she was still as deeply in love with the National Bard, now being given an honoured burial, as she had been with wild Rab Mossgiel all those years before. As his wife Jean had worked hard to make a home fit for a poet, although she knew nothing about poets or poetry.

Jean, from beginning to end, had always been willing to give herself totally to Burns in spite of everything; young Robert, nearly ten, and Maxwell, who now lay in her arms, were proof of this. He had left her with a fine crop of boys, but she had known the sorrow of losing every daughter she had borne him – all four of them. Lizzie Paton's daughter was growing up at Mossgiel and Ann Park's child was the only one of Rab's girls still with her and she would continue to rear this little Elizabeth because she was Robert's.

On 25 July 1796, as they buried her husband, Jean's mind was not on the past, but on the future, the bleak outlook of rearing her children with little or no money. She need not have feared, for in death, Burns still had many friends, none more faithful than John Syme in Dumfries and Alexander Cunningham in Edinburgh, who both worked tirelessly to ensure that Jean and the children would never be in need.

Two days before the Poet's death Syme had written to Cunningham suggesting they should do something for the family of the dying poet, and the following day, 20 July, unaware of Syme's action, Cunningham sent off a similar letter to him: 'We must think on what can be done for his [Burns'] family. I fear they are in a pitiable condition,' Syme told the Edinburgh lawyer, who had remained a faithful friend to the Poet right to the end. 'All that can be done shall be done by me,' Cunningham said in his letter. 'We must do the thing instantaneously and while the pulse of the Public will beat at the name of Burns.' Cunningham proposed a subscription for Jean and the children, and that the Poet's works, letters and songs should be sold to a London bookseller to raise more money. He felt sure that Burns could not have disposed of the copyright of his later work to Creech, and suggested they investigate the position, but without letting the wily Creech know. 'Creech must not be consulted or dealt with,' he warned.[2]

Within a week seventy guineas had been subscribed in the Dumfries district, but further afield the plan met with less enthusiasm, especially in Edinburgh, where Cunningham said people offered him only 'cold civility and humiliating advice'. Unfortunately, rumours were circulating in the city to the effect that the Excise and government were looking after Jean, so many felt they need do no more than take a guinea out of their pocket for the fund.

Ayrshire was no more generous: the parsimony of Burns' native county angered Syme. 'Col. Fullarton etc. in Ayrshire have as yet done nothing. Nay, those friends in Ayr etc. whom the Bard has immortalized have not contributed a sou!!! By heavens, they should be immortally d—d, and a list of the d—d should be made out.'

In England the response was better, thanks mainly to two men, James Currie, a Dumfriesshire-born doctor now living in Liverpool, and James Shaw in London. But even so, by the following spring, Syme had raised no more than £500 with a promise of a few hundred more. However, thanks to the unflagging work of Syme and his little band, Jean was never in want for a day. The government never gave Burns' widow a grant of any kind, but small annuities were paid later to some of the Poet's sons and grandchildren.

Jean lived on comfortably in Dumfries until her death in 1834, having outlived her husband by thirty-eight years. She did make a number of journeys to visit members of the family around Scotland and in 1828 George Thomson persuaded her to come to Edinburgh, where she not only saw many of her husband's friends, but also met Sir Walter Scott and 'Clarinda'. What Agnes McLehose and Jean Burns had to say to one another was never disclosed, but they could have had little in common except the love of Robert Burns, and neither would be prepared to let any secrets about that out.

Jean's son, Maxwell, died in 1799 at the age of three, and Francis just four years later, in 1803. Robert, her firstborn, had a career in the Stamp Office in London, but retired to Dumfries in 1833, the year before his mother's death. He died in 1857. William Nicol and James Glencairn both joined the East India Company and eventually retired to Cheltenham, where James died in 1865, and William, the longest-lived of all Jean's children, in 1872.

Betty, Lizzie Paton's child, who grew up at Mossgiel, married John Bishop, factor at Polkemmet, East Lothian, and they had seven children. She died in 1817, some said in childbirth. The other Elizabeth, Ann Park's child, whom Jean mothered, married a private in the Stirlingshire Militia, who became a handloom weaver after he left the service. She was the longest-surviving of all Burns' children, dying in 1873.

Burns' reputation fared worse than his family's finance. Maria Riddell, with acute womanly intuition, knew there were some who would savage the Poet's reputation, so she immediately wrote a 'Memoir Concerning Burns' for the *Dumfries Journal*, which described his character in the warmest terms, yet did not flinch from the truth, and summed up his failings with her remark about being disturbed by the dust on the gem, but not noticing that the pebble is soiled.

Maria was right: Thomson, for whom Burns had written so many songs for little or no payment, rewarded the Poet with that obituary notice for the Edinburgh and Glasgow newspapers that spoke of the Poet's 'frailties, which rendered them (his extraordinary endowments) useless to himself and his family.'[3] This set the pattern for other writers, including Robert Heron, who had been the target of Burns' satire, and now took his revenge. Heron's 'Memoir' appeared in the *Monthly Magazine* during the first half of 1797, and was reprinted elsewhere. Although it gave a shrewd assessment of the Poet's work, the 'Memoir' damned him as a drunkard, a fornicator and a boor. It belittled his work as a farmer and exciseman and said he preferred the company he found in taverns and brothels to that of the rich and great. Nothing could have been more carefully calculated to alienate those best able to help Jean and her children.

Syme struggled against this tide of lies and half-truths to ensure Jean's financial security and to preserve the poet's good name by producing a book of Burns' work, which would raise money for the fund and record the true facts of his life. Syme was no expert and was uncertain as to what kind of book should be published, but he felt it ought to be more than simply a volume of Burns' poetry. Dr Currie in Liverpool agreed, and became so enthusiastic that he volunteered to write a life of the Poet, which could be included with the poems. No sooner had Currie made his offer than he realized that he was not qualified for such an undertaking, so he wrote to Syme suggesting that some scholar such as Dugald Stewart should undertake the work. No volunteer came forward, so Currie was pressed to write the *Life*, and the result was a much-criticized first full biography of the Poet.

Currie produced his work from a disorganized mass of papers (the sweepings of the Poet's desk, he called them) and his aim, it must be remembered, was to raise money for Jean. Currie bowdlerized or cut letters or poems, which he thought not quite decent, and he repeated some of the criticisms of the Poet's character. Currie was obsessed by the drinking and sexual side of Burns' life and peppered his work with innuendo, which attracted the worst possible interpretation.

> He who suffers the pollution of inebriation, how shall he escape other pollutions? But let us refrain from the mention of errors over which delicacy and humanity draw the veil.[4]

Ignoring this side of Burns' life might have done him little harm had Currie not been so careless as to lose many of the papers, or so prudish as to destroy others and thus deny future biographers the opportunity of presenting a truer portrait of the Poet. As a result of Currie's actions, and correspondents who were so sensitive about their own characters that they destroyed their letters, much material which might have shed light on the Poet's life was lost. Currie's work raised nearly £2,000 for the Poet's family, but future generations have thought the cost to his reputation too high.

It is easy enough to judge the poetry of Robert Burns after two hundred years because its quality and content have made him immortal. His songs continue to spread his reputation not just across Scotland but around the world. The songs which filled the latter part of his life were Burns' crowning achievement and amounted to nothing short of a miraculous rescue of Scottish folk-song and the re-establishment of it as an element of the nation's vital cultural life. Burns was self-taught but his command of Scottish folk-song was breath-takingly broad: having mastered it, he fused his own genius to it to turn it into a collection beyond price. For that alone, he deserves immortality.

Love was the most vital single element in Burns' folk-song writing. His love songs are a legend and Burns was a legendary lover, but others had to pay the price for the inspiration that took him to the mountain peaks of lyric-writing.

Every generation has set Robert Burns' love life against the mores of its own time, rather than the century in which he lived. The most blatant exercise of such censorship can be found in Henley and Henderson's centenary 'life' of Burns, where they described the 'scalade' letter as in some parts 'too curious for a Victorian page.' Quoting the part about the actual 'scalade of horse-litter' they could not bring themselves to finish the sentence. 'She did all this like a good girl and . . .' – 'The rest is unquotable,' they wrote, ending the matter there just as surely as Currie had ended it nearly a century before.[5]

In Scotland attitudes to illegitimacy in Burns' time were probably closer to those of the present day than any time in between, with sexual intercourse outside marriage a widely accepted fact of life. In the eighteenth century country girls had no rights or aspirations, and consequently were docile and accepted what life brought, and if that was a love-child into the house, then so be it. The Kirk might rail and summon transgressors to stand on the cutty stool, but there was little it could do to alter the situation especially in Burns' West of Scotland, where folk had minds of their own. Every Kirk Session minute book in Ayrshire at that time solemnly records men and women who had fallen foul of the church by committing the sins of fornication or adultery, but that did not curb either.

So far as we know, after the Kirk and community had their say, life went on very much as usual for most girls who had a child by Robert Burns. Only poor Jenny Clow seems to have suffered, and the Poet tried to put matters right for her.

Burns' approach to sex was aggressive, as was his approach to every situation in his life, and it was well in tune with the military metaphors through which he described each sexual campaign – the infantry and the big guns went into battle together, and too often they conquered easily. Yet he could show profound tenderness towards the female sex, and he dearly loved the children they gave him, whether in or out of marriage. Shortly after Jean Armour's first set of twins was born he expressed his feelings to his friend John Kennedy. ''Tis there, Man is blest,' he told Kennedy:

'Tis there, my Friend, man feels a consciousness of something within him, above the trodden clod! The grateful reverence to the hoary, earthly Authors of his being – The burning glow when he clasps the Woman of his Soul to his bosom – the tender yearnings of heart for the little Angels to whom he has given existence – These, Nature has pour'd in milky streams about the human heart: and the Man who never rouses them into action by the inspiring influences of their proper objects, loses by far the most pleasureable [*sic*] part of his existence.[6]

267

He respected women, too, as he demonstrated when he wrote an address for the actress Louisa Fontenelle's benefit night at Dumfries Theatre on 26 November 1792. For the actress, whom he admired greatly, he chose the theme, 'The Rights of Woman,' and opened his address grandly:

> While Europe's eye is fix'd on mighty things,
> The fate of empires and the fall of kings;
> While quacks of State must each produce his plan,
> And even children lisp the Rights of Man;
> Amid this mighty fuss just let me mention,
> The Rights of Woman merit some attention.

*The Rights of Woman* was inspired by Tom Paine's recent *Rights of Man*, of course, and it may not have taken the women's liberation movement, as we know it, very far forward, but it was a recognition that women have rights at a time when they enjoyed very few. Even a woman's property belonged to her husband.

Burns' faltering step along the women's liberation road, spoken by Mrs Fontenelle, listed three rights only – protection, care and admiration. Some of the sentiments expressed must have sounded strange to her audience who would have been aware that they came from the pen of the man who, only the year before, had fathered one child by his wife and another by the Globe Inn barmaid within a fortnight.

> There was, indeed, in far less polished days,
> A time, when rough rude Man had naughty ways:
> Would swagger, swear, get drunk, kick up a riot,
> Nay, even thus invade a lady's quiet!

At the end Burns could not resist drawing in his political opinions, by quoting the cry of the French revolutionaries, *'Ça ira!'*

> Let Majesty your first attention summon,
> Ah! *ça ira!* THE MAJESTY OF WOMAN![7]

In the real world outside Dumfries Theatre Royal, Robert Burns was well aware of the rights of women and respected them. He accepted the women he met on their merits and treated them as equals, which few other men of his time were prepared to. When he met an intelligent, intellectual woman such as Peggy Chalmers or Maria Riddell, he enjoyed her company, wit and conversation as freely as he would have done that of his intellectual male friends.

From Robert's earliest days, when Nell Kilpatrick interrupted his harvest-work at Mount Oliphant and Peggy Thompson upset his trigonometry at Kirkoswald, his tinder heart was easily ignited by the girl who was currently in his life. His boundless passion led to extreme pain when she or he moved on, or in the case of 'Highland Mary' Campbell, years of remorse after she died.

Jean, the ever faithful wife, accepted all this with equanimity, although Catherine Carswell suggests that Jean might not have been as complaisant as history suggests. She must have been a very docile woman, however, to accept her husband's way of life, for she never stood in the way of his friendships which took him out to dine and drink with important people around Dumfries, and she certainly never hankered after being a part of that life. Jean was content to make a home for him, and provide the background against which he could write. Why did she accept all this so meekly?

The answer may simply have been that she understood her husband's passion, after all she had joyed in it many times herself, and she loved him enough to accept him for what he was rather than for what she would have liked him to be. Jean's contribution to her husband's work was more than to hum over a few tunes to him: by her quiet, constant support she made his song-writing possible.

Robert Burns never ceased to write songs from boyhood in the fields at Mount Oliphant until his final days in Mill Hole Brae in Dumfries. From beginning to end, love fired his muse. Like the Stewart dynasty, Burns' song-writing came with a lass and it went with a lass. He began with handsome Nell Kilpatrick, and when Jessy Lewars, sister of his Excise colleague, nursed him as he was dying, Burns wrote one of his simplest, yet tenderest songs for her. His strength had already ebbed away and he knew his heart could not hold out much longer; even the fires of passion had all but burned themselves up at last. All too aware of his own vulnerability and the financial worries which filled his thoughts, he hummed over an old tune *Lennoxlove to Blantyre*, until he had composed one of the very best songs he ever wrote to fit the air. It was the touching song of comfort and devotion, *O, Wert Thou in the Cauld Blast*.[11] No song could have provided a more fitting end to Robert Burns' career as a singer of songs, not just for Scotland, but for the whole of humanity:

> O, wert thou in the cauld blast
>   On yonder lea, on yonder lea,
> My plaidie* to the angry airt*,                    *shawl *direction
>   I'd shelter thee, I'd shelter thee.

Or did Misfortune's bitter storms
  Around thee blaw, around thee blaw,
Thy bield\* should be my bosom,                       \*shelter
  To share it a', to share it a'.

Or were I in the wildest waste,
  Sae black and bare, sae black and bare,
The desert were a Paradise,
  If thou wert there, if thou wert there.
Or were I monarch o the globe,
  Wi thee to reign, wi thee to reign,
The brightest jewel in my crown
  Wad be my queen, wad be my queen.

# *Notes*

The following texts have been used with the publisher's and editor's permission:

*Complete Letters of Robert Burns*, ed. James Mackay (Alloway Publishing, Darvel, 1987). Referred to as *Complete Letters*.

*Complete Works of Robert Burns*, ed. James Mackay (Alloway Publishing, Darvel, 1986). Referred to as *Complete Works*.

## CHAPTER ONE: AULD SANG – NEW SONG

1 *'Why Shouldna Poor Folk Mowe'. Complete Works*, p.476

2 Robert Burns to Dr John Moore, 2 August 1787. *Complete Letters*, p.255

3 David Daiches calls 1785 Burns' *annus mirabilis* (*Robert Burns*, p.186), when most of the poems in the Kilmarnock Edition and many others were written

4 *'Epistle to John Rankine'. Complete Works*, p.82

5 Mauchline Kirk Session Minutes, 3 January 1773. Scottish Record Office

6 Ibid. 3 January to 6 May 1773

7 Ian D. Whyte, *Scotland Before the Industrial Revolution*, pp.118–19

8 *'The Holy Fair'. Complete Works*, p.135

9 Mauchline Kirk Session Minutes, 6 March 1786. SRO

10 *Statistical Account of Scotland* (ed. Sir John Sinclair), Parish of Mauchline, compiled by Revd William Auld, vol. II, pp.110–16

11 *'Adam Armour's Prayer'. Complete Works*, p.198–9

12 Mauchline Kirk Session Minutes, 6 March 1786. SRO

13 Ian D. Whyte, *Scotland before the Industrial Revolution*, p.332

14 Revd John Mitchell, *Memories of Ayrshire about 1780* pp. 255–6. Quoted in *Ayrshire at the Time of Burns*. Collections of Ayrshire Archaeological and Natural History Society, vol. 5. p.35

15 Colonel William Fullarton, *Board of Agriculture Report*, 1793, p.14

16 Hans Hecht, *Robert Burns, The Man and his Work* (1981 edn), pp.vi–vii

17 RB to George Thomson, 7 February 1795. *Collected Letters*, p.671

18 James Currie, *The Works of Robert Burns* (1819 edn), vol I. pp.219–20

19 *Glenriddell Manuscript.* Quoted Thomas Crawford, *Burns, A Study of the Poems and Songs*, p.252

20 RB to Dr Moore, 23 March 1789. *Complete Letters*, p.259

21 *'Ode, Sacred to the Memory of Mrs. Oswald of Auchencruive'*, *Complete Works*, p.343

22 Cyril Pearl, *Bawdy Burns*, pp.15–16

23 R.B. Cunninghame-Grahame, quoted in Moray Maclaren, *Understanding the Scots*, p.127

24 Christina Keith, *The Russet Coat*, p.177

25 *'To the Guidwife of Wauchope House'.* *Complete Works*, pp.271–2
26 Robert Chambers, *Life and Works of Robert Burns*, vol. I. pp.170–1
27 Thomas Crawford, *Burns, A Study of the Poems and Songs*, p.133
28 *'The Birks of Aberfeldie'. Complete Works*, pp.288–9
29 RB to John Tennant, Jr, of Glenconner, 13 September 1784. *Complete Letters*, p.72
30 RB to John Richmond, 9 July 1786. *Complete Letters*, p.77
31 RB to James Smith, late July/early August 1786. *Complete Letters*, p.117
32 *'A Poet's Welcome to his Love-Begotten Daughter'. Complete Works*, p.112
33 *Robert Burns' Common Place Book* (ed. Raymond Lamont-Brown), republished from the 1872 edition, p.3
34 Ibid
35 *Eden Scenes on Crystal Jed.* BBC Radio 3, 25 January 1980
36 William J. Murray, *'The women in Burns' poems and songs: the poet as liberationist'. Burns Chronicle*, 1982, p.70
37 Mrs Dunlop to RB, 18 March 1789. W. Wallace, *Burns and Mrs Dunlop*, p.153
38 Ibid
39 Ibid, p. 154

40 *'Ae Fond Kiss'. Complete Works*, p.434
41 *'Of A' the Airts the Wind can Blaw'. Complete Works*, p.329
42 John Richmond to James Grierson of Dalgoner, December 1817. Grierson Mss, University of Edinburgh Library
43 *'Highland Mary'. Complete Works*, p.470
44 Thomas Carlyle, reviewing J.G.Lockhart's *Life of Robert Burns. Edinburgh Review*, vol. XLVIII (1828), p.287. I am indebted to Thomas Crawford, *Burns. A Study of the Poems and Songs* (p.336) for this reference
45 See: T. Crawford, *Burns, A Study of the Poems and Songs*, pp.366–8
46 A. Angellier, *Robert Burns: La Vie, Les Oeuvres*, vol. I, p.531
47 *'I'm O'er Young to Marry Yet'. Complete Works*, p.307
48 *'John Anderson, my Jo'. Complete Works*, p.391
49 *'I Hae a Wife o my Ain'. Complete Works*, p.450
50 Although Robert spelt his surname Burns, his father used the form Burnes, which was usual among his family in the north-east of Scotland. Family papers and other documents give a variety of spellings, including Burness, Burnace, Burnase and Burnece.

## CHAPTER TWO: APPRENTICE TO LOVE

1 *Robert Burns' Common Place Book* (ed. R. Lamont Brown), p.3
2 Brown, sometimes spelt Broun, in Scotland the name was (and is still) often pronounced Broon
3 Agnes Burnes described by her daughter Isabella Burnes (Begg), R. Chambers/W. Wallace, *Life and Works of Robert Burns*, vol. 1, p.42 note
4 R. Chambers, *Life and Works of Robert Burns*, vol. 1, p.334
5 John Ramsay of Ochtertyre, *Scotland and Scotsmen in the Eighteenth Century*, vol. 2, p.554
6 RB to Dr Moore, 2 August 1787. *Complete Letters*, p.249

7 James Mackay examines Burns' pedigree fully in *A Biography of Robert Burns*, pp. 17–23
8 J.C. Muir, Burns in Kirkoswald, *Burns Chronicle*, 1906
9 RB to Dr Moore, 2 August 1787. *Complete Letters*, p.249
10 A.M. Boyle, *The Ayrshire Book of Burns Lore*, p.69
11 RB to Captain Francis Grose, about June 1790. *Collected Letters*, pp.557–9
12 *'Tam O' Shanter'. Complete Works*, p.412
13 RB to James Dalrymple, February 1787. *Complete Letters*, p. 270
14 *'O, Can Ye Labour Lea'. Complete Works*, p.465

15  J. Currie, *Works of Robert Burns* (1819 edn), vol. I, p.89

16  H. Hecht, *Robert Burns the Man and his Work* (1981 edn), p.178

17  Catherine Carswell, *The Life of Robert Burns*, p.38

18  J. Mackay, *A Biography of Robert Burns*, p.32

19  RB to Dr Moore, 2 August 1787. *Complete Letters*, p.249

20  J. Currie, *Works of Burns* (1819 edn), vol. 1, p.87

21  'The Cotter's Saturday Night'. *Complete Works*, pp.147–51

22  RB to Dr Moore, 2 August 1787. *Complete Letters*, pp.250–1

23  *Common Place Book* (ed. R. Lamont Brown), p.6

24  'Handsome Nell'. *Complete Works*, p.43

25  'To the Guidwife of Wauchope House', *Complete Works*, pp.271–2

26  James Mackay has unravelled the mystery of Handsome Nell's identity. See *A Biography of Robert Burns*, pp.50–2

27  RB to Dr Moore, 2 August 1787. *Complete Letters*, pp.252–3

28  A.M. Boyle, *The Ayrshire Book of Burns-Lore*, p.70

29  RB to Dr Moore, 2 August 1787. *Complete Letters*, p.253

30  J. Mackay, *A Biography of Robert Burns*, p.59

31  RB to Thomas Orr, 11 November 1784. *Collected Letters*, p.50

32  'To an Old Sweetheart'. *Collected Works*, p.250

33  'Now Westlin Winds'. *Complete Works*, p.44

34  RB to Dr Moore, 2 August 1787, p.250

35  Same to same, 2 August 1787. *Collected Letters*, p.250

36  'The Twa Dogs'. *Collected Works*, p.142

37  J. Currie, *Works of Robert Burns* (1819 edn), vol. 1, p.63

38  RB to Dr Moore, 2 August 1787. *Collected Letters*, p.253

39  J. Currie, *Works of Robert Burns* (1819 edn), vol. 1, p.72

40  RB to Dr Moore, 2 August 1787. *Collected Letters*, p.252

41  Ibid

## CHAPTER THREE: SILK PURSES AND SOWS' LUGS

1  'The Lass o' Ballochmyle'. *Complete Works*, p.199

2  Glenriddell Mss, vol. 1, p.198

3  R. Chambers, *Life and Works of Robert Burns*, vol. 1, p.51

4  'The Ronalds of the Bennals'. *Complete Works*, p.77–8

5  J.C. Hill, *The Love Songs and Heroines of Robert Burns*, p.12

6  'The Tarbolton Lasses'. *Complete Works*, pp.78–9

7  R. Chambers/W. Wallace, *Life and Works of Robert Burns*, vol. 1, p.69

8  'Epitaph on a Noisy Polemic'. *Complete Works*, p.70

9  'Death and Dr Hornbrook'. *Complete Works*, pp.96–100

10  RB to John Wilson, 11 September 1790. *Collected Letters*, p.566

11  Saunders Tait published his poems in 1790. *Burns at Lochly* is quoted from *Saunders Tait* by J.L. Hempstead. *Burns Chronicle*, 1981, p.76

12  Bachelors' Club Rules. J. Currie, *Works of Robert Burns* (1819 edn), vol. 1, pp. 359–63

13  RB to Dr Moore, 2 August 1787. *Collected Letters*, p.252

14  R. Chambers, *Life and Works of Robert Burns*, vol. 1, p.51

15  RB to Dr Moore, 2 August 1787. *Complete Letters*, p.252

16  *Common Place Book*, p.31

17  RB to William Niven, 3 November 1780. *Collected Letters*, p.38

18  Same to same, 12 June 1781. Ibid, p.39

19  R. Chambers, *Life and Works of Robert Burns*, vol. 1, p.54

20 *'The Lass of Cessnock Banks', Complete Works*, pp.51–2

21 R.H. Cromek, *Reliques of Burns*, p.42 note

22 I am grateful to James Mackay for permission to paraphrase his theory as published in *A Biography of Robert Burns*, pp.86–91

23 RB to Alison Begbie, 1781? *Complete Letters*, p.43

24 Same to same. Ibid, p.44

25 Same to same. Ibid, pp.46–7

26 Same to same. Ibid, p.47

27 RB to Dr Moore, 2 August 1787. *Complete Letters*, pp.252–3

28 RB to William Niven, 29 July 1780. *Complete Letters*, p.38

29 *The Glasgow Mercury*, 16–23 January 1783

30 RB to Dr Moore, 2 August 1787. *Complete Letters*, p.254

31 Ibid

32 RB to William Burnes, 27 December 1781. *Complete Letters*, pp. 41–2

33 *'Stanzas on the Same Occasion'. Complete Works*, p.54

34 A.M.Boyle, *The Ayrshire Book of Burns Lore*, p.62

35 RB to Dr Moore, 2 August 1787. *Complete Letters*, p.254

36 Josiah Walker, *Poems by Robert Burns*, vol.II, pp.261–3

37 R. Chambers/W. Wallace, *Life and Works of Robert Burns*, vol. 1, pp.109–10

38 *'Epitaph on my Honoured Father'. Complete Works*, p.71

## CHAPTER FOUR: SEX AND SENSIBILITY

1 *'The Rigs o Barley'. Complete Works*, p.49

2 R. Chambers/W. Wallace, *Life and Works of Robert Burns*, vol.I, p.119

3 Ibid

4 *'My Girl She's Airy'. Complete Works*, p.82

5 RB to Dr Moore. *Complete Letters*, p.255

6 RB to Thomas Orr. *Collected Letters*, p.50

7 *'Epistle to John Rankine'. Collected Works*, pp.82–4

8 Ibid

9 David Daiches, *Robert Burns*, pp.172–3

10 Christina Keith, *The Russet Coat*, p.62

11 *'A Poet's Welcome to his Love-Begotten Daughter'. Complete Works*, p.113–14

12 *'The Rantin Dog, the Daddie o't'. Complete Works*, p.174

13 *'The Cotter's Saturday Night'. Complete Works*, pp.147–51

14 *'Hallowe'en'. Complete Works*, pp.151–7

15 *'The Vision'. Complete Works*, pp.114–21

16 *'The Jolly Beggars'. Complete Works*, pp.182–91

17 *'The Twa Dogs'. Complete Works*, pp.140–46

18 *'The Auld Farmer's New-year Morning Salutation to his Auld Mare, Maggie'. Complete Works*, pp.158–61

19 D. Daiches, *Robert Burns*, p.139

20 *'To a Mouse'. Complete Works*, pp.131–2

21 *'To a Mountain Daisy'. Complete Works*, pp.203–4

22 *'To a Louse'. Complete Works*, pp.181–2

23 *'Epistle to a Young Friend'. Complete Works*, pp.221–3

24 T. Crawford, *Burns: A Study of the Poems and Songs*, p.103

25 *'Scotch Drink'. Complete Works*, pp.165–8

26 *'The Author's Earnest Cry and Prayer'. Complete Works*, pp.174–80

27 D. Daiches, *Robert Burns*, p.119

28 *'Address to the Deil'. Complete Works*, pp.161–4

29 *'The Holy Fair'. Complete Works*, p.139

30 RB to Richard Brown, 4 November 1789. *Complete Letters*, p.422

31 Alan Dent, *Burns in his Time* pp.105–9

32 RB to John Tennant, Jr, 13 September 1784. *Complete Letters*, p.72

33 RB to William Burns, 5 May 1789. *Complete Letters*, p.516

34 Same to same, 10 February 1790. *Complete Letters*, p.518

35 R. Chambers/W. Wallace, *Life and Works of Robert Burns*, vol. III, p.164

36  Ibid
37  RB to Peter Hill, 2 February 1790. *Complete Letters*, p.315

38  *'Lines Written under the Picture of the Celebrated Miss Burns'. Complete Works*, p.375

## CHAPTER FIVE: THE MAUCHLINE LADY

1  *'To the Guidwife of Wauchope House'. Complete Works*, p.272
2  RB to John Arnot. No date, probably April 1786. *Complete Letters*, p.109
3  *'The Libel Summons'. Complete Works*, pp.227–30
4  RB to Mrs Dunlop, 21 August 1788. *Complete Letters*, pp.154–5
5  *'The Mauchline Wedding'. Complete Works*, pp.157–8
6  T. Crawford, *Burns, A Study of the Poems and Songs*, p.115
7  *'Holy Willie's Prayer'. Complete Works*, pp.93–5
8  *'Epistle to the Rev. John McMath'. Complete Works*, pp.129–31
9  *'O, Leave Novels'. Complete Works*, p.79
10  *'A Fragment'. Robert Burns' Common Place Book* (ed.R. Lamont-Brown) August 1785, p.47. *'The Mauchline Lady'. Complete Works*, p.80
11  *'The Belles of Mauchline'. Complete Works*, p.79
12  A.M. Boyle, *The Ayrshire Book of Burns-Lore*, p.8
13  RB to Margaret Chalmers, 16 September 1788. *Complete Letters*, p.238
14  Yvonne Helen Stevenson, *Burns and His Bonnie Jean*, p.10

15  *Common Place Book*, p.50
16  Ibid, pp.50–1
17  John McDiarmid, *Widow of Burns, her Death, Character and Funeral*
18  *'Their Groves of Sweet Myrtle'. Complete Works*, p.550
19  RB to Mrs Dunlop, 10 August 1788. *Complete Letters*, p.149
20  *'Epistle to Davie, a Brother Poet'. Complete Works*, p.88
21  RB to John Richmond, 17 February 1786. *Complete Letters*, p.76
22  William Jolly, *Burns at Mossgiel*, p.69
23  Mauchline Kirk Session Minutes, 2 April 1786. *Burns Chronicle*, 1893, p.56
24  Mauchline Kirk Session Minutes, 9 April 1786. *Burns Chronicle*, 1893, p.56
25  RB to Gavin Hamilton, 15 April 1786. *Complete Letters*, p.66
26  *'The Cotter's Saturday Night'. Complete Works*, p.147
27  RB to Gavin Hamilton, 15 April 1786. *Complete Letters*, p.66
28  RB to John Arnot. No date, but probably April 1786. *Complete Letters*, pp.107–10
29  *Glenriddell Manuscript*, vol. 1, p.9

## CHAPTER SIX: ST MARY OF ARGYLL

1  *'Bonnie Mary of Argyll'*. Words by G.C. Jeffreys (1807–65), music by S. Nelson (1800–62). Popular in music halls, drawing-rooms and among drinkers in Scottish pubs. The subject was Burns' 'Highland Mary'
2  *'I'll Go and be a Sodger'. Complete Works*, p.56
3  RB to Maria Riddell, November 1793. *Complete Letters*, p.604
4  *'Epistle to John Rankine'. Complete Works*, pp. 83–4

5  DeLancey Ferguson, *Pride and Passion*, p.191
6  RB to John Arnot, April 1786. *Complete Letters*, p.110
7  RB to Dr Moore, 2 August 1787. *Complete Letters*, p.255
8  Ibid
9  RB to John Arnot, April 1786. *Complete Letters*, p.110
10  J. Mackay, *Biography of Robert Burns*, pp.212–13
11  *Burns Chronicle*, 1893, p.55

12  *Burns Chronicle*, 1893, p.57

13  *'The Jolly Beggars'. Complete Works*, pp.190–1

14  RB to John Arnot, April 1786. *Complete Letters*, p.110

15  J. Mackay, *Biography of Robert Burns*, pp.205–7

16  Robert H. Cromek, *Reliques of Robert Burns, consisting of Original Letters, Poems and Critical Observations on Scottish Songs*, p.237

17  RB to George Thomson, 14 November 1786. *Collected Letters*, p.621

18  *'Highland Mary'. Complete Works*, p.470

19  RB to David Brice, 12 June 1786. *Complete Letters*, p.111

20  Mauchline Kirk Session Minutes, 18 June 1786. *Burns Chronicle*, 1893, p.56

21  RB to John Richmond. 9 July 1786. *Complete Letters*, p.77

22  Mauchline Kirk Session Minutes, 28 June 1786. *Burns Chronicle*, 1893, p.56

23  RB to John Richmond, 9 July 1786. *Complete Letters*, p.77

24  RB to David Brice, 17 July 1786. *Complete Letters*, p.112

25  Mauchline Kirk Session Minutes, 6 August 1786. *Burns Chronicle*, 1893, p.56

26  RB to David Brice. *Complete Letters*, p.111

27  John Gay, *The Beggar's Opera*, Act II, Scene xiii

28  RB to John Richmond, 30 July 1786. *Complete Letters*, p.78

29  *'Deed of Assignment'. Complete Letters*, p.115

30  RB to James Smith, 1 August 1786. *Complete Letters*, p.117

31  The document is now in the Scottish Record Office, Edinburgh

32  RB to John Richmond, 30 July 1786. *Complete Letters*, p.78

33  RB to James Smith, 14 August 1786. *Complete Letters*, p.118

34  *Glenriddell Manuscript*, vol. 2, pp. 63–4

35  RB to William Niven, 30 August 1786. *Complete Letters*, p.40

36  James T. Gray, *Maybole – Carrick's Capital*, pp.294–5

37  RB to John Richmond, 1 September 1786. *Complete Letters*, p.78

38  Same to same, 3 September 1786. *Complete Letters*, p.79

39  Train Mss, University of Edinburgh Library

40  RB to Robert Muir. 8 September 1786. *Complete Letters*, p.87

41  RB to Mrs Dunlop. 24 September 1792. *Complete Letters*, p.200

42  RB to John Kennedy. 26 September 1786. *Complete Letters*, p.85

43  R. Chambers/W. Wallace, *Life of Robert Burns*, vol. I, p.428

44  Robert H. Cromek, *Reliques of Robert Burns*, p.237

45  RB to George Thomson, 26 October 1792. *Collected Letters*, p.619

46  *'Will ye go to the Indies, My Mary'. Complete Works*, p.469

47  *'Highland Mary'. Complete Poems*, p.470

48  RB to Mrs Dunlop, 8 November and 13 December 1789. *Complete Letters*, pp.180–2

49  *'Thou Lingering Star'. Complete Works*, pp.372–3, quoted in letter to Mrs Dunlop, 13 December 1789. *Complete Letters*, p.182

50  *'Highland Mary's Grave', Greenock Telegraph* (no date). Quoted in *Burnsiana* (John D. Ross, compiler), p.33

51  Hilton Brown, *There Was a Lad*, p.150

52  Ibid, p.247

53  *The Greenock Telegraph*, 4 January 1921

54  C. Carswell, *The Life of Robert Burns*, p.205

55  F.B. Snyder, *The Life of Robert Burns*, p.143

56  H. Brown, *There Was a Lad*, p.251

57  Ibid, p.252

58  Maurice Lindsay, *Burns: The Man, his Work, the Legend*, p.113

59  *Blackwood's Magazine*, v. 67, 1850, p.309

60  M. Lindsay, *The Burns Encyclopaedia*, p.66

61  J. Currie, *Works of Robert Burns* (1819 edn), vol. I, p.125

62  A. Angellier, *Robert Burns, La Vie*, pp.161–2

63  Ian McIntyre, *Dirt and Deity*, pp.440–1

64  Grierson Ms, University of Edinburgh Library

## CHAPTER SEVEN: 'THE MOST VALUED FRIEND'

1 William Wallace, *Burns and Mrs Dunlop*, p.428

2 Robert Heron, *A Memoir of the Life of the Late Robert Burns*. Reprinted in H. Hecht, *Robert Burns, the Man and his Work* (1981 edn), p.266

3 Ibid

4 Lord Cockburn, *Memorials of his Times* (1936 edn), p.20

5 C. Carswell, *The Life of Robert Burns*, pp.201–2

6 A. M. Boyle, *The Ayrshire Book of Burns-Lore*, p.123

7 RB to Mrs Catherine Stewart, September 1786. *Complete Letters*, pp.125

8 Ibid, pp.125–6

9 RB to Mrs Stewart, October 1891. *Complete Letters*, p.126

10 RB to Mrs Dunlop, 5 February1789. *Complete Letters*, p.166

11 'Sweet Afton'. *Complete Works*, p.351

12 'Prayer – O Thou Dread Power'. *Complete Works*, p.261

13 'The Night was Still'. *Complete Works*, p.262

14 RB to Dr Moore, 2 August 1787. *Complete Letters*, p.256

15 'On Meeting with Lord Daer'. *Complete Works*, pp.254–5

16 RB to John Richmond, 27 September 1786. *Complete Letters*, p.80

17 RB to Robert Aiken, early October 1786. *Complete Letters*, p.92

18 W. Wallace, *Burns and Mrs Dunlop*, p. 152

19 'The Cotter's Saturday Night'. *Complete Works*, p.151

20 RB to Mrs Dunlop, 2 August 1788. *Complete Letters*, p.150

21 RB to Mrs Dunlop, 15 November 1786. *Complete Letters*, pp.131–2

22 Mrs Dunlop to RB, 21 May 1787. W. Wallace, *Burns and Mrs Dunlop*, p. 25

23 Same to same, 26 February 1787. Ibid, p.11

24 Mrs Dunlop to RB, 30 December 1786. Ibid, p. 4

25 'The Twa Dogs'. *Complete Works*, p.141

26 Mrs Dunlop to RB, 12 July 1791. W. Wallace, *Burns and Mrs Dunlop*, p.325

27 H. Brown, *There Was a Lad*, p.167, Note 7

28 RB to Mrs Dunlop, 12 February 1788. *Complete Letters*, p.139

29 RB to Mrs Dunlop, 30 April 1787. *Complete Letters*, p.136

30 RB to Mrs Dunlop, 15 January 1787. *Complete Letters*, p.132

31 Mrs Dunlop to RB, 9 September 1787. W. Wallace, *Burns and Mrs Dunlop*, p.28

32 RB to Mrs Dunlop, 10 August 1788. *Complete Letters*, p.151

33 RB to Mrs Dunlop, 30 or 31 July 1787. *Collected Letters*, p.137

34 RB to Mrs Dunlop, 10 August 1788. *Complete Letters*, p.148

35 RB to Mrs Dunlop. 8 November 1789. *Complete Letters*, p.180

36 'Thou Lingering Star'. *Complete Works*, p.372

37 Mrs Dunlop to RB. W. Wallace, 29 March 1787. *Burns and Mrs Dunlop*, p.16

38 RB to Mrs Dunlop, 25 March 1789. *Complete Letters*, p.170

39 Ibid

40 RB to Mrs Dunlop, 6 September 1789. *Complete Letters*, p.178

41 RB to Mrs Dunlop, 6 March 1790. *Complete Letters*, p.184

42 RB to Mrs Dunlop, 1 November 1790. *Complete Letters*, p.192

43 M. Lindsay, *Burns Encyclopedia*, p.219

44 RB to Mrs Dunlop, 14 January 1792. *Complete Letters*, p.197

45 Mrs Dunlop to RB, 15 March 1793. W. Wallace, *Robert Burns and Mrs Dunlop*, p.380

46 Mrs Dunlop to RB, 23 September 1792. W. Wallace, *Burns and Mrs Dunlop*, p.363

47 RB to Mrs Dunlop, 5 January 1793. *Complete Letters*, p.204

48 Mrs Dunlop to RB, 16 March 1793. W. Wallace, *Burns and Mrs Dunlop*, p.379

49 RB to Mrs Dunlop, 25 June 1794. *Complete Letters*, p.210

50  Mrs Dunlop to RB, 8 September 1784.
W. Wallace, *Burns and Mrs Dunlop*, p.407
51  RB to Mrs Dunlop, 20 December
1794–12 January 1795. *Complete Letters*, p.214

52  RB to Mrs Dunlop, 31 January 1796.
*Complete Letters*, p.214
53  RB to Mrs Dunlop, 10 July 1796.
*Complete Letters*, p.215

## CHAPTER EIGHT: FROM GREENLAND TO RAPTURE

1  Journal of the Border Tour. *Robert Burns' Tour of the Borders* (ed. Raymond Lamont-Brown), p.19
2  RB to George Reid, 29 November 1786. *Complete Letters*, p.220
3  Train Mss. University of Edinburgh Library
4  RB to John Ballantine, 14 January 1787. *Complete Letters*, p.101
5  RB to John Ballantine, 14 January 1787. *Complete Letters*, p.100
6  *The Lounger*, December 1786
7  RB to John Ballantine, 14 January 1787. *Complete Letters*, p.101
8  Craig-Brown, T., *Letters and Memoir of Her Own Life by Mrs Alison Rutherford or Cockburn*, pp. 187–8
9  John McVie, *Robert Burns and Edinburgh*, p.27
10  RB to Peter Stuart, 13 April 1789. *Complete Letters*, p. 521
11  M. Lindsay, *Burns Encyclopedia*, p.348
12  RB to William Chalmers, 27 December 1786. *Complete Letters*, p.219
13  'Address to Edinburgh'. *Complete Works*, p.263
14  Agnes McLehose to RB, 22 February 1788. W.C. McLehose, *The Correspondence of Burns and Clarinda*, p.233
15  M. Lindsay, *Burns Encyclopedia*, p.46
16  RB to Alexander Cunningham, 23 January 1791. *Complete Letters*, p.460
17  'Elegy on the Late Miss Burnet of Monbodo'. *Complete Works*, p.416
18  RB to Mrs Dunlop, 7 February 1791. *Complete Letters*, pp.193–4
19  'Elegy on the Late Miss Burnet of Monbodo'. *Complete Works*, p.416
20  RB to Robert Muir, 15 December 1786. *Complete Letters*, p.88
21  RB to Gavin Hamilton, 7 January 1787.

*Complete Letters*, p.67. Verse from *'The Jolly Beggars'. Complete Works*, p.190
22  Same to same, 7 January 1787. *Complete Letters*, p.67
23  RB to James Dalrymple of Orangefield, February 1787. *Complete Letters*, p. 270
24  J. Mackay, *Biography of Robert Burns*, pp.300–1
25  RB to Provost Robert Maxwell of Lochmaben, 20 December 1789. *Complete Letters*, p.548. I am indebted to Cyril Pearl's *Bawdy Burns* and to *The Merry Muses of Caledonia*, edited by James Barke and Sydney Goodsir Smith, for background information of Burns' bawdry
26  RB to John Ballantine, 13 December 1786. *Complete Letters*, p.99
27  R. Chambers/W. Wallace, *Life and Works of Robert Burns*, p. 51
28  'To The Guidwife of Wauchope House'. *Complete Works*, p.272
29  'Rantin, Rovin Robin'. *Complete Works*, p.268
30  'To Miss Isabella MacLeod'. *Complete Works*, p.273
31  RB to Mrs Dunlop, 22 March 1787. *Complete Letters*, p.134
32  'Written by Somebody on the Window of an Inn at Stirling, on Seeing the Royal Palace in Ruin'. *Complete Works*, p.286
33  RB to James Johnson, 4 May 1787. *Complete Letters*, p.292
34  RB to James Johnson, 1791? *Complete Letters*, p.296
35  'Epigram to Miss Ainslie in Church'. *Complete Works*, p.277
36  *Robert Burns' Tour of the Borders*, ed. Raymond Lamont-Brown, p.24
37  Ibid, p.23
38  Ibid, p.19
39  Ibid, p.20

40   RB to William Nicol, 1 June 1787. *Complete Letters*, p.343
41   R. Chambers/W. Wallace, *Life of Robert Burns*, vol.II, p.121
42   RB to Robert Ainslie, about 1 June 1787. *Complete Letters*, p. 332
43   RB to Robert Ainslie, 23 July 1787. *Complete Letters*, p.328
44   RB to Robert Ainslie, 25 June 1787. *Complete Letters*, p. 328
45   RB to Robert Ainslie, 29 July 1787. *Complete Letters*, p.329
46   RB to William Nicol, 18 June 1787. *Complete Letters*, p.344
47   R. Chambers, ed.W. Wallace, *Life of Robert Burns*, vol. II, p.125

## CHAPTER NINE: THE PASSIONATE PILGRIM

1   'The Bard at Inverary'. *Complete Works*, p.281
2   RB to James Smith, 30 June 1787. *Complete Letters*, pp.119–21
3   Ibid
4   RB to William Cruikshank, 3 March 1788. *Complete Letters*, p.360
5   RB to James Hoy, 20 October 1787. *Complete Letters*, p.361
6   RB to Patrick Miller, 28 September 1787. *Complete Works*, p.241
7   RB to his 'countrywoman' (probably Margaret Chalmers), about January 1787. *Complete Letters*, p.230
8   RB to James Smith. 30 June 1787. *Complete Letters*, p.120
9   Ibid
10   Ibid
11   J. Currie, *Works of Robert Burns* (1819 edn), vol. 1, p.165
12   Ibid, pp.165–6
13   RB to Margaret Chalmers, 21 October 1787. *Complete Letters*, p.231
14   'The Banks of the Devon'. *Complete Works*, p.298
15   RB to Margaret Chalmers, probably 6 November 1787. *Complete Letters*, p.232
16   'My Peggy's Charms'. *Complete Works*, p.297
17   RB to Margaret Chalmers, probably 6 November 1787. *Complete Letters*, p.232
18   RB to Margaret Chalmers, 16 September 1788. *Complete Letters*, p.237
19   'Blythe Was She'. *Complete Works*, p.295
20   J. Currie, *Works of Robert Burns* (1819 edn), vol. 1, p.170
21   RB to John Richmond, 25 October 1787. *Complete Letters*, p.81
22   Ian McIntyre, *Dirt and Deity. A Life of Robert Burns*, pp.169–70
23   'A Rose-bud by My Early Walk'. *Complete Works*, p.318
24   RB to Margaret Chalmers, 21 October 1788. *Complete Letters*, p.231

## CHAPTER TEN: CLARINDA, MISTRESS OF MY SOUL

1   RB to Agnes McLehose, 21 January 1788. *Complete Letters*, p.388
2   Agnes McLehose to RB, 8 December 1787. W.C. McLehose, *Correspondence of Burns and Clarinda*, pp. 82–3
3   Her birth date is usually given as 17 April 1759, but James Mackay traced it in Glasgow records as 26 April 1758 (*A Biography of Robert Burns*, p.369)
4   See page 75 for the full verse and the letter Burns wrote to Peter Hill about the incident
5   RB to Agnes McLehose, 6 December 1787. *Complete Letters*, pp.371–2
6   RB to Agnes McLehose, 8 December 1787. *Complete Letters*, p.372
7   Agnes McLehose to RB, 8 December 1787. W.C. McLehose, *Correspondence of Burns and Clarinda*, p.84
8   RB to Agnes McLehose, 12 December 1787. *Complete Letters*, p.372
9   Agnes McLehose to RB, 16 December 1787. W.C. McLehose, *Correspondence of Burns and Clarinda*, p.87

10  RB to Agnes McLehose, 20 December 1787. *Complete Letters*, p.373

11  *Burns Chronicle*, 1934, p.74

12  RB to Agnes McLehose, 21 December 1787. *Complete Letters*, p.374

13  RB to Agnes McLehose, 20 December 1787. *Complete Letters*, p.373

14  Glenriddell Manuscript, vol. 1, p.125

15  *'Sylvander to Clarinda'. Complete Works*, p. 301–2

16  RB to Agnes McLehose, 21 December 1787. *Complete Letters*, p. 374

17  RB to Richard Brown, 30 December 1787. *Complete Letters*, p. 419

18  Agnes McLehose to RB, 1 January 1788. W.C. McLehose, *Correspondence of Burns and Clarinda*, p.104

19  Agnes McLehose to RB, 3 January 1788. W.C. McLehose, *Correspondence of Burns and Clarinda*, p.107

20  *On Love and Friendship* by Clarinda. W.C. McLehose, *Correspondence of Burns and Clarinda*, pp. 106–7

21  RB to Agnes McLehose, 4 January 1788. *Complete Letters*, p.376

22  RB to Agnes McLehose, 2 January 1788. *Complete Letters*, p.375

23  *Talk Not of Love*, by Clarinda. *The Scots Musical Museum*, vol. II, p.194

24  RB to Agnes McLehose, 5 January 1788. *Complete Letters*, p.378

25  RB to Agnes McLehose, 10 January 1788. *Complete Letters*, p.380

26  Agnes McLehose to RB, 10 January 1788. W.C. McLehose, *Correspondence of Burns and Clarinda*, p.135

27  Agnes McLehose to RB, 13 January 1788. W.C. McLehose, *Correspondence of Burns and Clarinda*, p.141

28  Agnes McLehose to RB, 2 February 1788. W.C. McLehose, *Correspondence of Burns and Clarinda*, p. 193

29  *To a Blackbird Singing on a Tree.* Enclosed with letter, Agnes McLehose to RB, 2 February 1788. W.C. McLehose, *Correspondence of Burns and Clarinda*, p. 289

30  RB to Agnes McLehose, 27 January 1788. *Complete Letters*, p.390

31  RB to Agnes McLehose, 20/21 January 1788. *Complete Letters*, pp.386–7

32  RB to Mrs Dunlop, 21 January 1788. *Complete Letters*, p.139

33  RB to Margaret Chalmers, possibly 22 January 1788. *Complete Letters*, p.235

34  RB to John Richmond, 7 February 1788. *Complete Letters*, pp.81–2

35  RB to Agnes McLehose, 3 February 1788. *Complete Letters*, p.392

36  RB to Agnes McLehose, 13 February 1788. *Complete Letters*, pp. 394–5

37  RB to Agnes McLehose, Midnight, 13 February 1788. *Complete Letters*, p. 395

38  *'Clarinda, Mistress of my Soul'. Complete Works*, pp. 320–1

39  RB to Agnes McLehose, 14 February 1788. *Complete Letters*, pp.396–7

40  RB to Agnes McLehose, 15 February 1788. *Complete Letters*, p.397

41  RB to Margaret Chalmers, 17 February 1788. *Complete Letters*, p. 237

## CHAPTER ELEVEN: FARTHING TAPER . . . MERIDIAN SUN

1  W.E. Henley and T.F. Henderson, *Poetry of Robert Burns*, vol. 4, p. 307

2  RB to Agnes McLehose, 18 February 1788. *Complete Letters*, p. 398

3  RB to Richard Brown, 24 February 1788. *Complete Letters*, pp. 419–20

4  RB to Agnes McLehose, 22 February 1788. *Complete Letters*, pp. 398–9

5  RB to Agnes McLehose, 23 February 1788. *Complete Letters*, p. 399

6  Ibid

7  Agnes McLehose to RB, 19 February 1788. W.C. McLehose, *Correspondence of Burns and Clarinda*, p. 223

8  Agnes McLehose to RB, 22 February 1788. W.C. McLehose,

*Correspondence of Burns and Clarinda,*
p. 231

9 Agnes Mclehose to RB, 5 March 1788.
W.C. McLehose, *Correspondence of Burns and Clarinda*, p. 236

10 RB to Agnes McLehose, 23 February 1788. *Complete Letters*, p. 399

11 RB to Agnes McLehose, 2 March 1788. *Complete Letters*, p. 400

12 RB to Patrick Miller, 3 March 1788. *Complete Letters*, p. 242–3

13 RB to William Cruikshank, 3 March 1788. *Complete Letters*, p. 360–1

14 RB to Robert Ainslie, 3 March 1788. *Complete Letters*, pp. 331–2

15 H. Hecht, *Robert Burns, the Man and his Work* (1981 edn), p. 137

16 Ian McIntyre, *Dirt and Deity, A Life of Robert Burns*, p. 205

17 DeLancey Ferguson, *Pride and Passion*, p. 168

18 Agnes McLehose to RB, 5 March 1788. W.C. McLehose, *Correspondence of Burns and Clarinda*, p. 238

19 See J. Mackay, *A Biography of Robert Burns*, pp. 403–4. I am indebted to Dr Mackay's sources for information he located in Register House, Edinburgh, on the children

20 RB to Agnes McLehose, 6 March 1788. *Complete Letters*, p. 401

21 Agnes McLehose to RB, 5 March 1788. W.C. McLehose, *Correspondence of Burns and Clarinda*, p. 236

22 RB to Agnes McLehose, 7 March 1788. *Complete Letters*, p. 402

23 RB to Richard Brown, 7 March 1788. *Complete Letters*, pp. 420–1

24 W.E. Henley and T.F. Henderson, *Poetry of Robert Burns*, vol. 4, p. 309

25 C. Carswell, *The Life of Robert Burns*, p. 322

26 RB to Margaret Chalmers, 16 September 1788. *Complete Letters*, pp. 237–8

27 Agnes McLehose to RB, 5 March 1788. W.C. McLehose, *Correspondence of Burns and Clarinda*, p. 236

28 Old Parish Records, Mauchline, vol. 604/2, 304. New Register House, Edinburgh

29 RB to Margaret Chalmers, 14 March 1788. *Complete Letters*, p. 236

30 RB to Agnes McLehose, 14 March 1788. *Complete Letters*, p. 404

31 Agnes McLehose to RB, 5 March 1788. W.C. McLehose, *Correspondence of Burns and Clarinda*, p. 236

32 'Verses to Clarinda'. *Complete Works*, p. 321

33 RB to Agnes McLehose, 18 March 1788. *Complete Letters*, p. 405

34 RB to Richard Brown, 20 March 1788. *Complete Letters*, p. 421

35 Raymond Lamont-Brown, *Clarinda*, p. 182

36 RB to Robert Ainslie, 30 June 1788. *Complete Letters*, p. 334

37 RB to Agnes McLehose, 9 March 1789. *Complete Letters*, pp. 405–6

38 'Thine am I, My Faithful Fair'. *Complete Works*, p. 505

39 RB to Agnes McLehose, July 1791? *Complete Letters*, p. 407

40 Agnes McLehose to RB, November 1791. W.C. McLehose, *Correspondence of Burns and Clarinda*, p. 245

41 RB to Agnes McLehose, 23 November 1791. *Complete Letters*, p. 408

42 'Ae Fond Kiss'. *Complete Works*, p. 434

43 Agnes McLehose to RB, 25 January 1792. W.C. McLehose, *Correspondence of Burns and Clarinda*, p. 276

44 R.L. Brown, *Clarinda*, pp. 63–5

45 RB to Agnes McLehose, about March 1793. *Complete Letters*, p. 410

46 'Monody on a Lady Famed for her Caprice'. *Complete Works*, p. 511

## CHAPTER TWELVE: A WIFE O' MY AIN

1 'I Hae a Wife o My Ain'. *Complete Works*, p. 450

2 RB to William Dunbar, 30 April 1788. *Complete Letters*, p. 282

3 RB to William Stewart, 21 March 1788. *Complete Letters*, p. 444

4 'The Chevalier's Lament'. *Complete Works*, p. 322

5 RB to Robert Cleghorn, 21 March 1788. *Complete Letters*, p.274

6 RB to William Dunbar, 7 April 1788. *Complete Letters*, p.283

7 RB to Margaret Chalmers, April 1788.*Complete Letters*, p.237

8 Revd James Steven, who preached at Mauchline Church on the text, 'And Ye shall go forth, and grow up, as Calves of the Stall' (Malachi iv.2). For a wager with Gavin Hamilton, Burns wrote the poem *'The Calf'*

9 *Burns Chronicle*, vol.V, 1896, pp.74–5

10 RB to James Smith, 26 June 1788. *Complete Letters*, p.122

11 Mauchline Kirk Session Minutes, 5 August 1788. *Burns Chronicle*, 1893, pp.56–7

12 RB to Robert McIndoe, Silk Merchant, Glasgow, 5 August 1788. *Complete Letters*, p.476

13 *'I Hae a Wife o My Ain'*. *Complete Works*, p.450

14 RB to James Smith, 28 April 1788. *Complete Letters*, p.122

15 RB to Robert Ainslie, 26 May 1788. *Complete Letters*, p.332

16 RB to James Johnson, 25 May 1788. *Complete Letters*, p.293

17 Mrs Dunlop to RB, 4 June 1788. W. Wallace, *Robert Burns and Mrs Dunlop*, p.64

18 RB to Andrew Dunlop of Dunlop, 31 May 1788. *Complete Letters*, p.452

19 RB to Mrs Dunlop, 13 June 1788. *Complete Letters*, p.148

20 RB to Mrs Dunlop, 10 August 1788. *Complete Letters*, p.149–50

21 R. Chambers/W. Wallace, *Life and Works of Robert Burns*, vol. II, p.335

22 RB to Samuel Brown, 4 May 1788. *Complete Letters*, p.451

23 RB to Mrs Dunlop, 13 June 1788. *Complete Letters*, p.149

24 *'Of A' The Airts the Wind Can Blaw'*. *Complete Works*, p. 329

25 RB to Margaret Chalmers, 16 September 1788. *Complete Letters*, pp.237–9

26 *'Epistle to Hugh Parker'*. *Complete Works*, pp.322–3

27 *'O, Were I on Parnassus Hill'*. *Complete Works*, p.329

28 RB to Robert Ainslie, possibly June 1788. *Complete Letters*, p.333

29 W.E. Henley and T.F. Henderson, *Complete Works*, p.330

30 RB to Mrs Dunlop, 2 August 1788. *Complete Letters*, pp.150–1

31 RB to Robert Graham of Fintry, 10 September 1788. *Complete Letters*, pp.425–7

32 RB to Jean Armour Burns, 12 September 1788. *Complete Letters*, p.478

33 RB to Robert Graham of Fintry, 23 September 1788. *Complete Letters*, p.427

34 RB to Jean Armour Burns, 14 October 1788. *Complete Letters*, p.478

35 RB to Thomas Boyd, 8 February 1789. *Complete Letters*, p.513

36 RB to Thomas Boyd, 1 March 1789. *Complete Letters*, p.513

37 R. Chambers/W. Wallace, *Life and Works of Robert Burns*, vol. III, p.98

38 R. Chambers/W. Wallace, *Life and Works of Robert Burns*, vol. III, p. 98

39 RB to Robert Graham of Fintry, 13 May 1789. *Complete Letters*, p.428

40 RB to Robert Graham of Fintry, 31 July 1789. *Complete Letters*, p.429

41 RB to Mrs Dunlop, 19 August 1789. *Complete Letters*, p.177

42 RB to Gilbert Burns, 11 January 1790. *Complete Letters*, p.358

43 R.W. Macfadzean, *'Burns's Excise Duties and Emoluments'*, *Burns Chronicle*, 1898, pp.111–12

44 RB to Mrs Dunlop, 7 February 1791. *Complete Letters*, p.193

45 RB to Mrs Dunlop, 19 August 1789. *Complete Letters*, p.177

46 J. Mackay, *A Biography of Robert Burns*, p.444

47 RB to William Burns, 10 November 1789. *Complete Letters*, p.517

# CHAPTER THIRTEEN: WHITTLING CHERRY-STONES

1 Robert Louis Stevenson, *Some Aspects of Robert Burns*. In *Familiar Studies of Men and Books*, 2nd edn, 1886, pp.74–5

2 RB to Alexander Cunningham, 11 March 1791. *Complete Letters*, p.461

3 R.L. Brown, *Robert Burns's Tours of the Highlands and Stirlingshire*, p.26

4 DeLancey Ferguson, *Pride and Passion*, p.269

5 RB to George Thomson, 16 September 1792. *Complete Letters*, p.617

6 Same to same, 26 October 1792. *Complete Letters*, p.618

7 Same to same, July 1793. *Complete Letters*, p.631

8 'Scots Wha hae'. *Complete Works*, p.500

9 RB to George Thomson, about 30 August 1793. *Complete Letters*, p.638

10 *Edinburgh Evening Courant* and *Glasgow Mercury*, 23 July 1796

11 'Auld Lang Syne'. *Complete Works*, p.341

12 RB to George Thomson, about 19 October 1794. *Complete Letters*, p.658

13 RB to Jean McMurdo, July 1793. *Complete Letters*, p.693

14 'Bonie Jean'. *Complete Works*, pp. 493–4

15 'Lovely Polly Stewart'. *Complete Works*, p.523

16 M. Lindsay, *Burns Encyclopedia*, p.344

17 'The Rigs o Barley'. *Complete Works*, p.49

18 'The Ronalds of the Bennals'. *Complete Works*, p.76

19 RB to Deborah Duff Davies, June? 1793. *Complete Letters*, p.592

20 'Bonie Wee Thing'. *Complete Works*, pp.446–7

21 T. Crawford, *Burns, A Study of the Poems and Songs*, p.272

22 'Blythe was She'. *Complete Works*, p.295

23 Introduction to song, 'Blythe was She'. *Complete Works*, p.295

24 'My Peggy's Charms'. *Complete Works*, p.297

25 'Fairest Maid on Devon Banks'. *Complete Works*, p.568

26 RB to Alexander Cunningham, 10 September 1792. *Complete Letters*, p.466

27 RB to George Thomson, 2 July 1793. *Complete Letters*, p.631

28 Same to same, 19 October 1794. *Complete Letters*, p.659

29 'The Mauchline Lady'. *Complete Works*, p.80

30 'Louis, What Reck I by Thee'. *Complete Works*, p.345

# CHAPTER FOURTEEN: MY SPIRITS FLED!

1 John McDiarmid, *Dumfries Monthly Magazine*, No. 1, 1825

2 RB to Thomas Sloan, 1 September 1791. *Complete Letters*, p.577

3 C. Carswell, *The Life of Robert Burns*, p.380

4 RB to Robert Ainslie, November 1791? *Complete Letters*, p.339

5 William McDowell, *Robert Burns in Dumfriesshire*, pp.597–8

6 'Yestreen I had a Pint o Wine'. *Complete Works*, p.407

7 Allan Cunningham, *Complete Works of Robert Burns*, vol.IV, p.337

8 H. Hecht, *Robert Burns, the Man and his Work*, p.148

9 C. Carswell, *The Life of Robert Burns*, p.367

10 H. Brown, *There was a Lad*, p.109

11 I am indebted to the researches of James Mackay for details of Ann Park's background and fate. See *A Biography of Robert Burns*, p. 458

12 H. Hecht, *Robert Burns, the Man and his Work*, pp.148–9

13 'On the Late Captain Grose's Peregrinations thro Scotland'. *Complete Works*, p.373

14 RB to Francis Grose, 1 December 1790. *Complete Letters*, pp.559–60

15 RB to William Smellie, 22 January 1792. *Complete Letters*, p.597

16  Angus MacNaghten, *Burns' Mrs Riddell*, p.26

17  Maria Riddell to her mother, 30 January 1792. In Hugh S. Gladstone, *Maria Riddell, the Friend of Burns*, p.16

18  RB to William Smellie, 22 January 1792. *Complete Letters*, p.597

19  RB to Maria Riddell, February 1792. *Complete Letters*, p.601

20  Same to same, February 1792. *Complete Letters*, p.601

21  W. McDowall, *History of the Burgh of Dumfries*, p.598

22  *'Farewell, thou Stream'. Complete Works*, p.486

23  RB to Maria Riddell, April 1793. *Complete Letters*, p.603

24  *'On Mrs Riddell's Birthday, 4 November, 1793'. Complete Works*, p.508

25  RB to Maria Riddell, late November or December 1793. *Complete Letters*, p.605

26  Same to same, December 1793. *Complete Letters*, p.606

27  RB to Mrs Riddell (almost certainly Elizabeth Riddell), January 1794. *Complete Letters*, pp.697–8

28  RB to Maria Riddell, January 1794. *Complete Letters*, p.606

29  Same to same, 12 January 1794. *Complete Letters*, p.606

30  *'On Maria Riddell'. Complete Works*, p.501

31  *'Pinned to Mrs Walter Riddell's Carriage'. Complete Works*, p.514

32  RB to Agnes McLehose, 25 June 1794. *Complete Letters*, p.411

33  *'Monody on a Lady Famed for her Caprice'. Complete Works*, pp.511–12

34  RB to John Clark, 21 April 1794. *Complete Letters*, p.706

35  *'Inscription at Friar's Carse Hermitage'. Complete Works*, p.513

36  RB to Maria Riddell, March? 1795. *Complete Letters*, p.609

37  Same to same, October/November 1795. *Complete Letters*, p.611

38  *'Craigieburn Wood'. Complete Works*, pp.436–7

39  RB to John Gillespie, 1791? *Complete Letters*, p.572

40  James Hogg and William Motherwell (eds) *The Works of Robert Burns*, vol. 5. pp. 364–5. Quoted in *Burns, Jean Lorimer and James Hogg*, by David Groves, *Burns Chronicle*, 1987, p. 13.

41  RB to George Thomson, 19 October 1794. *Complete Letters*, p.658

42  RB to William Burns, 5 May 1789. *Complete Letters*, p.516

43  *'Lassie wi the Lint-white Locks'. Complete Works*, p.528

44  RB to George Thomson, November 1794. *Complete Letters*, p.665

45  *'Sae Flaxen were her Ringlets'. Complete Works*, p.520

46  *'I'll Ay Ca' in by Yon Toun'. Complete Works*, p.585

47  *'Sleep'st Thou'. Complete Works*, p.526

48  RB to Maria Riddell, Spring 1795. *Complete Letters*, p.609

49  RB to Robert Cleghorn, January 1796. *Complete Letters*, p.665

50  RB to James Johnson, about 1 June 1796. *Complete Letters*, p.303

51  RB to Maria Riddell, 1 June 1796. *Complete Letters*, pp.611–12

52  RB to Alexander Cunningham, 7 July 1796. *Complete Letters*, p.473

53  RB to Mrs Dunlop, 10 July 1796. *Complete Letters*, p.215

54  RB to Gilbert Burns, 10 July 1796. *Complete Letters*, p.358

55  RB to James Armour, 10 July 1796. *Complete Letters*, p.722

56  RB to James Armour, 18 July 1796. *Complete Letters*, p.722

57  RB to James Burness, 12 July 1796. *Complete Letters* p.63

## CHAPTER FIFTEEN: THE RIGHTS OF WOMAN

1  *'Memoir Concerning Burns'*, *Dumfries Journal*, August 1796

2  Syme–Creech correspondence, *Burns Chronicle*, 1934–36, Part 2, 1934, pp 40–1

3  *Edinburgh Evening Courant* and *Glasgow Mercury*, 23 July 1796

4   J. Currie, *Works of Robert Burns* (1819 edn), vol. I, p.215

5   Henley & Henderson. *Poetry of Robert Burns*, vol. 4, p.309

6   RB to John Kennedy, 26 September 1786. *Complete Letters*, p.85

7   *'The Rights of Woman'. Complete Works*, pp.471–2

8   *'Thou Lingering Star'. Complete Works*, p.372

9   *Life and Works of Robert Burns* ed. W. Scott Douglas, p.333

10   *'Handsome Nell'. Complete Works*, p.43

11   *'O, Wert Thou in the Cauld Blast'. Complete Works*, p.567

# Bibliography

Adams, James, *Burns Chloris: A Reminiscence*, Morison, Glasgow, 1893

Angellier, Auguste, *Robert Burns: La Vie, Les Oeuvres*, 2 vols, Hachette, Paris, 1893

Angus-Butterworth, L.M., *Robert Burns and the 18th-Century Revival in Scottish Vernacular Poetry*, Aberdeen University Press, 1969

Ayrshire Archaeological and Natural History Society Collections, vol. 5, 1959, 'Ayrshire at the Time of Burns'

Boyle, A.M., *The Ayrshire Book of Burns-Lore*, Alloway Publishing, Ayr, 1985

Brown, Hilton, *There was a Lad*, Hamish Hamilton, London, 1949

Brown, Raymond Lamont, *Clarinda: The Intimate Story of Robert Burns and Agnes MacLehose*, Martin Black, Dewsbury, 1968

——. (ed.). *Robert Burns's Tour of the Borders*, Boydell Press, Ipswich, 1972

——. (ed.). *Robert Burns's Tours of the Highlands and Stirlingshire, 1787*, Boydell Press, Ipswich, 1973

Burns, Robert, *Common Place Book*. Raymond Lamont-Brown (ed.). Republished from the 1872 edition by S.R. Publishers, Wakefield, 1969

——. *Complete Letters*. James Mackay (ed.), Alloway Publishing, Darvel, 1987

——. *Complete Poetical Works*. W. Scott Douglas (ed.), 2 vols., John McKie, Kilmarnock, 1871

——. *Complete Works*. Allan Cunningham (ed.), 2 vols, George Virtue, London, 1834

——. *Complete Works*. James Mackay (ed.), Alloway Publishing, Darvel, 1986

——. *Complete Works*. Ross Roy (ed.), Clarendon Edition, 4 vols, Oxford University Press, Oxford, 1985

——. *Life and Works of Robert Burns*. Robert Chambers (ed.), 3 vols, W. & R. Chambers, Edinburgh, 1850

——. *Life and Works of Robert Burns*. Robert Chambers (ed.). Revised William Wallace, 4 vols, Chambers, Edinburgh, 1896

——. *The Merry Muses of Caledonia*. James Barke and Sydney Goodsir Smith (eds). W.H. Allen, London, 1965

——. *Poems and Songs*. Oxford Standard Authors. James Kinsley (ed.), 4 vols, Oxford, 1979

——. *Poetry of Robert Burns*, W.E. Henley and T.F. Henderson (eds), Centenary Edition, 4 vols, T.C. & E. C. Jack, Edinburgh, 1896

——. *Works of Robert Burns*. James Currie (ed.), 4 vols, Cadell and Davies, London, 1800. Also 1819 edition

——. *Works of Robert Burns*, James Hogg and William Motherwell (eds) 5 vols, Fullarton, Glasgow, 1834–5.

*Burns Chronicle*, published annually by The Burns Federation, Kilmarnock

Carswell, Catherine, *The Life of Robert Burns*, Chatto and Windus, London, 1930

Chambers, Robert. See *Burns Robert, Life and Works*

Crawford, Thomas. *Burns, A Study of the Poems and Songs*, Oliver and Boyd, Edinburgh, 1960

Cromek, Robert H., *Reliques of Burns, consisting of Original Letters, Poems and Critical Observations on Scottish Songs*, Cadell and Davies, London, 1817

Cunningham, Allan, *See* Burns, Robert, *Complete Works*

Currie, James, *See* Burns, Robert. *Works of Robert Burns*

Daiches, David, *Robert Burns*, André Deutsch, London, 1966

Dent, Alan, *Burns in his Time*, Nelson, London, 1966

Dick, J.C., *The Songs of Robert Burns*, Henry Frowde, London, 1903

Donnelly, Pauline E., *Rob Mossgiel, Bard of Humanity – An Exploration of some Aspects of Burns' Poetry, Burns Chronicle*, 1984

Douglas, Hugh, *Robert Burns. A Life*, Robert Hale, London, 1976

Douglas, W. Scott. *See* Burns, Robert, *Complete Poetical Works*

Edgar, Reverend A., *Lectures on Old Church Life in Scotland*, 2 vols, Gardner, Paisley, 1885/6

*The Edinburgh Review*

Ferguson, J. DeLancey, *Pride and Passion. Robert Burns 1759–1796*, Oxford University Press, New York, 1939

Ford, Robert, *The Heroines of Burns and their Celebrating Songs*, A. Gardner, Paisley, 1906

Fullarton, Colonel William, *Board of Agriculture Report*, 1793

Gladstone, Hugh S., *Maria Riddell, The Friend of Burns*, Privately printed, Dumfries, 1915

*Glenriddell Manuscript*

Gray, James T., *Maybole – Carrick's Capital*, Maybole Town Council, 1972

Hecht, Hans, *Robert Burns, the Man and his Work*, William Hodge, London, 1936. Alloway Publishing, Darvel, 1981

Henley, W.E. & Henderson, T.F. *See* Burns, Robert. *Poetry of Robert Burns*

Heron, Robert, *A Memoir of the Life of the Late Robert Burns*, T. Brown, Edinburgh, 1797

Hill, John C., *The Love Songs and Heroines of Robert Burns*, J.M. Dent, London, 1961

Jolly, William, *Robert Burns at Mossgiel*, A. Gardner, Paisley, 1881

Keith, Christina, *The Russet Coat*, Robert Hale, London, 1956

Kinsley, James, *See* Burns, Robert. *Poems and Songs*

Lindsay, Maurice, *Robert Burns. The Man, His Work, the Legend*, MacGibbon & Kee, London, 1954

——. *The Burns Encyclopedia*. Robert Hale, London, 3rd edn. 1980

Little, Janet (The Scottish Milkmaid Poet), *Poetical Works*, Wilson, Ayr, 1792

Lockhart, John Gibson, *Life of Robert Burns*, Constable, London, 1828

Low, David, (ed.), *The Songs of Robert Burns*, Routledge, London, 1993

Low, Donald A., *Critical Essays on Robert Burns*, Routledge and Kegan Paul, London, 1975

McDiarmid, John, 'Memoranda, from Jean's dictation: Affecting circumstances connected with the history of the family of Burns', *Dumfries Monthly Magazine*, vol. I, 1825

——. 'Widow of Burns, her Death, Character and Funeral'. *Dumfries Courier*, 1834. Reprinted in the *Burns Chronicle*, 1934

McDowell, William, *Robert Burns in Dumfriesshire*, A. & C. Black, Edinburgh, 1870

Macfadzean, R.W., 'Burns's Excise Duties and Emoluments'. *Burns Chronicle*, 1898

McIntyre, Ian, *Dirt and Deity: A Life of Robert Burns*, Harper Collins, London, 1995

Mackay, James, *A Biography of Robert Burns*, Mainstream, Edinburgh, 1992

McLehose, William C., *The Correspondence of Burns and Clarinda*, W. Tait, Edinburgh, 1843

MacNaghten, Angus, *Burns' Mrs Riddell*, Volturna Press, Peterhead, 1975

McVie, John, *Robert Burns and Edinburgh*, The Burns Federation, Kilmarnock, 1969

Marchbanks, Agnes, 'A Poet's Inspiration'. In *Scottish Art and Letters*, Edinburgh, 1901

Mitchell, Reverend John, 'Memories of Ayrshire about 1780'. Scottish History Society *Miscellany*, vol VI, 1939

Muir, Reverend J. C., 'Burns in Kirkoswald'. *Burns Chronicle*, 1906

Muir, James, 'Burns till his 17th Year'. *Kilmarnock Standard*, 1929

Munro, Archibald, *The Story of Burns and Highland Mary*, A. Gardner, Paisley, 1896

Paterson, James, *The Contemporaries of Burns*, H. Paton, Edinburgh, 1840,

Pearl, Cyril, *Bawdy Burns, The Christian Rebel*, Frederick Muller, London, 1958

Ramsay, John, of Ochtertyre, *Scotland and Scotsmen in the Eighteenth Century*, Alex. Allardyce (ed.), Edinburgh, 1888

Ross, John D. (compiler), *Burnsiana*, Alexander Gardner, Paisley, 1892

——. *The Poems of Clarinda*, Eneas Mackay, Stirling, 1929

Skinner, Basil C., *Burns: Authentic Likenesses*, Oliver & Boyd, Edinburgh, 1963

Snyder, Franklyn Bliss, *Life of Robert Burns*, Macmillan, New York, 1932

*The Statistical Account of Scotland* Sir John Sinclair (ed.), 21 vols, W. Creech, Edinburgh, 1791–9

Stevenson, Robert Louis, 'Some Aspects of Robert Burns' in *Familiar Studies of Men and Books*, 2nd edition, Chatto and Windus, London, 1886

Stevenson, Yvonne H., *Burns and His Bonnie Jean*, Gray's Publishing, Sidney, B.C., Canada, 1966

Strawhorn, John & Andrew, Ken, *Discovering Ayrshire*, John Donald, Edinburgh, 1988

Thornton, R.D., *James Currie the Entire Stranger and Robert Burns*, London, 1963

Wallace, William, *Burns and Mrs Dunlop*, Hodder & Stoughton, London, 1898

Westwood, Peter J., *Jean Armour*. Creedon Publications, Dumfries, 1996

Whyte, Ian D. *Scotland before the Industrial Revolution; An Economic and Social History c.1050–c.1750*, Longman, London, 1995

Wood, John Maxwell, *Robert Burns and the Riddell Family*, Robert Dinwiddie, Dumfries, 1922

# Index of Poems and Songs quoted or referred to in the text

Q=quotation
R=reference
Italicised numbers denote illustrations

*A Man's a Man for a' That* R 118
*Adam Armour's Prayer* Q 5 R 6, 271
*Address to Edinburgh* Q 136 R 141, 279
*Address to the Deil* R 15, 70, 80, 275
*Address to the Unco Guid* R 15, 70
*Ae Fond Kiss* Q 19, 200, 202 R 272, 283, *31*
*Ah, Chloris* R 258
*Anna Thy Charms* R 127
*Auld Farmer's New-year Morning Salutation to his Auld Mare, Maggie, The* Q 67 R 68, 275
*Auld Lang Syne* Q 232, 233, 285 R 22
*Author's Earnest Cry and Prayer, The* R 69, 275

*Banks of the Devon, The* R 237, 280
*Bard at Inveraray* Q 153 R 280
*Behold the Hour, the Boat Arrive* R 200
*Belles of Mauchline, The* Q 80, 81 R 203, 275, *10*
*Birks of Aberfeldie, The* Q 14 R 272
*Blue-eyed Lassie, The* R 234
*Blythe Hae I been on Yon Hill* R 236
*Blythe was She* Q 162 R 285
*Bonie Jean* Q 234 R 238, 285
*Bonie Peggy Alison* R 54
*Bonie Wee Thing* Q 236 R 239, 285

*Calf, The,* Q 67 R 68, 104

*Castle Gordon* R 136
*Chevalier's Lament, The* Q 204 R 283
*Clarinda, Mistress of my Soul* Q 179, 199 R 127, 282
*Cotter's Saturday Night, The* Q 32, 33 R 15, 66, 86, 121, 175, 273, 275, 276, 278, *12*
*Court of Equity, The* R 140
*Craigieburn Wood* Q 56 R 286

*Death and Dr Hornbrook* Q 47, 48 R 274

*Elegy on the Late Miss Burnet of Monbodo* Q 137 R 279
*Elibanks and Elibraes* R 242
*Epigram to Miss Ainslie in Church* Q 145 R 280
*Epistle to a Young Friend* Q 68, 69 R 86, 275
*Epistle to Davie, a Brother Poet* R 276
*Epistle to Hugh Parker* Q 214 R 284
*Epistle to the Rev. John McMath* R 275
*Epistle to John Rankine* Q 64 R 271, 274, 276
*Epitaph on Holy Willie* R 15
*Epitaph on my Honoured Father* Q 61 R 275
*Epitaph on a Noisy Polemic* Q 47
*Epitaph on the Death of Sir James Hunter Blair* R 226

# Index